Loyalty, memory and public opinion in England, 1658–1727

Manchester University Press

Politics, culture and society in early modern Britain

General Editors

PROFESSOR ALASTAIR BELLANY
DR ALEXANDRA GAJDA
PROFESSOR PETER LAKE
PROFESSOR ANTHONY MILTON
PROFESSOR JASON PEACEY

This important series publishes monographs that take a fresh and challenging look at the interactions between politics, culture and society in Britain between 1500 and the mid-eighteenth century. It counteracts the fragmentation of current historiography through encouraging a variety of approaches which attempt to redefine the political, social and cultural worlds, and to explore their interconnection in a flexible and creative fashion. All the volumes in the series question and transcend traditional interdisciplinary boundaries, such as those between political history and literary studies, social history and divinity, urban history and anthropology. They thus contribute to a broader understanding of crucial developments in early modern Britain.

Recently published in the series

This England PATRICK COLLINSON

Sir Robert Filmer (1588–1653) and the patriotic monarch CESARE CUTTICA

Doubtful and dangerous: The question of succession in late Elizabethan England
SUSAN DORAN and PAULINA KEWES (eds)

Brave community JOHN GURNEY

'Black Tom' ANDREW HOPPER

Reformation without end: Religion, politics and the past in post-revolutionary England ROBERT G. INGRAM

Revolution remembered: Seditious memories after the British Civil Wars
EDWARD JAMES LEGON

Royalists and Royalism during the Interregnum JASON MCELLIGOTT and
DAVID L. SMITH

Laudian and Royalist polemic in Stuart England ANTHONY MILTON

The crisis of British Protestantism: Church power in the Puritan Revolution, 1638–44 HUNTER POWELL

The gentlewoman's remembrance: Patriarchy, piety, and singlehood in early Stuart England ISAAC STEPHENS

Exploring Russia in the Elizabethan Commonwealth: The Muscovy Company and Giles Fletcher, the elder (1546–1611) FELICITY JANE STOUT

Full details of the series are available at www.manchesteruniversitypress.co.uk.

Loyalty, memory and public opinion in England, 1658–1727

EDWARD VALLANCE

Manchester University Press

Copyright © Edward Vallance 2019

The right of Edward Vallance to be identified as the author of this work has been asserted by him in accordance with the Copyright, Designs and Patents Act 1988.

Published by Manchester University Press
Altrincham Street, Manchester M1 7JA, UK
www.manchesteruniversitypress.co.uk

British Library Cataloguing-in-Publication Data is available

ISBN 978 0 7190 9703 4 hardback
ISBN 978 1 5261 6023 2 paperback

First published by Manchester University Press in hardback 2019

This edition published 2021

The publisher has no responsibility for the persistence or accuracy of URLs for any external or third-party internet websites referred to in this book, and does not guarantee that any content on such websites is, or will remain, accurate or appropriate.

Typeset by Newgen Publishing UK

Contents

LIST OF FIGURES—*page* vi
ACKNOWLEDGEMENTS—vii
ABBREVIATIONS—ix

Introduction: addressing, petitioning and the public   1

1   Petitions, oaths and addresses: subscriptional activity during the civil wars   21

2   Cromwell's trunks: the origins of the loyal address, 1658–61   40

3   Addresses, abhorrences and associations: subscriptional culture and memory in the 1680s   66

4   Adversarial addressing, 1701–10   93

5   Who were the 'public'? Identifying the addressers   120

6   The performance of loyalty: ritual in loyal addressing   160

7   From subjects to objects: the language of loyalty   184

Conclusion   207

BIBLIOGRAPHY OF ARCHIVAL AND MANUSCRIPT MATERIAL CONSULTED—215
INDEX—220

Figures

1	Loyal address of the 'well-affected' of Leicestershire to Richard Cromwell, Bodleian Library MS Rawl A 61* f. 164–86, image reproduced by permission of the Bodleian Library, The University of Oxford	*page* 125
2	Distribution of subscription to 1658 address to Richard Cromwell in Leicestershire	126
3a	Image of the Stoke Golding address, Bodleian Library MS Rawl A 61* f. 175, reproduced by permission of the Bodleian Library, The University of Oxford	130
3b	Image of the Stoke Golding Hearth Tax return, The National Archives, Kew, E 179/251/4/8 f. 230, reproduced by permission of The National Archives, Kew	131
4	Variant broadsheet declarations of the gentry of Norfolk to General Monck (1660), BL Thomason 669 f. 23 [21]; 190 g. 13 [148], reproduced by permission of the British Library	139
5a	Printed version of the address of the Dorset nobility and gentry to Charles II, BL Thomason 669 f. 25 [44], reproduced by permission of the British Library	144
5b	Excerpt from the manuscript address of the Dorset nobility and gentry to Charles II in 1660, TNA SP 29/1 f. 55–6, reproduced by permission of The National Archives, Kew	145

Acknowledgements

I would like to thank the following people and organisations for their help in writing this book. A number of people have very generously shared references with me, including Ed Legon, Blair Worden, Jason Peacey, Philip Loft and Gavin Robinson. My Roehampton colleague Andrew Wareham gave me some very helpful pointers on the Hearth Tax and related records. Katrina Navickas made a very useful suggestion in relation to OCR software. I am also grateful to Ed and Blair, along with Tony Claydon, Brian Cowan and Mark Knights, for sharing their work with me, including work-in-progress. Mike Braddick, Simon Dixon, John Spurr and Brodie Waddell provided me with insightful comments on draft chapters and articles. I am particularly grateful to Mark Knights for his generosity in both sharing his own work (published and unpublished) on addressing, and in commenting on draft chapters of mine which have come his way. Very helpful feedback has also been given by seminar, workshop and conference audiences in Boston, London, Lyon, Paris, Portland, Toulouse, Erfurt, Oxford and Reading. Initial research in to this topic was supported by the award of a British Academy Small Research Grant. The University of Roehampton provided two terms of research leave which were critical to enabling me to complete this project. Access to *Nouvelles Ordinaires de Londres* at the Beinecke Library, Yale, was assisted through the award of a Lewis Walpole Library Fellowship. I would like to thank the many librarians and archivists who have assisted me with my research, particularly Dr Joan Unwin for sharing her expertise on the Cutlers' Company. I am grateful to the Northumberland Estates for permission to consult and quote from their papers. Some portions of Chapter three were published earlier in 'Petitioning, addressing and the historical imagination: the case of Great Yarmouth, England 1658–1784', *Parliaments, Estates and Representation*, 38 (2018) 364–77. Elements of Chapter six have been published in 'Une démonstration stratégique de loyauté dans l'Angleterre de la fin des Stuart: le cas des couteliers du Hallamshire', *Revue Histoire, Économie et Société*, 38, no. 1 (2019) 67–84. I am grateful to these journals for

Acknowledgements

permission to reproduce them here. I would like to thank the series editors at Manchester University Press for their understanding as delivery deadlines were shifted, and for their support through the writing process. Finally, I would like to thank the person who helped me most in completing this book, my wife Linnie. Writing a book is a stressful and time-consuming exercise. People involved in writing a book are not always the most fun to be around. I am indebted to Linnie for her support, patience, love and understanding while I bashed away at book number four.

Abbreviations

Unless otherwise stated, works published before 1800 are printed in London.

BL	British Library
Bodl.	Bodleian Library, Oxford
C. J.	Commons Journals
C.S.P.D.	Calendar of State Papers, Domestic
EEBO	Early English Books Online
ESRO	East Sussex Record Office Collections, The Keep, Brighton
HMC	Historical Manuscripts Commission
HRO	Hampshire Archives and Local Studies, Record Office
Leics RO	Record Office of Leicestershire, Leicester and Rutland, Wigston, Leicestershire
LRO	Lancashire Archives, Lancashire Record Office
NRO	Norfolk Record Office
ODNB	Oxford Dictionary of National Biography
TNA	The National Archives, Kew
VCH	Victoria County History
WYAS	Archives Services, West Yorkshire Joint Services

Introduction: addressing, petitioning and the public

> Why on earth is this a 'humble address' in this age? Are the royal family superior beings to the rest of us? Are we inferior beings to them? This was the feeling of the House seven centuries ago when we accepted [the] rule under which we speak now. We live in an egalitarian time where we recognise the universality of the human condition, in which royals and commoners share the same strengths and frailties ... If these occasions are to be greatly valued, it should be possible for members to utter the odd syllable that might be critical. The sycophancy described by the Prime Minister ... is something that must sicken the royal family when they have an excess of praise of this type.
>
> Paul Flynn MP (8 June 2011).[1]

The avowedly republican Labour MP Paul Flynn made this intervention in a Commons debate on delivering a humble address to Prince Philip on the occasion of his ninetieth birthday. Flynn's comments were markedly out of step with the sentiments of his parliamentary colleagues on both sides of the House: the opposition leader Ed Miliband had instead celebrated the Duke's 'unique turn of phrase' while the then Prime Minister David Cameron spoke of the royal consort's 'down-to-earth, no-nonsense approach' which endeared him to the British public.[2] A year later, another royal celebration, the Queen's Diamond Jubilee, prompted a further round of loyal addresses, with twenty-seven 'Privileged Bodies' (religious organisations, universities and civic corporations) sending their congratulations to Elizabeth II. Again, in among the general chorus of praise for the Queen, a few dissonant voices could be heard. The British Quakers were one of the groups invited to produce an address honouring the Jubilee but the acceptance of the invitation prompted consternation and criticism from some Friends. Central to this was the perceived clash between the Quaker ideal of equality and the celebration of the rule of a hereditary monarch. The form of an address itself pushed Quakers into employing the Queen's title when Friends generally employ only the given names of individuals. Some Quakers wondered how celebrating the rule of a monarch who was also Commander-in-Chief of the British armed forces could be squared with the Society of Friends' commitment to pacifism. In spite of this controversy, British Quakers did deliver an address congratulating the Queen on her sixty-year reign but they used the text of the address to raise issues of current concern to the Society of Friends (environmental sustainability and marriage equality). It was also reported that Jocelyn Dawes who read the address to the Queen did not curtsey before Elizabeth II but only bowed her head.[3]

As the British Monarchy's own website explained, though loyal addressing was now essentially 'ceremonial in nature' and used only on 'very special Royal occasions', it had once been a 'valuable and important privilege' which had provided a means of 'letting the authorities know what people at large, or at any rate an organised section of them, thought and felt about current political questions, or the conduct of Government'.[4] The responses of Paul Flynn MP and later the Quakers seemed to hark back to this previous role – both Flynn and the Society of Friends sought to use these texts to convey criticisms or demands to the Crown. In both instances, they chose to debate the address publicly, in Parliament or through the press. In the case of the Quakers' address, the presentation of the text itself was arguably an extension of this political argument with Dawes breaching normal royal etiquette by instead honouring Quaker traditions of 'social testimony'.

In the context of the summers of 2011 and 2012, dominated by the public celebration of Britain's monarchy, these critical voices were rare indeed. The majority of addresses, which saw the Queen's Jubilee as no more than an occasion for national celebration, were nonetheless connected to that earlier tradition of loyal addressing. The very process of addressing, with the presentation of the text followed by the delivery of royal thanks and acknowledgement, resonated with the historic role of this form as a 'point of contact' between the centre and the localities; and while the addresses were reported online, in the press and on television, they were also publicised in the same fashion as they would have been three centuries ago – in the pages of the *London Gazette*.[5]

Paul Flynn's attack on the Commons' 'Humble Address' as nauseating flattery represented another continuity between the addresses of 2011–12 and those of the seventeenth century. This book, however, will demonstrate that these addresses were much more than a mechanism for showering sycophantic praise upon authority: they were an integral part of what the historian Karin Bowie has termed the 'opinion politics' of the early modern period.[6] This book focuses on mass loyal addressing, from its emergence as a form of political communication towards the end of the Cromwellian Protectorate to its zenith as a vehicle for controversy at the turn of the eighteenth century. Public opinion, as represented in loyal addresses, was utilised to legitimate the actions and ideals of the political centre. The processes, rituals and ceremonies that surrounded addressing, however, suggested a reciprocal relationship between addresser and addressee, and addresses frequently voiced criticism of, and placed demands upon authority. Likewise, the exploitation of popular political participation to support government ultimately gave power to the judgement of 'the public' in political affairs. Addressing consequently raised major questions about representation, sovereignty and the nature and extent of public involvement in the political process.

In these respects, addressing shared many features with a related and more extensively researched political activity: petitioning. While not denying the important role of petitions as vehicles for articulating and representing public opinion, it will be argued here that particular features of the address encouraged a developing awareness of a political public. In contrast to often localised petitioning activity, addressing campaigns were typically national (and sometimes international) in scope. Connected to royal accessions, the waging of war and the securing of peace, addresses connected local communities to a broader national narrative. This facilitated the growth of a persistent public memory of addressing activity, providing a record of both corporate and individual political action. Although the language of loyal addressing was often highly emotional and the controversies articulated through these texts fiercely contested, this memory enabled these texts to be used critically to guide political action and to hold people and communities to account. Consequently, a political form ostensibly designed to flatter authority paradoxically played an integral role in the emergence of a critical, political public.

This book contributes to recent research that has identified forms of political communication closely related to addressing – petitioning – as facilitating the growth of the early modern public sphere. Petitioning, after a period of neglect, has become a vogue topic again, exemplified by recent work from (among others) Peter Lake, David Zaret, John Walter, James Daybell, Beat Kümin and, for the later period, Mark Knights.[7] However, in contrast to petitioning, loyal addresses have received relatively little attention, even though in the later seventeenth century they unquestionably overtook the petition as a mode of mass political communication. The exceptions have been the work of Knights, both in his first monograph, *Politics and Opinion in Crisis* and in his more recent *Representation and Misrepresentation in Later Stuart England*, and for Scotland the work of Karin Bowie.[8] Recently, Scott Sowerby has explored the use of loyal addresses to build political coalitions in support of James II's tolerationist policies.[9]

One reason for this relative lack of research is simply that in contrast to petitioning, already well established as a political practice by the late medieval period, addresses were of a more recent vintage. John Oldmixon, in his *History of Addresses* (1709), identified the practice of offering humble addresses to the Crown as originating in the Cromwellian era.[10] As Mark Knights has noted, large numbers of addresses were issued congratulating Richard Cromwell on succeeding his father as Lord Protector (discussed in more detail in Chapter two).[11] In contrast to petitions, that is communications which made a request or entreaty to authority, addresses were ostensibly only an expression of feeling, delivering the congratulations or thanks of a particular community. The two forms nonetheless remained closely related. In an important recent article, Derek Hirst has observed that groups petitioning the Protectorate developed the ploy of attaching their petitions to humble addresses as a means of ensuring that their grievances were heard.[12]

Given their apparent novelty, it is perhaps unsurprising that fewer formal rules (if any) seem to have been developed with reference to addressing. As with petitions, no address should be presented that deals with matters currently before Parliament. A humble address has now also become the standard response to the Queen's speech.[13] During the Exclusion Crisis, however, addresses from Parliament to the monarch were less formulaic and more explicitly confrontational, calling for the removal of royal ministers deemed to be obstructing exclusion bills and even for the removal from the Court of members of the royal household – specifically Catherine of Braganza and her Catholic attendants. (This more contentious use of parliamentary humble addresses has recently been revived as an opposition strategy. In November 2017, the Labour party issued a 'motion for return', an order for the production of papers, traditionally framed as a humble address, in a bid to force the government into releasing details of its Brexit impact case studies.)[14] As we will see, addresses from counties and boroughs could also make assertive demands, whether it was to bind MPs to particular election promises or to call for frequent parliaments or the protection of the Church of England. In fact, there appears to have been little official protocol about how addresses should be produced (Steven Poole has suggested that formal procedures for presenting addresses to the Crown only developed in the wake of deluge of addresses sent to William IV during the 'May Days' of 1832) and in this sense, their format and content appears to be less proscribed in principle than that of petitions.[15]

There were significant differences, though, in terms of the supposed catalysts for petitions as opposed to addresses. To put it simply, addresses were normally meant to be initiated from the top down, petitions from the bottom up. Josef Redlich defined an address as the traditional form of response to 'solemn messages from the Crown'.[16] So it might be argued that petitions were inherently more 'popular' in nature. They were at least supposed to emerge from communities and communicate grievances to the political centre (although we know that many petitions were produced at the centre to give the impression of local support for national causes). In contrast, the issuing of loyal addresses was often a product of prompting by the Court itself – as in the case of those in the wake of the dissolution of the Oxford Parliament, after the Rye House Plot, in response to James II's second Declaration of Indulgence and following the assassination plot of 1696.[17]

Even so, one surprising feature of these addresses is the fact that wholescale plagiarism of texts was relatively uncommon. This supports the impression that, though often prompted by the Crown, loyal addresses were actually local productions. This in turn fits with Karin Bowie's observation of Scottish addressing campaigns, that, in order for them to be influential, 'elite-sponsored messages still had to resonate with local grievances, attitudes and loyalties'.[18] Moreover, it was not the case that addresses were only drawn up at the instigation of the Court. Oldmixon's *History* was written in response to a Tory/High Church addressing campaign warning of 'the Church in danger'. That campaign, essentially sympathising with the clergyman Henry Sacheverell, impeached for his inflammatory sermon *The Perils of False Brethren*, was certainly not initiated by the Crown or the governing Whig ministry.[19] The similarities between petitioning and addressing in this period were testified to by the extent to which they were deemed synonyms of one another. The 1661 act that attempted to prohibit mass petitions had the full title of 'An Act Against Tumults and Disorders upon Pretence of Preparing or Presenting Public Petitions or other **Addresses** to His Majesty or the Parliament' and referred to the problems posed by 'petitions, complaints, remonstrances and declarations, and other **addresses** to the King'.[20]

PETITIONING, ADDRESSING AND THE PUBLIC SPHERE

It is worth noting here that the Restoration monarchy was attempting to regulate petitioning and addressing, rather than suppress it altogether. Even that proved impossible in the crisis decade of the 1680s, as it had before in the 1640s. The development of mass printed petitions as a permanent feature of the political landscape has been seen by some historians as indicative of wider changes in communicative practice. David Zaret argues that during the English Revolution, petitions 'simultaneously constituted and invoked public opinion'.[21] Examples of 'parrot petitions' (petitions from the localities which aped the substance of London petitions), petitions that were printed and sent out for subscription and then issued in a second printing with all the names attached, but most importantly the impact of mass printing of these petitions, led to the imposition of what Zaret calls 'dialogic order'. For Zaret, cheap print, through the ability to swiftly reproduce texts in massive numbers, to refer to other texts, excerpt chunks from them and comment upon them, created an ordered but rapidly evolving public political debate. According to Zaret, petitioning effectively constituted a public sphere as framers of petitions 'produced texts for an anonymous audience of readers, a public presumed not only to be capable of rational thought but also to possess moral competency for resolving rival political claims'.[22]

Mark Knights, whose work follows chronologically on from Zaret's investigation of petitioning in the 1640s, also sees petitioning and addressing as enabling greater political participation; however, he is more cautious about the degree to which these changes were sustained over time and the extent to which they altered normative assumptions about the role of the public in political debate.[23] Knights notes that while the addressing campaigns of the later seventeenth and early eighteenth century were truly national in scale and often invoked the idea of having captured the 'sense' or 'voice' of the kingdom, the authenticity of these addresses as representative of public opinion was highly contested. As Knights sees it, though the fact of greater popular participation was indisputable, the value of that involvement remained uncertain. Many feared that what these addressing campaigns really demonstrated was the ease with which the public could be swayed, not by reason, but by 'partisan polemic'.[24]

Knights' and Zaret's reading of petitioning and addressing reflects a wider scholarly engagement over the last twenty years with Jürgen Habermas' idea of a 'public sphere'. Since the publication in 1989 of an English translation of his 1962 work, a plethora of books have examined his claim that a 'public sphere that functioned in the political realm arose first in Great Britain at the turn of the eighteenth century'.[25] The responses of early modern scholars have ranged from enthusiastic adoption of the concept to outright rejection.[26] In a major recent article, Peter Lake and Steven Pincus have suggested that the appeal of the concept of the public sphere has been in no small part because it appears to offer a historiographical 'third way' between revisionism and older, 'Whiggish' interpretations.[27] They see the concept as not only allowing authors to employ a broader palette of primary sources (moving away from revisionist insistence on the primacy of manuscript evidence) but also encouraging historians to tackle longer-term historical development.[28] In the case of the subject of this study, the emphasis on cheap print (in the form of published petitions and addresses) and its role in fostering a more 'democratic' political culture could be seen as supporting Lake and Pincus' characterisation of the recent historiography.

Lake and Pincus' reading of the early modern public sphere does not represent a 'rigid application' of Habermas' scheme but rather offers 'variations on and applications of some [of his] basic themes and categories'.[29] The work of Knights and Zaret can also be seen as operating in a dialogue between Habermas and the empirical evidence of communicative practice in early modern England. Zaret, for example, defined his mission as attempting to find a 'viable compromise' between 'revisionist historiography' urging that historians must return to the sources, free of any theoretical preconceptions, and 'sweeping theories of the public sphere that simply cannot be squared with individual-level observations offered by meticulous, revisionist scholarship'.[30]

The idea of offering a re-reading of Habermas, informed by empirical studies of late seventeenth- and early eighteenth-century England, however, is not without its problems. As J. A. Downie has rightly noted, these approaches often tend to present Habermas' 'bourgeois public sphere' as if it were an ideal type rather than something that was particular to a specific time (the late seventeenth and early eighteenth century) and a specific place (England).[31]

Overlooking this fact has allowed historians to claim that a public sphere also existed in Elizabethan and early Stuart England as well.[32] As one historian has joked, on the basis of the discovery of a Tudor public sphere, it will not be long before an equivalent is found for the Palaeolithic era too.[33] More important, the ability to see the public sphere as a moveable feast has arguably been a symptom of the tendency of historians to treat it as description of communicative practice and to reify it, collapsing an intellectual concept into concrete arenas for debate (coffeehouses) and particular forms of expression (pamphlets, petitions). Such treatments assume that 'public opinion' can be identified in the conglomeration of individual viewpoints found in the historical record.[34] This view has long been challenged by philosophical and sociological treatments of the concept which suggest that it is futile to attempt to disaggregate the process of identifying 'public opinion' with the construction or representation it.[35] Other studies seek to limit their focus to shifts in political practice. For example, although Lake and Pincus acknowledge ideological/intellectual change, their account of the public sphere largely remains a 'depiction of communication' and not primarily a discussion of changing understandings of the 'public' or 'public opinion'.[36] Although they discuss the emergence of new fields of public enquiry – notably political economy – their analysis is mainly devoted to charting the growth and increased reach of forms of political communication.[37]

The difficulty with such an approach, at least as far as they seek to remain in dialogue with the Habermasian public sphere, is that Habermas' concept is not represented by a particular social group, form of political communication or type of real discursive space. Rather, as Michael Warner has eloquently put it, the Habermasian public sphere is,

> an imaginary convergence point that is the backdrop of critical discourse in each of these contexts and publics – an implied but abstract point that is often referred to as 'the public' or 'public opinion' and by virtue of that fact endowed with legitimacy and the ability to dissolve power. A 'public' in this context is a special kind of virtual social object, enabling a special mode of address.[38]

This study consequently follows the approach of Geoff Kemp in seeing an analysis of the emergence/existence of an early modern public sphere as requiring the investigation of changes in beliefs and ideas as well as practices.[39] The approaches of Knights and Zaret also acknowledge this, viewing addresses and petitions, in Zaret's words as 'devices that mediate between nominal and real moments of public opinion'.[40]

As Jason Peacey's recent work demonstrates, however, this does not mean that an investigation of the emergence of public opinion must be an exercise in intellectual history: the experience of popular political activity could itself generate radical thought.[41] Moreover, Kemp's study of the Tory propagandist and censor Roger L'Estrange demonstrates that the development of the idea of public opinion could be the product of seemingly conflicting impulses and beliefs – L'Estrange's drive to suppress the popular voice simultaneously gave acknowledgement to the judgement of the public in political and religious debate.[42] Popular addressing and petitioning had formed part of L'Estrange's attack on courting the multitude, his *Observator* complaining of the practice of getting 'half a dozen Schismaticall Hands to a Petition, or Address in a corner, and then call[ing] it, the sense of the Nation'.[43] L'Estrange's comments here support Knights' observation regarding growing concerns about the reliability of petitions and addresses as guides to public opinion. Knights' interpretation follows Habermas' own reading of the role of these devices in the early eighteenth century. Habermas noted that in this period:

> it became usual to distinguish what was then called 'the sense of the people' from the official election results. The average results of the county elections were taken to provide an approximate measure of the former. The 'sense of the people', 'the common voice', 'the general cry of the people', and finally 'the public spirit' denoted from this time onward an entity to which the opposition could appeal – with whose help, in fact, it more than once forced Walpole and his parliamentary majority to concessions.

However, Habermas was clear that the identification of 'the sense of the people',

> must not be construed prematurely as a sign of a kind of rule of public opinion. The true power constellation is more reliably gauged by the ineffectiveness of the numerous mass petitions organized since 1680. To be sure, in 1701 as well as in 1710, the dissolution of Parliament actually followed upon corresponding petitions; but these were basically mere acclamations of which the King made use.[44]

A number of features of loyal addresses do seem to make them a poor fit with the idea of a public sphere. As Habermas conceived it, the public sphere was essentially a critical space, separate from and in opposition to the monarchical State.[45] As already noted above, however, addressing activity was frequently initiated from the centre, by the Crown and/or its ministers. This was clearly a form of political communication in which the State was an active participant, not merely the passive object of public criticism. Though Habermas saw education and wealth as dictating that those who participated in the public sphere of critical debate would primarily be bourgeois men, crucially the normative values of this space held that social status was, in itself, no barrier to participation.[46] Addresses, on the other hand, were often keen to demonstrate their social credentials, marketing themselves as coming from the nobility, gentry and freeholders.[47] Conversely, those who sought to undermine the credibility of addresses would often claim that they were texts that had simply been foisted upon an ignorant rabble. Consequently, addresses also seem irreconcilable with another characteristic of Habermas' public sphere – the public's critical use of reason as the arbiter of debate.[48] Addresses instead could appear either insufficiently critical, reflecting their ostensible purpose as acclamations, overly emotional, conveying public feeling rather than rational thought, or dependent upon either the social clout of subscribers and/or sheer weight of numbers.

This study will show, nonetheless, that in a number of important respects, loyal addresses assisted the development of features of political debate that Habermas saw as integral to the emergence of the early modern public sphere. While it is true that they frequently remained indebted to notions of social hierarchy, it will show that addresses were, in practical terms, often very inclusive, incorporating adult males across the social scale. Equally, though they often may have been prompted by the initiative of the State, addressing activity, mirroring as it frequently did major political events, repeatedly commented upon such *'arcana imperii'* as the succession of the Crown, the status of Parliament and the conduct of foreign policy.[49] Following on from this, addresses demonstrated another quality – reflexivity – that Habermas and other scholars, notably Michael Warner, have felt is integral to the public sphere. For Habermas, the public that read and debated coffeehouse periodicals such as the *Spectator* 'read and debated about itself'.[50] For Warner, the emergence of 'temporally structured' publications was critical to the development of a public sphere, encouraging a self-awareness of the flow of debate and creating the sense of discussion 'currently unfolding in a sphere of activity'.[51] As mentioned above, the role of major events in prompting the issue of addresses ensured that a sense of timeliness was built into this form of political communication. Yet, these were more than ephemeral publications. As we will see, addressing activity quickly developed a consciousness of its own past through collections and histories of addressing which collated and commented upon these texts.

Most important, addressing activity directly engaged with and helped transform the role of the public in political affairs. This study will not dispute Knights' point that concerns were often raised about the reliability not only of addresses as quantitative indicators of public opinion but also as indicative in qualitative terms of the public's views. It will suggest, however, that these concerns need to be treated with caution and recognised not, perhaps, as the appeal of reasoned debate against the verdict of a majority swayed by partisan polemic, but instead as (in J. A. Downie's words) 'the sort of *ex post facto* rationalization which seeks to obscure party prejudice or self-interest'.[52] Ultimately, even the severest critics of 'Modern Addresses' (Daniel Defoe, John Oldmixon) held back from condemning addressing *tout court*. The reason, as we will see, was twofold. First, although the change was gradual, the increasing role of public opinion in politics did lead to a shift in the normative values surrounding 'popular' involvement in politics. This study argues that the reign of James II did not represent a potential turning-point in which this process might have unfolded differently: in place of the 'culture of incessant public adulation coupled with a sophisticated print-based propaganda regime' which Lake and Pincus see as indicative of his reign, this study will show that the practices of the 1680s were, in many ways, simply developments from and elaborations upon the tactics of the 1650s and 1660s.⁵³ While, to a certain degree, addressing campaigns might be stage-managed from the centre, the role of the public extended beyond simply shoring up authority. The implicit acknowledgement of the public involved in these exercises ultimately had a significant ideological impact. Popularity shifted from being a negative political value to one that was largely accepted and seen as a positive reflection of the nature of English government as founded on public consent. As Defoe remarked to Robert Harley in a letter of 1704:

> A Man Can Never be Great That is Not Popular, Especially in England. Tis Absolutely Necessary in the Very Nature of Our Constitution, where the People have So Great a Share in the Govornment.⁵⁴

Acknowledging that government was fundamentally 'popular' was not, though, as we will see, the same thing as legitimising mass participation in political life. Indeed, one of the arguments of this book is that by the end of the seventeenth century, a substantial consensus had developed around limiting popular engagement in subscriptional activity.

Second, from the earliest use of loyal addresses at the end of the Cromwellian Protectorate, the State became actively involved in the promotion of these devices. This helps explain the continued expansion of media and spaces for public discussion in the post-Restoration era. As Lake and Pincus have described it, the State 'could not put the genie back in the bottle'.⁵⁵ One reason for this was that the Stuart monarchy had recognised the 'genie' of public opinion could be very useful. Yet addressing could never be employed solely to legitimise power. As Lex Heerma Van Voss has noted, petitioning activity authorised the intervention of the centre in the administration of the periphery.⁵⁶ At the same time, however, as James Scott has observed, languages of legitimation could also place obligations on authority, while subordinate groups could exploit the deferential discourse of the 'public transcript' to achieve certain goals or concessions.⁵⁷ The reciprocal nature of addresses, demonstrated through their issue and response, and the giving and acknowledgement of thanks, meant that they could simultaneously be used to place demands upon authority and reap rewards from it.⁵⁸ Equally, the language deployed in addresses, frequently presented loyalty as constituting bonds of mutual love between subject and sovereign. As Defoe elaborated in the same letter to Harley, a truly 'popular' government was that which gained 'General Esteem Founded upon Good Actions, Truly Meriting the Love of the People'.⁵⁹ This reciprocal, affective understanding of loyalty was a consequence of the fundamentally emotional nature of addresses: while petitions were ultimately requests that authority *do* something, addresses were ostensibly expressions of feeling (gratitude, hope, love).

This study consequently complements the Habermasian theory of the public sphere in seeing the normative acceptance of the critical role of public opinion as fundamental. It also follows Habermas in locating the key moment of ideological change as coming in the late seventeenth to early eighteenth century. It supports Lake and Pincus' revised treatment of the early modern public sphere, however, in seeing this change as being in part facilitated by the participation of the State in public debate. It also sees the political 'public' that developed as both far more socially inclusive than envisaged by Habermas (including those on the margins of early modern society) and, at the same time, rhetorically more exclusive (often defined by status, gender, political affiliation and confessional identity). In this sense, though, as Geoff Kemp has noted, the early modern public was no different from its modern equivalent: it conceived of its 'audience as both the mass of the population and a coterie of discerning judges, a compound replicated in the imagined community of the modern political public'.[60] Critically, though, the question had shifted from being whether public opinion mattered to identifying who belonged to that discerning political public.

SOURCES, METHODS AND STRUCTURE

In making these claims, this book utilises a range of both printed and manuscript sources. The approach taken in this book is not to privilege either manuscript or printed evidence but to recognise the important role that both print and manuscript played in addressing activity, the former being critical to representing public opinion, the latter to the authenticating of texts as the genuine production of the communities they purported to come from. From the late 1650s onwards, loyal addresses were reproduced in great number in contemporary newsbooks, as well as being printed as separate broadsheets and collated into collections or compendia of texts. The value of this printed material is considerable. It provides us with a clear sense of the scale of these addressing campaigns, both in terms of the number of texts produced and also through reports of the numbers of individuals subscribing to these addresses. Analysis of these printed texts also provides us with an opportunity to see how addresses were used as vehicles for political and religious controversy. As well as preserving the content of addresses, print provides us with evidence of how these texts were produced and presented to authority, and often provides commentary on the disputes that sometimes arose in communities over issuing addresses. Cross- and counter-addresses provided clear evidence of partisan divisions, and print also played its part in fashioning political identity, attaching labels to different texts and assigning them to particular political or religious groupings ('Whig' or 'Tory', 'High Church' or 'Low Church').

Of course, this evidence needs to be treated with care. Addresses were most commonly reproduced in 'authorised' newsbooks – under the

Protectorate, *Mercurius Politicus*, after 1660 in the *London Gazette*. There is some evidence of under-reporting of particularly critical texts, with these addresses either omitted entirely or given only cursory notice. Addresses were unquestionably employed as a form of propaganda. Nonetheless, texts do not appear to have been simply fabricated. Comparison with manuscript addresses, for example, shows that the numbers of individuals reported to have subscribed to texts usually bore close relation to the actual number of subscribers. Instead, printed newsbooks, broadsheets and collections sought to 'spin' texts to demonstrate that public opinion was behind them. The repacking and editorialising of texts, as we will see, at times may have misrepresented the content of addresses. Yet, it also provides us with an indication of the importance of showing where the weight of public opinion lay. More than this, the process of identifying different addresses (and addressers) with particular positions, and recording this in print, embedded addressing activity in public memory. As will be shown later, printed addresses in newsbooks provided critical source material for collections and histories of addressing material which sought to provide a national and historical perspective on this activity. These texts in turn helped develop an awareness of shifts in public opinion over time, heightening a sense of the public as an independent, critical force.

Printed evidence is limited, however, in a number of respects. It offers us at best partial evidence of the actual process of production and subscription. This study employs manuscript returns and correspondence to shed light on how texts were prepared and then tendered to the public. Combined with other sources, such as parochial and tax records, this evidence also enables us to identify the social, religious and political background of subscribers. While this provides important proof of the social breadth of addressing activity and of the potential for addresses to be employed in the construction of political coalitions, the records of subscription in manuscript addresses can be deceptive. 'Fair copies' of addresses, for example, can give a misleading impression regarding the timing of subscription, conveying the sense that a document was subscribed in one sitting whereas sometimes a number of names were added at a later date. In addition, records of subscription, whether in originals or fair copies, provide very little evidence either about the motivations of subscribers or how individuals experienced addressing activity. For this reason, the book also makes use of 'ego texts' (diaries, memoirs and personal letters) to explore how contemporaries viewed addresses. Given the status of a number of these texts as private 'histories' or 'remembrances', such evidence also gives us a further insight into the relationship between addresses, memory and history.

The book begins by placing the loyal address in the context of other 'subscriptional genres' (to use Mark Knights' phrase), specifically petitions and oaths.[61] Reviewing the extensive historiography relating to both oath-taking

Introduction

and petitioning, Chapter one notes similarities between the impact of this activity and addressing. As with oaths and petitions, addresses could also be used to mobilise popular support and to represent that support publicly. In addition, addressing campaigns, as in the case of oath-taking and petitioning activity, could be employed to broadcast political and religious arguments from the centre to the localities. Finally, addressing campaigns, as in the case of petitioning and oath-taking, could include those normally excluded from the political process. This expansion of the political nation, while temporarily expedient, could also encourage a sense of popular agency. Without denying the importance of either oath-taking or petitioning to popular politics in early modern England, the chapter points towards some distinctive features of addressing activity. In particular, the inherently public and national nature of addressing campaigns distinguishes them from petitioning. These aspects of addresses, it is argued, made them peculiarly mnemonic texts, facilitating the connection of local with national history. While mass subscription was also a feature of addressing, the 'acclamatory' nature of addresses appeared to confer less political agency upon individual subscribers. Moreover, while there is good evidence of the social breadth of addressing as well as petitioning activity, addresses, unlike oaths and petitions, do not appear to have been subscribed by women. This particular feature of addresses would become more important in the eighteenth century.

The next three chapters of the book explore chronologically several key addressing campaigns. Chapter two focuses on the addresses issued to Richard Cromwell on his accession as Lord Protector in September 1658, a moment often identified as critical to the development of the loyal address as a political form. The chapter supports Mark Knights' observation that addresses operated as both 'accession' and 'succession' literature: that is that they both acknowledged and also debated the legitimacy of the new ruler.[62] In the case of the addresses to Richard Cromwell, the texts sent to him also engaged in broader debates around the Protectoral settlement, particularly concerning religious policy. Together, these texts point towards a late Cromwellian 'succession crisis', national in scope and, through instances of mass subscription, reaching down the social scale. Though Richard's Protectorate was notoriously short, the value of addresses as vehicles for political coalition building appears to have been recognised in the campaigns for a 'free Parliament'. The value of these devices as legitimating tools was also acknowledged by the restored Stuart monarchy which encouraged and welcomed congratulatory addresses from many English counties. The final, critical legacy of the Cromwellian period was to establish the public memory of addressing activity: the Cromwellian addresses were swiftly collected and critiqued in a number of largely hostile texts. The story of Richard Cromwell's trunks, in which he reputedly preserved the original addresses sent to him, would long stand as an example of the unreliability of these texts as evidence of genuine popular affection.

The impact of the memory of addressing activity in the Cromwellian period is explored in greater detail in Chapter three. The 1680s represented the most intensive decade of addressing activity during the period covered by this book. These campaigns frequently engaged with the history of popular subscriptional activity, both petitioning and oath-taking, identifying it as a prime cause of the civil wars and revolution. Loyal addressing was presented as an antidote to 'tumultuous' petitioning and conspiratorial oaths and covenants. The addressing activity of the 1650s provided Whigs in particular with an alternative historical narrative that could be deployed not only to attack individuals, such as the press censor and propagandist Sir Roger L'Estrange, but also to question the legitimacy of loyal addresses as expressions of public opinion. The politics of memory were also critical to the difficulties experienced by James II in deploying addresses to support his tolerationist policies. In seeking to emancipate Roman Catholics and dissenters, James' strategy of forming alliances with these groups cut against the now well-established connection between sedition, Popery and nonconformity. These controversial addressing campaigns would generate their own persistent memory which would be redeployed after the revolution of 1688 to humiliate, undermine and criticise individuals and communities for their former readiness to proclaim loyalty to the exiled Catholic Stuart dynasty.

As Chapter four demonstrates, the successive waves of addresses in support of very different royal policies was also used to question the value of addresses as indicators of authentic public opinion, just as the repeated tendering of oaths of allegiance during the civil wars had been used to criticise the worth of these devices. Addressing activity, nonetheless, continued after 1688 and arguably increased its political influence as it came to be directly tied to electioneering. These campaigns, however, were successfully employed by the government's opponents as well as its supporters, mirroring the use of these texts in contemporary Scotland. The success of opposition campaigns led the government's supporters to again use the past history of addressing activity, especially its more notorious moments during the rule of Richard Cromwell and the reign of James II, to attempt to discredit the practice. While the criticisms of addresses were far-reaching, they did, however, stop short of calling for an end to the activity. Indeed, though addresses acted as vehicles for the heated partisan rhetoric of the 'Rage of Party', the tone of these campaigns concealed a broader consensus on the legitimacy of petitioning and addressing, as well as the necessity of maintaining legal restrictions on popular political activity.

The subsequent chapters then examine different facets of addressing activity thematically. Chapter five explores the evidence of subscription to loyal addresses to uncover how these texts were circulated and who subscribed to them. Focusing in particular on one manuscript text, the address of

Introduction

the 'well-affected' inhabitants of Leicestershire to Richard Cromwell, the chapter demonstrates how subscription patterns mapped onto the geography of political allegiance and religious affiliation. The Leicestershire address also provides us with an unusual example of a cross- or counter-text existing within the same return and its very survival (within the papers of Cromwell's Secretary of State John Thurloe) may be explained as a consequence of the political suspicions the more equivocal text may have raised. It certainly demonstrates the social depth of addressing activity. Through a comparison of this manuscript with Hearth Tax records, the chapter shows that many of those subscribing to the Cromwellian address probably came from a significant but marginal section of society: those too poor to pay taxes but wealthy enough that they were not recipients of local relief or formal tax exemption. While addresses were occasionally very inclusive in terms of social status, in contrast to petitions and oaths, they appear to have been distinctively exclusive in terms of gender: female subscribers have been identified on only one manuscript address. Addresses issued immediately post-Restoration reacted to the petitions and addresses of the civil wars and interregnum by emphasising social exclusivity and hierarchy. This emphasis, however, was not maintained in the 1680s as popular petitioning and addressing was once again utilised to mobilise support. Even so, no serious attempt was made to remove the statutory limitations on mass petitioning and addressing of Parliament. After 1688, these legal restrictions on petitioning and addressing Parliament remained in place and the popularity of addresses was also usually presented in clearly qualified terms with subscribers identified as exclusively the freeholders of a particular area. Subscriptional activity was thereby accommodated within an environment in which government was accepted as being founded on public consent but in which that political public was often clearly circumscribed so as to exclude women and plebeian men.

Chapter six further explores the surviving manuscript evidence to examine the performance of addressing in drafting, delivering and presenting these texts. It shows that producing an address involved making a number of potentially fraught political choices, not only about the content of the text but also concerning who were the appropriate people from the locality to deliver this text to authority and who should be approached to introduce these texts at Court. The last question involved some understanding of politics at the centre as well as in the locality. Addressing was also potentially costly in financial as well as political terms: there were fewer opportunities for cost-cutting in comparison with petitioning, especially immediately after the Restoration, when addresses were also frequently accompanied with cash gifts. Such expenditure did not necessarily signal ideological commitment: the chapter employs the case study of the Hallamshire Cutlers to demonstrate that groups employed addressing as a strategy to buy political access and influence (in their case in a bid to secure tax exemption for their forges). There remained benefits for authority in securing such addresses, even if the communities had been motivated by pragmatic concerns rather than heartfelt loyalty. Addressing required a public performance of loyalty which could then be publicised through 'official' media such as the *Gazette*. More than this, the ceremonial itself, especially during the reign of Charles II, provided opportunities to control and manage public opinion through the careful filtering of political access. These strategies were employed less sensitively during the reign of James II but the difficulties that James experienced also demonstrate the degree to which successful addressing campaigns were dependent on cooperation with local elites.

The final chapter of the book looks at the changing language of loyalty over the period under consideration. It follows recent philosophical and historical work on loyalty to see this value as being consistently articulated in emotional terms. Chapter seven employs corpus analysis software to explore the language of addresses as contained in printed compendia of texts produced over the period 1659 to 1756. This analysis demonstrates that the affective register of loyalty remained although the objects of loyalty shifted after 1688. In the post-revolutionary era, loyalty was more frequently identified with ideas (liberty) and institutions (the State). The tendency of addressing campaigns to generate new political vocabularies was noted by critical observers who suggested that the fluidity of the political lexicon threatened the credibility of addresses. Authors such as Daniel Defoe, John Oldmixon and Benjamin Hoadly, however, stepped back from either discrediting loyal addresses or the emotional language in which they were frequently framed. Indeed, Oldmixon suggested that addresses needed to be evaluated in terms of the authenticity of the feelings expressed within them. The chapter demonstrates that the emotional understanding of loyalty was, if anything, heightened by the post-revolutionary context in which sincerity was prized over correctness of belief and legitimate political organisation was seen as being founded on voluntary association.

As the conclusion to this volume demonstrates, addressing adapted not only to the post-revolutionary political context, but also to the emergence of mass (male) democracy in the nineteenth century. The survival of loyal addressing demonstrates its particular suitability for a democratic nation in which public life, nonetheless, remains centred on a hereditary monarchy. The greatest paradox, of course, is that this enduring means of demonstrating public loyalty to the Crown had its origins in the papers kept in Richard Cromwell's trunks.

NOTES

1 MP Paul Flynn decries Duke's Birthday Address', Wales Online, 6 August 2011, www.walesonline.co.uk/news/wales-news/2011/06/08/mp-paul-flynn-decries-duke-s-birthday-address-91466-28846585/, accessed 12 August 2013.

2 'MPs' tribute to Prince Philip's "unique turn of phrase"', BBC News online, 8 June 2011, www.bbc.co.uk/news/uk-politics-13698601, accessed 12 August 2013.
3 'Quakers Divided Over Loyal Address to Monarch', *Ekklesia*, 27 March 2012, www.ekklesia.co.uk/node/16464, accessed 12 August 2013.
4 www.royal.gov.uk/RoyalEventsandCeremonies/Addresses/Addresses.aspx, accessed 12 August 2013.
5 *London Gazette*, 2 June 2012, no. 60160, www.thegazette.co.uk/London/issue/60160?supplement/4, accessed 5 May 2017.
6 K. Bowie, *Scottish Public Opinion and the Anglo-Scottish Union, 1699–1707* (Woodbridge: Boydell and Brewer, 2007), p. 1.
7 B. Kümin and A. Würgler, 'Petitions, gravamina and the early modern state: local influence on central legislation in England and Germany (Hesse)', *Parliaments, Estates and Representation*, 15 (1995), 39–60; J. Walter, 'The English people and the English Revolution revisited', *History Workshop Journal*, 61 (2006), 171–82; J. Walter, 'Confessional politics in pre-civil war Essex: prayer books, profanations and petitions', *Historical Journal*, 44 (2001), 677–701. J. Daybell (ed.), 'Introduction: rethinking women and politics in early modern England', *Women and Politics in Early Modern England, 1450–1700* (Aldershot: Ashgate, 2004), ch. 1; M. Knights, 'London's "Monster" Petition of 1680', *Historical Journal*, 36 (1993), 39–67; David Zaret, 'Petitions and the "invention" of public opinion in the English revolution', *American Journal of Sociology*, 101 (1996), 1497–555; Zaret, *Origins of Democratic Culture: Printing, Petitions and the Public Sphere in Early-Modern England* (Princeton, NJ: Princeton University Press, 2000).
8 M. Knights, *Politics and Opinion in Crisis 1678–81* (Cambridge: Cambridge University Press, 1994), esp. chs 8 & 9; M. Knights, *Representation and Misrepresentation in Later Stuart Britain* (Oxford: Oxford University Press, 2005), pp. 109–62; Bowie, *Scottish Public Opinion*, esp. ch. 6.
9 S. Sowerby, 'Forgetting the repealers: religious toleration and historical amnesia in later Stuart England', *Past and Present*, 215 (2011), 85–123; Sowerby, *Making Toleration: The Repealers and the Glorious Revolution* (Cambridge, MA: Harvard University Press, 2013).
10 [John Oldmixon], *The History of Addresses. By One Very Near a Kin to the Author of the Tale of a Tub* (1709), p. 2.
11 Knights, *Representation and Misrepresentation*, p. 149.
12 D. Hirst, 'Making contact: petitions and the English republic', *Journal of British Studies*, 45 (2006), 26–50.
13 E. May, *Treatise on the Law, Privileges, Proceedings and Usage of Parliament (Parliamentary Practice)*, ed. Sir C. Gordon (20th edn, London: Butterworth's, 1983), pp. 635–9.
14 https://constitution-unit.com/2017/11/10/labours-motion-for-a-return-what-and-why/, accessed 6 April 2018.
15 S. Poole, *The Politics of Regicide in England 1760–1850: Troublesome Subjects* (Manchester: Manchester University Press, 2000), p. 31.
16 J. Redlich, *The Procedure of the House of Commons* (3 vols, London, 1908), ii, pp. 246 and 244–8 more generally for addresses to the Crown.
17 Knights, *Representation and Misrepresentation*, p. 117 features a useful table indicating the major occasions on which addresses were created and see also Knights, 'Participation and representation before democracy: petitions and addresses in

pre-modern Britain', in I. Shapiro, S. C. Stokes, E. J. Wood, and A. S. Kirshner (eds), *Political Representation* (Cambridge: Cambridge University Press, 2009), pp. 35–57 at pp. 45–8.
18 Bowie, *Scottish Public Opinion*, p. 6.
19 Knights, *Representation and Misrepresentation*, p. 118.
20 A. Browning, *English Historical Documents 1660–1714* (London: Eyre and Spottiswood, 1966), p. 66 for the text of the act.
21 Zaret, 'Petitions and the "Invention" of Public Opinion', 1517.
22 Ibid., 1532.
23 Knights, *Representation and Misrepresentation*, pp. 115–16.
24 Ibid., pp. 162–3.
25 J. Habermas, *The Structural Transformation of the Public Sphere*, trans. T. Burger (Cambridge: Polity Press, 1992), p. 57.
26 For the former, see the earlier work of Steven Pincus, '"Coffee politicians does create" coffeehouses and Restoration political culture', *Journal of Modern History*, 67 (1995), 807–34, and for the latter J. A. Downie, 'Public and private: the myth of the bourgeois public sphere', in C. Wall (ed.), *A Concise Companion to the Restoration and Eighteenth Century* (Oxford: Blackwell, 2005), pp. 58–79.
27 Lake and Pincus, 'Rethinking the public sphere in early modern England', in Lake and Pincus (eds), *The Politics of the Public Sphere in Early Modern England* (Manchester: Manchester University Press, 2007), pp. 1–31; p. 2.
28 Ibid., p. 3.
29 Ibid.
30 Zaret, *Origins of Democratic Culture*, p. 11.
31 Ibid., p. 59.
32 See here the important work of Natalie Mears, *Queenship and Political Discourse in the Elizabethan Realms* (Cambridge: Cambridge University Press, 2005).
33 B. C. Cowan, 'What was masculine about the public sphere? Gender and the coffee-house milieu in post-Restoration England', *History Workshop Journal*, 51 (2001), 127–57 at 128.
34 See for an example of this Bob Harris' review article, 'Historians, public opinion and the "public sphere"', *Journal of Early Modern History*, 1 (1997), 368–77 at 377 where public opinion is described as 'articulated by real people whose perceptions and languages cannot be encapsulated in any general sociological model'.
35 J. D. Peters, 'historical tensions in the concept of public opinion', in T. L. Glasser, and C. T. Salmon (eds), *Public Opinion and the Communication of Consent* (New York, London: Guilford Press, 1995), p. 3–33; P. Bourdieau, 'Public opinion does not exist', in A. Mattelart and S. Siegelaub (eds), *Communication and Class Struggle* (2 vols, New York: International General, 1979), pp. 124–30.
36 Lake and Pincus, 'Public sphere', p. 3.
37 Ibid., pp. 13–14 for political economy, pp. 18–19 for scale and scope of public sphere.
38 Michael Warner, *Publics and Counterpublics* (New York: Zone Books, 2002), p. 55.
39 Geoff Kemp, 'L'Estrange and the publishing sphere', in J. McElligott (ed.), *Fear, Exclusion and Revolution: Roger Morrice and Britain in the 1680s* (Aldershot: Ashgate, 2006), pp. 67–91, at p. 69. For another approach from a history of ideas

perspective see Geoff Baldwin, 'The "public" as a rhetorical community in early modern England', in A. Shepard and P. Withington (eds), *Communities In Early Modern England: Networks, Place, Rhetoric* (Manchester: Manchester University Press, 2000), pp. 199–215.

40 Zaret, *Origins of Democratic Culture*, p. 220; Knights, *Representation and Misrepresentation*, p. 160.
41 J. Peacey, *Print and Public Politics in the English Revolution* (Cambridge: Cambridge University Press, 2013).
42 Kemp, 'L'Estrange and the publishing sphere', p. 89.
43 *Observator*, 13 April 1681, no. 1. On L'Estrange and petitioning see M. Knights, 'Roger L'Estrange, printed petitions and the problem of intentionality', in J. Morrow and J. Scott (eds), *Liberty, Authority, Formality, Political Ideas and Culture, 1600–1900, Essays in Honour of Colin Davis* (Exeter: Imprint Academic, 2008), ch. 6.
44 Habermas, *Structural Transformation*, pp. 64–5. Of course, Habermas here forgets that the 'King' in 1710 was a queen.
45 Ibid., p. 51 he describes it as a 'sphere of criticism of public authority'.
46 Ibid., p. 54.
47 The social make-up of Scottish addresses is tabulated in Karin Bowie, 'Scottish Public Opinion and the Making of Union' (PhD dissertation, Glasgow University, 2004), vol. 2, appendix I.
48 Habermas, *Structural Transformation*, p. 54.
49 Ibid., pp. 52–3.
50 Ibid., p. 43.
51 Warner, *Publics and Counterpublics*, pp. 95–6.
52 Downie, 'Public and private', p. 73.
53 Lake and Pincus, 'Rethinking the public sphere', p. 12, perhaps, again, influenced by Habermas' reference to 'plebiscitarily manipulated assent', *Structural Transformation*, pp. 67–8.
54 *The Letters of Daniel Defoe*, ed. G. H. Healey (Oxford: Clarendon Press, 1955), p. 33. Contrast this with earlier treatments of 'popularity' as a threat to the State: P. Lake, 'The politics of "popularity" and the public sphere: the "monarchical republic" of Elizabeth I defends itself'; and P. Hammer, 'The smiling crocodile: the earl of Essex and late Elizabethan "popularity"', both in Lake and Pincus (eds), *The Politics of the Public Sphere*, chs 3 & 4.
55 Lake and Pincus, 'Rethinking the public sphere', p. 18.
56 L. Heerma Van Voss, 'Supplications between politics and justice: the northern and central Italian states in the early modern age', in Heerma van Voss (ed.), *Petitions in Social History* (Cambridge: Cambridge University Press, 2002), pp. 35–56, at p. 55.
57 J. C. Scott, *Domination and the Arts of Resistance: Hidden Transcripts* (New Haven, CT: Yale University Press, 1990) and for an important collection applying Scott's ideas to the context of early modern England, see M. J. Braddick and J. Walter (eds), *Negotiating Power in Early Modern Society: Order, Hierarchy and Subordination in Britain and Ireland* (Cambridge: Cambridge University Press, 2001).
58 On this aspect of legitimation see M. J. Braddick and J. Walter (eds), 'Introduction. Grids of power: order, hierarchy and subordination in early modern society', *Negotiating Power in Early Modern Society*, pp. 1–42, esp. pp. 9–12.

59 *Letters of Defoe*, ed. Healey, p. 41.
60 Kemp, 'L'Estrange', p. 87; See on this Warner, *Publics and Counterpublics*, p. 106.
61 Knights, *Representation and Misrepresentation*, p. 109.
62 M. Knights, 'The loyal address: prose panegyric 1658–1715', in A. McRae and P. Kewes (eds), *Stuart Succession Literature: Moments and Transformations* (Oxford: Oxford University Press: 2018), ch. 16, p. 326. I am grateful to Mark Knights for letting me see a copy of his chapter prior to publication.

Chapter 1

Petitions, oaths and addresses: subscriptional activity during the civil wars

> ... all these petitions for a translation, both of Church and State, with so little fear of the Halter, that they would thinke themselves neglected, if they had not thanks for their care for the Re-publicke; only he that desires the ratification of an old Law, or of a long setled Eccelsiastick Government, looked as if the Halter were his share.[1]

This Royalist commentary on the Parliamentarian petitioning of 1640–2 in support of first 'Root and Branch' reform of the church and then the Protestation of 1641 and Grand Remonstrance, explicitly connected this activity with revolutionary change. Recent scholarly treatments of petitioning and oath-taking during the 1640s have drawn similar conclusions: the subscriptional texts that proliferated during this period have been seen as fostering a democratic political culture, making public opinion 'the ultimate ground of legitimacy for a legislative agenda';[2] devices such as the Protestation 'offered agency to an active citizenry and authority to the Parliament';[3] and the incorporation of subscribers normally excluded from political processes on the grounds of social status or gender pointed to a radical expansion of the boundaries of the political nation.[4] These transformations were underwritten by technological change (especially the growth of printed petitions), leading to fundamental shifts in political practice which, it is argued, were not reversed by the restoration of monarchy in 1660.[5]

This chapter places loyal addressing within the context of these broader developments in English subscriptional culture. Beginning with a discussion of the historiography of popular petitioning, it moves on to consider mass oath-taking during the civil war. Loyal addresses certainly shared a number of features with these other subscriptional texts: print was critical to the practice of addressing and to the impact of addresses upon contemporary understandings of the 'public'. Many loyal addresses were also subscribed (or reputed to be subscribed) in very large numbers and, as with petitions, mass subscription was used as evidence that these texts were representative of public opinion. As with petitions, however, claims to representativeness were in tension with contemporary understandings of who could exercise political agency. Yet, as both petitions and addresses could generate cross- or counter-texts, subscriptional activity also generated an awareness of political and religious difference, while encouraging the audience for these texts to adjudicate between rival claims. These subscriptional texts were also far from ephemeral: oath-taking, petitioning and addressing, as critical, popular forms of political activity, all generated a public memory of political loyalty and mass grievance. Print facilitated this memorialising process for both petitions and addresses, enabling the creation of compendia or catalogues of texts directed at delivering the sense of national public opinion at particular moments. This same aspect of subscriptional texts also meant that they were often included within both manuscript and printed histories.

Given these similarities and the common contemporary practice of treating 'petitions' and 'addresses' as synonymous (noted above), this book will not attempt to maintain a hard and fast division between addressing and other forms of subscriptional activity. In this and subsequent chapters, however, it will also be argued that a number of particular features of addressing activity set it apart from other types of subscriptional texts and made addresses critical to the development of an awareness of public opinion.

Foremost among these was the primary purpose of the address in displaying collective public loyalty before authority. This emphasis on collective loyalty was important for two reasons: first, because it lessened the stress on individual agency and second, because it suggested texts should be evaluated on the basis of the loyalty of the subscribers. Claims were made on the basis of an emotionally laden language of loyalty, rather than on the grounds of rights and responsibilities which invited rational adjudication.

The relationship between addresses and print was also distinct from that in petitioning. Whereas print might be used as part of discreet lobbying strategies, in addressing activity, print was almost exclusively employed to publicise the loyalty of the addressers (and by extension, the level of public support enjoyed by the regime in question). These connections between addressing, printing, publicity and central authority meant that addressing was a peculiarly mnemonic genre. Prompted by events such as the succession of a new ruler, the birth of royal heirs and military victories, the content of addresses ostensibly tackled national history in a relatively homogenous fashion. This in turn readily enabled the anthologising and historicising of these texts, embedding addressing activity in public memory. Histories and anthologies of addressing activity provided testimony of the growing importance of public opinion as an authoritative force in early modern politics. The nature of addressing activity, however, meant that the acknowledgement of public opinion did not involve an acknowledgement either that the scope of the political nation had been fundamentally transformed or that participation in this kind of popular political activity conferred the characteristics of citizens upon the participants. While the 'sense of the nation' was now critical to legitimating authority, the rise of public opinion, it is argued, should be separated from notions of emergent liberal democracy or expanding understandings of citizenship.

MASS PETITIONS DURING THE CIVIL WARS

Petitioning, both at the time and subsequently, has been seen as critical to the political history of the 1640s. Edward Husbands' highly influential *An Exact Collection* of Parliament's declarations and votes included both parliamentary and extra-parliamentary petitions as part of its anthology of the key texts produced from 1640–2.[6] Since the 1980s at least, historians, though they may differ over the precise significance of petitioning the 1640s, have rejected the older assumption that this activity was purely the product of elite orchestration and manipulation.[7] For Anthony Fletcher, petitions instead deserved 'recognition as an authentic expression of deeply felt local opinion'. Far from being 'parrot petitions', cooked up at the political centre, the similarities between petitions could be explained by the process of local communities acting 'one after another as they heard what friends and neighbours were doing'.[8] Similar processes, as we will see, can be observed in the case of loyal addresses.

In contrast to addressing, of course, petitioning was anything but a new or uniquely English practice. Studies of petitioning range from ancient Egypt to Khrushchev's Soviet Union.[9] Some of the earliest handwritten texts in Britain take a petitionary form: the seventy-eight 'curse tablets' discovered by the archaeologist Barry Cunliffe beneath the Roman springs at Bath are petitions to the Gods etched in lead, calling on them to exact vengeance against those who had wronged the supplicants.[10] Early modern England might be described as a petitioning society: very large numbers of manuscript petitions survive both centrally (in parliamentary archives or State papers for example) and in local record offices; petitions survive from individuals across the social scale and from women as well as men; petitioning activity was woven into the administration of manorial estates and advice on constructing petitions was a key element of epistolary manuals; and while the costs of producing a written petition meant that this form of the activity was not open to everyone, the degree of participation in petitionary activity was extensive.[11] Petitioning, as Brodie Waddell has described it, was a political form well-suited to a society which valued equity but not equality.[12] One volume of Protectoral State papers held at Yale captures their variety: from a petition from the well-affected of York in 1648 calling on Parliament to execute justice especially against 'such as are guilty of polluting a land with blood', to petitions to the Protector from the widows and wives of Royalists seeking to compound for their estates, to petitions against the schoolmaster and anti-Trinitarian John Biddle.[13]

The sheer variety and ubiquity of petitioning activity poses its own problems for historians. As David Zaret has observed, the fact that women and even slaves could petition, indicates that the right to petition was not a 'right in the modern sense but related instead to medieval conceptions of liberty'. It was a privilege, granting (under certain conditions) the freedom to communicate with and make requests to social and political superiors.[14] This 'right' consequently was not a badge of citizenship. The appropriate content and tenor of petitions to Parliament by the seventeenth century was well-defined: petitions were to be couched in deferential terms and it was widely agreed that petitions should not attempt to dictate terms to Parliament. As Lord Digby commented in response to the London 'Root and Branch' petition: 'What can there be of greater presumption, than for a multitude to teach a parliament what and what is not government according to God's word.'[15]

The creation of a petition was supposed to be a spontaneous act, driven by immediate experience of a pressing issue or problem, not a deliberative (and thereby more political) public reflection on a particular grievance. Matters of broader public concernment were, in any case, to be left to petitions from the relevant institutions of local government and private individuals were to restrict themselves to matters that directly concerned them so as to avoid accusations of conspiratorial or factional activity.[16] The norms that surrounded petitioning have led Amanda Whiting to argue that most petitions, deferential and submissive in tone, and limited in scope, tended to make use of a 'feminine speaking position'. In this sense, women's use of petitioning was only slightly more constrained than that of other petitioners.[17]

Identifying a particular, unmediated 'voice' through petitions is also problematised by their formulaic and uniform nature. Petitions have been identified as vital source for exploring the social as well as the political imaginary. The vast majority of 'pauper petitions', however, were written by scribes on behalf of the petitioners. As Jonathan Healey and Steve Hindle have argued, what these sources offer instead are 'hybrid voices', the product of the intersection of the petitioners' experiences and demands, the scribes' cultural world and the expectations of authority.[18] The proliferation of petitions to Parliament by the fourteenth century, with an accompanying rise in the use of scriveners and lawyers to compose them, led to a similar uniformity in these texts as well.[19] The content of the petition followed an established order, beginning with the address to the intercessor (exordium), followed by the identification of the applicant, the statement of the complaint, the request for remedy and form that the remedy should take (narratio or proposito), before closing with the petition proper or peroratio (the appeal for the remedy).[20] By this point, petitioning activity had become further regularised by the creation of groups of receivers and auditors to handle petitions, and by the establishing of the distinction between 'common' (those which addressed matters of broader concernment) and 'private' petitions.[21]

The growth of parliamentary petitioning in the late medieval period did not simply reflect growing demand that Parliament hear and act upon public grievances, but also the value of petitioning activity to the Crown in bolstering its authority and extending its legal 'reach'. According to Gwilym Dodd,

> by introducing a legal channel by which men (or women) of lesser status could seek redress without resorting to local judicial structures (which could be dominated by powerful interest groups), Edward [I] not only made local government accountable, but in doing so significantly increased the power and control that the Crown wielded over its servants.[22]

Successful petitioning activity, as noted by Brodie Waddell, typically required a combination of assertiveness and deference, a readiness to demand that authority fulfil its obligations and remedy grievances, while at the same time acknowledging that the intercessor alone was authorised to resolve the problems the petition outlined.[23]

During the 1640s this delicate balance between submissiveness and complaint became destabilised. As we will see, in the post-Restoration period, popular petitioning was frequently identified (in the words of the 1661 act against tumultuous petitioning) as 'a great meanes of the late unhappy Wars Confusions and Calamities in this Nation'.[24] The qualitative shift in the nature of public petitioning was noted in a number of areas: the exponential increase in the number of persons involved in petitioning activity; the increasing resort to print to publicise the petitioners' complaints and to counter other opposing petitions; and the shift in the tone of petitioning, from the articulation of requests for action made with due deference to authority, to the expression of assertive demands grounded on the assumption that authority had an obligation to the public to satisfy them.

Mass petitioning not only appeared to challenge one of the accepted conventions of petitioning – that petitions should be generated and subscribed by those directly affected by/concerned in the matter of the petition – but also seemed to attack the notions of social and political hierarchy inherent in petitioning activity. As Leoline Jenkins commented to Lord Chief Justice North during the Exclusion Crisis:

> What was there in the beginning and progress of the last war more designing against lawful authority and more pernicious in the consequences than popular petitions? The artifice in them is so much more un-ingenious, as that the suffrages, that is the judgment of Tag and Rag, are made equal to those of the greatest men.

Whiting notes that these kinds of comments were not exclusive to the Royalist side.[25] The 1661 act which curbed popular petitioning post-Restoration was heavily indebted to a 1648 Parliamentary Declaration 'against tumultuous Assemblies, under Pretence of preparing petitions'.[26] As we will see, these reservations about mass petitioning remained in the post-Restoration era, even as this practice re-emerged during the Exclusion Crisis, and survived the Revolution of 1688.

Popular petitioning was encouraged, however, both as a means of mobilising support and as a tool for exerting pressure on political opponents. There was an air of both intimidation as well as pomp around the presentation of some mass petitions such as the Buckinghamshire petition, delivered with 3,000 participants on horseback, with sword at their sides and copies of the Parliament's Protestation in their hats or held in their hands.[27] The reference here to the Protestation makes clear that petitioning in the years 1641–42 was being combined with other subscriptional genres, namely oaths, to mobilise the population effectively in support of Parliament. Indeed, John Walter's research has suggested that the imprecision in the Parliament's orders for subscription to the Commons' Protestation, especially the absence of gendered language, may have been deliberate: a means of harnessing both male and female support for Parliament at a moment in which it was under threat from a Royalist coup.[28] This strategy may, in turn, have been inspired by the prominence of women in the Scottish covenanter movement.[29]

The use of such strategies also secured the same benefit for the English Parliament as parliamentary petitioning had done for the medieval Crown in legitimating and extending its authority.[30] In order for this aspect of petitioning to be fully realised, however, such activity had to be publicised. The role of print in petitioning during the civil wars has been the most commented upon facet of this activity. Petitions were reproduced as broadsheets and within pamphlets; they were also incorporated into newsbooks and reprinted as collections of texts.[31]

Jason Peacey has shown that not all printed petitions were directed at publicising the content of the petition to a broad public audience. Instead printing could offer a more affordable means of targeting a select group of individuals, for example MPs, that the petitioners wished to lobby.[32] John Rees has noted that the printing of petitions was sometimes employed to facilitate gathering subscriptions, to mobilise individuals to join a cause rather than simply to publicise it.[33] As David Zaret has argued, however, the printing of petitions did have wider political ramifications. Print not only broadcast the petitioners' concerns to a wider audience nor simply reflected the level of support for policies, such as the reform of the English church, but also, Zaret contends, encouraged both petitioners and their readers to participate in public debate.[34] This discursive aspect to petitioning was facilitated by the 'dialogic order' imposed by print: the citing and reproducing of texts in opposing works as a form of criticism; the creation of 'counter' or 'cross' positions which acknowledged a divided rather than harmonious, consensual political and religious landscape; and the encouragement to the readership of these petitions to employ their reason in adjudicating between these competing truth claims.[35] Printed petitions also helped generate a record of political activity and its consequences, with later texts complaining of the failure of earlier petitions and contemporary newsbooks reporting on petitioning activity.[36] According to Zaret, printing also had the effect of separating popular petitioning from its physical sites of discussion and subscription. This was advantageous as these sites (alehouses for example) could be associated with seditious and/or libellous activity. Furthermore, the 'backstage' work of petitioning was frequently used to undermine the credibility of petitions (by claiming that subscribers were forced or bribed into signing, or unable to form a judgement about the matter of the petition because they were drunk or illiterate).[37]

One other, currently less commented upon feature of petitioning activity was the way in which it quickly became embedded into the history of the civil wars. There was a long-standing interrelationship between petitioning and history, identified by Andy Wood in his examination of Elizabethan manuscript civic histories deposited in Great Yarmouth's town archive, the 'Yarmouth Hutch'. One practical rationale for compiling these histories was to provide a resource that could be a store of 'good Presidentes lefte unto them in the tyme of there necessities to make and frame there sutes and peticions'.[38] This pragmatic use of history in petitioning was followed by a more ideological deployment of subscriptional texts in historical works both during and after the civil wars. The godly London wood turner Nehemiah Wallington's collection of petitions had been gathered, he said, so that,

> generations to come ... may see and behold what our God hath done in the stirring up of the people of all counties, and of all sorts, high and low, rich and poor, of both sexes, men and women, old and young, bond and free, both in cities and countries, for to go up to Westminster ... with their petitions.[39]

These processes of collecting were facilitated by print and especially by the reproduction of material in contemporary newsbooks.

Wallington's consumption of news, therefore, was driven by a desire to preserve a historical record of God's work in England through his people. Much of the recent work on early modern news media, on the other hand, has focused on the importance of 'contemporaneity' – the significance of an emerging sense of the 'now'. Daniel Woolf has argued that early modern news media created a 'de-temporalised zone' which encouraged critical debate of contemporary politics in ways analogous to a Habermasian public sphere.[40]

In many respects, as we will see, the print media used to promote and disseminate addressing campaigns display the characteristics of flow, density and commonality Woolf argues were critical to the conception of the present as a defined period rather than a fleeting moment.[41] As has been suggested in a recent article by Tony Claydon, however, the 'permanent separation of news from history' identified by Daniel Woolf was, perhaps, less final than he contends.[42] This was not least, as Noah Millstone has demonstrated, because early modern printed newsbooks, in both England and continental Europe, were frequently specifically designed to be collected and collated, with these collections providing vital reference works for the writing of history.[43] Collections of this kind, however, could be catalogues of infamy as well as glory: the 1642 compendium of petitions in defence of the church was reprinted twice, first in 1660 and then again in 1681. The text issued during the Exclusion Crisis noted on its revised title page that these petitions had been 'Occasioned by the many Libellous Petitions, then secretly set on Foot both against Church and State ... and now again publish'd to precaution the ill-meaning Zealots of this Age'.[44] The self-referential nature of petitioning activity, noted above, helped fashion a public memory of political conduct which could be deployed later to defend or critique activity in the present moment.

Nehemiah Wallington's intention in collecting petitions was clearly also more than archival. The 'stirring up of the people' may have been part of a divine plan but the activity of ordinary men and women was clearly critical to this design. While petitioning did provide opportunities for authority to extend its political reach, mass petitioning also conferred agency on subscribers who were otherwise formally excluded from political life. The tone of petitioning shifted, with the language of humility and submission before authority replaced in some instances with the frank expectation that grievances would be addressed by a Parliament that was acting in the service of the people.[45] As Alice Rolph asserted in her 1648 petition, the Parliament was 'chosen and betrusted by the people to provide for their Weal but not for their Woe; and to maintain their Laws and Liberties, which you have often promised, sworn and declared to do'.[46]

Even when the language of petitions remained deferential, the public displays of submissiveness usually anticipated as accompanying their presentation were flouted, as petitioners crowded, haranged and harassed MPs.[47] If the right to petition was not itself a mark of citizenship, the expansion of political petitioning during the civil war certainly appears to have had a role to play in the development of the political identity of some petitioners. While Ann Hughes has observed that many petitions from women continued to deploy traditional feminine roles as wives and mothers, some, such as the Leveller women's petition of May 1649, made bold and radical statements of equality with men.[48] Even the less controversial petitions for relief produced by widows during and after the civil wars involved making political claims, asserting their loyalty and that of their family in order to secure restitution.[49]

OATHS OF LOYALTY

Other subscriptional texts also appear to have imbued their subscribers with a sense of political identity and authority, and legitimised their political activism. Oath-taking, like petitioning, was a very well-established feature of public life by the seventeenth century. It was integral to office-holding, with public servants from the great offices of State to lowly parish constables expected to swear oaths to perform their duties diligently.[50] Prior to the civil war, oaths of loyalty had already undergone a transformation in both nature and scope. The personal oath of fealty was replaced by a range of tests which required subscribers to assent to particular ideological positions (for example the supremacy of the English Crown over the Church.)[51] The social range of those expected to declare their loyalty to such positions also dramatically broadened: according to the Earl of Huntingdon 'a great number of inferior quality' subscribed to the Bond of Association in defence of Elizabeth I in 1584, a claim borne out by subsequent historical analysis of the returns of this solemn bond.[52] By the end of the seventeenth century, returns for the 1696 Association to William III (an oath of loyalty consciously modelled on its Elizabethan predecessor) were so vast in scale that they may have included the entirety of some counties' adult male populations.[53]

The frequency of these exercises in canvassing public loyalty reached its highest pitch during the civil wars, as the Parliamentarians devised successive and distinct loyalty tests both to mobilise support and to help identify opponents. Counter-oaths were also tendered on the Royalist side, though on a seemingly less ambitious scale.[54] As their roles as 'Shibboleths' (the Biblical allusion employed by John Pym in describing the Protestation) indicates, the language of these texts was grounded in an adversarial idiom of the 'well-affected' pitched against the 'malignants'. As Tom Leng has noted, the sort of activism encouraged by these texts was focused upon combating an enemy: in place of much overt discussion of citizenship was an emotional language focused on zeal for the cause and hatred for its opponents.[55] In some parishes, subscription to the Protestation was combined with the process of securing contributions to the Parliament's collection for the 'distressed [Protestant] subjects of the Kingdom of Ireland', providing an opportunity for parishioners to show individual support for the struggle against the forces of Popery.[56] Consequently, it is unsurprising that devices such as the Protestation and the Solemn League and Covenant seemed to some subscribers to also provide them with the justification to undertake direct action without further authorisation from Parliament. Acts of iconoclasm in some parishes followed subscription first to the Protestation and then the Solemn League and Covenant.[57] It was also used to justify other forms of popular politics, namely the drawing up of mass petitions.[58] There were similarities too with popular petitioning in the importance of printing both in giving practical directions as to who should subscribe, and when and where they do so, and in enabling subscription itself through the mass production of printed texts of the oaths.[59]

Parliament's oaths, covenants and associations provided it with a vital means to project its political and religious vision into the localities both via print but also orally, through the extensive sermonising that accompanied the tendering of these tests.[60] Tellingly though, some individuals, such as Alice Rolph mentioned above, stressed that these tests placed obligations upon Parliament, as well as upon the subscribers. Similar arguments were adopted by the most celebrated radical groups of the 1640s: the Levellers and the Diggers.[61] The inclusion of women in particular on oath returns was arguably a more transgressive act than women's petitioning, given the association between oath-taking and traditional male roles (public office and, during the civil war, military service).[62] As Sara Mendelson and Patricia Crawford have argued, the subscriptions of some women appear to have been a conscious assertion of an independent political identity.[63] In broader terms, David Cressy has described the Protestation as a 'practical mobilisation of citizenship' which gave subscribers 'a stake in the outcome' of the English revolution.[64] I have suggested elsewhere that the process of subscribing to oaths and covenants promising to defend the rights and liberties of the subject, as well as the privileges of Parliament, may have helped inform radical proposals for constitutional change, namely the various iterations of the 'Agreement of the People'.[65] Given the emphasis placed on individual agency, the publicising of these tests through print and sermons and their role as vehicles for Parliamentarian 'mission statements', it is unsurprising that mass oath-taking, as with petitioning, embedded itself in public memory.[66] After the Restoration, the Solemn League and Covenant of 1643, for example, came to be emblematic of the 'Good Old Cause'.[67]

Subscriptional activity during the civil wars played a significant role in broadening political participation. Oaths and mass petitions presented a significant challenge to authority by seemingly permitting the public a voice in matters, such as Church government, that had previously been the preserve of Crown and Parliament. Unquestionably, for some individuals, involvement in this activity had a radicalising effect, enhancing their own sense of political independence. Some even went so far as viewing the Parliament's oaths and covenants as social contracts which made allegiance conditional on the fulfilment of certain conditions. While some scholars, notably David Zaret, have seen these devices as fostering a democratic political culture, the relationship between these devices and citizenship was not straightforward. As noted by Walter above, the involvement of women as subscribers (for example) appears to have been driven by expediency rather than any weakening of patriarchal values. Indeed, women petitioners consistently received better treatment when they employed traditional feminine tropes and when their petitions focused upon matters (the home, the family, 'women's work') that were seen as appropriate to their station. As demonstrated in Tom Leng's work, these texts were also dominated by the language of partisanship. Even in more radical reformulations of the subscriptional text, such as the Levellers' 'Agreements of the People', partisan loyalty was a key qualifier for the enjoyment of the full rights of citizenship.[68] There was certainly, then, 'subversive potential' in subscriptional activity (as the historian Susan Zaeske has put it) but this was often constrained by the hierarchical and patriarchal values ingrained in oath-taking and petitioning.[69]

THE LOYAL ADDRESS

Loyal addresses were much more recent creations than either oaths or petitions, though they shared some features with both. As will be discussed later, the loyal address was widely seen as originating during the Cromwellian Protectorate, as counties and boroughs sent in their expressions of loyalty to first Oliver Cromwell and then his son Richard. Contemporaries could, therefore, distinguish between the address and other subscriptional forms. In this book, however, the loyal address is not treated as a completely discrete political genre. As noted above, it was particularly closely related to the petition and there are instances of addresses which appear more like petitions (in that they were used to place demands upon authority) and, vice versa, petitions which appear more like loyal addresses. (Take for example the 'Humble petition' of the corporation of Great Yarmouth, which spent most of the text heaping praise on the Commonwealth before belatedly making a request for a reduction in the town's monthly assessment.)[70] Indeed, when the term 'address' first appeared to be ascribed to subscriptional texts in the late 1640s, it seems only to have been used as an equivalent for 'petition', as in *The humble address of the agitators of the army to his excellency Sir Thomas Fairfax* (1647), which requested that 'all and every person, that have sate in that pretended Parliament, or adhered to them or their Votes ... might ... be declared against, as persons incapable of sitting or voting in this Parliament'.[71] Similarly, the three 'addresses' sent by John Lilburne to Oliver Cromwell were also 'humble petitions' which asked the Lord General to suspend the judgment previously passed against the Leveller by the Rump.[72]

If we follow Amanda Whiting's suggestion that petitioning should be thought of as a particular tone, mood or voice, rather than as a form, then addressing was accented by acclamation rather than grievance.[73] The address, while developing as a political form during the Cromwellian Protectorate, was notable for conveying public affection, thanks and congratulations. As with petitions, addresses therefore involved an acknowledgement of the authority to which they were directed. Yet, unlike petitions, addresses were defined by the absence of grievances and requests for their remedy from authority. In short, they offered submission without supplication. Of course, as we will see, many addresses were far less acclamatory than this, conveying veiled or overt criticism of authority. Some contained requests for assistance or were promoted as a means of gaining the political access and influence that could then deliver that assistance.

Consequently, the similarities between petitioning and addressing were numerous. The process of drafting, subscribing and presenting addresses, outlined in more detail in Chapters five and six, was very similar to that employed in the production of public petitions. Formal or informal meetings of the local elite, often conducted in cooperation with and through direction from the locality's representatives in Parliament, generated the text of the address which was then circulated for subscription before being delivered to authority in a performance of deference and submission.[74] As this indicates, addresses were predominately corporate texts, issued from official and unofficial groups rather than individuals. There was a tension in addressing activity, as with petitioning, between the desire to show that texts were authoritative (the production of borough corporations or county benches), and the impulse to demonstrate that they enjoyed popular support (through the reporting of mass subscription). The emphasis upon the loyalty of corporate bodies rather than individuals, however, limited the degree of agency conferred through the subscription process. The almost complete absence of women from the records of subscription to these addresses may also be explained by their function in representing communities rather than in mobilising people.

Print was also critical to addressing activity in the 1650s and onwards as it had been in the 1640s for petitioning. As with petitions, addresses were issued as broadsheets, gathered together in collections and compendia of texts, and reproduced in contemporary newsbooks. Similar patterns of recording and reproduction of addressing activity can be found, as with petitions, in printed newsbooks, manuscript collections and newsletters. We will see that addressing activity was also incorporated into historical narratives whether personal (such as memoirs) or national.

In other respects, however, addressing was closer to oaths of loyalty in that addressing campaigns, as those for subscription to oaths of loyalty, were centrally directed. Subscribers to addresses, especially those holding public office, occasionally treated these devices as if they were loyalty tests and, in some instances, for example in 1696 where oath-taking was combined with the production of loyal addresses, the distinction between subscription to the address or to the oath became blurred. As already noted, addressing was also, like covenanting and oath-taking, a practice shared across England and Scotland. As with oaths and covenants, partisan language predominated. Addresses largely depicted a political landscape divided between the loyal and the disloyal, the well-affected and the disaffected. The role of oaths in mobilising the public and fostering active political engagement was also shared with loyal addresses which, as the work of Scott Sowerby has shown, were critical to the formation of political and religious alliances in the post-Restoration period.[75]

Loyal addresses, however, were more than simply another variety of subscriptional text in early modern England. Distinctive features of loyal addresses, it is argued, played a particular role in developing the sense of 'the public' in late Stuart and early Hanoverian England. The nature of loyal addresses as documents typically prompted by national and international events and concerns (the succession of a new leader, matters of national religious and political policy, the birth of new heir, military victories and peace treaties) meant that addressing, even more than petitioning, provided ready source material for historical writing. This mnemonic quality was enhanced further by the different uses of print in addressing campaigns. Whereas, as Jason Peacey has shown, print in petitioning campaigns was not always deployed for reasons of publicity, in addressing campaigns geared towards generating statements of public support, the reproduction of manuscript texts in newsbooks, broadsheets and collections was the prime aim of printing. Addresses were nominally supposed to be free of representations of grievances or requests for their remedy, and the presentation of the manuscript original or fair copy of the address to authority represented the vital opportunity to seek concessions from authority. In this way, addressing activity accentuated the legitimating effect of petitioning by making a public display of loyalty and submission critical to securing the greatest benefit from addressing (both for the individual addressers and for the community as a whole).

Loyal addresses could therefore be seen as a development of earlier subscriptional practices, designed to limit the 'subversive potential' of petitioning and oath-taking while retaining their value in mobilising public support and legitimating authority. Combined with legal measures to limit popular petitioning and open criticism of the republican regime, they could be regarded as part of a broader attempt to carefully manage media and public opinion during the interregnum.[76] (We will see in subsequent chapters that although mass petitioning and addressing did re-emerge post-Restoration, the legal restrictions against mass petitioning of Parliament remained in force, even after 1688.) In this way, the role of addresses in generating a sense of the 'public' followed the State-driven expansion of the political nation noted by John Walter in relation to the Protestation.[77] Of course, as with popular petitioning and oath-taking, measures to manage the public's response were not wholly successful: communities could choose not to respond, or to respond equivocally or even critically, to the prompt to produce addresses. Such prompts could build coalitions in support of government policy but they could also reveal and exacerbate divisions within communities.

Loyal addressing, nonetheless, significantly outlasted other subscriptional forms, notably the oath of loyalty. This survival raises some questions about the relationship between subscriptional texts, the public sphere and citizenship. The emphasis placed by Zaret, following Habermas, on the use of reason in controversies over petitioning seems at odds with contemporary anxieties (noted by Knights) that political discourse in addressing disputes had been subverted by deeply subjective 'partisan polemic'.[78] This study, however, suggests that partisanship was integral to the role of addresses in developing a sense of the public in early modern England. Recent work on modern publics has suggested that Habermas' emphasis on 'communicative rationality' might be regarded as potentially exclusionary, focusing on the 'rightness' of particular speech acts. 'To treat contest and partisanship as evil or inherently defective', Gerard Hauser has suggested, 'is to prejudge the terms of almost all disputes, along with their less than ideal solutions.'[79] Certainly, some of these early modern texts were discredited on the grounds of their tone as much as their content. We will also see that loyalty in these addresses was often defined in emotional terms. This emotional content, rather than being evidence of their irrationality, may instead explain the effectiveness and significance of addressing activity. Hauser persuasively argues that public engagement is often a product of emotional engagement, itself based on what is deemed rhetorically reasonable at a given historical moment.[80]

This emotional identification and engagement with addressing can be seen in the prominence of this activity in some diaries and memoirs. This is true even in the case of texts written by women, namely the 'Remembrances' of Elizabeth Freke. Addressing provided a means of connecting individual and local histories to the history of the nation, it is argued, even in instances where there was no personal involvement in this activity. The importance of memory to partisan identities, especially the memory of the civil wars and interregnum, and the way in which addressing activity itself fed into the memory of political activity was fundamental, it will be proposed, to the growth of a self-aware political public. Moreover, in rendering legitimate political activism dependent on a shifting definition of loyalty, addressing activity simultaneously limited the 'subversive potential' of subscriptional activity, while at the same time providing sufficient flexibility to permit the inclusion of normally excluded groups when expedient. The following chapter explores the moment when addressing activity was first fixed in the public memory at the end of the Cromwellian Protectorate.

NOTES

1. *A collection of sundry petitions presented to the Kings most excellent majestie ... published by his speciall command* (1642), 'The collector to the Reader'.
2. Zaret, *Origins of Democratic Culture*, p. 265.
3. J. Walter, *Covenanting Citizens: The Protestation Oath and Popular Political Culture in the English Revolution* (Oxford: Oxford University Press, 2016), p. 250.
4. S. Mendelson and P. Crawford, *Women in Early Modern England, 1550–1720* (Oxford: Oxford University Press, 1998), p. 399; J. Walter, 'The English people and the English Revolution revisited', p. 179; Vallance, *Revolutionary England and the National Covenant: State Oaths, Protestantism and the Political Nation: 1553–1682* (Woodbridge: Boydell and Brewer, 2005), p. 110.
5. D. Zaret, 'Petitioning places and credibility of opinion in the public sphere of seventeenth-century England', in Beat Kümin (ed.), *Political Space in Pre-industrial Europe* (Farnham: Ashgate, 2009), ch. 6; Peacey, *Print and Public Politics*, pp. 393–413; Zaret, *Origins of Democratic Culture*, conclusion.
6. *An exact collection of all remonstrances, declarations, votes, orders, ordinances, proclamations, petitions, messages, answers, and other remarkable passages betweene the Kings most excellent Majesty, and his court of Parliament* (1642).
7. For an early challenge to this idea see B. Manning, *The English People and the English Revolution* (London: Penguin, 1978 edn), p. 32 'It is not very likely that the

8 A. Fletcher, *The Outbreak of the English Civil War* (London: Edward Arnold, 1985 edn), p. 192. See also R. Ashton, *Counter-revolution: The Second Civil War and its Origins, 1646–8* (New Haven, CT: Yale University Press, 1994), esp. ch. 4; K. Lindley, *Popular Politics and Religion in Civil War London* (Aldershot: Scholar Press, 1997); J. Rees, 'Leveller Organisation and the Dynamic of the English Revolution' (PhD dissertation, University of London, 2014), ch. 4.

9 M. Dobson, *Khrushchev's Cold Summer: Gulag Returnees and the Fate of Reform* (New York and London: Cornell University Press, 2009), ch. 2; B. Kelly, *Petitions, Litigation and Social Control in Roman Egypt* (Oxford: Oxford University Press, 2011).

10 C. Higgins, *Under Another Sky: Journeys in Roman Britain* (London: Jonathan Cape, 2013), pp. 103–4.

11 R. A. Houston, *Peasant Petitions: Social Relations and Economic Life on Landed Estates 1600–1850* (Basingstoke: Palgrave Macmillan, 2014).

12 Brodie Waddell, 'Was early modern England a petitioning society', paper delivered at 'Addressing Authority: Petitions and Supplications in Early Modern Society' workshop, 18 March 2016, Birkbeck, University of London; for a summary see https://manyheadedmonster.wordpress.com/2016/11/07/was-early-modern-england-a-petitioning-society/#_edn9, accessed 5 May 2017, and see Waddell, *God, Duty and Community in English Economic life, 1660–1720* (Woodbridge: Boydell and Brewer, 2012), ch. 2, esp. pp. 87, 137. I am grateful to Brodie Waddell for sharing notes of his talk with me.

13 Yale University Library Manuscripts, MS 753 Box 2, English Miscellaneous Manuscripts Collection, 1362–1945.

14 Zaret, *Origins of Democratic Culture*, p. 88 and for similar comments in relation to petitioning more broadly see J. Healey, *The First Century of Welfare: Poverty and Poor Relief in Lancashire, 1620–1730* (Woodbridge: Boydell and Brewer, 2014), p. 97.

15 Fletcher, *Outbreak of the English Civil War*, p. 123; Zaret, *Origins of Democratic Culture*, pp. 90–2.

16 Ibid., pp. 92–7.

17 A. J. Whiting, *Women and Petitioning in the Seventeenth-Century English Revolution: Deference, Difference and Dissent* (Turnhout: Brepolis, 2015), p. 296.

18 Quoted in Healey, *First Century of Welfare*, p. 93 and see ch. 3; S. Hindle, *On the Parish? The Micro-Politics of Poor Relief in Rural England c. 1550–1750* (Oxford: Clarendon Press, 2004), pp. 156–63; 407–28.

19 Zaret, *Origins of Democratic Culture*, p. 82–3; R. C. Bailey, *Popular Influence upon Public Policy: Petitioning in Eighteenth-Century Virginia* (Westport, CT: Greenwood Press, 1979), pp. 44–5 for petitioning by slaves and free blacks.

20 Whiting, *Women and Petitioning*, p. 8; P. Jones and S. King, 'From petition to pauper letter: the development of an epistolary form', in Jones and King (eds), *Obligation, Entitlement and Dispute under the English Poor Laws* (Newcastle: Cambridge Scholar, 2015), ch. 3, pp. 59–60.

21 Bailey, *Popular Influence upon Public Policy*, pp. 10–11.

22 G. Dodd, *Justice and Grace: Private Petitioning and the English Parliament in the Late Middle Ages* (Oxford: Oxford University Press, 2007), p. 33.

23 Waddell, *God, Duty and Community*, p. 137.
24 'Charles II, 1661: An Act against Tumults and Disorders upon p[re]tence of p[re]paring or p[re]senting publick Petic[i]ons or other Addresses to His Majesty or the Parliament', in *Statutes of the Realm: Volume 5, 1628–80*, ed. John Raithby (s.l, 1819), p. 308. British History Online www.british-history.ac.uk/statutes-realm/vol5/p308, accessed 11 July 2017.
25 Quote and comment from Whiting, *Women and Petitioning*, p. 5.
26 'May 1648: Declaration against tumultuous Assemblies, under Pretence of preparing Petitions', in *Acts and Ordinances of the Interregnum, 1642–1660*, C. H. Firth and R. S. Rait (eds) (London, 1911), p. 1139. British History Online www.british-history.ac.uk/no-series/acts-ordinances-interregnum/p1139, accessed 11 July 2017. I am grateful to Philip Loft for bringing this ordinance to my attention.
27 Fletcher, *Outbreak of the English Civil War*, pp. 196–7.
28 Walter, *Covenanting Citizens*, p. 204.
29 See L. Stewart, *Rethinking the Scottish Revolution: Covenanted Scotland, 1637–1651* (Oxford: Oxford University Press, 2016), pp. 110–14.
30 On this see Whiting, *Women and Petitioning*, p. 207.
31 For example, *Severall petitions presented to the honourable Houses of Parliament now assembled* (1641), Thomason E.135 [31].
32 Peacey, *Print and Public Politics*, pp. 280–98.
33 Rees, 'Leveller Organisation', pp. 126–7.
34 Zaret, *Origins of Democratic Culture*, p. 217.
35 Ibid., pp. 250–2, 261–2.
36 Rees, 'Leveller Organisation', pp. 131, 134.
37 David Zaret, 'Petitioning places', pp. 188–92.
38 Andy Wood, 'Tales from the "Yarmouth Hutch": civic identities and hidden histories in an urban archive', *Past & Present*, 230 (Supplement 11) (2016), 213–30, quote at 218.
39 Quoted in Whiting, *Women and Petitioning*, pp. 11–12.
40 Daniel Woolf 'News, history, and the construction of the present in early modern England', in S. A. Baron and B. Dooley (eds), *The Politics of Information in Early Modern Europe* (London: Routledge, 2001), pp. 80–108, at p. 108.
41 Woolf, 'Construction of the Present', pp. 84–5.
42 Ibid., p. 98; T. Claydon, 'Daily news and the construction of time in late Stuart England, 1695–1714', *Journal of British Studies*, 52 (2013), 55–78 at 74.
43 N. Millstone, 'Designed for collection: early modern news and the production of history', *Media History*, 23 (2017), 177–98. For newspaper collecting see also U. Heyd, *Reading Newspapers: Press and Public in Eighteenth-century Britain and America* (Oxford: Voltaire Foundation, 2012), ch. 6.
44 *A collection of sundry petitions presented to the Kings most Excellent Majesty* (1681) Wing A4076.
45 Whiting, *Women and Petitioning*, p. 12.
46 *To the chosen and betrusted knights, citizens and burgesses assembled in Parliament at Westminster: the humble petition of Alice Rolph* (1648) Thomason 669 f. 12 [73].
47 J. Walter 'Body politics in the English Revolution', in S. Taylor and G. Tapsell (eds), *The Nature of the English Revolution Revisited* (Woodbridge: Boydell and Brewer, 2013) ch. 4; and see, for example, the report of the presentation of

'The Petition of many civilly disposed women', in *Mercurius Civicus, Londons Intelligencer* (1643), p. 88.

48 A. Hughes, 'Gender and politics in Leveller literature', in S. Amussen and M. Kishlansky (eds), *Political culture and cultural politics in England: essays presented to David Underdown* (Manchester: Manchester University Press, 1995), pp. 162–88; Ann Marie McEntee '"The [un]civill-sisterhood of oranges and lemons": female petitioners and demonstrators, 1642–1653', *Prose Studies*, 14 (1991), 92–111; Patricia Higgins, 'The reactions of women with special reference to women petitioners', in B. L. Manning (ed.), *Politics, Religion and the English Civil War* (London: Edward Arnold, 1973), pp. 179–224. A. Button, 'Royalist women petitioners in south-west England, 1655–62', *Seventeenth Century*, 15 (2000), 53–66.

49 Hindle, *On the Parish*, pp. 162–4; H. Worthen, 'Supplicants and guardians: the petitions of Royalist widows during the civil wars and Interregnum, 1642–1660', *Women's History Review*, 26 (2017), 528–40.

50 On this see C. Condren, *Argument and Authority in Early Modern England: The Presupposition of Oaths and Office* (Cambridge: Cambridge University Press, 2006).

51 I discuss these transformations in my *Revolutionary England and the National Covenant*, pp. 17–28. See also D. Martin-Jones, *Conscience and Allegiance in Seventeenth-Century England: the Political Significance of Oaths and Engagements* (Rochester, NY: University of Rochester Press, 1999).

52 Roger Turvey, '"An Ill-considered invitation to violence and vengeance": Pembrokeshire and the Bond of Association 1584', *Journal of the Pembrokeshire Historical Society*, 21 (2012), 35–53 at 43.

53 See D. Cressy, 'Binding the nation: the Bonds of Association, 1584 and 1696', in D. J. Guth and J. M. McKenna (eds), *Tudor Rule and Revolution: Essays for G.R. Elton from his American Friends* (Cambridge: Cambridge University Press, 1982), pp. 217–34 at p. 231 and for more detail on the Suffolk returns Cressy, *Literacy and the Social Order: Reading and Writing in Tudor and Stuart England* (Cambridge: Cambridge University Press, 1980), pp. 98–105. The total population of the county in the 1670s has been estimated at only 125,000, J. Patten, 'Population distribution in Norfolk and Suffolk during the sixteenth and seventeenth centuries', *Transactions of the Institute of British Geographers*, 65 (1975), 45–65. For more on the 1696 Association and its scale see S. Pincus, *1688: The First Modern Revolution* (New Haven, CT: Yale University Press, 2009), ch. 14, Knights, *Representation and Misrepresentation*, pp. 154–60.

54 For a short introduction to these oaths see Vallance, 'Protestation, vow, covenant and engagement: swearing allegiance in the English civil war', *Historical Research*, 75 (2002), 408–24.

55 Tom Leng, 'Citizens at the door: mobilising against enemies in civil war London', in M. Braddick and G. Rivett (eds), *Journal of Historical Sociology Special Issues: Activism, Mobilisation and Political Engagement*, 28 (2015), 26–48; Tom Leng, 'The meanings of "malignancy": the language of enmity and the construction of the parliamentarian cause in the English revolution', *Journal of British Studies*, 53 (2014), 835–58.

56 Walter, *Covenanting Citizens*, p. 161. For an example, see the Protestation return for Middle Claydon, Bucks, TNA SP 28/148 pt 1. f. 151 transcribed by

Gavin Robinson here http://webarchive.nationalarchives.gov.uk/+/http://your archives.nationalarchives.gov.uk/index.php?title=Middle_Claydon,_Bucks,_Protestation_Return, accessed 13 July 2017. I am grateful to Gavin Robinson for bringing this document to my attention.

57 Walter, *Covenanting Citizens*, pp. 218–25; Vallance, *Revolutionary England and the National Covenant*, pp. 111, 128–9; J. Spraggon, *Puritan Iconoclasm During the English Civil War* (Woodbridge: Boydell and Brewer, 2003), p. 188; D. Cressy, 'The protestation protested, 1641 and 1642', *Historical Journal*, 45 (2002), 251–79 at 263.
58 Walter, *Covenanting Citizens*, pp. 213–16.
59 Zaret, *Origins of Democratic Culture*, pp. 248–9; Walter, *Covenanting Citizens*, pp. 120–1, 252–3.
60 Ibid., p. 252; Vallance, *Revolutionary England and the National Covenant*, pp. 121–3.
61 Vallance, *Revolutionary England and the National Covenant*, ch. 6.
62 Walter, 'Rethinking the English Revolution', p. 179.
63 Crawford and Mendelson, *Women in Early Modern England*, p. 399.
64 Cressy, 'Protestation protested', p. 253.
65 E. Vallance, 'Oaths, covenants, associations and the agreements of the people: the road to and from Putney', in P. Baker and E. Vernon (eds), *The Agreements of the People: The Levellers, the Army and the Constitutional Crisis of the English Revolution* (Basingstoke: Palgrave Macmillan, 2012), ch. 1.
66 Walter, *Covenanting Citizens*, pp. 246–50.
67 Vallance, *Revolutionary England and the National Covenant*, ch. 8; E. Legon, 'Remembering Revolution: Seditious Memories in England and Wales, 1660–1685' (PhD dissertation, University College London, 2015), pp. 98–100. I am grateful to Ed Legon for sharing his thesis with me.
68 I. Gentles, 'The *Agreements of the People* and their political contexts 1647-48', in M. Mendle (ed.), *The Putney Debates of 1647: The Army, the Levellers and the English State* (Cambridge: Cambridge University Press, 2001), ch. 8, p. 162.
69 S. Zaeske, *Signatures of Citizenship: Petitioning, Antislavery & Women's Political Identity* (Chapel Hill and London: University of North Carolina Press, 2003), p. 12.
70 HMC 9th Report, Appendix, p. 320.
71 Daniel Hincksman, *The Humble Address of the Agitators of the Army to His Excellency Sir Thomas Fairfax* (1647), p. 5.
72 J. Lilburne, *The banished mans suit for protection to his excellency the Lord Generall Cromwell. Being the humble address of Lieutenant Colonel John Lilburn* (1653); Lilburne, *A second address directed to his excellency the Lord General Cromwell* (1653); Lilburne, *A third address to his excellency the Lord Generall Cromwell* (1653). For another petition-like 'address' see C. Cheesman, *Berk-shires agent's humble address to the honourable commissioners for compounding* (1651), discussed in Peacey, *Public Politics*, pp. 293–4.
73 Whiting, *Women and Petitioning*, p. 143; and see Knights, *Representation and Misrepresentation*, p. 162.
74 See here Fletcher, *Outbreak of the English Civil War*, pp. 193–7.
75 Sowerby, *Making Toleration*; Sowerby, 'Forgetting the repealers'.
76 On which see J. Peacey, 'Cromwellian England: a propaganda state?', *History*, 91 (2006), 176–99.

77 Walter, *Covenanting Citizens*, p. 260.
78 Zaret, *Origins of Democratic Culture*, p. 15; Knights, *Representation and Misrepresentation*, p. 162.
79 G. A. Hauser, *Vernacular Voices: The Rhetoric of Publics and Public Spheres* (Columbia: University of South Carolina Press, 1999), pp. 52–3, at p. 53.
80 Ibid., pp. 50–51, 61. Hauser uses the contrast between the minimal impact of scientific papers on the ecological impact of pesticides with the national and international impact of Rachel Carson's personal narrative *A Silent Spring* (1987).

Chapter 2

Cromwell's trunks: the origins of the loyal address, 1658–61

According to the collection *A true catalogue* (1659), probably written by the Welsh Independent minister Vavasor Powell, the address of the Army to Oliver Cromwell on his accession as Lord Protector represented the starting point of loyal addressing as a political activity: 'the wicked foundation and rise of all the following Addresses both to himself, and his Son after him.'[1] Certainly, the 'Addresses and Approbacon of the Nacon from several Countys and Citys' was urged in Parliament as a reason for recognising the Protectoral constitution in 1654, though other MPs countered that these texts had only expressed relief that the 'Extremitys and Confusions' endured during the life of the Nominated Assembly had been brought to an end.[2] The emergence of the address during the Protectorate was not accidental: Mark Knights has argued that its form was specifically tailored to the government of a single person.[3] The presentation of a loyal address formed part of a public ceremonial in which the adulation of the subject was returned with the thankfulness of the magistrate. Bulstrode Whitlocke, for example, in his *Memorials* recorded with barely concealed pride that he had been 'pitched upon' by the gentlemen and freeholders of Buckinghamshire to present the county's address to Richard, which he noted, the new Protector received with 'a very good prudent answer'.[4] Addressing activity therefore emerged as a means of supporting, legitimating and endorsing the authority of the Protectoral regime against the attacks of those who regarded its followers as 'apostates' (in the terms of *A true catalogue*) from the 'Good Old Cause'.[5] These texts were clearly employed as propaganda for the Protectorate. Addresses were publicised via government-controlled newsbooks such as *Mercurius Politicus*, *The Publick Intelligencer* and the Protectorate's French language newsbook, *Nouvelles Ordinaires de Londres*. Some, more critical texts may have been censored. The York ministers' address, discussed in detail in *A true catalogue* and other contemporary pamphlets, was not fully reproduced in printed newsbooks or published as a separate broadsheet.[6]

Contemporaries certainly questioned the authenticity of these Cromwellian texts. The uniformity of these addresses led the author of *A Second Narrative of the Late Parliament* (1659) to question whether they were not, in fact, 'rather hatch'd at the Court by Secretary *Thurlo*, and the old malignant Pamphleter, lying, railing *Rabshakeh*, and Defamer of the Lords people, *Nedham*'.[7] Some historians have suggested conversely that these addresses demonstrate genuine public support for Richard's Protectorate. Ronald Hutton has claimed that there 'is not a scrap of evidence in either central or local archives that this response was anything but spontaneous'.[8] While this, we will see, is arguably an overstatement, neither is the similarity of these texts evidence of government manipulation. As Godfrey Davies suggested, the regular practice of reproducing address in printed newsbooks, rather than central coordination, contributed much to the homogeneity of addresses as texts, as corporations and counties played a political game of 'follow the leader'.[9] This is not to deny that the Cromwellian regime certainly encouraged the production of these loyal texts and exploited them for propaganda purposes. These addresses were, however, far less adulatory and uniform than may appear at first glance. The homogeneity of these texts which contemporaries found so suspicious, on closer examination proves to be deceptive: revealing widespread political and religious divisions, the variations between these texts demonstrated public uncertainty over the legitimacy of Richard's succession.

Richard Cromwell's succession to the Protectoral office has become the subject of recent scholarly debate. Peter Gaunt and Jason Peacey have made the case for Richard being identified as successor through his increasingly public and prominent role before Oliver's death in September 1658. Jonathan Fitzgibbons, on the other hand, has cast serious doubt on whether Oliver ever formally named Richard as his heir.[10] Whether or not Oliver did name his son as successor, the addresses produced to Richard from late 1658 to early 1659 suggest that the debate over the new Protector's legitimacy was not limited to the political elite but was national and public in scope and character. Moreover, the content of these addresses demonstrates how they were employed as media for engaging in religious as well as political controversy, as the succession of a new Protector also re-energised disputes over the Cromwellian Church settlement. Given the equivocal nature of many of the supposedly 'loyal' texts sent to Richard, it was unsurprising that the second Lord Protector's period in office was so notoriously brief. Nonetheless, the value of addresses both as legitimating devices and campaigning tools was recognised by first the restored Rump, then by those campaigning for a 'free' Parliament and finally by the Stuart monarchy itself. Although the congratulatory addresses sent to Charles II sought to differentiate themselves from their interregnum predecessors, emphasising the social status of subscribers, their debt to the subscriptional culture of the Cromwellian period was clear.

ADDRESSING THE CROMWELLIAN PROTECTORATE

Accusations of elite manipulation of subscriptional activity were not new: as Jason Peacey has shown, they had also been aimed at mass petitioning campaigns in the 1640s.[11] There is certainly evidence that considerable effort was put into ensuring that Richard was proclaimed Lord Protector throughout the British Isles and its colonies.[12] Counties that failed to proclaim Richard as Protector, such as Rutland and Northamptonshire, were reminded very firmly of their duties by the Council of State.[13] Evidence from the letterbooks of Sir John Fitzjames and from the 'Diary' of Bulstrode Whitelocke suggests that official guidance was being sought by local administrators concerning the content, form and even timing of loyal addresses to Richard. In a letter to the Protectorate's chief propagandist, Marchamont Nedham, Fitzjames expressed regret that,

> I could enjoy your Company noe other wise then I did when I had the happiness to see you last: Amongst all yt Greate Unexpected Crowde I had not ye Oppertunity then to mind you of your promise of a patterne for an Address &c I humbly beff [sic.] your assistance therein & with all your Advise concerning the time of ye Tender whether before, or assoone as ye Black Solemnity [meaning Oliver Cromwell's funeral] is over. Or whether it will bee more seasonable imediately after ye Inauguration if any such Pomp bee Intended.[14]

Whitelocke, appointed keeper of the great seal by Richard Cromwell, recorded that he was contacted by several counties about the drafting of addresses.[15] It is also clear that addresses from the army acknowledging Richard's title were developed with similar care and in coordination with central government. Henry Cromwell's letters show the effort that was made to ensure that the army pledged loyalty to Richard through addresses produced in September 1658. His correspondence also demonstrates, however, that the issue quickly became divisive, with different loyal texts being developed. Five days after Oliver's death, Charles Fleetwood wrote to Henry notifying him of an address to be subscribed by the army in England, Scotland and Ireland so that 'all 3 armyes might joyn in one'.[16] Henry wrote to Richard on the eighteenth of the same month informing him that a seemingly different text of an address had been circulated among the army officers in Ireland as a 'witness against the treachery and falsehood of any officers of this army'.[17] For Henry Cromwell, these addresses were something like a test of loyalty for the army, a view, as we shall see, shared by other leading Cromwellians. A later letter from George Monck revealed that another address distinct from Fleetwood's had been drafted for the Scottish army too.[18] *Nouvelles Ordinaires* reported, however, that on receiving Fleetwood's address 'pour témoigner l'harmonie &, la grande correspondence qui est entre les Officiers des 3 nations, en leur obéissance & fidélité envers S. A. P. vous aves eu la teneur de ladite adress en nôtre précédente.'[19] Fleetwood meanwhile was still attempting to secure subscriptions to his text. On the twenty-first he wrote to Henry Cromwell telling him that an address had been made, 'the title of which was named Scotland and Ireland, because of both armyyes'. Fleetwood hoped that Henry Cromwell would join in this address, for it was 'our duty to be earnest for him [Richard Cromwell], that he may be kept up to walke in his father's paths with that integrity, as may manifest by what spirit he is ledde forth by'.[20] A letter from Fauconberg to Henry Cromwell in cipher reinforces the sense that these addresses were already being used for factional purposes: 'This last week the cabal I mentioned lately was delivered of a thing they cal the armies address; it's indeed pretty well featur'd promises all good in shew; but in the end I feare wil prove a serpent.' The claim that it represented the army in Ireland and Scotland, was also specious, Fauconberg said, as only 'Two or three officers at Ireland and Scotland [were] present at signing'. For Fauconberg however, the text presaged further division in the Council of State, predicting that none would 'hereafter ... be admitted members there, or of the army that pronounce not Shibboleth'.[21] Fauconberg's use of the term Shibboleth here not only had a clear Biblical allusion but also a powerful contemporary resonance as the same term had been used to describe the Commons' Protestation of 1641.[22]

The texts of Fleetwood's and Henry Cromwell's addresses, both of which appeared in the pages of *Mercurius Politicus*, were clearly different. Fleetwood's text referred to the frame of government as being established in the Humble Petition and Advice, and prayed for God to give Richard the strength to maintain it.[23] Henry Cromwell's (by his own acknowledgement) shorter text did not specifically refer to the Humble Petition and Advice but instead spoke of Richard as the nations' providentially appointed governor.[24] The address promoted by Fleetwood, however, did contain intimations of the kind of political and military purge Fauconberg saw as being threatened: it urged Richard to maintain officers in the army who were,

> of honest godly principles free to adventure all that is dear unto them by all lawful ways and means to maintain an equal just liberty to all persons that profess godliness, that are not of turbulent spirits as to the peace of these Nations, nor disturbers of others, though differing in some things from themselves according to the true intent of the *Humble Petition and Advice*.

Similar care was urged in the appointment of civil magistrates. As both Godfrey Davies and Austin Woolrych noted, although Fleetwood's address superficially seemed to want to appease all political factions, it clearly intimated that the army had a right to direct the nation's chief magistrate.[25] To paraphrase Fleetwood's own words, the address appeared to be giving the new Protector a rule to walk by.

Rather than being uniform texts, concocted at Westminster, the army addresses to Richard became part of a factional struggle almost as soon as he assumed the title of Lord Protector. (That this was the case is also suggested by the fact that both Fleetwood's and Henry Cromwell's texts were published in newsbooks before the process of subscription had been completed, indicating that publication was part of the process of mobilising support not a signal that the process had been completed.) Instead of being seen as 'vehicles of servile adulation', as J. T. Rutt, the editor of Thomas Burton's parliamentary diary, described them, these texts were instead part of the succession crisis that gripped the Cromwellian regime in the autumn and winter of 1658/9.[26] Regardless of whether Oliver did name his son as successor, many of the addresses produced to Richard in late 1658/early 1659 indicate that there was considerable public doubt about the matter and that support for his appointment as Lord Protector was equivocal at best. This becomes clearer if we look at the basis on which Richard was proclaimed Lord Protector in September 1658. The proclamation, acknowledging the providence of God in taking away his father, declared that Oliver had named Richard as Protector 'according to the humble petition and advice' and declared him 'rightful' Protector of England, Ireland and Scotland, due obedience according to law and the constitution established by the humble petition.[27] While there was a muted reference to providence here, the heaviest emphasis was laid on Richard's legal title as established by the second protectoral constitution, which gave the Protector power to name his successor, subject to the approval of the Privy Council. In contrast, the addresses that appeared in the pages of *Mercurius Politicus* and the *Public Intelligencer* were laden with providential language. The Biblical allusion to the elder Cromwell as Moses and his son as Joshua, begun with Fleetwood's army address, was repeated so frequently that *A true catalogue* chose to mark these instances up to indicate what the author saw as the artificial uniformity of the Cromwellian texts.[28] Other communities, perhaps fearful of appearing too derivative, sought different religious comparisons: the address from Poole depicted Oliver as Asa and Richard as Jehosaphat, while the text from St Albans carried apocalyptic overtones – identifying Richard with the prophet Elijah whose return would be a harbinger of the day of judgement.[29]

The use of providential language indicates that the publication of the army address promoted by Fleetwood had served to provide a template for other communities to follow. In addition, the heavy emphasis on providence was also indicative of the role of these addresses in attempting to shape the religious policy of Richard's Protectorate. The text presented by Thomas Goodwin on behalf of 'above a Hundred Congregational Churches' was delivered at the same time as the Protector was also given the Savoy Declaration, drafted by Goodwin in conjunction with other leading divines. The Declaration reaffirmed the role of the civil magistrate in curbing blasphemy and error as defined in the Westminster Confession of 1646 but it also reminded the Protector of the Humble Petition and Advice's commitment to religious toleration and aimed at presenting the 'Congregational Way' as compatible with the Presbyterian 'classis' system established in the 1640s.[30] Several other addresses, such as that from the 'gentlemen, ministers, freeholders and others inhabiting within the County of Sussex', however, gave voice to more conservative religious aspirations, expressing the hope that Richard's succession would prompt further reformation and lead to the stamping out of blasphemy, heresy and vice. These texts, though, also departed from the supposedly acclamatory form of the address by effectively placing demands on the new Protector. The address from Sussex called in Miltonic terms for him to take action against those who turned 'Liberty into Licentiousness'. More significantly, the Sussex address called for the Protector to encourage greater 'Christian union', a request which at this time connected with Presbyterian initiatives to secure an 'accommodation' with Independency (typically understood to mean the 'comprehension' of congregational churches within a strengthened classis system).[31] Similarly, the address from the 'well-affected' inhabitants of Taunton, Somerset, suggested that the toleration afforded under the Protectoral constitution needed to be reined in, urging Richard to deal not only with those whose public behaviour was immoral but also with those 'who being outwardly cleer from the lusts of the flesh; are yet defiled with the lusts of the mind.'[32] This call for the vigorous monitoring of religious belief was in stark contrast to the address from England's Baptist churches, which mourned the elder Cromwell as a 'nursing father' to their churches but which also thanked the new Protector for his proclamation promising protection for 'tender consciences'.[33]

The addresses to Richard Cromwell were clearly being employed as part of a confessional struggle between Independency and Presbyterianism, a struggle heightened by his appointment as head of State but initiated earlier: Richard's more conservative religious outlook had already been signalled as Chancellor of the University of Oxford, when he replaced John Owen as Vice-Chancellor in favour of the Presbyterian John Conant.[34] Derek Hirst has suggested that religious division, as much as political differences between Cromwellians and 'Commonwealthsmen', may help explain the fractiousness of Richard's Parliament.[35] As will be discussed in Chapter five, confessional divisions may also help explain the geography of subscriptions to these texts. Finally, the religious backdrop to the addressing campaign may provide further evidence that Vavasor Powell was the author of *A true catalogue*. Powell had been approached to participate in the Savoy Conference but had declined, warning his fellow Independents of becoming too involved with 'political and worldly interests'.[36] Both the Quaker William Caton and the author of *A true catalogue* attacked the 'time-serving' of pro-Cromwellian Independents such as Goodwin.[37] Nonetheless, the author of *A true catalogue* clearly felt that some of these godly addresses were sincere, arguing that the Scarborough address's desire that the nation should be 'governed by the Laws of God' (a hope that chimed with Powell's Fifth Monarchist ideals) was 'too honest an expression for Thurloe or Nedham to have a hand in'.[38]

The religious language of the Cromwellian addresses also revealed public division over the legitimacy of Richard's succession. It was noticeable that the near universal reference to divine providence in these texts was not matched by a similarly ubiquitous recognition of Richard's title as lawful under the terms of the Humble Petition and Advice. Of forty-four non-military addresses published in *Mercurius Politicus* from September 1658 to April 1659, only six made references to Richard being rightfully or lawfully Protector, while just eight specifically mentioned the Humble Petition and Advice. The author of *A true catalogue* presumably complemented material taken from the Protectorate's English newsbooks with the discussion of addresses in its French language newsbook, *Nouvelles Ordinaires de Londres*, edited by William Dugard. This reproduced a further twenty-six addresses in full and provided short notices of another twenty-four. Only half of those printed in full provided any explicit acknowledgement of Richard's title.[39] This is not to deny that in the seventeenth century, providence itself was widely seen as legitimising political authority. The example of Great Yarmouth, however, suggests that in the case of some of the Cromwellian addresses it was being used strategically to avoid explicit endorsement of the Protectoral regime. While the corporation received the proclamation announcing Richard's succession in early September and celebrated the event shortly afterwards, it would not be until November 1658 that the town would agree on the wording of the address, and only in early 1659 that the text appeared in print.[40] In some counties, as will be discussed below, delays in presenting addresses were caused by the desire to secure as many subscriptions as possible. In the case of Yarmouth, however, it is notable that when Charles II was restored to the throne, the corporation was able to appoint the committee to produce an address and agree the text all on the same day.[41]

In emphasising the role of divine providence communities were not only relieved from having to comment on the legality of the succession, but also, in the case of some addresses, provided with a vehicle for implicit criticism of Richard's suitability, through overemphasis of the quality of his father (in the words of the Barnstable address, 'that choice Jewel whereof the World was not worthy') and the depth of loss felt at his passing.[42] Even some of those addresses which did place more emphasis upon Richard's legal title might have made less than reassuring reading for the new Protector. If the Protectorate itself represented a return to older ways of governing, some addresses seemed to hint that monarchy itself might soon be restored. The address from Dorchester did not explicitly mention the Humble Petition and Advice but instead owned 'the foundation upon which your Highness stands, namely the form of Government by a single person and Parliament'.[43] Avoiding the now clichéd references to Moses and Joshua, the address from Warwickshire chose a somewhat surprising historical allusion in comparing Richard's succession to that of James VI and I following the death of Elizabeth.[44]

POPULARITY, ADDRESSES AND THE DOWNFALL OF RICHARD CROMWELL

Equivocal though some of these loyal addresses were, they nonetheless found their way into the pages of the Protectorate's semi-official newsbook, *Mercurius Politicus* and its French language equivalent, *Nouvelles Ordinaires*. The very fact that it was deemed worthwhile to reproduce these addresses in translation in a semi-official newsbook indicates that the Cromwellian regime wished to demonstrate public support for the Protectorate internationally as well as nationally. As we will see, this would not be the last time that addressing campaigns were employed to represent popular opinion beyond the domestic arena. This is not to say that these addresses were simply uncensored. It may be significant that the unpublished York ministers' address was presented by the leading Presbyterian clergyman Edward Bowles, who would later urge General Monck to publically declare for the restoration of Charles II.[45] In this way, both the author of *A true catalogue* and his target, Marchamont Nedham, were engaged in a similar enterprise. Both authors chose to gloss over the criticisms and reservations contained in many of these addresses and instead presented these texts as uniform pledges of loyalty to Richard. The only difference was in the degree of insincerity detected by *A true catalogue*.

The reproduction of these texts in official media reflected the importance that was again being attached to addresses as legitimating devices. This became clearer still in the debate over the Act of Recognition, introduced by Thurloe into Parliament on 1 February 1659 in attempt to bring an end to disputes over Richard's title and the extent of his authority. G. B. Nourse viewed Thurloe's bill as a tactical mistake, providing the Protectorate's opponents with an opportunity to question Richard's legitimacy.[46] These disputes, however, may already have been affecting the Protectorate's ability to govern: a letter from Edward Nicholas to John Evelyn indicated that judges were refusing to take up their offices until Richard had been formally recognised by Parliament.[47] Richard's supporters invoked the addresses as evidence of the people's acceptance of him, as had Oliver's five years earlier. George Starkey stated that,

> The main objection is, that it appears not that his Highness was declared. I believe some here can satisfy you. But, *cui bono*, the people have manifested their satisfaction already, both by addresses, and by sending us hither. They have sent us hither to represent them, by his Highness's call. We have owned him in our assembling, in taking our oaths at the door, and there is a greater acknowledgment in that.[48]

The argument here went beyond mere popular acclamation to suggest that both the Protectoral title and the authority of Parliament rested upon a sovereign people. Starkey's claims were perhaps meant as a Cromwellian rebuttal to the extensive arguments of 'Commonwealthsmen' such as Sir Arthur Hesilrige that opened the debate on the bill of recognition. We can, however, see a similar desire to demonstrate that popular opinion was behind Richard in the references in newsbooks to the numbers subscribing these loyal addresses, most notably the 'above six thousand hands' that were reputed to have signed or marked the Lincolnshire address.[49] Few manuscript versions of these addresses appear to have survived and some may have been deliberately destroyed: the press reported that Northamptonshire's address to Richard was publically burnt as part of the county's celebrations of Charles II's birthday in 1661, though this may only have been a reference to the printed copy.[50] The address from Leicestershire preserved in Thurloe's papers, discussed in detail in Chapter five and extending to twenty-three sheets of signatures and marks, nonetheless, seemed to justify press reports of it being appended with 'some Thousands of hands'.[51] Similarly, Fitzjames claimed that the Dorset address had already secured 'allmost 2000 hands' by November 1658.[52] Equally, the emphasis placed on the quality of those signing, that the address came not only from the 'well-affected' but from gentlemen, ministers and county and civic officials was also intended to increase the credibility of the addresses as indicators of the public mood.[53]

Opponents of the bill of recognition were quick to deny that these subscriptions legitimised Richard's rule. Major-General Packer claimed that he would not 'lay much store in ye Addresses. If ye K. of Scots were landed at Dover, & had a force, he [would] have as many Addresses. [They are] easily obtained. [The] people [are] like a flock of sheep.' The people were only truly represented through Parliament, not via the addresses carefully 'husbanded' into the Protectorate's newsbooks.[54] Others urged that the addresses did not deliver the sense of public opinion as individuals had either been misled into subscribing or the presenters had misrepresented who the address had been produced by. Thomas Challoner complained that the addresses were 'not valuable, because we know how they were procured, if there were a Comittee of Addresses as there is of Priviledges, there would be as many Complaints for false Addresses as for fals Eleccons.'[55] Robert Reynolds, MP for Whitchurch and former attorney general under the Commonwealth, described the addresses as 'an evil measure to measure the people's affections by: not for his Highnesse's service: full of flatteries'. He alleged that one address had come to his hands, 'pretending to contain the sense of the whole country, that they would stand up to defend the good old cause with all that sat in the Long Parliament', and 'for defence of your Highness's person and government' but in fact 'drawn by a young minister'.[56] Similar accusations were made retrospectively by the leading Presbyterian divine Richard Baxter. Baxter claimed that though an address was forthcoming from his home county of Worcestershire, 'none of us in Worcestershire, save the Independants, medled in it.'[57]

As these debates ensued, addresses continued to come in that tackled other opposition schemes, including the attempt to remove Richard as commander-in-chief.[58] Yet, though Richard's supporters succeeded in securing parliamentary recognition of his title, neither this vote nor the addresses in his favour could keep him in office. While *Mercurius Politicus* continued to reproduce the texts of loyal addresses to Richard, *Nouvelles Ordinaires* noticeably shifted to only acknowledging that a certain borough, county or group had addressed the Protector, claiming that no further space was necessary as 'toutes au même effet de celes que vous avez euës ci-devant'.[59]

Richard's effective deposition did not bring an end to the practice of mass addressing. Indeed, Richard's government was first directly challenged via a 'subscriptional text', a petition from the republican merchant and Barebones MP Samuel Moyer presented to Parliament in February 1659 and addressed to the 'Commonwealth of England' with no mention of the Protector or Upper House.[60] The revived Commonwealth itself employed very similar strategies to attempt to legitimate its own authority. The humble petitions made to the restored Rump were fewer in number than those made to Richard Cromwell (Ruth Mayers has identified thirty-four in total) and they came from a more geographically restricted range (mostly from southern England).[61] Although Mayers has identified one manuscript petition from this period with 800 signatures on it, and though other addresses claimed great popularity, there appear to have been no humble petitions to the Rump as heavily subscribed as those from Lincolnshire and Leicestershire to Richard.[62] The petitions were also largely styled as coming from informal groups of the 'well-affected' or 'Assertors of the Good Old Cause' (as a text from Buckinghamshire put it), a feature of them which may also indicate the difficulty of the restored Rump in securing the formal approval of local officialdom.[63]

Of course, the language of ideological purity employed in these petitions cut against straightforward claims to popular support and some, like the Buckinghamshire petition, were clear that the Commonwealth had to be protected from the 'giddiness of the multitude'. Others, pre-empting the tone of *A true catalogue* denounced the 'apostacy' of those 'Backsliders' who had supported the Protectorate.[64] As with the Cromwellian addresses, however, it was alleged at the time, and assumed by some historians, that these were not spontaneous productions but documents concocted at Westminster.[65] These pro-Rump humble petitions also served very similar ends to Richard's addresses – to present the image of public support for the new regime, to foster alliances with groups of potential supporters and to identify and neutralise potential opponents.[66] These petitions foreshadowed future addressing campaigns as well as looking back to their subscriptional predecessors: the Rump's employment of humble petitions to purge and reform the militia represents a precursor of James II's use of loyal addresses to secure support for the repeal of the Test and Corporation Acts (a move which will be discussed below).[67] This strategy was no more successful for the Rump in perpetuating its existence than it was for Richard Cromwell and the Protectorate. Addresses and other similar subscriptional forms were nonetheless employed to call first for a 'free' Parliament and, after this had been achieved, to celebrate the restoration of the Stuart monarchy.[68]

LOYALTY, MEMORY AND THE RESTORATION

The period from 1658 to 1660 was one of profound political instability. In such a situation, it is scarcely surprising that the insecure regimes of the time sought any means available, however seemingly ineffective, to give their government the air of legitimacy. The dizzying fluctuations in public loyalty were used, as in *A true catalogue*, to question the integrity of the authors of these addresses and the value of the genre as a whole as an indicator of the nation's mood. Accusations of disingenuous behaviour proliferated as the Rump's authority crumbled. A 1659 pamphlet alleged that two Guernsey jurats, Peter and William de Beauvoir, had been the architects of the island's address to Richard Cromwell though both were Royalists, William even having borne arms for the King in the first civil war.[69] Peter de Beauvoir was certainly one of the Guernsey officials who left for London in May 1660 to await the arrival of Charles II. If this doesn't necessarily confirm his 'Royalism' the pamphlet offers an important reminder of the way in which past addressing activity soon came to be employed to mount political attacks.[70] *Mercurius Politicus* and its counterpart *The Publick Intelligencer* regularly denounced petitions for a 'free Parliament' as really Royalist productions, no more than a 'designe to promote the Interest of C. Stuart'.[71]

In this vein, we might see Sir John Fitzjames as acting in bad faith in promoting the Dorset address to Richard Cromwell given that two years later he not only signed but also presented the county's congratulatory address to Charles II on his Restoration.[72] Before labelling Fitzjames a hypocrite or turncoat, however, it is worth considering how he promoted the address to Richard among the Dorset elite. In his letters, Fitzjames stressed the role of the address as a device to secure 'ye unity & Peace of ye County' and assumed that the address would be signed by all the 'peaceably minded'.[73] There was little in Fitzjames' letters that spoke of deep ideological commitment to the Protectoral regime. Instead, the address and, by extension, Richard's succession were seen as means to ensure the stability and security of the county, a view that Baxter ascribed to individuals of a variety of political and religious persuasions in the wake of Oliver's death.[74]

These sorts of accommodations were predictable in the turbulent years following Oliver Cromwell's demise and make charges of hypocrisy or dissimulation seem in many cases unjust and unrealistic. In this way, the language of providence utilised in many addresses might not only have been convenient but also perhaps sincere.[75] More significant than any unreasonable expectations of absolute ideological constancy was the way in which addressing activity clearly created a powerful public memory. Several counties that issued congratulatory addresses to Charles II felt obliged to excuse their past activity. The 'declaration and vindication of the loyal-hearted nobility, gentry, and others of the county of Kent, and the City of Canterbury' sought to cleanse the community from the taint of 'many several Petitions, Remonstrances, Declarations, and other like Addresses' which had been previously issued in the county's name 'framed or rather forged by a few disloyal, factious and seditious time-servers'.[76] The address from the city of Lincoln apologised that 'through the general defection of your Majesties Subjects in this your Kingdome from their Alleigance ... they were therein involved with the rest of your Majesties Subjects' and appealed to the King's recently issued general pardon and indemnity for absolution and protection.[77] Other congratulatory addresses sought to excuse the purchase of Crown fee-farms during the interregnum, typically offering to restore these revenues plus arrears to their rightful owner.[78]

Conversely, several addresses highlighted their community's lack of involvement in previous addressing campaigns as evidence of unwavering loyalty: the petition from the mayors and bailiffs of the Cinque Ports asserted that their reputation had never been tarnished 'by any Address or Application whatsoever, to testifie our Assent to any Government imposed upon us'.[79] The address presented to Charles II from the city of Chester claimed that its inhabitants had 'never temporized w[it]h any irregular power, by any Address made to them; since ye death of your most Royall Father'.[80] The loyal address from the Gloucestershire gentry boasted that they had never been brought to 'flatter with any Address whatsoever, any usurped power which hath been over us'.[81] The clergy of Kent asserted that they 'never did formerly make the least Addresses to those prodigious Usurpers'.[82] Similarly, that from the borough of Totnes used their early and committed support for a free Parliament (in which cause, the address stated, two of their inhabitants were killed) to show their devotion to the Royalist cause.[83]

Some of these protestations displayed a somewhat selective memory: Gloucestershire may not have sent an address but the city of Gloucester certainly promised loyalty to Richard in a text that was reproduced in *Nouvelles Ordinaires* in January 1659, and while the inhabitants of Chester do not appear to have pledged their lives and fortunes to the Protector, two variant addresses were sent in the name of the county of Cheshire.[84] Post-Restoration loyal addresses can be seen as a corporate equivalent of such texts as petitions for relief in that both sought to refashion the community or the individual's political identity.[85] In both cases, circumstances required that these identities were as uncompromised as possible. In some instances, the very public nature of addressing made acknowledging disloyal actions necessary but these could be excused by explaining that addresses were unrepresentative of the true community and/or had been fraudulently obtained. Undoubtedly, some of these expressions of loyalty were incredibly contrived: one can only marvel at the tortuous logic on display in the army address, signed by the regicide Richard Ingoldsby, which assured the King that former Parliamentarian soldiers were 'his Majesties best and most loyal Subjects'.[86] Yet, at the same time, these texts revealed the very varied backgrounds and aspirations of those who congratulated Charles II on his Restoration. The address from the clergy of Kent, for example, was subscribed by both Thomas Plume and John Beadle. Both men had previously made some accommodation with the Cromwellian regime but the Presbyterian Beadle would shortly to be ejected from his parish for refusing to submit to the terms of the Act of Uniformity, while the conformist Plume would retain his living.[87] Similarly, while some congratulatory addresses, such as that from Devon and Exeter ministers praised the King for his care for 'tender consciences' as expressed in the Declaration of Breda, others, such as that from Northamptonshire, made clear that they sought the restoration of a national, episcopal church as well as the monarchy.[88] Beneath their surface uniformity, addresses continued to contain a multitude of demands and aspirations.

CROMWELL'S TRUNKS: THE LOYAL ADDRESS ORIGIN STORY

The succession of loyal addresses and humble petitions which had accompanied the shift from Protectorate to Commonwealth to monarchy came to an end in 1661 with the passage of the 'Act against Tumults and Disorders upon Pretence of Preparing or Presenting publick Peticions'. The statute placed this activity within a historical narrative, identifying popular petitioning as a cause of the 'late unhappy wars Confusions and Calamities in this Nation'.

Yet the act was arguably not just a retrospective condemnation of the mass petitioning of the 1640s but was also targeted at more recent subscriptional activity. As has been noted, the act included addresses as well as petitions within its terms and the requirements it established for lawful petitioning, that petitions subscribed by twenty or more individuals had to be approved by three or more justices or the majority of the grand jury, seemed directly aimed at the humble petitions and addresses sent to the restored Rump from informal groups of the 'well-affected'.[89] Even before this bill passed into law, many of the congratulatory addresses sent to Charles II seemed determined to draw back from the overt populism of some of the Cromwellian addresses. As will be discussed in greater detail later, instead of seeking to record the greatest number of subscribers, these addresses emphasised that they were socially exclusive productions, signed only by the gentry and nobility.[90] These gentry addresses, however, may have been a reaction to popular Royalism as well as Parliamentarian petitioning and addressing initiatives: as both *Mercurius Politicus* and the *Publick Intelligencer* had been keen to report, calls for a free Parliament had led to rioting and disorder.[91] The legislation, then, did not intend to suppress all petitioning and addressing activity, not least because it had been made clear that this could be a very useful weapon in defence of the monarchy. Instead, the act gave the Restoration monarchy a statutory instrument (as already noted, built on a Parliamentarian precedent) through which to regulate and contain popular subscriptional activity. As we will see later, even in controversies which displayed deep ideological divisions, it often proved possible for the disputants to agree that some form of regulation of petitioning and addressing was both legal and necessary.

The memory of addressing activity during the Cromwellian Protectorate was also critical to shaping responses to subsequent campaigns. *A second narrative of the late Parliament* denounced the 'blasphemous, lying, flattering Cycophant Addressors in City, Countrey, [and] Army' who had recently pledged their loyalty to the new Lord Protector, Richard Cromwell.[92] The pamphlet went on to mock those addresses that portrayed Richard Cromwell as a new Joshua to his father's Moses: 'Is Hawking, Hunting, keeping Race-horses, and riding Horse-matches to the endangering of the lives both of Horses and Men ... such a demonstration' the author asked 'of those noble vertues and high endowments you so speak of to be in him?'[93]

These attacks on the addresses to Richard Cromwell as absurd, manufactured hyperbole were quoted approvingly in *A true catalogue*. The chief purpose of this anthology of 'lying, flattering addresses' was to bring those who had been the main architects and promoters of these texts into 'publique view'.[94] The collection would demonstrate,

> that such pitiful, inconsiderable, uncertain spirited, principled persons as these, are not fit to be trusted for the future, by no sort of men whatever, having upon all accounts (take them which way you will) proved so unstable, deceitful and treacherous, both to God, and man.[95]

The compendium singled out particular individuals for heavy criticism, most notably the former Royalist journalist turned Cromwellian propagandist Marchamount Nedham. The decision to employ Nedham, the author said (once again borrowing the wording of *A second narrative*) 'stinks in the Nostrils of God, and his faithful people, The good Old Cause of Christ needs no liars to be employed to help bear it up'.[96] Overall, the author asked whether those that had publically proclaimed Oliver and Richard as Lord Protector should now be tried under the treason laws of 1649 which had forbidden the promotion of government by a single person.[97] A similar work by William Caton, *Truths caracter*, published a year later, collected thirty county and borough addresses to Richard, which Caton presented as really the product of Baptist and Independent churches. The addresses showed, Caton argued, how like 'subtil & cunning merchant-men' these Baptists and Independents were, always ready to 'change their merchandize to continue their trade'.[98]

The intent of these collections was not only to identify and denounce those who had previously professed loyalty to the Cromwellian regime but also to question the value of these addresses as evidence of public support for the

Protectorate. In this way, the collections began a consistent trend evident in later compendia of loyal addresses of analysing and commenting upon their claims to speak for the people of a particular locality. For example, the author of *A true catalogue* stated that the Norwich address's claim to have been based on the 'general consent' of the people of that city was a 'notorious lye'.[99] The collection suggested that these addresses were not the spontaneous creation of the localities themselves but part of a coordinated propaganda campaign originating with the Protector's court, 'the offspring of *Thurloe* and *Nedham*', an accusation that would be levelled (rightly or wrongly) at a number of later addressing initiatives.[100]

The collection was written from the perspective of a godly supporter of the 'Good Old Cause', attacking the back-sliding of the Cromwellian years. Both the author of *A true catalogue* and William Caton employed the texts of addresses to demonstrate the inconstancy of the architects of these documents. English corporations in particular were so pusillanimous, the author urged, that not only would they readily swear allegiance to a tyrannical, apostatising Protectorate but 'should the Lord suffer a wicked power to break in upon us, as would set up, and impose the Mahomitan Religion, Popery, or Atheism in the Nation, yea, even Belzebub himself', there were no 'substantial grounds or security' to believe that corporations 'would not also fall in, and bow down to that too'.[101] (These attacks on English corporations may also have been a reflection on the decision to revert to an older franchise for elections to Richard's Parliament which, in the words of Edmund Ludlow, gave more seats to 'mean and decayed boroughs.')[102]

The Cromwellian addresses were recalled well into the eighteenth century. *A true catalogue* was reprinted in 1702, though this time with significant amounts of its 'godly' commentary cut out, and it continued to attract attention throughout the eighteenth century.[103] Those sceptical of the value of addresses as indicators of the public opinion were keen to note that the practice began under the Cromwellian 'usurpation'. (The decision to reprint the text in 1702 was itself in all probability an implicit criticism of the recent Williamite addressing campaign inspired by Louis XIV's recognition of the Old Pretender.) The fact that Richard Cromwell's succession was heralded with so many addresses (*A true catalogue* had identified ninety-four in total) was often cited as clear evidence that these texts were fundamentally untrustworthy. As *An impartial account of the nature and tendency of the late addresses* (1681), sometimes attributed to the Earl of Shaftesbury, stated,

> no Applications of this nature to the *Regnant* person are to be esteem'd of any great weight or significancy, if you do but consider the Result of the many Addresses Three and twenty year ago to *Richard Cromwell*, and how they only served to render him secure till he was undermined and supplanted. For of all the *Sixteen hundred thousand* that vow'd to Live and Dye by him, not so much as one man drew a Sword in his favour when he came to be laid aside.[104]

Writing in the early eighteenth century, John Oldmixon made the same point through an anecdote concerning Richard's last days in power. While two men were assisting Cromwell in clearing his belongings from the Protectoral lodgings, Oldmixon said that he instructed them to take special care of 'two old *Trunks*':

> The Men wonder'd why he was so solicitous for their Preservation, since by their Appearance, and the Place they were put in, they did not seem to contain a Treasure of such Consequence. And one of his Friends hearing him inquire after them with more Concern than for any other part of the Lumber, ask'd him, What was in them that made him value them so much? *Why, no less*, says *Richard, than the Lives and Fortunes of all the Good People of England*. It seems the Addresses that had been presented him, were thrown in there: and we all know that 'tis a poor Address, that has not *Lives* and *Fortunes* in it.[105]

The politically dubious origins of addressing activity were discussed by high Tory commentators as well as Whigs. The antiquary Thomas Hearne reported a conversation between Richard Cromwell and a mutual acquaintance Walter Garrett. In later life, Cromwell had told Garrett that he,

> looked upon addresses as nothing, and that he was addressed to once as much as any prince had been, and that he had a great many of the original addresses then by him, which he had a mind to send to the Bodleian library, on purpose to be preserved, to shew the temper of this nation, and the readiness of the greatest members to complement people on purpose of secular interest.[106]

Hearne's account gives Richard Cromwell rather more credit as a judge of the true value of these addresses than Oldmixon's. In a similar vein, the loyalist historian Mark Noble, in his late eighteenth-century collective biography of the Cromwell family, reported that Richard liked to bring the trunk out as an after dinner entertainment, encouraging guests to ride upon it and then warning the uninitiated that they should take care because the chest carried the 'lives and fortunes' of the English people within it.[107] These stories may even have a germ of truth within them. In 1706, Richard Cromwell gave written instructions that his 'little shagreen truncke' should be given on his death to his sister Mary, countess of Fauconberg; and Richard's modern biographers have speculated that this might be the trunk full of addresses mentioned by Oldmixon, Hearne and Noble.[108]

What the 1659 compendium asserted and what these subsequent anecdotes concerning Richard Cromwell's trunks drove home, was that the pledges of loyalty embodied in loyal addresses were insubstantial and manufactured, and that addressing campaigns gave little indication of the strength of support for a particular individual. The addresses of the late 1650s, as has been shown, were more than examples of vapid court sycophancy. The identification of the origin of the strategy of mass addressing with the Cromwellian Protectorate was nonetheless significant. It demonstrated the extent to which addressing was very quickly identified as a practice that was related to but distinct from other forms of communication, especially petitioning. This in turn revealed the way an awareness and reflectiveness about addressing as a practice rapidly developed which was itself a consequence of the very public nature of mass addressing. The actual content of the addresses to Richard Cromwell was also far less uniform and adulatory than the 1659 compendium or William Caton's 1660 text suggested. Instead, these addresses were part of the wider debate over the legitimacy of Richard's succession and of the Protectorate in general.

The language of loyalty was also deceptive, as Derek Hirst has noted in relation to petitions and addresses in this period, because it concealed the extent to which communities were employing this discourse strategically, to win concessions from authority or, at least, avoid potentially being penalised for appearing disloyal.[109] The depiction of addresses as expressions of hollow obsequiousness was significant in another respect, in showing how the process of editing and compiling these texts could allow authors to repackage their content to make it appear more uniform than it actually was. These were, however, not texts which simply existed in printed compendia or within the pages of newsbooks such as *Mercurius Politicus* or *The Publick Intelligencer*. They were, in Mark Knights' words, 'subscriptional' texts and the process of subscription left its own imprint on public memory. Subscription could not only be used to demonstrate the level and quality of public support but also to identify opponents, build political alliances and later hold 'backsliders' to account.

CONCLUSION

The oft-repeated story of Richard Cromwell's trunks was meant to prove that addressing was fundamentally unreliable as an indicator of 'public opinion', given the deep gulf between the multiple and vehement professions of loyalty to him in print and the near total indifference which the public appeared to greet his fall from power. Addresses are certainly not straightforward indicators of popular support. Thinking about public opinion in purely numerical terms, however, is surely to diminish that 'public' to little more than, in Gerard Hauser's expression, a 'data set'.[110]

Addressing activity reveals a more complex and self-aware political public. The relative uniformity of addresses reflected less central coordination and manipulation than the ability of communities to engage with and respond to arguments, ideas and phrases in public discourse. In the case of 1658–9, these were clearly not boiler-plate encomiums but varied texts which, beneath the repeated use of providential tropes (themselves not mere empty verbiage), revealed the issues at stake in the struggle over Richard Cromwell's succession: not just the legitimacy of his title but the whole Cromwellian settlement in both Church and State. Instead of simply seeing these promises of loyalty as disingenuous, we can see many of them as agile rhetorical exercises, employing the public transcript of acclamation to deliver criticisms and make demands. This strategic use of the medium continued after Richard Cromwell's fall: addresses that urged a 'free parliament' occasionally did so through the use of the language of the 'Good Old Cause', a phrase formerly associated with republicanism and the sects, but which was now being appropriated by Presbyterians to call for the return of the 'secluded' members.[111] As the congratulatory addresses to Charles II demonstrated, the public nature of addressing and its direct connection with what would now be called regime change made it a particularly mnemonic form, bearing the attributes of Warner's reflective, temporally structured public sphere. So, while these texts cannot straightforwardly indicate the contours of popular support at a particular historical moment, they do reveal the engagement of local communities with national politics and contemporary political rhetoric, as well as documenting, contrary to the Habermasian model, the role of the political centre in facilitating the growth of the public sphere.

The Cromwellian period established not only the form of the loyal address itself but also the discourses both negative and positive surrounding the genre. From the 1650s onward, each addressing campaign would witness the assertion in print that these texts either embodied popular will and sincere loyal affection, or that they contained nothing more than fraudulent, and manufactured, obeisance. Neither claim was wholly true, though some Cromwellian addresses were signed by thousands, and certainly some governmental influence was brought to bear on the content and form of these texts. More important, as will be shown in subsequent chapters, the very heated disputes over the value of these texts and their reliability rarely, if ever, went so far as to question the legitimacy either of 'public politics' (to use Jason Peacey's term) or some types of addressing and petitioning. It was also in the 1650s that print strategies were devised to increase the impact of these texts – the use of newsbooks to disseminate texts, mobilise opinion and secure subscriptions which in turn facilitated the creation of compendia to 'spin' the meaning of these texts.

As has already been argued, these strategies encouraged the rapid development of a self-awareness and reflectiveness concerning addressing as genre. An indication of this was not only the creation of compendia but the growth of parody texts aping the form of the loyal address. These included *The humble petition of Richard Cromwell, late Lord Protector of England, Scotland and Ireland, to the Councel of Officers at Walingford House*. Here Richard complained that despite,

> the Address of many thousands of these nations, faithfully promising to establish me on my Fathers usurped Seat, and protesting before God to live and die for me, whom they stiled their *Joshua* ... [the army] were guilty of such insolent and contrary proceedings as to turn me out of my place before I was well warm, under the specious pretence of setting up the *Good old Cause*.[112]

Yet, while Richard Cromwell's reign was famously brief, the long-lived second protector survived to see addressing develop as a major mode of popular political communication. Contrary to Habermas' view, the emergence of addressing was very much a recognition of the rule of public opinion. The dizzying changes in public loyalty might be invoked to demonstrate the credulity and/or fickleness of the people. Commentators would certainly continue to debate who exactly constituted that legitimate political public. As the creation of collections and histories of addressing showed, however, addresses ultimately acknowledged the emergence of 'opinion politics' in early modern England. At the same time, addressing and petitioning, as already noted, provided a pretext for the centre to intervene in the administration of the localities, as much as it gave the periphery an avenue through which to place demands upon government. In the late 1650s, addressing campaigns were employed to relatively limited success in this regard – attempts by the Rump to reform the militia through networks developed via addressing activity foundered with the restored Commonwealth's own downfall. As will be demonstrated in the next chapter, however, in the 1680s much more concerted and ultimately successful attempts were made by the Crown to deploy addresses to help purge and reform local government and to build alliances which would back radical shifts in religious policy.

NOTES

1. *A true catalogue, or, an account of the several places and most eminent persons in the three nations, and elsewhere, where and by whom Richard Cromwell was proclaimed Lord Protector* (1659), p. 6. The text is attributed to Powell in C. H. Firth, 'Richard Cromwell', in L. Stephens and S. Lee (eds), *Dictionary of National Biography* (60 vols, London, 1885–1900); it was earlier attributed to Powell by Mark Noble, *Memoirs of the Protectoral House of Cromwell* (3rd edn, 2 vols, 1807), i, p. 180. The attribution seems plausible given Powell's Fifth Monarchist beliefs, his public hostility to the Cromwellian Protectorate and also the specific attacks within the tract on Powell's opponent, the loyalist Welsh Independent Walter Cradock, see *A true catalogue*, p. 10.
2. BL Add MS. 5138, f. 9–9v, Guybon Goddard's diary; 'Guibon Goddard's Journal: September 1654', in J. T. Rutt (ed.), *Diary of Thomas Burton Esq*, (4 vols, London, 1828), i, pp. xvii–xliv www.british-history.ac.uk/burton-diaries/vol1/xvii-xliv, accessed 18 December 2014.
3. Knights, 'Loyal Address', p. 322.
4. B. Whitelock, *Memorials* (4 vols, Oxford, 1853) iv, p. 337. Whitelock noted the presentation of addresses to Richard with some care in his *Memorials* – see pp. 336–8 and to Rump pp. 350–4 and see also Chapter six below. For evidence of the care taken at a local level over the presentation of addresses see Gloucestershire Archives, GBR/H/2/3, p. 255.
5. Besides the works listed in the notes below, valuable overviews of the Protectorate can be found in B. Coward, *The Cromwellian Protectorate* (Manchester: Manchester

University Press, 2002); B. Worden, *God's Instruments: Political Conduct in the England of Oliver Cromwell* (Oxford: Oxford University Press, 2012).
6   *A true catalogue*, p. 45; W. Caton, *Truths caracter of professors and their teachers* (1660), p. 46; A notice of the York address was provided in *Nouvelles Ordinaires de Londres* but not the full text, 14–25 November 1658, no. 444. See also the Cumberland address, of which there is only a notice in *Nouvelles Ordinaires de Londres*, 24 February to 5 March, no. 458 but which is discussed in detail in Caton, *Truth's caracter*, pp. 48–9. This also suggests that these suppressed texts were being circulated in manuscript.
7   *A second narrative of the late Parliament (so-called)* (1659), p. 37. The attribution of this pamphlet to Sir George Wharton seems hard to sustain. It seems far more a product of a 'commonwealthsman'. I am grateful to Bernard Capp for discussing the pamphlet's authorship with me. For this pamphlet, see also Knights' 'Loyal address', p. 319.
8   R. Hutton, *The Restoration: A Political and Religious History of England and Wales, 1658–1667* (Oxford: Oxford University Press, 1985), p. 22.
9   G. Davies, *The Restoration of Charles II, 1658–1660* (San Marino: Huntington Library, 1955), p. 11.
10 P. Gaunt, 'Cromwell, Richard', ODNB; J. Peacey, '"Fit for public services": the upbringing of Richard Cromwell', in P. Little (ed.), *Oliver Cromwell: New Perspectives* (Basingstoke: Palgrave, 2009), ch. 10; and see also Peacey 'The Protector Humbled: Richard Cromwell and the Constitution', in P. Little (ed.), *The Cromwellian Protectorate* (Woodbridge: Boydell and Brewer, 2007), ch. 3; Jonathan Fitzgibbons, '"Not in any doubtfull dispute?" Reassessing the nomination of Richard Cromwell', *Historical Research*, 83 (2010), 281–300. See also P. Little and D. L. Smith, *Parliaments and Politics during the Cromwellian Protectorate* (Cambridge: Cambridge University Press, 2007), ch. 7; P. Little, 'Cromwell and Sons: Oliver Cromwell's intended legacy', in J. A. Mills (ed.), *Cromwell's Legacy* (Manchester: Manchester University Press, 2012), ch. 1.
11 J. Peacey, *Politicians and Pamphleteers: Propaganda during the English Civil Wars and Interregnum* (Farnham: Ashgate, 2004), p. 252.
12 TNA PRO 31/17/33, Transcript of the Council of State Order Book, 3 September 1658 to 18 January 1658/9, pp. 3–9 and see p. 27 for order that Richard be proclaimed Protector in Virginia. Bodl. MS Rawl A 61/1 f. 87, includes a report of the proclamation of Richard in the United Provinces and the congratulation of the States General, ibid. f. 95.
13 TNA PRO 31/17/33, pp. 38–40.
14 The Archives of the Duke of Northumberland at Alnwick Castle, DNP: MS 552, f. 35 (BL Loan Microfilm 331), Letterbooks of Sir John Fitzjames;. I am grateful to Blair Worden for bringing this source to my attention and to the Northumberland Estates for permission to consult the microfilms at the British Library.
15 R. Spalding (ed.), *The Diary of Bulstrode Whitelocke, 1605–1675* (British Academy, Records of Social and Economic History, NS, XIII, 1990), p. 500 and see also pp. 517, 519 for Whitelocke being consulted regarding petitions to the restored Rump.
16 Thomas Birch (ed.), *A collection of the state papers of John Thurloe, Esq* (7 vols,1742), vii, p. 375. See also P. Gaunt (ed.), *The Correspondence of Henry Cromwell 1655–1659 from the British Library Landsowne Manuscripts* (Camden Soc., 5th series, vol. 31, 2007), pp. 405–7.

17 Thurloe State Papers, vii p. 400. A true catalogue claimed that an ensign in the garrison at Waterford was punished for refusing to acknowledge Richard Cromwell, p. 23.
18 Thurloe State Papers, vii, p. 411.
19 Nouvelles Ordinaires de Londres, 30 September to 7 October 1658, no. 437.
20 Thurloe State Papers, vii., p. 405.
21 Ibid., vii, p. 406.
22 Vallance, Revolutionary England and the National Covenant, p. 52.
23 Mercurius Politicus, 16–23 September 1658, no. 434.
24 Mercurius Politicus, 23–30 September 1658, no. 435; Thurloe State Papers, vii, p. 426.
25 Mercurius Politicus, 16–23 September 1658, no. 434; Davies, Restoration, p. 9; Woolrych, 'Introduction', Complete Prose Works of Milton, Don. M Wolfe (ed.), (8 vols, New Haven, CT: Yale University Press, 1953–1982), vii, p. 12.
26 'Introduction' to Diary of Thomas Burton, iii, pp. iii-viii. For the problems with Rutt's edition see J. R. Fitzgibbons, 'Reconstructing the debates of the Protectorate parliaments: The pitfalls of J. T. Rutt's edition of "Thomas Burton's" diary', Parliamentary History, 35 (2016), 221–41.
27 John Prestwich, Prestwich's respublica, or a display of the honors, ceremonies, ensigns of the Common-Wealth under the Protectorship of Oliver Cromwell (1787), pp. 204–6; TNA PRO 31/17/33, pp. 3–4.
28 A true catalogue, pp. 37–8. For examples see Devizes, Mercurius Politicus, 28 October to 4 November 1658, no. 440; Leicester, Mercurius Politicus, 4–11 November 1658, no. 441; Coventry, Mercurius Politicus, 11–18 November 1658, no. 442.
29 (Poole), Mercurius Politicus, 25 November to 2 December 1658, no. 444; (St Albans) Mercurius Politicus, 11–18 November 1658, no. 442.
30 A. G. Matthews (ed.), The Savoy Declaration of Faith and Order, 1658 (London: Independent Press Ltd, 1959), pp. 70–1, pp. 107–8.
31 N. H. Keeble and G. Nuttall (eds), Calendar of the correspondence of Richard Baxter (2 vols, Oxford: Clarendon Press, 1991), i., pp. 367, 378.
32 (Sussex), Mercurius Politicus, 30 September 7 October 1658, no. 436; (Taunton) Mercurius Politicus, 21–28 October 1658, no. 439; And for similar calls to suppress blasphemy see the address from Marlborough, Wiltshire, Nouvelles Ordinaires de Londres, 18–25 November 1658, no. 444.
33 Mercurius Politicus, 10–17 February 1649, no. 554.
34 Matthews, Savoy Declaration, p. 10 and see also Little and Smith, Parliaments and Politics, p. 151.
35 D. Hirst, 'Concord and dischord in Richard Cromwell's House of Commons', English Historical Review, 103 (1988), 339–58 at 341–2.
36 Mathews, Savoy Declaration, pp. 16–17.
37 A true catalogue, p. 44, Caton, Truth's caracter, A2.
38 A true catalogue, p. 47.
39 Ibid., p. 45; Caton, Truth's caracter, p. 46; Some internal evidence points to the author of A true catalogue making use of Nouvelles Ordinaires de Londres, see p. 17 where it refers to the 'cruel Jaylour of the Lords people', Major Bull of the Isle of Wight. Bull is referred to in Nouvelles Ordinaires de Londres, 23–30 September 1658, no. 436. Similarly, on p. 36, A true catalogue provides details

of the presenter of the address from the officers and soldiers of Portland, Weymouth and Sandfort not given in *Mercurius Politicus* or the *Publick Intelligencer* but present in *Nouvelles Ordinaires de Londres*, 13–20 January 1659, no. 452.

40 NRO, Y/C 19/7, f. 312, Yarmouth corporation assembly book, 1642–1662, 6 September 1658 (receipt of proclamation announcing Richard's succession); ibid., f. 315v., 8 November 1658 (appointment of a committee to draw up the address); ibid., f. 316 18 November 1658 (address agreed and order given for it to be presented). *Nouvelles Ordinaires de Londres*, 7–16 September 1658, no. 434, reports celebrations of Richard's succession in Yarmouth; *Mercurius Politicus*, 30 December to 6 January 1658/9, no. 548, reproduces Yarmouth address. See also *Nouvelles Ordinaires de Londres*, 24 February to 5 March 1659, no. 458.

41 NRO, Y/C 19/7 f. 356v-357, Yarmouth corporation assembly book, 1642–1662, 8 August 1660.

42 (Durham) *Mercurius Politicus*, 2–9 December 1658, no. 445 (Barnstable), *Mercurius Politicus*, 24 February 3 March 1659, no. 556.

43 *Mercurius Politicus*, 25 November to 2 December 1658, no. 444.

44 *Mercurius Politicus*, 17–24 February 1659, no. 555.

45 Stephen Wright, 'Bowles, Edward', ODNB; John Price, *The Mystery and Method of his Majesty's Happy Restauration. Laid Open to Publick View* (1680), p. 79. R. Baxter, *Reliquiae Baxterianae*, M. Sylvester (ed.), (1696), p. 218 notes that Bowles was also one of the Presbyterian ministers to visit Charles II in Holland before his return to England.

46 G. B. Nourse, 'Richard Cromwell's House of Commons', *Bulletin of the John Rylands Library*, 60 (1977), 95–113, at 107.

47 BL Add MS 78195 f. 148, Evelyn Papers vol XXVIII, 16/26 October 1658. See also Bodl. MS Rawl A. 61/2 f. 281, Letter of Thomas Lilburne 11 October 1658, intimating delay and division at the Durham sessions in producing an address, which Lilburne blamed on the sheriff who did not come to the session, 'nor kept that correspondence with the Justices in there sessions'.

48 *Diary of Thomas Burton*, iii, pp. 85–118 www.british-history.ac.uk/burton-diaries/vol3/pp85-118, accessed 18 December 2014. See also BL Add MS 15862, Parliamentary Diary of Thomas Burton 1656–59. Jonathan Fitzgibbons identifies Starkey as a 'new Presbyterian', one of those MPs who defended the Humble Petition and Advice, Fitzgibbons, *Cromwell's House of Lords: Politics, Parliaments and Constitutional Revolution, 1642–1660* (Woodbridge: Boydell Press, 2018), p. 169 and pp. 180–1 for 'new Presbyterians'.

49 *Mercurius Politicus*, 17–24 March 1659, no. 559.

50 *Kingdomes Intelligencer*, 3–10 June 1661, no. 23; *Mercurius Publicus*, 6–13 June 1661, no. 23. Manuscript addresses to Richard have been identified for Gloucester, Gloucestershire Archives, GBR/H/2/3, p. 255 and Great Yarmouth, TNA SP 18/184 f. 145–145v; NRO, Y/C 19/7 f. 406–407, Yarmouth corporation assembly book, 1642–1662, 'Taken from a very Old Copy Penes Joseph Cotman'. For further discussion of deliberate destruction of manuscript addresses to Richard see Chapter three for the Yarmouth address.

51 Bodl., MS Rawl A. 61*, f. 164–87; A. G. Matthews, *Calamy Revised: Being A Revision of Edmund Calamy's Account of the Ministers and Others Ejected and Silenced, 1660–2* (Oxford: Clarendon Press, 1988 edn), p. lxxi. *Mercurius Politicus*,

14–21 October 1658, no. 438. See also Hirst, 'Making Contact', 47–8 for the elaborate preparations made for presenting the Leicester address.
52 Alnwick Castle, DNP: MS 552, f. 47 (BL Loan Microfilm 331). The address was reproduced in *Nouvelles Ordinaires de Londres*, 16–23 December 1658, no. 448.
53 See *Mercurius Politicus* 30 September to 7 October 1658, no. 436 where the address from Sussex is described both as being subscribed by thousands and being from the 'Gentlemen, Ministers, Freeholders and others' of the county.
54 BL Add MS 15682, Diary of Thomas Burton 1656–1659, unpaginated and out of chronological order 9 Feb 1658/9. I have preferred the text of the original MS here as Rutt's version includes the interpolation 'and by another sort of people' not present in the manuscript. I read Packer's argument as suggesting that *anyone* could be brought to address Charles II, not just Royalists: *Diary of Thomas Burton*, iii, pp. 152–94 www.british-history.ac.uk/burton-diaries/vol3/pp152-194, accessed 20 December 2014.
55 BL Add MS. 5138, f. 71, Guybon Goddard's diary, 7 February 1659.
56 *Diary of Thomas Burton*, iii, pp. 201–33 www.british-history.ac.uk/burton-diaries/vol3/pp201-233, accessed 18 December 2014.
57 Baxter, *Reliquiae*, Sylvester (ed.), p. 100. See *Nouvelles Ordinaires de Londres*, 4–11 November 1658, no. 442, for address from JPs and Grand Jury of Worcestershire.
58 That from Lord Howard's regiment, *Mercurius Politicus*, 20–27 January 1659, no. 551 and see also the draft addresses in Henry Cromwell's letters,BL Lansdowne MS 823 f. 375–80.
59 *Nouvelles Ordinaires de Londres*, 24 February to 5 March 1659, no. 458 and similar statement in no. 460, 10–17 March 1659.
60 A. H. Woolrych, 'The good old cause and the fall of the Protectorate', *Cambridge Historical Journal*, 13 (1958), 133–61 at 138. *Diary of Thomas Burton*, iii, pp. 288–96; Godfrey Davies, 'The army and the downfall of Richard Cromwell', *Huntington Library Bulletin*, 7 (1935), 131–67, at 146.
61 R. E. Mayers, *1659: The Crisis of the Commonwealth* (Woodbridge: Boydell and Brewer, 2004), pp. 98–102 but see also Hutton, *Restoration*, pp. 46–7. Richard in contrast was addressed by colonies as well as various parts of the British Isles, *Mercurius Politicus*, 24–31 March, no. 560, address from Barbados.
62 BL, Egerton MS. 1048, fols. 163–9. The petition contains the signature of a young Benjamin Keech, the Particular Baptist minister, see fo. 169; Mayers, *1659: The Crisis of the Commonwealth*, p. 102.
63 *Mercurius Politicus*, 26 May to 2 June 1659, no. 569.
64 *Mercurius Politicus*, 12–19 May 1659, no. 567 (Hertford); 19–26 May 1659, no. 568 (Durham Militia).
65 Hutton, *Restoration*, p. 46; Sir G. F. Warner (ed.), *The Nicholas Papers: Correspondence of Sir Edward Nicholas Secretary of State vol. IV, 1657–1660* (Camden Soc., 3rd series, xxxi, 1920), pp. 151–2.
66 E. Vallance, 'Harrington, petitioning and the construction of public opinion', in G. Mahlberg and D. Wiemann (eds), *Perspectives on English Revolutionary Republicanism* (Farnham: Ashgate, 2014), ch. 7.
67 Vallance, 'Construction of public opinion' and see below Chapter three.
68 W. L. Sachse (ed.), *The Diurnal of Thomas Rugg* (Camden Soc., 3rd series, xci, 1961), pp. 31–2. For collections of these broadside addresses see BL 190. g. 12 and

C. 112. h. 4. For the declarations in support of a 'free Parliament' see B. Worden, 'The campaign for a free Parliament, 1659–1660', *Parliamentary History*, 36 (2017), 159–84; Worden, 'The demand for a free parliament, 1659–60', in G. Southcombe and G. Tapsell (eds) *Revolutionary England, c. 1630-c. 1660: Essays for Clive Holmes* (Abingdon: Routledge, 2016), ch. 11 and Worden, '1660: restoration and revolution', in J. Clare (ed.), *From Republic to Restoration: Legacies and Departures* (Manchester: Manchester University Press, 2018), ch. 1. I am grateful to Blair Worden for sharing his work on the free Parliament campaign with me prior to publication.

69 *An epitomie of tyranny in the island of Guernzey* (1659), p. 4.
70 See G. E. Lee (ed. and trans) *Note-book of Pierre Le Roy, Schoolmaster of S. Martin's Parish in the Island of Guernsey 1600–1675* (Guernsey: Guernsey Historical and Antiquarian Society Publications, 1893), p. 25 and n.
71 *Mercurius Politicus*, 9–16 February 1660, no. 607, referring to the Leicester address for a free parliament. *Publick Intelligencer*, 30 January to 6 February 1660, no. 214, referred to the Kent declaration for a free Parliament as the production of 'old Cavaliers'. For a different perspective on the promoters of these texts see Price, *Mystery and method*, p. 84.
72 TNA SP 29/1/f. 55–6 printed as *To the King's Most Excellent Majesty ... the Humble Address of the Nobility and Gentry of Dorset* (1660) (Thomason 669.f 25[44]). The differences between the MS and printed versions will be discussed in a subsequent chapter.
73 Alnwick Castle, DNP: MS 552 f. 48 (BL Loan Microfilm 331), Fitzjames to John Hardy, 11 November 1658.
74 Baxter, *Reliquiae*, p. 100.
75 See here Derek Hirst's comments on providentialism and de factoist ideas in Richard's Parliament, 'Concord and dischord', 353, 357.
76 Thomason 669. f. 25 [19]; see also for this address, Knights, *Representation and Misrepresentation*, p. 121.
77 *Mercurius Publicus*, 5–12 July 1660, no. 28.
78 TNA SP 29/1/f. 52 (Coventry); TNA SP 29/3 f. 17 (Oxford); *Mercurius Publicus*, 26 July to 2 August 1660, no. 31 (Preston); *Parliamentary Intelligencer*, 2–9 July 1660, no. 28 (St Albans) and see also n. above for Lincoln.
79 *Mercurius Publicus*, 2–9 August 1660, no. 32.
80 TNA SP 29/1 f. 50.
81 Thomason 669. f. 25 [8].
82 Thomason 669. f. 25 [76].
83 TNA SP 29/1 f. 90; printed in *Mercurius Publicus*, 2–9 August 1660, no. 32.
84 *Nouvelles Ordinaires de Londres*, 6–13 January 1659, no. 451; *Mercurius Politicus*, 10–17 February 1659, no. 554, address of High Sheriff, Justices of Peace, Grand Jury, Gentlemen, Freeholders and Soldiers of the County of Chester; *Mercurius Politicus*, 17–24 February 1659, no. 555, 'Humble address of several justices of the peace, gentlemen, ministers and many other of the freeholders of the county of Chester'. The editor explained that 'The following Address was some weeks ago presented to his Highness, but its not coming to my hand, is the reason why it was not published till now.' These variant addresses may also reflect the very divided nature of the county at this time, Little and Smith, *Parliaments and Politics during the Protectorate*, p. 74.

85 On which see Matthew Neufeld, *The Civil Wars After 1660: Public Remembering in Late Stuart England* (Woodbridge: Boydell and Brewer, 2013), ch. 2 and works by Hindle and Worthen noted in ch 1. For an individual example see the petition of Benjamin Worsley to Lady Clarendon in which he claimed that he had never made any public address, protestation or engagement to the Cromwells, P. Elmer, *Miraculous Conformist: Valentine Greatrakes, the Body Politic, and the Politics of Healing in Restoration Britain* (Oxford: Oxford University Press, 2013), p. 71.
86 Thomason 669 f. 25[5].
87 T. Webster, 'Beadle, John', ODNB; H. R. French, 'Plume, Thomas', ODNB.
88 TNA SP 29/1 f. 54 [Devon and Exeter ministers] f. 79–80 [Northamptonshire] and see also f. 78 [North Wales gentry].
89 'Charles II, 1661: An Act against Tumults and Disorders upon p[re]tence of p[re]paring or p[re]senting publick Petic[i]ons or other Addresses to His Majesty or the Parliament', in John Raithby (ed.), *Statutes of the Realm: Volume 5, 1628–80* (s.l, 1819), p. 308 www.british-history.ac.uk/statutes-realm/vol5/p308, accessed 3 September 2015.
90 See below and for one example *A Letter and Declaration of the Lords, Knights, Gentlemen and Ministers, of the County of York, and of the Lord Mayor, Aldermen and Common-Councell of the City of York, presented to Generall Monck, Feb. 17th 1659. at his quarters at Drapers Hall London* (1660).
91 *Publick Intelligencer*, 6–13 February 1660, no. 215; 13–20 February 1660, no. 216; *Mercurius Politicus*, 2–9 February 1660, no. 506 and see Worden, 'Campaign for a free Parliament', 165.
92 *A second narrative*, p. 39.
93 Ibid., p. 40.
94 *A true catalogue*, p. 3.
95 Ibid., p. 5.
96 Ibid., p. 14; *A second narrative*, p. 35.
97 *A true catalogue*, p. 19.
98 Caton, *Truths caracter*, epistle to the reader.
99 *A true catalogue*, p. 29.
100 Ibid., p. 74 and quotation at p. 5. Again, note the similarity with the wording of *A second narrative*.
101 *A true catalogue*, p. 72.
102 Quoted in Little and Smith, *Parliaments and Politics during the Cromwellian Protectorate*, p. 72; see also Clive Holmes, 'John Lisle, Lord Commissioner of the Great Seal, and the last months of the Cromwellian Protectorate', *English Historical Review*, 498 (2007), 918–36.
103 *A collection of several remarkable addresses to Richard Cromwell* (1702). The collection claimed to be taken out of the 'Diurnal of those Times' but it was clearly based on the 1659 pamphlet given the inclusion of editorial commentary from the original edition on some pages, pp. 23, 31, 41; for later references to the collection see *The Parliamentary or Constitutional History of England, vol. 21* (1762), p. 232n. where it was attributed only to a 'zealous Fifth Monarchy Man'.
104 [Attrib Earl of Shaftesbury] *An impartial account of the nature and tendency of the late Addresses in a letter to a gentleman in the country* (1681), p. 4.
105 [Oldmixon], *History of Addresses* (1709), p. 8. Although Oldmixon discussed the Cromwellian addresses in some detail, his source material was Bulstrode

Whitlocke's *Memorials* not the 1659 compendium. See also [D. Defoe], *A new test of the sence of the nation: Being a modest comparison between the addresses to the late King James, and those to her present majesty* (1710), p. 16 and [Benjamin Hoadly] *The high church mask pull'd off or, the modern addresses anatomized* (1710), p. 7 for further references to the addresses to Richard Cromwell.

106 *Reliquiae Hearnianae: The Remains of Thomas Hearne M.A.*, ed. Philip Bliss (vol. 1., London, 1869), pp. 257–8.
107 Noble, *Protectoral House of Cromwell*, i, pp. 181–2. Noble's own source material here was an MS note on a copy of Powell's compendium by the Rev. George North.
108 Sir R. Tangye, *The Two Protectors: Oliver and Richard Cromwell* (London: S. W. Partridge & Co, 1899), p. 238. P. Lyon, *Our Gentleman: The Life and Times of Richard Cromwell* (London: Regency Press, 1979), p. 135.
109 Hirst, 'Making contact', 26–50.
110 Hauser, *Vernacular Voices*, p. 197.
111 [Attrib William Prynne], *The Remonstrance of the Noble-men, Knights, Gentlemen, Clergy-men, Free-holders, Citizens, Burgess and Commons of the late Eastern, Southern, and Western Associations, who desire to shew themselves Faithfull and Constant to the Good Old Cause* (1659) (Thomason, 669 f. 22[11]); Worden notes that this language remained divisive, 'Campaign for a free Parliament', 175–8.
112 Thomason 669 f. 22 [34].

Chapter 3

Addresses, abhorrences and associations: subscriptional culture and memory in the 1680s

On 12 July 1676, Richard Bower, a Great Yarmouth coffeehouse keeper, wrote to Secretary Williamson enclosing,

> our towne's Address to Rich., Protector (wch came from one yt was formerly of theire Assembly), where you will finde severall of our new militia officers, as our Coll, Sr George England, our Maior, Bayliff Thaxter: & Capt. Richard Huntington, besides severall of ye old Presbiterian gang, that are at present justices & aldermen of our towne, whoo are marked wth P. there is alsoe ye chiefe of our Independts now in towne marked wth I ... if you please to p[er]use ye Address from this towne to Richard, Protector: you will finde those cheifly concerned in yt Address, to have ye greatest share in the government of this towne from ye yeare '65 to this present day, from whence the Nonconformists here, tooke encouragement to contemne both ye laws & ye King's Comands & to grow So numerous as now they are.[1]

Richard Bower was a regular correspondent of Charles II's Secretary of State and chief intelligence gatherer, Sir Joseph Williamson. Between 1662 and 1679 he provided Williamson with information concerning two essential topics: shipping and, the issue which exercised him most, the activities of the town's non-conformists. Bower's concern with the influence wielded by men such as England and Thaxter unquestionably bordered on the obsessive, and the accusations he made within his letters clearly overstepped the mark: the material Bower fed Williamson about Yarmouth's dissenters would eventually lead to him facing serious reprisals.[2] Nonetheless, Bower's letter is indicative of the persistence of the memory of the addressing activity of the Cromwellian period and its importance to political debates in the latter years of Charles II's reign, especially during the Exclusion Crisis.

It was remarkable, in the first place, that the address had come into Bower's possession at all. Yarmouth corporation had ordered on 3 January 1661 that 'the Addresse made to Richard Cromwell (the late pr[e]tended Protector[)] by this house be utterly disclaimed obliterated and made void'.[3] Bower's letter suggests that this order may have been as much motivated by a desire to conceal the past actions of those civic officers who survived the post-Restoration purges, as out of loyalty to the new monarch, and that some members of the corporation had preserved a copy of the address, sensing that it might prove useful at a later date. If so, they were not alone: a pamphlet printed in 1682, detailing disputes over the production of a loyal address to Charles II from the borough of Wells, Somerset, compared this text with that produced from the same borough to Richard Cromwell. As in Bower's letter, it used the records of subscription to the Cromwellian address to intimate that those who had signed it were the fathers of the civic officers who had recently sought to obstruct the loyal text to the King.[4]

The employment of the example of Cromwellian addressing activity connected with the broader invocation of the memory of the civil wars and interregnum at this time, noted by historians such as Jonathan Scott, Mark Knights and Matthew Neufeld among others.[5] As we will see, however, the example of the Cromwellian addresses was more frequently invoked by Whigs than by their loyalist/Tory opponents such as Bower. For Whig writers, the Cromwellian addresses had an important role to play in the broader debate over the legitimacy of revived strategies of popular petitioning; strategies that their Tory opponents were keen to connect in turn to the political turmoil of the 1640s.

As Bower's letter also indicates, though, the memory of addressing could serve other purposes. In Bower's case, it provided a means of determining contemporary political and religious loyalties. The 1680s represent the most sustained and intense period of petitioning and addressing activity in early modern England: over a thousand loyal addresses were presented over the course of this decade to Charles II and James II.[6] This activity, publicised through the pages of the *London Gazette* and other newsbooks, as well as being catalogued in printed compendia, generated its own record of the loyalties of communities and individuals. As in the 1650s, such subscriptional activity could be deployed to embarrass, stigmatise or discriminate.

While the origins of the loyal address during the Cromwellian Protectorate remained an important reference point, the addressing activity of the 1680s developed a strong and lasting public memory of its own. Here the memory of addressing in the 1680s fused with the broader deployment of the memory of the civil war: addresses denouncing 'fanaticism' and 'Commonwealth Principles', issued in their hundreds during the reign of Charles II, would pose considerable problems later in the decade as James II sought to generate public support for the repeal of the Test and Corporation Acts. Both contemporaries and some historians, notably Peter Lake and Steven Pincus, have seen the 1680s as a key period for subscriptional culture and the viability of a critical public sphere. In 1680 Parliament viewed the right to petition itself as under threat from the Court and its agents. For Lake and Pincus, such moves are indicative of a late Stuart monarchy intent on replacing the relatively open and fiercely contested political discourse of the period of the Exclusion

Crisis with a well-regulated propaganda state in which the public was only ushered onto stage to deliver state-managed adulation.[7] Yet, James II's use of addresses was not novel either in its tactics or its results, baring close comparison to the subscriptional strategies employed by the restored Rump Parliament as it attempted to shore up its authority. Moreover, even during the reign of James II, addressing activity remained more spontaneous and varied in its content than might initially seem. Equally, while the right to petition was once again seen to be under threat at the end of the decade and the right to petition the Crown reasserted in the English Bill of Rights, the fierce polemical exchanges of the early 1680s concealed considerable agreement about the parameters of legitimate subscriptional activity. This agreement was unsurprising given that both the Stuart monarchy's supporters and its opponents readily employed mass petitioning and addressing campaigns to political effect.

THE REVIVAL OF MASS PETITIONING AND ADDRESSING

The frenetic mass petitioning and addressing activity of the 1680s was preceded by a marked shift in the register of communication between Crown and Parliament. A compilation of the addresses made by the Commons to the Crown since the Restoration published in 1680 revealed a formal means of communication between the monarchy and the lower house which was being brought under considerable strain as the addresses became increasingly assertive in their demand for Charles to act against the perceived threat of popery and arbitrary government.[8]

In 1678, the Commons addressed Charles urging him to declare war on France, to remove ministers such as Secretary Williamson from his presence and to dismiss all Catholics from Whitehall, including the Queen, her family and attendants.[9] These addresses invaded areas typically seen as part of the royal prerogative – the appointment of ministers, the management of the royal Court and foreign policy, especially the waging of war. The parallels with demands made of Charles I by the Long Parliament did not go unnoticed: as one pamphleteer asked, 'Is not this Writing after the 41 Copy? Is not this striking at His Majesty and the Government through his Ministers sides?'[10] Another pamphlet, attributed to Edmund Bohun, thought the tone of the Commons' addresses to the King, 'not much unlike those who remonstrated to his Majesties Father till they at last fairly brought him to the Block'.[11]

Assertive addressing in Parliament was followed by frenetic mass petitioning and addressing activity outside of Westminster. Petitions issued in 1679 calling for Parliament to sit to address questions of foreign policy, the royal succession, the Church and redress of public grievances were followed by anti-petitions or addresses condemning the petitioners for intruding on the King's right to summon, prorogue and dissolve parliaments.[12] These were followed in quick succession by addresses to MPs issued prior to the calling of the Oxford Parliament in March 1681 urging members (among other things) to use the next session to ensure the defence of the Protestant religion, the extirpation of popery and the prosecution of the Popish Plot, the exclusion of all possibility of a popish successor, and the protection of the subject's right to petition itself.[13] The surprise dissolution of the Oxford Parliament in April of the same year was followed by some 210 addresses giving thanks for Charles II's royal declaration explaining his reasons for doing so.[14]

These addresses were swiftly followed by another mass addressing campaign, this time 'abhorring' the allegedly treasonable 'Association' found among the Earl of Shaftesbury's papers. More 'abhorrances' were issued in 1683 in response to the discovery of the Rye House Plot to kill Charles II and his brother and raise a general insurrection.[15] The accession of James II brought hundreds more addresses which combined with those congratulating the King on the suppression of the rebellion led by Charles II's illegitimate son, the Duke of Monmouth. These were succeeded by some one hundred and ninety-seven addresses ostensibly supporting James' declarations of indulgence.[16]

In the early 1680s, these addressing campaigns followed so quickly one after another that communities in the farther reaches of England's empire were still declaring their abhorrence of one thing, while counties and towns closer to the metropolis had already moved on to registering their disgust at something else: the grand jury of Barbados's address condemning the 'Association' arrived at the same time as Salisbury, Newark upon Trent, St Albans, Coventry, Andover, Rochester, Cowbridge in Glamorgan and the common councils of Worcester and Gloucester were presenting their texts abhorring the Rye House Plot.[17] References to loyal addresses were ubiquitous, reproduced in full in the *London Gazette*, as well as separate broadsheets and pamphlets and referenced in detail in contemporary printed newsbooks and manuscript newsletters.[18]

This subscriptional activity was highly contentious. For loyalists, popular petitioning was one more indication that Whigs and their dissenting allies were intent on resurrecting the strategies of the 1640s to achieve similar ends as the Parliamentarians of the civil wars. For the Whigs, loyal addresses and abhorrances sought to suppress the fundamental right of subjects to petition for the redress of grievances and were a prop to arbitrary rule. A royal declaration, issued on 12 December 1679, complained of the actions of:

> evil disposed Persons at this time, ... in several parts of this Kingdom, to Frame Petitions to His Majesty for specious ends and purposes relating to the Publick, and thereupon to Collect and Procure to the same, the Hands or Subscriptions of multitudes of His Majesties Subjects; Which Proceedings are contrary to the Common and known Laws of this Land, for that it tends to promote Discontents amongst the People, and to Raise Sedition and Rebellion.[19]

Soon after the issuing of this declaration, counter or anti-petitions were issued from grand juries, quarter sessions and justices in Berkshire, Devon, King's Lynn, Lancashire, Middlesex, Norfolk, Norwich and Westminster attacking popular petitioning activity calling for Parliament to sit.[20] The recorder of Norwich was reportedly put out of his place for refusing to subscribe to the address, a claim which the ousted official rebutted in print.[21] The address from Lancashire's grand jury attacked all 'manner of Association not by yourself [meaning the King] directed', opening up a broader attack on popular subscriptional activity that would be extended in subsequent years.[22] Those presenting these addresses were warmly received by the King: Sir Francis Withens, who delivered the Westminster address, was knighted for his services.[23] In contrast, those presenting petitions to the Crown calling for the sitting of Parliament were firmly rebuffed: Charles II reportedly told Henry Mildmay when he presented the petition from Essex that 'it was the old business of 41' (to which Mildmay responded that it was a petition from his county which had helped restore the king to the throne in 1660).[24] The connections between the petitioning activity of the civil wars and the strategies of the Whigs were drawn out by the leading Tory propagandist and press censor, Sir Roger L'Estrange in his *A Seasonable Memorial* (1680). L'Estrange described popular petitioning as 'the most necessary Link in the chain of a Rebellion'.[25] Irrespective of the content of popular petitions, they were always likely to provoke 'tumults' for 'the One [disorder] is but the Hot Fit of the other'.[26] From 'First to Last', L'Estrange claimed, the civil war had been driven on 'mainly by PETITIONS'.[27]

When Parliament was recalled in October 1680, it swiftly took action against so-called 'anti-petitioners' or 'abhorrers'. A number of members were censured for presenting addresses attacking petitions urging that Parliament should sit. Sir Francis Withens was expelled from the Commons for impugning the right of subjects to petition in the Westminster address.[28] Grand jurymen who had been involved in producing addresses or who had moved to prosecute petitioners were also censured.[29] The Commons treated both the King's declaration and the addresses condemning mass petitions urging Parliament to sit as an attack on the right to petition in general. The house resolved that it was the undoubted right of the subject to petition Parliament for redress of grievances and any who described such petitions as 'tumultuous' designed the alteration of the constitution and the bringing in of arbitrary government.[30] A committee was appointed to investigate who had advised the King to issue the royal declaration against tumultuous petitioning, identifying Sir Francis North, chief justice of common pleas, and resolving unanimously to bring impeachment proceedings against him.[31] Others who were seen to have impugned petitioning activity, including Roger L'Estrange, were forced to flee the country.[32]

With the end of the Oxford Parliament in April 1681, the Court's supporters took a similarly stringent line with those who were deemed to have attacked loyal addressing activity supporting the dissolution. Individuals were prosecuted for speaking against addressing activity, with prosecutions for seditious words uttered against the loyal addresses produced in Dorset and Devon.[33] The zealous Tory Gregory Alford, a former mayor of Lyme known for his vigorous prosecution of local dissenters, had already come to public attention for bringing indictments – despite, as a militia captain, having no clear legal authority to do so – against a person of the town for 'speaking very scandalously and unbecomingly of the Addresses in general' in July of 1681.[34] The addressing campaign also provided an opportunity for Alford to move against potential rivals, such as Henry Flory and Ferdinand Lucy or Lacey, for the lucrative post of customs surveyor which he held.[35] Alford accused Lucy of stating that 'nought but knaves, rascals and fools signed the Dorsetshire address [abhorring the Earl of Shaftesbury's 'Association'] to the King', even though Lucy was a respectable citizen who had recently been empanelled as part of the investigation into a smuggling riot. Alford's actions were, however, ultimately frustrated by the fact that the only justice in the vicinity, William Ellesdon, was bribed by Lucy not to arraign witnesses, leading to his punishment being remitted to a small fine.[36] Addresses issued to MPs prior to the calling of the Oxford Parliament, urging them to support the exclusion of the Duke of York, were also treated as seditious libels and the promoters prosecuted.[37] The Middlesex Grand Jury responded in kind by indicting the Norwich address of thanks to the King for his declaration as likewise a seditious libel and fining the printer who published it.[38]

These reprisals and counter-attacks against petitioners and addressers illustrate the political risks involved in subscriptional activity, notably that the record left by such activity provided evidence that could be used by opponents once circumstances had changed. As we will see, this was particularly true of addressing activity which was, by its nature, more public and more closely tied to national politics. They also demonstrate the connections that were being drawn between subscriptional activity during the Exclusion Crisis and mass petitioning during the civil war. It is worth stating here that these comparisons were not unwarranted, and some historians, notably Tim Harris, have suggested that these aspects of popular political activity were deeply indebted to the strategies and practices of the 1640s.[39] More than simply informing the practice of mass petitioning and addressing, Edward Legon has noted that the memory of subscriptional activity was critical for many of those who continued to feel a commitment to the 'Good Old Cause'.[40] These historical allusions, however, clearly also served a polemical purpose which was to connect oppositional political activity with the threat of rebellion and ultimately violent revolution. The accusation that the Whigs were again at 'the old business of '41' was made frequently by the Court and its supporters. The connection between Whig ideals and mid-century republicanism was explicitly drawn in the King's declaration justifying his dissolution of the Oxford Parliament, which compared exclusion to the regicide and warned of the threat posed by those attached to 'Commonwealth Principles'.[41] As Mark Knights has noted, the addresses which followed the declaration were quick to pick up on the cue to engage with the memory of civil war and interregnum.[42] Some followed the declaration in suggesting that, as in the 1640s, the defence of the subject's liberties was merely a pretext through which to seize power.[43] Many offered generalised recollections of the horrors and miseries of the 1640s and 1650s, such as that from Eye in Suffolk, which recalled that it was the King's restoration that delivered them from 'the cruel yoke of Tyranny and Usurpation'.[44] Others connected these sufferings directly to their locality. The address from Pontefract remarked that the physical reminders of the civil wars remained all around them in their 'once Princely, now ruined Castle, our present demolished Parish Church, shattered Houses, bare and tottering Walls, ... Testimonies of our past, and Obligations to our future Loyalty, that even those from those Honourable Scars, we may instruct our Posterity in our, and their unshaken Fidelity'.[45] Some expressed shame and contrition for their region's part in the internecine struggle – that from the Isle of Wight recalling with sadness that the island had once been a 'Prison to that Royal Martyr, Your Majesties most blessed Father of most Glorious Memory'.[46] These parallels between the activities of the Whigs and those of the Parliamentarians in the civil wars would be drawn even closer in subsequent addressing campaigns abhorring Shaftesbury's 'Association' (texts which compared that device to the oaths and covenants imposed by the Long Parliament) and the Rye House Plot (seen to provide evidence that the Whigs' intentions were one and the same with the regicides of 1649).[47] In the words of the address abhorring the Rye House Plot issued by the nobility and gentry of Kent, the conspiracy was hatched by 'a Party of Men of Fanatick and Antimonarchical Principles, first sprung from the Wicked Solemn League and Covenant, and since propagated by the late Devilish Association'.[48]

The memory of past addressing activity, specifically under the Cromwellian protectorate, however, also provided the Whigs with a means of employing the history of the civil war and interregnum against their opponents. As Mark Knights has shown, shortly after the Restoration, Roger L'Estrange used a published collection incorporating addresses to counter allegations that he had worked with the Cromwellian regime.[49] During the Exclusion Crisis, presumably as part of the general loyalist bid to connect Whig popular politics and parliamentarianism, L'Estrange reprinted some of his earlier works which had traced the origins of the civil war. One of these works was his *A Memento*, originally printed in 1662 and republished in 1682 in a slightly truncated edition by Joanna Brome, the widow of the original printer (and some alleged L'Estrange's mistress).[50] In this work, L'Estrange commented on the addresses sent to Oliver Cromwell, describing them as no more than 'Leagues Offensive, and Defensive Betwixt the Faction, and the Usurper'. 'These Numerous and Pretending Applications, were', L'Estrange said, 'but False Glosses upon his Power; and Cromwell was too wise to think them

Other: Gain'd by Contrivement, Force, or at least, Importunity. Half a Score pitiful wretches call themselves the People of such or such a County, and here's the Totall of the Reckoning.' Similar texts, L'Estrange noted, were brought in 'thick and threefold' by 'the Court-Interest' to honour Richard Cromwell at his accession 'but Those Complements had no Sap in them.'[51]

These comments were soon alighted upon by newsbooks and pamphlets which sought to discredit the addressing campaigns issued in support of Charles II. L'Estrange's comments clearly begged the question as to the value and reliability of contemporary addresses, especially given L'Estrange's reputation as the Court 'wire-puller' orchestrating these campaigns. (An image sustained in part by L'Estrange's own claims to have directed petitioning and addressing activity in support of the Restoration.)[52] As one pamphleteer argued:

> very person that is not only principally employ'd in framing the draughts which are remitted into the Countrey, where Lieutenants, Justices and Curates, are commissioned to prosecute subscriptions to them, but whose Province it is to publish their usefulness to the Government, and to make the world believe what security the State receiveth from them in order to its support in the pursuance of present Councels ... had different thoughts concerning Addresses some years ago when they came in sholes to Oliver Cromwell, and with great multitudes of hands subjoined to them, from what he now hath.[53]

L'Estrange's slip also provided opportunities for authors to revive allegations that the propagandist had once been in the employment of the Cromwellian regime, one newsletter writer noting that even L'Estrange's 'old master Cromwell' was too wise to take much notice of addressing.[54]

The same strategy was used against other addressers, such as the mayor of Gloucester, who, one author remarked, it was strange to see applauded for his loyalty, given that he had previously been congratulated for 'the good service which he did in fighting against Charles Stewart at Worcester (as the words inserted in their Town Book bear)'.[55] The *Impartial Protestant Mercury* similarly alleged that the magistrates who opposed the Taunton address to their MPs prior to the calling of the Oxford Parliament were 'all actually in Arms against His Late Majesty', or opposed 'our present Sovereigns happy Restauration, and one of them received a shot on the Back, which remains there to this day, a Token both of his Valor and Loyalty; another chosen to Guard King Charles the First to Execution &c.'[56] The Middlesex justice Sir William Smith or Smyth, a former Royalist colonel and a rigorous prosecutor of dissenters, was accused of having promoted an address to Richard Cromwell.[57] A pamphlet attributed to the Earl of Shaftesbury suggested that it was a breach of Act of Indemnity and Oblivion for loyalists to repeatedly invoke the memory of the civil wars, especially when 'most that were believed either the first fomenters of, or proved afterwards Actors in it, are dead and gone'. Damning by association, the author intimated that this was even less understandable given that children of Parliamentarians '(witness many of the most violent and high flown Clergy) ... are commonly found to be of Principles directly contrary to what they were'.[58]

The Cromwellian addresses were not simply employed, however, in an attempt either to discredit contemporary loyal addresses or to turn accusations of adherence to 'Commonwealth Principles' against their opponents. By identifying the dubious origins of addressing, authors sought to differentiate this particular form of subscriptional activity from legitimate mass petitioning, though, in fact, the terminology of 'address' had been used by both critics and supporters of the Court. Addresses, one pamphlet history of the genre urged, were useless, being 'rather stuffed with Flattery, than filled with Loyalty, as may be apparent from that of *Richard Cromwel*, who was visited with magnificent Addresses, but when Deposed, found not one of them faithfull Assistants'.[59] Mounting this historically grounded attack on addressing had the additional benefit of allowing the Court's opponents to recast themselves as the truly 'loyal'.

For the author of the pamphlet *An impartial account*, attributed to the Earl of Shaftesbury, however, it was the genre itself which was the problem, not merely its past usage. Addressing threatened legitimate forms of political expression, namely petitioning and voting. Unlike petitions, the content of these addresses was not limited to matters directly affecting the subscribers. Petitions, the author said, could 'represent their [the petitioners] wants and grievances, without prejudicing or giving offence to those who chuse silently to undergo them'.[60]

Addresses, in contrast, presumed to speak for whole communities, stigmatising those who protested against the content of these addresses as 'peevish and clamorous'.[61] Worse, addresses directed at the Crown suggested that all law was dependent on the 'Will and Pleasure' of the King and that Parliament itself existed only upon the monarchy's sufferance.[62] The true voice of the kingdom was delivered through Parliament via elections. Specific matters could be brought to the attention of Parliament through legitimate petitioning, but to address the Crown in the name of the kingdom or people was to subvert the power of Parliament:

> tho' it be lawful for any one man, and much more for any number of men, to represent to His Majesty their own wants and dangers, and accordingly beg redress and relief; yet to declare the State of the Nation, belongs to no number of private persons, whatsoever, but appertains only to the Parliament, as being the Representatives of the whole Kingdom. And therefore the Addressers, by assuming to themselves a Right and Authority to determine about the State of the Nation, and to judge concerning those things which the Trustees of all the people met in the great Councel, are only proper and by Law allowed to meddle with.[63]

There was, however, the author of *An Impartiall Account* said, at least some value to addresses: those signing them had put an 'everlasting infamy' upon themselves. The records of these addresses would 'make a Survey and obtain a List of all that were for the Duke of York'.[64] The notion that addresses might be used to identify the politically suspect worked against the idea of these texts representing whole communities and instead connected them with other subscriptional forms, notably oaths and covenants, used to purge and discriminate.

In some areas, addresses clearly were being used in this divisive fashion. In Coventry, lists were prepared of those that refused the city's address abhorring the Association, a list which included the name of one Edward Euell, who said 'hee Abhorred the Abhorrers.'[65] Grant Tapsell has noted increasing calls for political separation in the addresses produced abhorring both the Association and the Rye House Plot.[66] The contemporary press, including even the usually bland pages of the *London Gazette*, was filled with reports of inns of court, corporations and county benches divided over producing and subscribing addresses.[67] In some instances, pre-existing factional conflict threatened to prevent even the drafting of an address. In Rye, Sussex, struggles between Court and Country groupings had led to a disputed mayoral election between Thomas Crouch and Thomas Tournay in 1681 which was decided in favour of the Court candidate (Crouch) in September of 1681. Despite this decision, Tournay refused to hand over the mayoral regalia and in May of the following year, he and his supporters broke into the town hall, changed the locks and appropriated the town's records and insignia. Crouch died in August 1682 but Tournay again contested the mayoralty against Joseph Radford, an election which led to both candidates claiming victory.[68] This dispute caused problems when attempts were made to call a Guestling or Brotherhood of the Cinque Ports (the ancient body which represented the ports and associated towns) to offer a loyal address abhorring the Rye House Plot. The members for the town of New Romney wondered whether such a Brotherhood 'may p[er]happs prove of dangerous consequence in relacon to the difference that must necessarily happen betweene Those two persons that prtend to the speakershipp and Maiorality of Rye'. It might prove a dangerous precedent, assuming that Rye was unable to participate, they continued, if addresses were issued that couldn't be made under the Guestling's common seal.[69]

The repeated demands over the 1680s for communities to issue loyal addresses to the Crown caused greater problems as the Court moved from a religious policy designed to appease Tory/Anglican opinion to one which sought toleration for both Protestant dissenters and Catholics. The addresses prompted by the Crown in the early 1680s had frequently condemned the activities of 'fanatics' as well as 'Commonwealthsmen' and identified conventicles, as well as corporations, as 'Nurseries of Sedition and Rebellion'.[70] Roger Morrice noted growing discontent among loyalists now asked under James II to give their thanks for the King's declaration of indulgence, noting that one Mr Duck or Duckey in Devon asked to support an address to this effect responded that he 'had no reason to give thanks to the King for incourageing Fanaticks' and that he would instead prosecute them as 'publick enemies according to his Abhorrence and Addresses &c'.[71] Morrice reported that another zealous 'abhorrer', Mr. Gibbons, the sub-recorder of Norwich, was put out of his place for speaking 'very unmannerly, and scandalously of his Majesties Declaration and Addresses'.[72]

These incidents indicate that addressing activity across the 1680s developed its own memory. This should hardly be surprising. Not only was addressing activity very public, communicated, as we will see, through public ceremonial as well as through medium of print, it also required considerable investment in time and money from communities. The investment was potentially very worthwhile if the address was well received but, as the reception of some petitions and addresses in the early 1680s indicated, not without risk. Scott Sowerby has noted that addresses in support of James II's tolerationist policies were denounced, as earlier addressing campaigns had been, as manufactured and unrepresentative of local opinion.[73] In broader terms, the involvement of some groups, notably the Quakers, in supporting these addresses was used as a means of attacking them in the post-revolutionary period.[74]

As has been shown in the case of the Cromwellian addresses, one strategy for exploiting this 'back catalogue' of subscriptional activity was simply to reprint collections of old addresses whose content in the current context could be used to embarrass or criticise opponents. The reign of James II was ripe with such opportunities. A collection produced in 1700 – the year in which, with the death of Princess Anne's son, the Duke of Gloucester, the Hanoverian Succession became virtually assured – reprinted the addresses delivered on the birth of James Francis Edward Stuart in June 1688.[75] Similarly, the 1702 reissue of the addresses to Richard Cromwell may well have been timed as a further comment on the royal succession. Clearly this was a tactic that could not only be employed by the Whigs. In the wake of the Atterbury plot of 1722, a collection appeared reprinting addresses from Scottish and English Presbyterians congratulating James II on the birth of the Prince of Wales.[76] The conclusion to be drawn from these addresses was made plain by the compiler: 'I'm sure, whoever reads them, cannot think but the Addressers were the greatest Jacobites in the World'. Yet it was these same groups, the editor noted, who were the first to forsake James at the revolution, even though their earlier promises of loyalty contained no reservations 'unless Jesuitical or mental'.[77]

As well as being employed to target particular religious or political groups, the hostages to fortune left behind through James II's addressing campaigns were also used to attack individuals. Morrice noted that the court loyalist Sir John Trevor was silenced during a debate over the Corporation bill 'because some had a Gazette that mentioned a High Address to king James promoted and procured by him at Witch [Droitwich] in Worcestershire'.[78] White Kennett, the future bishop of Peterborough, was attacked in 1704 for a controversial 30

January fast sermon through the re-publication of the prologue to his translation of Pliny's 'Panegyricus'. Published in 1685 as *An address of thanks to a good prince*, Kennett's prologue had reflected on the timeliness of such a translation when 'the peevish news of petitioning was universally improv'd into the more generous humour of Addresses'.[79] The tone of the prologue was far out of step with Kennett's Whiggish 1704 sermon, which was highly critical of the rule of both Charles I and James II. The prologue denounced courting popularity, attacked resistance theory and denied the principle that the prince was subject to the law, 'the very Principle', Kennett said, 'our late Regicides proceeded on.'[80] Although the prologue was written while Charles II was still alive, a postscript by Kennett made clear that James was as, if not more worthy of such panegyric: 'A Monarch whose accomplishments are in each respect so admirable, that they surmount flattery, and defie the rankest malice.'[81] As the author of the hostile pamphlet *White against Kennet* noted, such expressions seemed far removed from his recent sermon which was more akin to the works of 'Milton and John Goodwin' and represented a public defence of the 'Language of Forty One'.[82]

ADDRESSING AND THE RIGHT TO PETITION

As we have seen, debates prompted by petitioning and addressing activity in the 1680s repeatedly invoked the memory of the civil war and interregnum. In turn, the addresses produced during the 1680s, as with their Cromwellian predecessors, became embedded in public memory. The memory of subscriptional activity was also critical to arguments over the legitimacy of petitioning and addressing. In contemporary and subsequent accounts, the addressing activity of the 1680s was frequently seen as a threat to the established right to petition, under attack from a court intolerant of the spontaneous expression of public opinion. There is certainly evidence that, as the Whigs had attempted to use the addresses to Richard Cromwell to delegitimise this form of subscriptional activity, so the Court's supporters employed the oaths and petitions of the civil wars to attack popular petitioning. The contrast in Kennett's sermons between 'peevish' petitions and 'generous' addresses was echoed in many other loyalist texts in the 1680s.

The addressing campaigns against the 'Association' and the Rye House Plot seemed at points to directly challenge the idea that any non-state controlled subscriptional activity could be legitimate. The address from the grand jury of Wiltshire abhorring the Association noted how 'fatal all Covenanting without the Royal Authority, hath been to this Kingdom'.[83] Despite the attempts of Shaftesbury's defenders to compare the Association instead with the Elizabethan Bond of 1584, as the remarks of the Wiltshire grand jury indicate, the parallel drawn most frequently by loyalist propagandists was between the Association and the Long Parliament's Solemn League and Covenant of 1643.[84]

Those that followed in the wake of the uncovering of the Rye House Plot continued to make this connection between associations, covenants and sedition.[85] Indeed, *The Weekly Discovery of the Mystery of Inquity*, published in serial form from 1681 onwards, went further in referring to the more moderate Commons' Protestation of 1641 as an 'Association ...a perfect infernal Fiend ... as indeed are all Associations, Covenants, Protestations or Engagements made without the consent, or against the good liking of the Sovereign'.[86]

It is also clear that in the later years of Charles II's reign and during the reign of James II, addressing activity was being used to identify opponents and purge them from office.[87] Addresses were also part of the process of borough charter revision designed to render English corporations more compliant. In Norwich, at the same time as the city's loyal address thanking the King for his declaration concerning the dissolution of the Oxford Parliament had been put forward, the city assembly had also formed a committee to overlook the process of charter revision. The aim was clear: the loyal addresses would serve the dual purpose of currying favour with the Crown while cowing potential opponents. Ultimately it was hoped that these overtures would result in a charter revision both politically and financially advantageous to the local Tory hierarchy.[88]

For some observers, such as Narcissus Luttrell, it was now clear that addressing activity alone would receive a favourable hearing from the Crown: 'those [addresses] meet with a kind reception at any time, these [petitions] are alwaies distastfull'.[89] Claims that petitioning activity was fundamentally threatened in the 1680s, however, ignored the fact that all parties continued to exploit subscriptional texts to advance their particular goals. Consequently, Mark Knights has wondered whether for a writer such as L'Estrange the distinction between legitimate and illegitimate petitioning was highly subjective, or at least heavily dependent on circumstances: 'The republican regime was illegitimate and therefore popular pressure, public remonstrances and a recourse to arms were necessary to restore the legitimate ruler.'[90]

Reading L'Estrange's *Seasonable Memorial*, however, it is possible to identify a general, as well as a circumstantial or subjective defence of popular petitioning. L'Estrange upheld private petitioning of authority for redress of grievances as unquestionably legitimate but he was also prepared to concede that there were grey areas where private petitioning might be deemed 'public', those 'Mixt Cases of Publick and Private; as in the Calamities of War, Pestilence, Fires, Inundations and the like'.[91] So L'Estrange conceded that there were some instances when it would be necessary for private persons to petition on matters of public concernment. Indeed, L'Estrange presented the problem with the Long Parliament's petitioning as being not only that they encouraged the 'rabble' to subscribe but that, hypocritically, they were perfectly ready to suppress popular petitions or addresses which challenged their authority: 'For so soon as ever any Petition appear'd that crost the Factions Interest ... there was presently a strict enquiry after the Authours and

Abettors of them, and the Design immediately crusht.'⁹² (As we have seen, this accusation had some substance to it, given the Long Parliament's own attempts to regulate 'tumultuous assemblies'.) In answering Whig critics of his *Seasonable Memorial*, L'Estrange was keen to stress that he thought that 'if the thing be Simply Good; the Petitioners Competent Judges of it; and every man keep himself to his own Post, I see no hurt in't.'⁹³ Retrospectively, Roger North's *Examen* took issue with White Kennett's presentation of the royal declaration of December 1679 as an assault on petitioning *in toto* to argue instead that it was only an attempt to keep public petitioning within its proper bounds.⁹⁴

Indeed, we can find evidence that the Court's opponents also sought to regulate and limit mass petitioning. It is certainly true that the second 'Exclusion' Parliament engaged in a strident defence of the subject's right to petition. It is worth noting, however, that there appears to have been no attempt to repeal the post-Restoration laws prohibiting tumultuous or seditious petitioning as there were parliamentary attempts (with accompanying addressing and petitioning campaigns) to reverse Elizabethan and Jacobean recusancy laws which were used against Protestant dissenters.⁹⁵

Contemporary and later observers noted that both petitioners and addressers made significant efforts to stay within the terms of the 1661 Tumultuous Petitioning Act, ensuring that the numbers presenting these texts did not exceed those prescribed by law.⁹⁶ Moreover, while they were equally keen to stress numerical support for their campaigns, both the Court's critics and its supporters resorted to attacks on mass petitioning and addressing which criticised these texts on the basis that they were subscribed by those unqualified to express judgement in such matters. The *Impartial Account* claimed that those signing them were 'persons of little interest, and most of them of a very small and mean figure in the Nation.'⁹⁷ Their support could easily be bought with food, drink or promises of money and favour:

> wheresoever there is either a little bankrupt Tradesman, a scandalous and disgrac'd Attorney, one whose necessity exposeth him to be biased by Crusts of Bread and Pots of Ale, any whose folly makes them pragmatical and impertinent, or whose prodigality and ambition forceth them to look for preferment beyond their merit, these are infallibly in the front of the Addressers.⁹⁸

Similar remarks were made of the loyal London apprentices who addressed the King in 1681: 'Ruffians and Beggerly Vermine, drawn in by Pots of Ale'.⁹⁹ The pamphlet *Vox Juvenilis* which sought to vindicate the actions of the 'loyal' London apprentices stated that their numbers were firmer than those of the rival address as they had,

> never cross'd the Water to the *Hope* on *Bear-Garden* days, to offer to get Hands there; nor were ever concerned to create a Bull-baiting, on purpose to draw the Rabble in, to fill up our Number, as some of the famous *Essex*-Patriots did to fill up their Petition for a Parliament. We never went to any Country-Fairs, amongst the

Ballad-Singers, nor in all Humility addressed our selves to the little Boys of a Free-School to pleasure us with two or three hundred Hands. We never hired any one to subscribe, nor ever told a Refuser that we would put him in our black Book, as Mr. S. H. did those that would not sign his *Good old Cause-Petition*. We never called a Conventicle, to get the Well-Wishers together: but honestly left our Papers where we thought fit, though the Republican Rats had so little Manners to gnaw them in pieces when they were full of Hands.[100]

As noted earlier, David Zaret argued that the places in which petitioning activity occurred (alehouses, inns and coffeehouses) made these kinds of accusations, associating subscribing to petitions with conspiratorial or seditious activity, more plausible. For Zaret, print provided a 'virtual space' distinct from the real geographical locations of subscription, thereby enabling the disassociation of petitions and addresses from political subversion.[101] The production of compilations of addresses took this distancing process a stage further, harmonising localised grievance, complaint or acclamation into one, unified national voice.[102]

However, we have seen that Whigs employed addresses as well as petitions during the Exclusion Crisis. They also produced their own collection of addresses, *Vox Patriae*, which, like its Tory equivalent, *Vox Angliae*, claimed to encapsulate the voice of the country. The collective sense of these addresses, it claimed, was,

so general and Unanimous, that they may justly be stiled the Voice of the Realm, which tho, for a great part, already abroad scatter'd and imperfect in several Prints, will undoubtedly not be unacceptable, thus decently gathered together; To remain as a Testimoney to all the World.[103]

Yet there was less conflict with the seeming arguments for popularity in this compendium and those attacks on the quality of the addressers than first appears. *Vox Patriae* described Parliaments as the pulse of the people, a phrase that had earlier appeared in a pamphlet, *The Long Parliament Dissolved*, attributed to Denzil Holles and published in 1676. This work had argued that the Cavalier Parliament had been dissolved as a result of its lengthy prorogation – a claim which led the printer to be fined £1,000.[104]

Vox Patriae therefore fitted in with Shaftesbury's vision of Parliament as the ultimate representative of the nation. This was underlined by the fact that the addresses contained within the collection were not directed at the Crown but instead to members of Parliament, thereby not falling foul of the *Impartial Account's* comments regarding the unreliability of addresses made to 'regnant' persons. These included instructions from the freeholders relating to the conduct of their representatives – in the case of that from the gentry and freeholders of Suffolk, demanding that their MPs prosecute the Popish Plot, resist the succession of the Duke of York through exclusion bills, call for frequent Parliaments and promote Protestant union.[105] The author was keen to stress that these addresses were openly and publicly consented to but they also stressed that it was the freeholders who gave the texts their backing. Speaking of the address from Essex:

> Tis observable That this Address being openly read to their Representatives, and confirm'd by the Unanimous and Loud Acclamations of the Freeholders, for further demonstration that it was the Sense of each individual person of that Numerous Assembly, it was offered, that so many as agreed to it, should say Ay; upon which, they all cried out Ay, Ay. And if any were otherwise minded, they were desired to express their Dissent by saying No: At which there was Altum Silentium, not one to be heard saying No.[106]

The distinction that the collection made between the legitimate approval of the freeholders and mere popular acclamation was clarified in the introduction. Against Tory claims that the Whigs pandered to the 'Rabble' the author complained that, to be accurate, these critics must either mean 'the meer Vulgar, the dregs of Mankind' 'or else they put the greatest Affront imaginable on the Body of a Nation, especially in England, where under the Title of Commoners, are included all degrees of Gentry, under Peerage, consisting not as in France and other Popish Countries of Sneaking Slaves and Clouted Boors.'[107]

These addresses were legitimate because they had come from the gentry and freeholders of England and were directed at their representatives in Parliament. They were, in turn, confirmed and authorised by the election of these members to the Oxford Parliament. The collection finished by assuring its readers that there were,

> many more Addresses of like Nature and Purport made from divers other Parts of the Realm, True Copies of which, are not yet come to our Hands: But indeed the Re-Election of so many of the former Members, is itself a General Address, and loudly speaks it, The Voyce of the People, which we trust, will be Ratified by the Voyce of Heaven. No Popish Successor, No French Slavery.[108]

These claims to social exclusivity were not the sole preserve of the Court's opponents. Similar arguments about the quality of subscribers can be found in pamphlets defending the loyal addresses sent to the Crown after the dissolution of the Oxford Parliament.[109] There remained, nonetheless, a tension noted by other historians, namely Knights, between the claims that subscriptional activity was and should be limited to those competent to exercise political judgement (the gentry and freeholders) and broader appeals to popularity.[110] At the same time as attacking the subscriptions of the 'rabble' acquired by alleged bribery, subterfuge and threats, both *Vox Angliae* and *Vox Patriae* emphasised the numbers who had subscribed to these addresses, numbers that appear to be supported by the few surviving manuscript originals of these addresses.[111] The compilation of rival Whig and Tory addresses in printed compendia was itself a means of attempting to assert the coherence and popularity of each grouping. As was the case with the compendia produced of the addresses to Richard Cromwell, however, these compendia were seeking to impose a false uniformity on these texts.

The extensive work that went into stimulating and managing petitioning and addressing campaigns, as texts were being formulated, during the subscription process and through publication of them has rightly led historians to be sceptical about their value as equivalents to early modern opinion polls. Even so, addressing campaigns were not divorced from the public mood, nor did they simply map on to the crude binary of political affiliations (Whig vs Tory, Court vs Country, Church vs Dissent) represented in the press. As Roger Morrice noted of the addresses issued in the wake of the dissolution of the Oxford Parliament, 'Notwithstanding all the Addresses made to the Duke, things go not in all points according to his desire.'[112] Mark Knights has observed that only 83 of the 210 addresses issued giving thanks for the King's declaration in 1681 promised to defend the King's lawful heirs and successors as well as Charles himself.[113] Both Knights and Harris have concluded that a range of political and religious positions can be detected within these addresses; a variety encouraged by the broad terms of the King's declaration itself, with its promises to call frequent parliaments, govern within the law, defend the Protestant religion and extirpate popery.[114] The number of addresses secured in response to the King's declaration, Knights has suggested, was in part a result of the moderation of the loyalist message being expressed in the declaration.[115] Contemporaries were aware of the significance, nonetheless, of the subtle differences in these responses to the declaration.[116] Similarly, the even larger numbers of addresses secured 'abhorring' the Rye House Plot, Harris suggests, can be explained in part because of the relatively uncontroversial nature of this campaign – only a small number of radical Whigs supported the kind of insurrectionary activity uncovered in 1683.[117]

Though James II certainly put considerable effort into carefully canvassing public support for his tolerationist policies, loyal addresses issued ostensibly in support of his declarations of indulgence also reflected a broader range of opinion than the pro-tolerationist views the King wished to solicit. The most obvious recalcitrants were the Anglican clergy who sent in addresses thanking the King for his promises to defend the Church of England but made no comment concerning the indulgences. This omission was not lost on James who scolded the bishops at the presentation of the address:

> Can you find nothing to give thanks for but that one clause that relates to yourselves, have you no sense of that kindnesse others have received thereby, Methinks you might have given thanks at least for that ease and relief your Protestant Brethren have received by it &c.[118]

Similar addresses, though, were also forthcoming from towns such as Ludlow, which sought to be as effusive in its praise for the King's resolution to defend the Church of England as others had in thanking him for his indulgence. Others, for example that from Richmond in Surrey, hinted at the threat of 'fanatick' government, raised by James' intrusion of Whigs and dissenters into office.[119] Overall, James secured 200 addresses notionally thanking him for his royal declarations of indulgence. As Harris argues, however, this was significantly less than the 346 which had greeted the King's accession and only eighty-three of the indulgence addresses were produced by boroughs or counties.[120]

Almost as many came from often very small groups of non-conformists. There is some evidence from manuscript addresses that dissenting groups were attempting to present their texts as representing a broader constituency than they did in reality: a 1686 address from Gloucestershire was initially titled 'The humble Addresse & Petition of severall psons (dissenting from the Church of England) in the County of Glouc singed [sic] on ye behalfe of themselves & severall others score more in the said County'. These lines were crossed out so that the address, signed by a mere fifteen people, simply read 'the Baptists'.[121] The fact that James had to resort to addresses from small sectarian churches led some contemporaries to view support for his tolerationist policies as 'no way considerable'.[122]

So while loyal addresses cannot be read as early modern opinion polls, there does appear to be some relationship between the number of addresses secured and the popularity of a particular measure or policy. Relatively uncontroversial matters, such as the accession of a new monarch, could garner large numbers of addresses in relatively quick succession. In the case of controversial policies (for example, James II's declaration of indulgence) it proved much harder to secure quickly large numbers of texts in support and greater 'creativity' was required in manufacturing the appearance of popularity. It may be significant that some areas known to be in the control of Court loyalists such as Hertford and Exeter, addressed the King multiple times.[123] Here we might extend some of Tim Harris' observations concerning the attempted management of public opinion during the reign of Charles I to the reign of his younger son James: it was not necessarily that these efforts to court public opinion were insubstantial or unsophisticated but they were in the service of policies that were simply too hard to sell.[124]

CONCLUSION

The revolution that led James to flee England in December 1688 was itself legitimised through subscriptional texts, including loyal addresses and even a loyal association (despite the approbrium heaped on armed associations of Protestants five years earlier) to the Prince of Orange.[125] (These addresses caused some embarrassment when James II inconveniently returned from his first abortive attempt to leave the kingdom.)[126] The English Bill of Rights reaffirmed the right of subjects to petition the Crown, a right which had seemingly been threatened by James' decision to treat the seven bishops' petition against reading his second declaration of indulgence as a seditious libel.

This chapter has argued, however, that subscriptional activity was not under serious threat during the 1680s. Instead, the reverse could be said to be true given the high level of petitioning and addressing activity across the decade. Of course, both addressers and petitioners faced reprisals, and there were thoroughgoing attacks launched on both popular petitioning and mass addressing. These critiques pulled back from urging the complete suppression of subscriptional culture, however, and instead tended to argue for this activity to be properly regulated and directed.

Again, it is worth noting here that neither the Exclusion Parliaments nor the revolution settlement sought to repeal the Restoration act against tumultuous petitioning. The Bill of Rights only protected petitioning the Crown and left the limitations on petitioning parliament untouched. For Whig writers in particular, the memory of the addressing activity of the Cromwellian era served a useful purpose in this regard: not only did it provide them with a means of attacking certain individuals, notably L'Estrange, it also helped to distinguish addressing from other forms of subscriptional activity. In this way, illegitimate addressing could be dismissed without seeming to undermine the Whig's own employment of strategies of mass petitioning. Of course, such a distinction ignored the fact that the terms 'address' and 'petition' continued to be used interchangeably on a regular basis and that these subscriptional forms shared many common features, to the extent that discriminating between them was sometimes artificial.

What the invocation of the memory of the Cromwellian addresses also demonstrated was, again, the reflective and self-aware nature of addressing activity. Its public nature and the ease with which these texts could be collated and compiled provided a ready record of past political conduct. Consequently, the multi-stage process of forgetting, which Scott Sowerby has argued gradually obscured public support for James II's policy of toleration, was nonetheless preceded by very active and critical remembering of the addressing activity in support of this policy.[127]

There were contemporary attacks on these addresses as manufactured and unrepresentative of the communities that they were supposed to originate from and, as has been suggested above, in some instances, these criticisms might have been justified. Yet, it was also the case that these kinds of criticisms had been levelled at addressing campaigns since the rule of Richard Cromwell which equally had not excised these texts from the public memory. The use of these strategies does lend weight to the argument of Peter Lake and Steven Pincus that James' reign threatened a potentially very different kind of public culture, one much more tightly controlled by the monarchy and in which critical voices were suppressed and replaced with unquestioning royal adulation. The downfall of the Stuart monarchy prevented such a possibility from being realised. Even so, James' strategies were not entirely novel: the combination of addressing with political re-organisation at a local level was a legacy of the so-called 'Tory reaction' of his brother's reign.

Equally, the building of alliances through addressing campaigns harked back to some of the tactics deployed (with similarly limited success) by the restored Rump Parliament in 1659. In fact, James II's difficulties in part were the product of past subscriptional activity and the persistent memory of loyal addressing. The consistent invocation of the memory of the civil wars and specifically the opprobrium heaped on those defending 'Commonwealth Principles' and 'fanatics' meant that the King's overtures towards both Whiggery and dissent in 1687–88 immediately seemed in conflict with the nature of loyalty as defined in the preceding seven years.

As we will see, after 1688, the rapid succession of one addressing campaign after another in this period was sometimes presented as evidence that the fickle public could be brought to address to anything and anyone. The reaction to James' campaign to repeal the test and corporation acts, however, indicates that some communities remembered past addressing activity all too well.

NOTES

1 TNA SP 29/383 f. 140–142. The copy Bower sent Williamson can be found in TNA SP 18/184 f. 145–145v, placed in the volume for December 1658, but with the names of subscribers clearly marked up as indicated above. See also Perry Gauci, *Politics and Society in Great Yarmouth, 1660–1722* (Oxford: Clarendon Press, 1996), pp. 103–4. Gauci, however, overstates the loyalty of the corporation to the new Protector as represented in this address. Yarmouth's text avoided direct acknowledgement of Richard's right to rule as conferred through the Humble Petition, instead, as with many others, preferring to emphasise the role of divine providence. For a printed version of the text see H. Swinden, *The History and Antiquities of the Ancient Burgh of Great Yarmouth in the County of Norfolk* (Norwich, 1772), pp. 578–9. I am grateful to Ed Legon for alerting me to Bower's correspondence and the address. See Legon, 'Remembering Revolution', pp. 76–7. For more on Bower's letter and the Yarmouth address, see my 'Petitioning, addressing and the historical imagination: the case of Great Yarmouth, England 1658–1784', *Parliaments, Estates and Representation*, 38(2018), 364–77.
2 See TNA SP 29/408 f. 37.
3 NRO, Yarmouth Corporation Assembly Book 1642–1662, Y/C 19/7 f. 371. C. J. Palmer, *The History of Great Yarmouth Designed as a Continuation of Manship's History* (Great Yarmouth and London, 1856), p. 245. The corporation also appears to have failed to carry out the order to deface the ordinance giving instructions for the presenting of the address, see NRO Y/C 19/7 f. 316, 18 November 1658.
4 *The proceedings of the grand jury at Taunton* (1682); the address was first reproduced in *Nouvelles Ordinaires de Londres*, 4–11 November 1658, no. 442

but without any details regarding the subscribers, indicating that the author of the pamphlet was working from either the original address or a manuscript copy. Unfortunately, the Wells Corporation Act Books for the years 1644–1662 have been lost; for more detail see D. Underdown, 'A case concerning bishops' lands: Cornelius Burges and the Corporation of Wells', *English Historical Review*, 78 (1963), 18–48; C. Burges, *A case concerning the buying of bishops lands* (1659), p. 36 provides a list of some of the corporation members during the 1640s. Legon also notes that the production of lists of political enemies, tied to the history of the civil wars, was not uncommon, 'Remembering Revolution', p. 77.

5   J. Scott, *England's Troubles: Seventeenth-century English History in European Perspective* (Cambridge: Cambridge University Press, 2000); M. Knights, 'The Tory interpretation of history in the rage of parties', *Huntington Library Quarterly*, 68 (2005), 353–73; Neufeld, *The Civil Wars After 1660*. See also E. Legon, 'Bound up with meaning: the politics and memory of ribbon wearing in Restoration England and Scotland', *Journal of British Studies*, 56 (2017), 27–50; Legon, 'Remembering Revolution'.

6   For a breakdown of numbers see Knights, *Representation and Misrepresentation*, p. 117. Aside from the titles listed below, important surveys of this period include J. Miller, *After the English Civil Wars: English Politics and Government in the Reign of Charles II* (Harlow: Longman, 2000); G. Southcombe and G. Tapsell, *Restoration Politics, Religion, and Culture: Britain and Ireland, 1660–1714* (Basingstoke: Palgrave, 2010); J. Spurr, *England in the 1670s: 'This Masquerading Age'* (Oxford: Blackwell, 2003).

7   Lake and Pincus, 'Rethinking the public sphere', p. 12.

8   *A true and perfect collection of all messages, addresses, &c. from the House of Commons to the kings most excellent majestie* (1680).

9   C. J., ix,; *The Entring Book of Roger Morrice, 1677–91*, general ed. Mark Goldie (6 vols, Woodbridge: Boydell and Brewer, 2007–9), ii, pp. 51–3; 63–5; 80–4.

10 T. B., *The loyalty of the last Long Parliament, or, a letter to an English gentleman at Florence* (1681), p. 10.

11 [Edmund Bohun], *Reflections on a pamphlet stiled, a just and modest vindication of the proceedings of the two last Parliaments, or, A defence of his majesties late declaration* (1683), p. 55.

12 M. Knights, *Politics and Opinion in Crisis*, ch. 8, 9; *The entring book of Roger Morrice*, ii, p. 231; Narcissus Luttrell, *A brief historical relation of state affairs from September 1678 to April 1714* (6 vols, Oxford: Oxford University Press, 1857), i, p. 31; For anti-petitions or addresses see *London Gazette*, 22–26 January 1680, no. 1480; *London Gazette*, 3–6 May 1680, no. 1509.

13 Collated in *Vox patriae: or the resentments & indignation of the free-born subjects of England, against popery, arbitrary Government, the Duke of YORK OR ANY POPISH SUCCESSOR* (1681) and for these texts see Knights, *Politics and Opinion in Crisis*, pp. 291–8; T. Harris, *Restoration: Charles II and his kingdoms, 1660–1685* (Penguin: London, 2006), pp. 185–6.

14 *Vox Angliae: or, the voice of the kingdom. Being a compleat collection of all those numerous addresses lately presented to his majesty* (1682) and for these texts see Harris, *Restoration*, pp. 267–76; Knights, *Politics and Opinion in Crisis*, pp. 329–45.

15 On these texts see P. Harth, *Pen for a Party, Dryden's Tory Propanganda in its Contexts* (Princeton, NJ: Princeton University Press, 1993), pp. 149–53, 213–14; Harris, *Restoration*, pp. 403–5.
16 Knights, *Representation and Misrepresentation*, pp. 122–3; for the campaign in support of James II's indulgence, see Sowerby, *Making Toleration* and Sowerby, 'Forgetting the Repealers'.
17 Luttrell, i, pp. 269–70.
18 Narcissus Luttrell's *Brief relation*, Roger Morrice's *Entring book* and Sir Richard Newdigate's newsletters all feature repeated references to addressing activity.
19 *A proclamation against tumultuous petitions* (1679) [Wing C3226].
20 *London Gazette*, 3–6 May 1680, no. 1509; *London Gazette*, 6–10 May 1680, no. 1510; *London Gazette*, 10–13 May 1680, no. 1511; Luttrell, i., pp. 43, 53.
21 *Whereas in the LONDON GAZZETTE, published from Thursday May the 6th to Munday May the 10th 1680* (n.p., n.d [1680]).
22 *London Gazette*, 10–13 May 1680, no. 1511.
23 Luttrell, i, p. 41.
24 *Domestick Intelligencer*, Tuesday, 27 January 1680, no. 59; Luttrell, i, p. 32; G. Hampson, G. Jaggar, 'Mildmay, Henry (1619–92)', in B. D. Henning (ed.), *The History of Parliament: The House of Commons* (Woodbridge: Boydell, 1983), www.historyofparliamentonline.org/volume/1660-1690/member/mildmay-henry-1619-92, accessed 2 August 2017; The reported words of the King here are very similar those in the Westminster address, Roger North, *Examen, or an enquiry into the credit and veracity of a pretended complete history* (1740), pp. 546–7.
25 [Sir Roger L'Estrange], *A seasonable memorial in some historical notes upon the liberties of the presses and pulpit: with the effects of popular petitions, tumults, associations, impostures and disaffected common-councils* (1680), p. 21. (References are to the London rather than Edinburgh printing of this pamphlet.) On this tract and L'Estrange's attitude to petitioning see M. J. Knights, 'Roger L'Estrange, printed petitions and the problem of intentionality', in J. Morrow and J. Scott (eds), *Liberty, Authority, Formality, Political Ideas and Culture, 1600–1900, Essays in Honour of Colin Davis* (Exeter: Imprint Academic: Exeter), ch. 6.
26 L'Estrange, *Seasonable memorial*, p. 22.
27 Ibid., pp. 36–7.
28 *C. J.*, ix, p. 656; Folger Shakespeare Library, Washington DC (hereafter Folger), L. c. 1000, Newdigate newsletters, 25 October 1680, 'Sr Fra: Withers was calld to ye bar & accusd of having calld ye late petions tumultuous to wch he sd he knew it was ye undoubted right of ye subjt to petion but thought it not seasonable.'; Folger, L.c. 1001, Newdigate newsletters, 29 October 1680. *The entring book of Roger Morrice*, ii, pp. 242–4. Roger North alleged that it was Withens' abject apology which resulted in his ejection going unchallenged, North, *Examen*, pp. 549–50.
29 Ibid., p. 561; *C. J.*, ix, p. 656; Folger, L.c. 871, Newdigate newsletters, 22 December 1679.
30 *C. J.*, ix, p. 643, Folger, L. c. 1000, Newdigate newsletters, 25 October 1680.
31 *C. J.*, ix, pp. 657, 662; North, *Examen*, pp. 551–4.
32 Knights, 'Roger L'Estrange', p. 116.

33 Harris, *Restoration*, p. 273. *C. S. P. D*, 1680–1, p. 570; Luttrell, i, 110, 113, 128. Some seditious words indictments sought to link Whiggery with the regicide, *Loyal Protestant and True Domestick Intellignce*, 30 July 1681, no. 42.
34 For Alford see J. G. Alford, *Alford Family Notes Ancient and Modern* (London, 1908), pp. 85–9; *London Gazette*, 21–25 July 1681, no. 1636; *London Gazette*, 4–8 August 1681, no. 1640.
35 P. J. Norrey, 'The Relationship between central and local government in Dorset, Somerset and Hampshire, 1660–1688' (PhD dissertation, University of Bristol, 1988), pp. 258–9.
36 *C.S.P.D.*, 1682, p. 80; Norrey, 'Central and local government in Dorset', p. 261. For a more detailed discussion of this case see E. Vallance, ' "From the hearts of the people": loyalty, addresses and the public sphere in the exclusion crisis', in T. Claydon and T. Corns (eds), *Religion, Culture and the National Community in the 1670s* (Cardiff: University of Wales Press, 2011), ch. 6.
37 *Loyal Protestant and True Domestick Intelligence*, 2 April 1681, no. 8.
38 J. T. Evans, *Seventeenth Century Norwich: Politics, Religion, and Government, 1620–1690* (Oxford: Clarendon Press, 1979), p. 273; Luttrell, i 91.
39 See for example T. Harris, 'The Leveller legacy: from the Restoration to the Exclusion Crisis', in M. Mendle (ed.), *The Putney Debates of 1647: The Army, the Levellers and the English State* (Cambridge: Cambridge University Press, 2001), ch. 11.
40 Legon, 'Remembering Revolution', p. 251.
41 *His majesties declaration to all his loving subjects touching the causes and reasons that moved him to dissolve the two last parliaments* (1681), pp. 7, 9.
42 Knights, *Politics and Opinion in Crisis*, pp. 321–2.
43 *Vox Angliae*, p. 45 (Leeds), 'the safety of the People pretended, made a Cloak to enslave the People'.
44 Ibid., p. 12 and for similar expressions see that from Clifton, Dartmouth and Harness in Devon, p. 15.
45 Ibid., p. 18.
46 Ibid., p. 19.
47 Harth, *Pen for a Party*, pp. 144–7; 148–53, 166–8, 211–28.
48 *London Gazette*, 27 September to 1 October 1683, no. 1864.
49 Knights, 'L'Estrange', pp. 113–15; [Roger L'Estrange], *L'Estrange his apology* (1660).
50 Roger L'Estrange, *A memento: treating of the rise, progress and remedies of seditions; with some historical reflections upon the series of our late troubles* (1682).
51 Ibid., p. 29.
52 *The addresses importing an abhorrence of an association. Pretended to have been seized in the E. Of Shaftsbury's closet, laid open and detected* (1682), p. 1. And see Knights, 'L'Estrange', pp. 120–1.
53 *Addresses importing an abhorrence*, p. 3.
54 *True Protestant Mercury*, 25–28 March 1681, no. 128.
55 *Addresses importing an abhorrence*, p. 2.
56 *Impartial Protestant Mercury*, 12 May 1681, no. 6.
57 Edward Whitacker, *The second part of the ignoramus justices* (1682), pp. 2–3, produced in response to Smith's 1682 charge to the Middlesex sessions of the peace, *The charge given by Sr. William Smith Brt.* (1682) and see Leonard Naylor and John P. Ferris, 'Smith (Smyth), William (1617–1697) of Radclive, Bucks,

and Stepney, Mdx.', in Henning (ed.), *The History of Parliament: The House of Commons 1660–1690*, www.historyofparliamentonline.org/volume/1660-1690/member/smith-%28smyth%29-william-1617-97, accessed 9 April 2018. I am grateful to Ed Legon for this reference.
58 [Attrib Earl of Shaftesbury] *An impartial account*, p. 26.
59 *An historical account of the rise and progress of addressing* (1681), p. 2.
60 *Impartial account*, p. 6.
61 Ibid., p. 7.
62 Ibid., pp. 15, 18–19.
63 Ibid., p. 39.
64 Ibid., pp., 9, 22.
65 TNA, SP 29/419, f. 51.
66 G. Tapsell, *The Personal Rule of Charles II, 1681–85* (Woodbridge: Boydell and Brewer, 2007), pp. 114–15.
67 See for example the disputes over the address from the Middle Temple, *Impartial Protestant Mercury*, 17–21 June 1681, no. 17; *Loyal Protestant and True Domestick Intelligence*, 18 June 1681, no. 30; *Loyal Protestant and True Domestick Intelligence*, 21 June 1681, no. 31; *London Gazette*, 20–23 June 1681, no. 1627; *A vindication of addresses in general* (1681), pp. 3–4; *The earl of Shaftsbury's grand-jury vindicated from the aspersions cast on them in the late address from some of the Middle-Temple* (1682) and see similar reports concerning the attempt to produce an 'abhorrence' from Gray's Inn in 1682, *True Protestant Mercury*, 11–15 February 1682, no. 116 and for reports of disputed address in the *London Gazette* see the counter-address from Middlesex Justices, 23–26 May 1681, no. 1619.
68 Michael Hunter and Annabel Gregory (eds), *An Astrological Diary of the Seventeenth Century: Samuel Jeake of Rye 1652–1699* (Oxford: Clarendon Press, 1988), pp. 30–2.
69 Kent Archives and Library Services, CP/Bp 286, Brotherhood papers, 1 June 1683. The Brotherhood did finally draft an address, Kent Archives and Library Services, CP/Bp 290, Brotherhood papers, 24 July 1683.
70 *Vox Angliae*, p. 20 (Newport, Isle of Wight), p. 23 (Penryn, Cornwall), p. 25 (Deal, Kent); *London Gazette*, 20–23 August 1683, no. 1853 (Grand Inquest of Southampton).
71 *The entring book of Roger Morrice*, iv, p. 24.
72 Ibid., p. 79.
73 Sowerby, 'Forgetting the Repealers', pp. 113–14.
74 Ibid., p. 112.
75 *A collection of the several addresses in the late King James's Time: Concerning the conception and birth of the pretended Prince of Wales* (1700), attributed by George Watson, *New Cambridge Bibliography of English Literature 1660–1800* (vol. 2, Cambridge: Cambridge University Press, 1971), p. 890 to Daniel Defoe but here dated 1710.
76 *A collection of addresses presented by the English and Scottish Presbyterians to King James VII. To which are added, two ADDRESSES of the Royal Burrows in Scotland on the birth of the then Prince of Wales* ('Re-printed in the Year 1722').
77 Ibid., p. 8.
78 *The entring book of Roger Morrice*, v, p. 365.

79 *An address of thanks to a good prince presented in the pangeyrick of Pliny, upon Trajan, the best of Roman emperours* (1685), p. iii. For this tract see also Knights, 'Loyal Address', p. 327.
80 Kennett, *An address of thanks*, pp. xi-xii, quote at p. xvii.
81 Ibid., pp. xxii.
82 *White against Kennet: or Dr. Kennet's panegyrick upon the late King James* (1704), p. v. For the controversy over the sermon see G. V. Bennett, *White Kennett 1660–1728: Bishop of Peterborough. A Study in the Political and Ecclesiastical History of the Early Eighteenth Century* (London: S.P.C.K, 1957), pp. 90–4.
83 *Loyal Protestant and True Domestick Intelligence*, 26 January 1682, no. 108; for a very similar address see that of New Sarum, *Loyal Protestant and True Domestick Intelligence*, 28 January 1682, no. 109. Comments which were pre-empted by those of L'Estrange in *A seasonable memorial*, p. 23.
84 Harth, *Pen for a Party*, p. 157. Philanax Misopapas pseud., *A Tory plot* (1682), p. 38; *Addresses importing and abhorrence*, p. 4.
85 *The humble address of the grand jury of and for the town and burrough of Southwark* (1683) which promised to defend the king against 'all Conspiracies, Associations, and CONVENTICLES'.
86 *Weekly Discovery*, 19 February 1681, no. 3.
87 For references to local officials losing office for refusing to address or discountenancing addresses see Luttrell, i, pp. 405, 457, reporting the dissolution of the corporation of Ipswich for refusing to address in support either of James II's declaration of indulgence or the birth of the Prince of Wales; *The entring book of Roger Morrice*, iv, p. 115.
88 Evans, *Norwich*, pp. 273, 281.
89 Luttrell, i, p. 108.
90 Knights, 'L'Estrange', p. 123.
91 L'Estrange, *Seasonable memoriall*, p. 18.
92 Ibid., p. 37.
93 Sir Roger L'Estrange, *L'Estrange his appeal humbly submitted to the king's most excellent majesty and the three estates assembled in Parliament* (1681), p. 17.
94 [White Kennett] *A Complete History of England: with the Lives of all the King's and Queens thereof* 3 vols (1706), iii, p. 382; North, *Examen*, pp. 546–7.
95 *Protestant (Domestick) Intelligence*, 25 Feb. 1681, no. 100; *Protestant (Domestick) Intelligence*, 11 March 1681, no. 104; *Protestant (Domestick) Intelligence*, 15 March 1681, no. 105. *Vox Patriae*, pp. 10, 13–15; *The address of the freeholders of the county of Middlesex* (1680 [1681]).
96 North, *Examen*, p. 542; *The Southwark address presented by several inhabitants of note, in the name of themselves and their loyal fellow-burghers to their burgesses* (1680), p. 2. See also Kent Archives and Library Service, Brotherhood papers, Cp/Bp/289 for the determinations of the Brotherhood concerning which of the representatives of the fourteen towns and ports should present the address 'not exceeding tenn men'.
97 *Impartial account*, p. 7.
98 Ibid., p. 12.
99 *Impartial Protestant Mercury*, 10–14 June 1681, no. 15.
100 *Vox juvenilis: Or, the loyal apprentices vindication of the design and promoters of their late humble address to his majesty* (1681 [2]), pp. 2–3; for similar accusations see *A*

friendly dialogue between two London-apprentices, the one a Whigg, the other a Tory, concerning the late addresses to my lord mayor (1681), pp. 2–3.

101 Zaret, 'Petitioning places', p. 176; print, though, raised its own problems of credibility, see George Savile, Marquis of Halifax, *A seasonable address to both Houses of Parliament concerning the succession* (1681), p. 17.

102 Although some commentators saw these collections themselves as providing evidence of a conspiracy, see R. L'Estrange, *Notes upon Stephen College ... the second edition* (1681), p. 45 'the same Pulse beats still in all their Pamphlets of Appeal to the Multitude; which speaks them clearly to be animated with the same soul, and directed to the same end. As *Vox Patriae* for the purpose (among forty others.) What is it, but under the Notion of *Petitions* and *Addresses*, in the name of the people of *England*, a certain *Compendium* of Instruction toward the Forming and carrying on of a *Conspiracy?*'

103 *Vox patriae*, 'To the reader'.

104 *The History and Proceedings of the House of Commons from the restoration to the present time* (14 vols, 1742–44), ii, p. 52.

105 *Vox Patriae*, p. 11; Mark Knights, 'Participation and representation', pp. 35–57 at p. 51 notes that these sorts of instructions were repeatedly issued in the eighteenth century. See also Knights, *Representation and Misrepresentation*, pp. 166–71.

106 *Vox Patriae*, p. 12.

107 Ibid., 'To the reader'.

108 Ibid., p. 20.

109 *The true Englishman, being a vindication of those many loyal addresses presented to his majesty for his late gracious declaration: In an answer to an impartial account of the nature and tendency of the late addresses* (1681), p. 13.

110 Knights, *Representation and Misrepresentation*, p. 137.

111 Compare here the numbers for the Kingston upon Thames address featured in *Vox Angliae*, pt 2, p. 4 (140) and those included on the original, Kingston History Centre, KB 10/1.

112 *The entring book of Roger Morrice*, ii, p. 312.

113 Knights, *Politics and Opinion in Crisis*, p. 340.

114 Harris, *Restoration*, p. 269.

115 Knights, *Politics and Opinion in Crisis*, pp. 345–6.

116 BL Add MS 75359, Althorp papers vol. I, unfoliated, 22 October 1681, Lord Windsor to Earl of Halifax, reports of the refusal to sign the Worcestershire clothiers' address because it did not include a promise to 'Elect acceptable men to his Majesty'.

117 Harris, *Restoration*, p. 319.

118 *The entring book of Roger Morrice*, iv., p. 78.

119 See E. Vallance, *The Glorious Revolution: 1688 Britain's Fight for Liberty* (London: Little, Brown, 2005), pp. 86–9. For these addresses see T. Harris, *Revolution: The Great Crisis of the British Monarchy, 1685–1720* (London: Allen Lane, 2006), pp. 216–24.

120 Ibid., pp. 216, 218 for the numbers.

121 Gloucestershire Record Office, D747-2. This is dated in the catalogue as 1687 but see *The entring book of Roger Morrice*, iv, p. 238.

122 Ibid., iv, p. 238.

123 Luttrell, i, pp. 408, 420, 422 (Hertford); i, pp. 428, 443 (Exeter).

124 T. Harris, 'Charles I and public opinion on the eve of the English civil war', in Taylor and Tapsell *English Revolution Revisited*, ch. 1.
125 For the association see Vallance, *Glorious Revolution*, pp. 131–2; for addresses to William see Royal Institution of Cornwall, MEN/146, and *The entring book of Roger Morrice*, v, pp. 377, 381, 393, 398.
126 Ibid., v, p. 399.
127 Sowerby, 'Forgetting the Repealers', 90–1.

Chapter 4

Adversarial addressing, 1701–10

On 10 June 1710, the Tory newsletter writer John Dyer reported that,

> one Mr. A— a Gentl[man] of ye Long Robe goeing to a Barbers to have some Superfluous Haires taken off & entring into a Dialogue wth Tonsor & his Lady about ye Loyal Addresses now on ffoot ye latter were of opinions of ye Addressers yt ye Queen has an Hereditary Right but ye Lawyer Strenuously denyed it & Said ye Same was in ye P[re]tender & yt Q's was a Parliamentary one &tc. of all wch Mr Tonsor gave informac[i]on & a Warrt. Of H. Treason was granted agt ye Lawyer who after two days doing penance in Custody was discharged being found in ye main [to] be a man of sound principles but not without an Admonic[i]on to take more care for ye [fu]ture & not to discourse ye Politicks wt Barbers.[1]

Whether apocryphal or not, Dyer's anecdote demonstrates the perceived importance of addressing activity to later Stuart politics. On one level, we can see it as showing how addresses facilitated the penetration of political ideas down the social scale. As we will see, the addressing campaigns of the early eighteenth century certainly encouraged the circulation and discussion of key phrases and concepts. Dyer's story also tells us something, however, about the complexity of these political debates. Loyalty was highly contested and so in Dyer's account it was the Whiggish lawyer who became a defender of the Pretender's hereditary right, while the barber and his wife were supporters of the Queen's title (though not primarily her parliamentary one). This is suggestive of the type of rhetorical strategies employed during the controversy and which influenced the texts of loyal addresses, whereby conventional political associations were inverted in order to secure ownership of the coveted identity of the loyal. Dyer's tale also reveals the way in which commentaries upon loyal addresses attempted to simplify and neatly categorise these texts: the barber and his wife becoming defenders of hereditary right, the lawyer of a title conferred by Parliament, overlooking the possibility of combining these positions or seeing the Queen's title as legitimated in other ways (by providence or possession).

This chapter explores the politics of loyal addressing during two moments when addressing became particularly contentious – in 1701 in the wake of the trial of the Kentish petitioners and in 1710 in the aftermath of Sacheverell's conviction for 'High Crimes and Misdemeanours'. It is arguably in this period that addressing reached its peak of political influence as first Whig and then Tory-inspired addressing campaigns forced changes in the ministry and helped shape the national electoral map.

While these campaigns remain relatively underexplored, current scholarship is divided on their character and significance. For Geoffrey Holmes, the addressing campaign of 1710 that followed the trial of Henry Sacheverell, though unquestionably effective, was very much of a piece: 'the words might vary ... the message was almost always the same.'[2] For Mark Knights, on the other hand, the polemical battles waged through these addresses were so intense that the stability of meaning in political discourse seemed itself to be under threat. Indicative here for Knights are Daniel Defoe's comments in his *A New Test of the Sence of the Nation* (1710). For Defoe, half a century of mass addressing had created a political culture in which it had grown 'preposterous to expect, that Men should be suppos'd to mean the same Thing to Day, that they meant yesterday by the same Words'.[3] Knights sees Defoe's comments as reflecting a moment of high anxiety about political identity in general, in which much energy was devoted to attempting to uncover the 'true' character of parties and individuals – an urge epitomised by the sermon that brought Henry Sacheverell to trial, *The Perils of False Brethren*, which contended that the real threat to Church and State came not from papists and Jacobites, but 'fanatics' and 'republicans'.[4] Defoe's attack on addressing in 1710 can also be connected to a broader trend identified by Knights in which the rise of the 'acclamatory' mode of the loyal address, in place of 'dialogic' mass petitioning, represented a significant challenge to an emergent early modern English 'public sphere'.[5]

It will be argued here, however, that the political addresses of the early eighteenth century were neither essentially univocal devices nor completely riven by partisan divisions. The addressing campaigns of 1701–2 and 1710 certainly displayed many of the characteristics that scholars such as David Zaret have associated with features of an emergent democratic culture. The speed with which they were produced encouraged a 'dialogic' culture of address and counter-address, while the replication of texts in a variety of media (newsbooks, newsletters, pamphlets, collections and histories) fostered the growth of a political debate that was reflexive and conscious of its own unfolding.

As Zaret has argued, these features of petitioning-like activity, especially the anthologising of texts, helped in the formation of group and party identities but, within these controversies, this chapter demonstrates the importance of separating out partisan commentary (in contemporary news media) from the content of address themselves.[6] The texts of these addresses often represented attempts to occupy a middle ground and avoid ideological overcommitment, and also conveyed specific local concerns as well as responding to and embedding national debates. In this chapter, I suggest that the crisis of political credibility identified by Knights was also partly a product of conscious rhetorical strategies which attempted to fashion the image of loyal moderation through the projection of an inverted extremism onto their opponents. In so doing, polemicists created the impression of a political debate that was starkly polarised and deeply unstable – an impression that did not tally with the content of many addresses. Indeed, in comparison with the positions advanced in the addressing campaign of 1701–2, the range of political opinions expressed in 1710 actually constituted a narrower and more moderate selection of views.

POPULAR PETITIONING AND ADDRESSING? THE CASE OF THE KENTISH PETITIONERS

The addresses issued in support of Henry Sacheverell, as noted by Geoffrey Holmes, built upon the earlier example of a successful pro-Whig addressing campaign initiated in 1701.[7] Like those sent to Queen Anne in 1710, these addresses were in part inspired by a celebrated court case initiated by Parliament. The case of the Kentish Petitioners, as with the case of Sacheverell later, raised important questions concerning the authority of Parliament, the nature of representation and the efficacy of loyal addresses and petitions. The five gentlemen of Kent who sent the petition in May 1701 implored the house to 'have Regard to the Voice of the People' and make good their own loyal addresses to the King by passing bills of supply that would allow William to raise a substantial standing army. The Tory-dominated Commons deemed the petitioners' requests insolent and seditious, and ordered the petitioners to be imprisoned until the end of the session. The case of the Kentish petitioners inspired an impressive Whig pamphleteering campaign. This was led by Daniel Defoe's *Legion's Memorial* which asserted that if Parliament betrayed the trust of the people it was 'the undoubted right of the people of England to call them to an account for the same, and by convention, assembly or force ... proceed against them as traitors and betrayers'. The tract *Jura populi Anglicani* (1701), presumed to have been written by the Whig grandee Lord John Somers, in a similar vein presented members of Parliament as 'delegates' of the people and cited John Locke to claim a natural right to petition.[8]

As we will see, these strident Whig arguments in support of assertive popular petitioning and addressing would come back to haunt Defoe in 1710 as Tory/High Church supporters exploited the same strategies. Yet, these arguments were themselves deceptive in terms of their apparent support for the popular voice and took place in a context in which it was the Whigs who were now defenders of the political status quo and the Tories the voice of the opposition – a fact reflected in the deployment of history in support of these positions. Tory critics of the Junto such as the MP Sir Henry Mackworth could even be found citing that classic statement on the mixed constitution, Charles I's Answer to the Nineteen Propositions, to demonstrate the limitations on royal authority.[9] Supporters of the Court Whigs, including the author of *Jura Populi Anglicani*, were accused in contrast of ransacking the arguments of their former opponents, such as Sir Roger L'Estrange.[10]

Nonetheless, Defoe's *Legion's Memorial* (1701) and *Jura Populi Anglicani* have usually been presented as reassertions of radical Whig ideology. The strident tone of Defoe's *Legion* is undeniable. Defoe here asserted that if,

> the House of Commons, in breach of the Laws and Liberties of the People do betray the Trust reposed in them, and act Negligently or Arbitrarily, and illegally, it is the undoubted Right of the People of England to call them to an account for the same, and by Convention, Assembly or Force may proceed against them as Traytors, and Betrayers of their Country.[11]

The imprisonment of men who were not members of the House and by a simple vote was, Defoe argued, a flagrant example of just such a breach of trust.[12]

The threat of popular revolution seemed to be encapsulated in the Biblical allusion in Defoe's title – 'My name is Legion, for we are many' (Mark 5:9). Defoe expanded on these arguments in a pamphlet published the following year, *The Original Power of the Collective Body of the People of England, Examined and Asserted* (1702). Here he seemed to echo Locke's account in his *Two Treatises* by suggesting that it was up to each individual to judge whether an action of the legislature might be unjust or unreasonable. The individual therefore retained a right to appeal to the legislature via petitions in such a case.[13]

All elements of the State held power in trust from the people:

> The People of *England* have Delegated all the Executive Power *in the King*, the Legislative in the *King, Lords and Commons*, the Soveraign Judicature *in the Lords*, the Remainder is reserv'd in themselves, and not committed, no not to their Representatives: All Powers Delegated are to one Great End and Purpose, and no other, and that is *the Publick Good*. If either or all the Branches to whom this Power is Delegated invert the Design, the End of their Power, the Right they have to that Power ceases; and they become Tyrants and Usurpers of a Power they have no Right to.

In such a situation, power 'retreats' back to its original, into the hands of the 'whole People' who, as Defoe had insisted in *Legion's Memorial*, might form a revolutionary convention to resolve on new constitutional arrangements.[14] *Jura Populi Anglicani* was less explicit regarding the consequences of such a breach of trust but likewise insisted that the 'The Knights, Citizens, and Burgesses, sent by the People of England to serve in Parliament, have a Trust reposed in them, which if they should manifestly betray, the People, in whom the power is more perfectly and fully than in their Delegates, must have a Right to help and preserve themselves.'[15] The author cited Locke to suggest that the right to petition was effectively a natural right, for if men had formed societies to protect their property, they must also have created mechanisms to ensure redress if that property was threatened or there would be no point to men organising in this fashion.[16]

From these statements it is easy to see why some scholars, such as Defoe's biographer Paula Backscheider, see Defoe's ideas in these tracts as 'radical Lockean' in character.[17] An alternative reading of these pamphlets, however, has been offered by Manuel Schonhorn, who has argued that they were, in fact, anti-populist.[18] Schonhorn's position is supported by the observation of Mark Knights that the right to petition itself was not at stake in the controversy over the Kentish Petition.[19] It is worth noting that neither Defoe nor the author of *Jura Populi Anglicani* contested that petitioning could be regulated by law. Both, in fact, justified the actions of the Kentish gentlemen on the basis that they were in conformity with the procedures for lawful petitions laid out in the 1661 act against tumultuous petitioning.[20] Both authors were agreed that laws regulating petitioning were necessary to prevent such activity leading to disorder or to being subverted for partisan ends. (The author of *Jura Populi Anglicani* predictably chose an example of pro-Tory mass addressing, the texts supporting the dissolution of the Oxford Parliament of 1681, to illustrate the dangerous consequences of unregulated petitioning.)[21] What was in dispute between Defoe, the author of *Jura Populi Anglicani*, and opponents such as Mackworth was not whether petitioning was lawful but whether this particular petition was in violation of the regulations set down in the 1661 statute.[22]

Both sides in this dispute were upholding a law which had essentially been created to bring an end to the assertive, popular petitioning of the English revolution. The lack of debate over the principle that petitioning was legitimate if properly regulated was indicative of the inherent anti-populism of Defoe's position. Critical here was Defoe's interpretation of 'property'. As Schonhorn has argued, Defoe's view of property was much narrower than Locke's. Rather than being, as James Tully has put it for Locke, 'a right to some thing such that it cannot be taken without the consent of the proprietor or the consent of his representatives', for Defoe, property referred simply to possession and, in terms of its relationship to political power, exclusively to the ownership of land.[23] When Defoe spoke of power reverting to the people, he therefore meant only a subset of 'the people' – the freeholders.

> I do not place this Right [the right to create a new constitution] upon the Inhabitants, but upon the *Freeholders*; the *Freeholders* are the proper Owners of the Country. It is their own, and the other Inhabitants are but Sojourners, like Lodgers in a House, and ought to be subject to such Laws as the Freeholders impose upon them, or else they must remove; because the Freeholders having a Right to the Land, the other have no right to live there but upon sufferance.[24]

Defoe was keen to exonerate the Kentish petitioners themselves from accusations that they had courted the mob. Of subscription to the petition he said, 'many Thousands of Hands might have been had to it, if the Justices had not declined it, refusing to add any more Rolls of Parchment, as insisting more upon the Merit of the Persons, than the Number of Subscribers.'[25] Indeed, supporters of the Junto in general were keen to paint their opponents and not the Court Whigs, as whipping up the populace. Jonathan Swift, for example, used classical allegory to show that 'popular Tyranny' 'never fails to be followed by the Arbitrary Government of a single person'.[26] There was, though, an obvious tension here. Writers such as Swift, Defoe and the author of *Jura Populi Anglicani* wished to stress the authoritative nature of *Vox Populi*. To do that, they had to show that the Kentish petition was representative of the will of that community. At the same time, however, they needed to demonstrate that it was only the legitimate political actors within that community – the freeholders – who had given their backing to the petition. Consequently, when the press did report mass subscription to these texts, as in the case of the five thousand who were said to have added their names to the Northamptonshire address, this was qualified by the statement that these were only the 'Gentlemen and Freeholders' of the county.[27]

Critics of the Kentish petition nonetheless claimed that it was not only unlawful and seditious but also unrepresentative. The author of the *Legionites Plot* argued that,

> never any wise King yet rely'd upon popular Addressing, they being incapable by Addresses to judg the true Sense of a Nation, for never yet one 8th part of the People sign'd such Addresses, which are generally promoted by Men designing and ambitious, forward and willing to make a Noise in the World and some profitable Bargain with the Prince they address.

This was demonstrated by using the by now familiar examples of mass addresses in support of first Richard Cromwell and then James II.[28] In fact, press reports of the numbers subscribing to these addresses appeared relatively infrequently in comparison with past campaigns, again perhaps indicating an attempt by the Court Whigs' supporters to counter accusations of populism.[29] Similarly, references to addresses being from 'the Inhabitants' or 'loyal subjects' of a particular area, or to coming from more informal bodies (charities or dissenting groups) suggested that a less restrictive definition of the political nation than Defoe's was being employed in these addressing campaigns.[30] Nonetheless, they fed into a vision of political representation which shared much with that outlined in *Legion's Memorial*. The addresses issued in support of war in the summer and autumn of 1701 often promised to choose MPs who would carry out their constituents' wishes by defending the King and the Protestant interest in Europe. As noted by Mark Knights, the notion that MPs were bound to follow the directions in these addresses was implied by the routine involvement of MPs in presenting these texts to the Crown and made explicit in some election 'Instructions' which specifically referred back to demands made in the county or corporation's loyal address.[31]

As Defoe himself recognised, however, such demands went somewhat against the nature of addresses themselves, distinct from petitions: while petitions were formal 'requests', addresses tended to be 'congratulatory' texts.[32] Addresses were therefore inherently emotional appeals. Consequently, it is not surprising that very few of those issued in 1701 spent much time discussing the nature or original of political power: the address from the West Riding of Yorkshire was unique in this instance in describing William's title as 'established by the Consent of Your People'.[33] Instead, these addresses were typically presented as emotional responses – expressions of gratitude and thankfulness to the King for rescuing Britain from 'Popery and Slavery' and of indignation and affront at the insult delivered by Louis XIV in recognising the title of the Pretender, James Francis Edward Stuart. The trust between monarch and people was founded on these emotional ties and replenished by the reciprocal activity of addressing itself – with the address often presented to the King in person and the addressers honoured and treated by the monarch in return.[34] Statements and practices of this kind were, of course, more politically ambiguous and consequently safer promises of support than those that entered into the specifics of William's title. Yet, they also invited broader political participation – all who enjoyed the King's protection and not just freeholders might give their thanks for his rule.

Defoe's comments on the Kentish Petition, far from being radically populist, limited ultimate political authority to English freeholders and upheld existing statutory limitations on popular participation in activity such as addressing and petitioning. In this sense, Defoe's arguments in *Legion's Memorial* and *The Original Right* may still be 'Lockeian' but in the sense that they fit with Mark Knights' recent observations concerning the political aspirations of Locke's circle. As Knights shows, Locke's 'college' had a keen interest in proposals for changing the electoral system. They supported such proposals, however, as means of regulating rather than reforming the system of representation. The aim was not to widen participation (indeed, in some areas these proposals would have made the franchise more limited than before), but to reform what were seen as the degenerate aspects of politics (the 'treating' of constituents for example) and to ensure the vote was placed in the hands of those typically responsible for government in the localities.[35] Similarly, Defoe saw the necessity of regulating activities such as addressing and petitioning at the very same time as he recognised their importance for making legislators accountable to their trustees, the freeholders of England.

This predominately Whig addressing campaign delivered impressive results: a Whig majority in the elections of November and December 1701, reversing the small Tory majority registered earlier in the year.[36] It also signalled public commitment to the war with France. In addition, the addressing campaign appeared, at least at first glance, to reaffirm William's title to the throne and to uphold the Protestant succession. The very public nature of mass addressing meant that these texts could represent popular loyalty to the regime not only in a national but also an international context. William ordered the City of London's address to be translated and dispersed throughout Europe. According to Luttrell 'the French king was much incens'd at the English addresses, and said he would chastise their insolence, and sett the prince of Wales on the throne of England, or lose his crown'.[37] The *Mercure Historique et Politique,* published in The Hague, likewise reported in December 1701 that 'Les Adresses que les Anglois ont presenté coup sur coup à leur Monarque, ont fait du chagrin au Roi de France, & on dit à ce sujet qu'il a déclaré publiquement qu'il n'abandoneroit jamais le Roi Jaques III.'[38]

Beneath the general picture of these addresses as a coup for the Whig party, however, a more complicated political landscape was visible. For one thing, there remained a significant number of addresses which made no clear acknowledgement of William's right to the throne.[39] Other addresses presented William's title as established not by law or hereditary right but by popular consent: the address from Chester spoke of William's 'Just and Lawful Title, begun by the Free Consent and Affectionate Desires of Your People, Established by several Acts of Parliament and Acknowledged throughout the World'.[40] What was particularly remarkable about these addresses, at least as far as William's title was concerned, was that only four of these texts (those from Lydd, Newcastle upon Tyne, Durham and the London Baptist ministers) made reference to the Association in defence of William III tendered in 1696.[41] This was surprising given that only five years prior to the 1701 addressing campaign, in the largest act of mass oath-taking in British history, the public had sworn that William was 'rightful and lawful King'.[42] The oath returns for the Association had also been frequently accompanied with loyal addresses, many of which promised (like those issued in 1701) to elect only MPs who would subscribe the association and/or were deemed loyal to the present government.[43] (Although one difference with the addressing campaign of 1701 was that addresses were only noted in the press in 1696 rather than being reproduced in full.)[44] The exercise was not completely forgotten: an election publication printed in 1701 included among the members who should be opposed in the upcoming contest those who were against the 'mutual Association' and had 'Impeached the Associators'.[45] As we will see, the Association returns would also be very important to later Whig arguments concerning popular support for the Revolution settlement. It was extraordinary, nonetheless, that an addressing and oath-taking campaign which had, in some areas, probably touched almost every adult male inhabitant, subsequently, in very similar circumstances, occasioned so little comment only five years later.[46] Indeed, in contrast to the addressing campaigns of the 1680s, the texts produced in 1701 included little historical reflection.[47]

The lack of a historical perspective within these addresses may be revealing, perhaps indicating an unwillingness to elaborate on the legitimacy of the events of 1688 in particular. Moreover, while some of these addresses were clearly aimed at tackling the perceived injustice of the judgment against the Kentish petitioners, other addresses more clearly sided with the Tory Commons. The address from New Windsor borough stated that they did not think themselves 'wise enough to advise Your Great Council in Parliament assembled; but shall always esteem their Resolutions, when stampt with Your Majesty's Authority, the unquestionable Rules of our Obedience, and not Matters fit for our Dispute'.[48] The Cornish address to their knights of the shire required them to investigate who had pressed for the dissolution of the last Parliament which, they felt, had acted 'entirely in the king and kingdoms interest'.[49] The addressing campaign of 1701–2 clearly represented a political victory for the Court Whigs but it also revealed a notable reluctance to engage in wider discussion of the revolution settlement, as well as a continued reticence about popular subscriptional activity. Both the meaning of the revolution of 1688 and the legitimate scope of loyal addressing would be explored much further in the next major addressing controversy.

LOYALTY AND PARTISANSHIP IN THE SACHEVERELL ADDRESSES

The addressing campaign of 1701, while it ostensibly delivered considerable gains to the Whig party, actually represented, on closer examination, a more equivocal display of loyalty, with many boroughs and counties, in spite of the experience of 1696, refusing to acknowledge clearly William's title to the throne.

The accession of Queen Anne in 1702 was greeted with hundreds of loyal texts and hundreds more followed the military victories of Blenheim and Ramillies. As will be discussed in more detail in Chapter six, the Union with Scotland provoked many addresses for and against. Although a mooted Jacobite invasion attempt in 1708 resulted in nearly four hundred addresses to the queen, assuring her of her subjects' loyalty, the lukewarm response to the capture of Tournay and the victory at Mons pointed to growing public disenchantment with the war with France.[50] Nonetheless, while the pro-Sacheverell addresses presented to the Crown in 1710 generally appeared to fit in with the increasingly critical public mood, there were significant, dissonant voices in here as well. These were not only expressed in the small number of Whig counter-addresses, which were easily outnumbered by those that seemed broadly supportive of Sacheverell, but also in the extensive commentary and editorialising upon these loyal addresses in the Whig press. What the addresses and the public discussion demonstrated was that, as argued by Mark Knights, the political ideas at stake in Sacheverell's trial (the right of resistance versus passive obedience, hereditary right versus contract theory, toleration versus 'indulgence') had penetrated down to a local and popular level.[51] More than this, that the language of Sacheverell's own highly controversial sermon itself had become integrated into the wording of addresses created by county grand juries and corporation common councils.

Henry Sacheverell already had a well-established reputation as a firebrand High Church preacher by the time that he came to give his explosive sermon, *The Perils of False Brethren* before the mayor, aldermen and common council of the city at St Paul's on 5 November 1709.[52] Sermons given on this date, as opposed to those offered on that other significant political anniversary, 30 January, the date of Charles I's execution, typically dwelt on the nation's double-deliverance from 'Popery', first by James VI and I and then William of Orange. Sacheverell's sermon proved controversial not only because of its specific content but because of the way in which it subverted the typical themes of 5 November sermons. Instead of 'papists' representing the great threat to Church and State, it was Protestant dissenters who were the true enemy within. According to Sacheverell, it was they who had brought Charles I to the scaffold, and their 'republican' principles continued to threaten the security of the Crown. On Sacheverell's reading, this was a monarchy which had been little altered by the 'revolution' of 1688: no genuine resistance had been made to James' rule and the throne had been transferred to William and Mary as a result of James' 'abdication', not through the actions of the Convention Parliament.

The assault on the Whig interpretation of the revolution and the flagrant disregard for the conventions of 5 November commemorations predictably aroused controversy but it was Sacheverell's not very veiled attacks on the governing Whig ministry that led to Parliament taking action. The content of the sermon was not incendiary enough to make a charge of seditious libel stick. Consequently, the ministry took the alternative tack of impeaching Sacheverell for high crimes and misdemeanours. Specifically, Sacheverell was charged with impugning the right of resistance (and thereby casting odium on the revolution itself), attacking toleration, falsely claiming that the Church was in danger and slandering members of the government by suggesting that they wished to subvert the constitution. The trial, when it began on 27 February 1710 at Westminster Hall, in front of both Houses of Parliament and over a thousand spectators, turned into a propaganda coup for the Tory opposition. Though Sacheverell was found guilty, the sentence constituted little more than a slap on the wrist: he was banned from preaching for three years. The news of the verdict was treated as if Sacheverell had been acquitted. Loyal addresses expressing support for the Church and opposition to the very 'revolution principles' the trial had attempted to vindicate (resistance, toleration) were produced before the proceedings had even been concluded – the first coming from Gloucestershire on 18 March.[53] Sacheverell himself began a progress around the country, ostensibly en route to his new living at Selattyn in Shropshire, his presence generally meeting with a rapturous public reaction. Like the addresses, his tour of counties and boroughs was clearly calculated at influencing the calling of a new Parliament and thereby securing a Tory majority.[54]

The addresses tendered to the Crown in the wake of Sacheverell's trial were unquestionably predominantly High Church/Tory in their political sympathies. John Morphew's compendium of these addresses, published first in serial form, collected some 141 of them but marked only twenty of these as Low Church/Whig in sympathy.[55] As with Sacheverell's progress, many of them were obviously targeted, as Abel Boyer noted, 'against the Ministry and Parliament, and the whole Moderate Party'.[56] (An interesting description which indicates how far commentators on all sides were attempting to repackage the middle ground.) Addresses, such as that from Warwickshire, promised the Queen that they would elect only 'such Representatives in Parliament as are *True* Sons of our Church, of Approv'd Loyalty to Your Majesty'.[57] Some, such as that from the borough of Fowey in Cornwall explicitly referred to the prospect of new elections.[58] Others, such as the address from the University of Oxford, hoped for an end to the Whig-supported war in Europe.[59] The pressure exerted by these addresses, and by pro-Sacheverell propaganda and public demonstrations, was successful: new elections were called, resulting in a clear Tory majority of about 150 and a new ministry which, in turn, initiated a cessation of hostilities in the War of Spanish Succession.[60]

The addressing campaign, as in 1701, was clearly integrated into election campaigning; the existence of counter-texts plus reports of disputes over addressing testified to the partisan contest which lay behind this activity. Morphew's collection of addresses revealed a number of areas in which competing, variant texts were produced, including Berkshire, Cambridge, Coventry, Hampshire, Hertford, Kent, the London Lieutenancy, Northamptonshire, Nottingham, Pembrokeshire, Shropshire, Westminster, Wiltshire, Worcester and Worcestershire, and Yorkshire. One of the most extensive disputes took place in Shropshire, not surprisingly perhaps given that this was the location of Sacheverell's new living and the end point of his 'tour'. The dispute reveals the importance of timing in addressing controversies, especially the significance of presenting the text at Court before any rival declarations could be received. It also emphasises the importance of demonstrating loyalty for both addressers and counter-addressers. Finally, the controversy illustrates the continuing desire to distance subscriptional strategies from accusations of 'popularity' or 'mobbing.'

There was evidence of popular opinion both for and against Sacheverell in the county. As noted by Nicholas Rogers, when Sacheverell arrived in Bridgnorth he was greeted by a pro-Whig crowd which brandished oranges on sticks at him, telling him that it was 'the best fruit that ever came into England'.[61]

It was a pro-Sacheverell mob, however, that acted as the catalyst for a dispute over the loyal addresses presented from the county. It was reported that one Thomas Yewde, a lay non-juror, had stirred up a riotous assembly at the Shrewsbury assizes in order to pressurise the grand jury into promoting a Tory loyal address.[62] Yewde was also accused of inciting public hostility towards Nicholas Lechmere, one of the managers of Sacheverell's trial and a staunch public advocate of a Lockeian vision of the revolution during the proceedings.[63] Yewde's subsequent refusal to take the oath of abjuration when tendered to him by Shropshire JPs added the taint of Jacobitism to his activities.[64] For the Whig *Observator*, the actions of Yewde at Shrewsbury offered proof that the Tory addresses were,

> no Manner of Proof that the Majority of the Nation is on their Side for we have no Reason to doubt that they are most, if not all, procur'd in the same Way as the Party in the County of Salop endeavour'd to procure theirs, which at last is dwindled into a Silly Address from the Town of Ludlow. It appears by a Letter from Ten Gentlemen to the Right Honourable the Earl of Bradford, Lord Lieutenant of that County, that the Rebellious and Tumultuous Mob endeavour'd to procure an Address from the Grand Jury there; but failing in that, the Faction, to shew that their Works were those of Darkness, sent their Address about to the Publick Houses of the Town about Ten a Clock at Night to procure Hands to it in a Clandestine and Unusual Manner.[65]

The accusations were repeated in a letter produced by a number of Shropshire gentlemen and sent to the Earl of Sunderland.[66] These claims clearly connected with well-established tropes in hostile commentaries on subscriptional activity, associating the physical performance of addressing with disorder, conspiracy and sedition.

Aware of the political capital to be made out of Yewde's intervention, this letter was published and reproduced in a number of English texts, as well as being translated into French and Dutch.[67] Further evidence of underhand tactics being used in this instance comes from a manuscript note on a British Library copy of Morphew's addresses. Towards the end of the address from the borough of Shrewsbury before the line, 'In Testimony whereof, we have hereunto affix'd our Common Seal, and subscrib'd our Names this 26th day of *May*, in the Ninth Year of Your Majesty's Reign' was inserted the text 'there it was to have ended. The rest was added by I do not know what hand.'[68] The marginal comment suggests that the address may initially have been completed without the addition of the borough seal indicating that this was an authentic address from the town. Accusations of corporate seals being added under duress were also made by Dyer in the case of some Whig counter-addresses.[69]

The first address to reach the Court from the county as a whole, however, was clearly sympathetic to the Whig ministry rather than Sacheverell. Presented by Henry, Lord Newport on 18 July at Kensington Palace, the text from the deputy lieutenants, justices of the peace and grand jury made clear its support for the Protestant Succession in the house of Hanover. The addressers also rejected the notion that the established Church was under threat: 'we can by no means join in any Insinuations of the Danger of the Church of England, which we stedfastly believe, by the Blessing of God, to be in perfect Safety and Prosperity.' Finally, they denounced attempts to disparage the present ministry or Parliament itself (which Whigs, as with the Tories in 1701, claimed was being treated with contempt by Sacheverell's supporters).[70]

There is evidence that the efforts of Whig supporters in Shropshire succeeded in suppressing addresses promoted by the pro-Sacheverell faction. A letter addressed to Sunderland sent on 5 April 1710 by John Lawne had warned the earl of an address 'carrying on by the high Sheriff &ca against the sence of your Friendes'. The letter also revealed how pressurised the controversy had become: Lawne sent his missive by private messenger to overtake any High Church text sent via the post.[71] This intervention seems to have been at least partially successful: it was not until 7 September that an address from the high sheriff, grand jury, justices of the peace, clergy, gentlemen and freeholders of Shropshire was presented at Court. The addressers clearly acknowledged the previous text sent from the county, expressing their desire to refute accusations that they had been promoting riots or disturbances of the peace:

> We, Your Majesty's most dutiful Subjects, being deeply affected with the Reproach underservedly cast upon our County, by a Representation laid before Your Majesty, in April last; whereby divers of Your Majesty's Faithful Subjects were unjustly traduc'd with the promoting of Tumults, and disturbing the Publick Peace:
>
> Humbly beg Leave to acquaint Your Majesty, that that Representation was *false* and *groundless,* and was maliciously compos'd, and design'd to draw down Your Majesty's Displeasure upon us.

The addressers promised that, contrary to insinuations in pamphlets and the press, their address had not been procured in a *'clandestine and unusual manner* but that we speak the Sense of our Country'. The address went on to denounce the 'Jesuiticall' doctrine of resistance which brought the Queen's 'Royal Grandfather to the Block' and stated that when the Queen was ready to call another Parliament they would send forward representatives that would give an unlimited obedience to her, 'with a firm Resolution of continuing the Succession in the Protestant Line, and of the Church of England as by Law establish'd'.[72] The address itself was reported as being composed at the quarter sessions on 3 August but not mentioned in the press until after its presentation at Kensington, suggesting further difficulties were encountered in promoting the document. Dyer had noted that there had been a major struggle over the choice of representatives for the county in that month but that ultimately the supporters of the 'Church Militant' had emerged triumphant.[73]

An earlier address, from the archdeaconry of Shropshire had, however, already attempted to give a different picture of the political leanings of the county, denouncing dissenting academies as 'Academies of Schism and Faction' which threatened the historical role of Oxford and Cambridge as 'the best Nurseries of Obedience to Governours'. The Shropshire clergy promised that they would 'always vindicate Your Hereditary Right to the Crown of Your Royal Ancestors, the Protestant Succession, and the Church of England as by Law establish'd, at the Expence of all that is dear to us'.[74] Moreover, the address from the county of Shropshire was clearly seen as important enough a propaganda coup for Dyer to unusually lead with its text rather than the summary of foreign news that typically began his letters. Referring to it as an 'Excell[en]t Address', he noted that the creation of this text had even convinced one non-juror, Lord Kilmorey, to take the oaths of allegiance to the Queen, a political conversion that was also reported in Morphew's collection.[75] The story served a clear purpose, tackling the taint of disloyalty thrown upon the Tory addressers by the involvement of the non-juror Yewde and instead showing Sacheverell and his followers as working to convert the disaffected back to allegiance to their true monarch.

The story of Kilmorey's conversion was, however, a relatively rare example of the Tory press commenting on these addresses. With the exception of Dyer's newsletters, Tory papers, particularly the *Post Boy*, preferred to simply reprint the addresses themselves as clear testimony of support for their cause. In contrast, Whiggish publications such as the *Observator* and the *Flying Post*, with admittedly far fewer supportive addresses to present, chose rather to editorialise and critique the more numerous Tory texts.[76] Dyer even suggested that the government's own papers, namely the *London Gazette*, simply ignored those addresses that criticised the administration.[77] In fact, very few notices of addresses, let alone their texts, featured in the *Gazette*, although those that did were also supportive of Sacheverell.[78]

Overall, Whig commentators sought to diminish the value of the large number of Tory addresses as an indicator of the public mood. One tactic (as we have seen by now well established in addressing campaigns), was to suggest that the majority of those whose names were added to these addresses were from the lowest and most credulous sections of society: '*Ignorance* has been the great *Mother* of this Addressing *Devotion*', and 'its the Weak, the Implicit Believers, the Priest-Ridden Bigots of the Nation, that have made up the Croud.' The seeming groundswell of support for Sacheverell was, they claimed, illusory as the signatories to the addresses would easily be dwarfed in number by the refusers or the silent majority who supported the government but were never asked for their hands. Defoe's *Review* wondered,

> What Candle-light Work was used, to get Hands to an Address – and away they went with the mighty Roll to her Majesty, boasting of a Thousand Hands ___ But had they made an exact List, of the Names of those that either they had not the Impudence to ask, or being ask'd flatly refused them, what a Roll would there have been?

Now, were I to advise these Gentlemen, how to act fairly and honestly, and how they shall give her Majesty a fair Account of the Division of the Nation, upon this Head, it should be thus; In every Town from whence they bring these Addresses, let them bring two Rolls up, one of the Addressers, and one of those that refuse to Address – and let them add a Scheme of the Estates, Substance, Trade and Character of the Men on both sides; and her Majesty will soon see, where the Weight of their Interest lies ___and where the substance of the Nation goes.[79]

These broader claims were underwritten by allegations of underhand tactics or force being used to procure pro-Tory address.[80] Once again, the memory of past addressing activity was invoked to delegitimise texts as authentic expressions of public opinion. The *Review* claimed that the Tories were 'mobbing' the nation into producing these addresses, just as the illegitimate and tyrannical regimes of Richard Cromwell and James II had once done.[81] As will be discussed in greater detail in Chapter six, histories of addressing produced by Defoe, John Oldmixon and Benjamin Hoadly employed this strategy in lengthier critiques of the pro-Sacheverell addresses. This also had the advantage of compensating for the relative lack of Whig counter-texts.

Another tactic adopted by the Whig press was to describe (without reprinting) Tory addresses as being 'seditious' in nature.[82] Inevitably, Tory writers and printers such as Dyer and Morphew responded by reprinting these addresses in full, alongside fulsome endorsements of their loyal nature.[83] This strategy of labelling addresses as seditious had other ramifications in that it allowed Whig authors to redefine which addresses were disloyal and which not. In the process, this both weakened the credibility of these addresses and encouraged the perception that these texts fitted into two essential categories – the loyal and the seditious. We can see this at play in the *Observator's* commentary on two variant addresses produced from New Windsor, one published in the Tory *Post Boy*, the other in the Whig *Flying Post*. It noted that while one of the addresses expressed an explicit abhorrence of the Pretender and his Jacobite adherents, the other only mentioned the Queen's hereditary title. The *Observator* went on to note that other addresses had chosen the tactic of only expressing their adherence to the Protestant succession 'as by law established'. This seemingly straightforward promise to abide by the terms of the 1701 Act of Succession was, however, too 'Ambiguous, considering we have a Party among us who own nothing to be Law that has been enacted since the Revolution', especially since there were other addresses, such as those from Westbury, Leicester, Brecon, Carnarvon, Lincoln and Abingdon which did not mention the succession at all. Equally, said the *Observator*, those that mentioned the Protestant Succession but not the House of Hanover were also suspect, 'since there are so many of the High-Church who are for the Pretender, and flatter themselves that he will profess himself a Protestant'.[84] An inverted version of the same strategy was employed by Tory writers as well, who argued that Whig addresses only founded the Queen's title on the revolution, with no acknowledgement of her hereditary right.[85]

This presentation of Whig and Tory argument fitted in with the polarised political landscape portrayed in some of the addresses, in which Tories and High Churchmen were really crypto-Jacobites whipping up a mob frenzy to weaken the State in preparation for a French invasion, and Whigs and dissenters were the intellectual descendants of civil war republicans and 'fanatics', unwavering defenders of the right of resistance.[86] To a considerable degree, this reflected the way in which the vision of politics and recent political history embodied in Sacheverell's controversial sermon had become integrated into the text of the addresses of 1710. *The Perils of False Brethren*'s very limited acknowledgement of the Toleration Act, encapsulated in the phrase 'consciences truly scrupulous' (with its obvious implication there were dissenting consciences that were not), appeared in a number of Tory addresses.[87] Similarly, a number of addresses also followed Sacheverell in singling out dissenting academies as one of the particular evils of the post-revolutionary landscape.[88] This was not only evident in Tory addresses but also those that were clearly Whig in political sympathy. The Whig variant address from Kent stated that they would in future elect representatives who would not only be loyal to the Queen but would protect the State from 'the more dangerous Perils of False and Seditious Brethren at Home', reversing Sacheverell's meaning and identifying the real fifth column as being the Tories and their High Church supporters.[89]

The use of such tactics of inversion in part helps explain Defoe's comments about the instability of meaning within the addresses of 1710, discussed in greater detail in Chapter seven.[90] Yet the employment of Sacheverell's own phrases within these texts also says something about their ambiguity and variety. Two further addresses, one from the grand jury of Durham, the other from Hampshire, made use of the phrase 'consciences truly scrupulous'. The Durham address, however, used this phrase in the context of promising to elect representatives who would uphold toleration as defined by law and also included sentences that seemed to question the shrills cries of 'the Church in danger', which were a stereotypical feature of pro-Sacheverell addresses.[91] The address from Hampshire similarly sought to find a compromise between political extremes: while it followed Sacheverell in connecting resistance theory with regicide, it also, unlike other Tory addresses which preferred not to talk of 1688 as a revolution at all, thanked God for 'all the advantages of the late Happy Revolution'. Similarly, it spoke of Queen Anne's title as founded on both hereditary right and statute law, and explicitly abjured the Pretender and upheld the Hanoverian succession.[92]

These two texts reflected the way in which, in broader terms, the addresses of 1710 represented a more equivocal demonstration of support for the established Church and the doctrines of non-resistance and passive obedience than has sometimes been acknowledged. Morphew marketed the first part of his collection of these addresses as demonstrating the 'Sense of the Kingdom ... for Her Majesty's *Hereditary Title* to the Throne'. The presentation of the compendium, with a different typeface (italic or Gothic) used for pro and anti-Sacheverell texts, suggested a starkly bifurcated political landscape. This typographical representation of political division was copied in Whig compendia as well.[93]

Many of the addresses Morphew featured, however, and not just those identified as Whig counter-addresses, did not specifically mention the Queen's right by lineal descent.[94] In fact, addresses which based the Queen's title solely on hereditary right, such as that from St Albans which seemed to revive the language of divine right absolutism, were rare (and, if reports are to be believed, also unpopular with Anne herself).[95]

In part, the majority of addresses were following the shifts in Sacheverell's own position: as Brian Cowan has argued, the doctor's speech at his trial carefully repackaged him as a more moderate figure who supported the Hanoverian succession and disclaimed any attempt to disparage the revolution of 1688.[96] Similarly, none of those addresses identified as being Whiggish in outlook attempted to claim that the Queen's title was established on the basis of some sort of Lockeian contract or gave explicit support to the right of resistance. The closest any of them came was the Kent address's statement that by Anne's 'undoubted title' they meant that 'Title which is founded on the Happy Revolution, and confirm'd by the indisputable Authority of Parliament'.[97] While we can see this as strategic, a way of countering the accusations of those such as the addressers of Fowey in Cornwall who set themselves against those who claimed the Queen's title was 'the sole gift of the People', it was also consistent with much contemporary Whig political theory.[98] Acceptance of first William, then Anne and the Hanoverian dynasty was often grounded upon a combination of divine providence, the recognition of their title in statute law and on the historic fact of the revolution (but not necessarily any of the more radical philosophical conclusions that were sometimes drawn from it).[99] Consequently, the Lichfield address, which promised to elect only MPs who rejected the right of the people to depose and/or try their princes, was largely aimed at straw men.[100]

These addresses not only reflected a more moderate range of political opinions than some commentators claimed but also demonstrated forms of loyalty that were largely separate from party politics. For example, the address from the Stannary Parliament of Cornwall dwelt mainly on giving thanks to the Queen for her 'late Contract with us for our Tinn at the time of our Extreamest Difficultyes', while at the same time hoping that the Crown would consider the burdens placed on their industry by export duties and the 'late Duty upon Candles which most sensibly affects Or Adventures'.[101] The nearest that this and a similar address from the Stannary Court of Devon got to high politics was in expressing a hope for a peace which would help revive their trade.[102] Other addresses were so bland that it was hard to see what, if any, political position that corporation, borough or county was taking.[103] While addressing disputes such as that which took place in Shropshire showed clearly that party political divisions had an impact at a local level, other county addresses may have been produced as a result of nothing more than a desire to be seen to be as loyal, if not more so, than other counties and boroughs.

At the same time, in a politically volatile period, it was no more than good sense to hedge bets in terms of the content of the address. The Brecon address, for example, praised the Queen for her care of the Church, the achievement of the union of Scotland and England and for her army's victory against the French (all of which might suggest Whiggish sympathies). Yet, while praying for Christian union (in echo of Anne's own speech to Parliament), they also expressed their detestation of 'Atheistical, Disloyal and Republican principles'.[104] Other addresses revealed no more than a concern that their locality might be deemed insufficiently loyal. A second address from County Durham stated that since 'Our last Address to Your Majesty being only from our Quarter-Sessions; we, Your Majesty's most Loyal and Obedient Subjects, think it our Duty, once more, to renew our former Assurances, at this greater, and more solemn Time of our Assizes'.[105]

As will be discussed in more detail in Chapter six, these assurances of loyalty were important: the presentation of an address represented an opportunity for preferment and/or the securing of royal favour upon the county and borough.[106] While the *Observator*, as we have seen, could suggest that such even-handed promises of loyalty were politically suspect for what they did not say, we might see these 'non-aligned' addresses as simply sensibly cautious: as we have already seen, the very public nature of loyal addressing meant that it was very easy for individuals and localities to over-commit themselves to a particular party or regime, leading to the addressers being brought to book (or at the very least publicly shamed) at a later date when political circumstances had changed.[107]

CONCLUSION

The addresses of 1710, while undeniably helping to deliver an election victory for the Tories, bringing down the Whig ministry and halting hostilities with France, were not all of a piece. As we have seen, though counter-addresses represented a small minority of those published, many others deemed 'loyal' by Tory printers and newsletter writers demonstrated a much less clear commitment to the goals of Sacheverell and his supporters. Moreover, even though many of these addresses did display a keen awareness not only of the political principles under dispute but also of the content of Sacheverell's sermon and the course of his trial, there were others that seemed almost entirely detached from the controversy. While the variety of these addresses reinforces the impression that generally these texts remained local productions and were not in any coherent way directed/dictated from the centre, the amount of variation did not render these addresses so unstable as to be meaningless. Rather, the nature of the rhetorical strategies used in these addresses meant that particular identities were often heavily contested: Whigs could contend that the real 'false brethren' were Tory crypto-Jacobites, Tories and Churchmen could argue that the real 'Jacobites' were those adherents of 'revolution principles' who would only acknowledge a hereditary right in the Pretender.

The use of these tactics of inversion was not just a way of avoiding expressing support for dangerous positions, whether that was the right of resistance or indefeasible hereditary succession. It also revealed the relatively moderate ideological positions that were incorporated within the political mainstream – Whigs who saw a Protestant monarchy essentially based on a mixture of providence, the law and history; and Tories who acknowledged the goodness of the revolution and supported the Hanoverian succession but who chose to view the fruits of 1688, such as the Toleration act, in different terms from their Whig opponents. As Robert Harley's (admittedly self-serving) plea for moderation, *Faults on both sides*, noted, many of the addresses of 1710 effectively tilted at a whole set of windmills:

> What a Noise do they make with their Nonsensical Addresses and Furious Insolent Sermons? We know that the Queen has both an Hereditary and Parliamentary Title, but without the later She had not now so happily fill'd the Throne: What do they mean then by crying up the Hereditary, and slighting the Parliamentary Title? And what Nonsense is it in them to lay so great Stress on the former, and yet at the same time to profess their Adherence to the Succession in the House of Hanover, which can pretend to no Claim but by Act of Parliament? But, if their own ignorant Partizans don't see, we know what the Contrivers intend by it; for one of their own Writers has told us plainly, that *Hereditary Right, and the Natural Allegiance due to it, is a stubborn thing, and will not bend even to an Act of Parliament, nor to a thousand Usurpations*. This is plain enough without a Comment. Why do they make such an Out-cry against Rebellion and Rebellious Principles, when (except the notorious *Jacobites* who herd with them, and what has lately appear'd on their own side) the whole Nation is full of Duty, Loyalty, and Hearty Affection to Her Majesty? To what end do they cry out against Republicans, when at this day there is not the least Appearance of any Party that affect any Change of the Establish'd Government?[108]

In 1701, an addressing campaign had been used successfully to support war with France and elect a Whig ministry. Nine years later, the Tories used the same tactic to remove the Whigs from office and bring a halt to that same conflict. In both instances, the addresses themselves reflected a certain degree of amnesia about recent public declarations of loyalty. For Defoe and for other critics of mass addressing, this meant that these texts were of minimal value in discerning the sense of the nation. The rapid switch in public loyalty from regime to regime, party to party provided 'evident Testimonies that Addressing the Sovereigns in England, from the Towns, Corporations, Counties, Grand Juries, &c. has for many Years past, been reckoned to stand for nothing; and is therefore, by Custom determin'd to be of no Manner of Signification'.[109]

Yet, if addressing campaigns during the first decade of the eighteenth century appeared to show a political nation whose affiliations fluctuated dramatically, this was no more than was suggested by the polls.[110] Moreover, as will be shown in Chapter seven, Defoe's image of a nation, which had lost all political faithfulness and whose political symbolism had ceased to signify anything constant, was itself a studied polemical stance: the adoption of the persona of the historian removed from party struggles. Employing this strategy allowed the partisan writer Defoe to appear objective as he questioned in its entirety the significance of a highly popular opposition addressing campaign. These attacks on addressing also revealed the limits of what was deemed legitimate popular political activity. The strident tone of Defoe's *Legion*, and the vociferous responses it generated belied a consensus over parliamentary petitioning, which essentially supported the limitations placed on mass subscriptional activity after the Restoration. This would be reemphasised following the succession of George I, as loyal addresses repeatedly denounced rioting and popular 'tumults' and linked them directly with Jacobite insurrection.[111] Yet, as this use of addresses to condemn and contain other forms of popular political activity indicates, even as harsh a critic of addresses as Defoe was reluctant to completely disown a political practice that had proved very useful to the Whigs at the turn of the eighteenth century and would prove so again in the wake of the Hanoverian succession.

NOTES

1. BL, Add MS. 70421, f. 135v–136, John Dyer's newsletters, 1709–1710 – the anecdote runs backwards in this newsletter. For Dyer's newsletters, see A. W. Barber, ' "It is not easy what to say of our condition, much less to write it." The Continued Importance of Scribal News in the Early 18th Century', *Parliamentary History*, 32 (2013), 293–316.
2. G. Holmes, *The Trial of Dr. Sacheverell* (London: Eyre Methuen, 1973), p. 250. For the trial see now also B. Cowan, *The State Trial of Doctor Henry Sacheverell* (Chichester: Wiley-Blackwell, 2012) and M. Knights (ed.), *Faction Displayed: Reconsidering the Impeachment of Dr Henry Sacheverell* (Chichester: Wiley-Blackwell, 2012), also published as *Parliamentary History*, 31 (2012). For literary discussions, L. Horsley, ' "Vox Populi" in the Political Literature of 1710', *Huntington Library Quarterly*, 38 (1975), 335–53. For the broader political background, besides the titles listed in the notes below see G. Holmes, *The Making of a Great Power: Late Stuart and Early Georgian Britain, 1660–1722* (London: Longman, 1993).
3. [Defoe], *A new test*, p. 2.
4. M. Knights, 'Introduction: the view from 1710', *Parliamentary History*, 31 (2012), 1–15 at 13–15.
5. Knights, *Representation and Misrepresentation*, ch. 3, esp. pp. 149–62.

6   Zaret, 'Petitions and the invention of public opinion'; Zaret, *Origins of Democratic Culture*, esp. ch. 8.
7   Holmes, *Sacheverell*, p. 238.
8   See. M. Goldie, 'The English system of liberty', in Goldie and R. Wokler (eds), *The Cambridge History of Eighteenth-Century Political Thought* (Cambridge: Cambridge University Press, 2006), pp. 40–78 at pp. 61–2; Knights, 'Participation and representation', pp. 44–51; J. A. W. Gunn, *Beyond Liberty and Property: The Process of Self-Recognition in Eighteenth-Century Political Thought* (Montreal: McGill-Queen's University Press, 1983), pp. 75–8; J. P. Kenyon, *Revolution Principles: The Politics of Party 1689–1720* (Cambridge: Cambridge University Press, 1977), pp. 57–60.
9   H. Mackworth, *A vindication of the rights of the Commons of England* (1701), p. 8.
10 [C. Davenant], *The true picture of a modern Whig* (1701), p. 41.
11 *Political and Economic Writings of Daniel Defoe*, eds. W.R. Owens and P. N. Furbanks (8 vols, London: Pickering and Chatto, 2000), ii, p. 45.
12 Ibid., ii, 42.
13 D. Defoe, *The original power of the collective body of the people of England, examined and asserted* (1702), p. 4.
14 Ibid., p. 17.
15 *Jura populi Anglicani*, p. 40.
16 Ibid., p. 25.
17 P. R. Backscheider, *Daniel Defoe: His Life* (London: Johns Hopkins Press, 1989), p. 81.
18 M. Schonhorn, *Defoe's Politics: Parliament, Power, Kingship and Robinson Crusoe* (Cambridge: Cambridge University Press, 1991), pp. 82–3.
19 Knights, *Representation and Misrepresentation*, pp. 132–3.
20 *Jura populi Anglicani*, p. 27; Defoe, *Political and Economic Writings*, ii., pp. 56,63; Defoe, *Original power*, p. 4.
21 *Jura populi Anglicani*, p. 36.
22 Mackworth, *Vindication*, p. 39.
23 J. Tully, 'Locke', in J. H. Burns (ed.), with M. Goldie, *The Cambridge History of Political Thought* (Cambridge: Cambridge University Press, 1991), ch. 21, at p. 629, Schonhorn, *Defoe's Politics*, pp. 80–1.
24 Defoe, *Original power*, p. 18.
25 Defoe, *Political and Economic Writings*, ii, p. 52.
26 Jonathan Swift, *A discourse of the contests and dissentions between the nobles and the commons in Athens and Rome with the consequences they had upon both those states*, Frank H. Ellis (ed.) (Oxford: Clarendon Press, 1967), p. 106.
27 *London Gazette*, 17–20 November 1701, no. 3759.
28 *The Legionites plot* (1702), p. 20.
29 *London Gazette*, 6–10 November 1701, no. 3756.
30 *London Gazette*, 10–13 November 1701, no. 3757; (London dissenting ministers); *London Gazette*, 17–20 November 1701, no. 3759 (Poor widows and children of clergymen); *London Gazette*, 1–4 December 1701, no. 3763 (Presbyterian ministers of Northern Ireland).
31 Knights, 'Participation and representation', p. 51; and on election advice generally see Knights, *Representation and Misrepresentation*, ch. 4. See *The electors*

right asserted: with the advices and charges of several counties, cities and boroughs in England (1701), pp. 6, 10; Luttrell, v, pp. 115, 119 for examples. The fact that some new MPs were given the task of presenting their constituencies' addresses strengthened the impression that these representatives were bound to abide by the terms of these texts *London Gazette*, 1–5 January 1702, no. 3772, see address from Clitheroe.

32 Defoe, *Political and Economic Writings*, iv, p. 178.
33 *London Gazette*, 23–27 October 1701, no. 3752.
34 For examples, see a number of the addresses included within *London Gazette*, 6–10 November 1701, no. 3756 (especially University of Cambridge; New Woodstock; Minehead) and see below chs 6 & 7 for the language and performance of loyalty.
35 M. Knights, 'John Locke and post-revolutionary politics: electoral reform and the franchise', *Past and Present*, 213 (2011), 41–86.
36 www.historyofparliamentonline.org/volume/1690-1715/parliament/1701, accessed 17/03/2013.
37 Luttrell, v, pp. 100, 114.
38 *Mercure Historique et Politique, Contenant l'etat present de l'Europe, ce qui se passé dans toutes les Cours ... Mois de Decembre* (A la Haye, 1701), p. 644. The *Mercure* reprinted a number of English addresses in French translation that month but not that from the City of London, see pp. 652–69. See Chapter five for discussion of the circulation of texts of addresses in French manuscript newsletters.
39 *London Gazette*, 13–16 October 1701; no. 3749, see the Lincoln, Nottingham and New Windsor addresses; *London Gazette*, 20–23 October 1701, no. 3751, Gloucester address; *London Gazette*, 23–27 October 1701, no. 3752; Maidstone and Devizes addresses.
40 *London Gazette*, 30 October – 3 November 1701, no. 3754; See also address from West-Riding of Yorkshire *London Gazette*, 27–30 October 1701, no. 3753.
41 For Lydd, *Post Boy*, 21–23 October 1701, no. 1004; For Newcastle upon Tyne, *London Gazette*, 6–10 November 1701, no. 3756; For Durham, *London Gazette*, 17–20 November 1701, no. 3759; For London Baptists, *London Gazette*, 25–29 December 1701, no. 3770.
42 For the association of 1696 see, among others, S. Pincus *1688: The First Modern Revolution* (New Haven, CT: Yale University Press, 2009), ch. 14; Knights, *Representation and Misrepresentation*, pp. 154–9; E. Vallance, 'Loyal or rebellious? Protestant associations in England 1584–1696', *The Seventeenth Century*, 17 (2001), 1–24; D. Cressy, 'Binding the nation: the bonds of association, 1584 and 1696', in DeLloyd J. Guth and John W. McKenna (eds), *Tudor Rule and Revolution: Essays for G. R. Elton from his American Friends* (Cambridge: Cambridge University Press, 1982), pp. 217–34.
43 Vallance, *Revolutionary England and the National Covenant*, p. 202.
44 A feature of these addresses commented upon at the time in contrast to those being published in France: *Post Man and the Historical Account*, 24–26 November 1696, no. 242, 'sure I am, they have not boasted very much in publick of those bold [English] Addresses, since they have not been printed in our Gazette, which was a very good way to spread it. We stand upon another bottom than France and therefore the French Gazetteer will never forget to give a long account of

the Audience the French King gives to the States of Languedoc and Britanny, because it is necessary for them.'
45 *A list of one unanimous club of members of the late Parliament, Nov 11. 1701, that met at the Vine Tavern in Long Acre.* (1701), p. 1.
46 The amnesia was perhaps all the more surprising given the currency of the term 'association' in political discourse in 1701–2, Gunn, *Beyond Liberty and Property*, p. 45; [Charles Leslie, sometimes attributed to Sacheverell], *The New Association* (1702), p. 12 which proposed imposing a loyalty test instead on dissenters. The 1701 Act for the Further Security of His Majesties Person revised the association of 1696 to account for James II's death, thereby retaining it as a requirement for office-holders at least, *Statutes of the Realm*, ed. Raithby, vii, pp. 747–50.
47 See for example the Newcastle upon Tyne address noted above which restricted its political commentary to the years after 1688.
48 *London Gazette*, 13–16 October 1701, no. 3749.
49 Luttrell, v. p. 121.
50 Knights, *Representation and Misrepresentation*, pp. 125–6.
51 Knights, 'The view from 1710', 7–8.
52 For a chronology of Sacheverell's career see Cowan, *State Trial*, ch. 2.
53 Holmes, *Sacheverell*, p. 238. My summary of Sacheverell's case and sermon is based on W. A. Speck, 'Sacheverell, Henry', *ODNB*.
54 Holmes, *Sacheverell*, pp. 141–8, pp. 243–4.
55 John Morphew, *A collection of the addresses which have been presented to the queen, since the impeachment of the Reverend Dr. Henry Sacheverell* (pt 1, 1710, pt 2, 1711); A. Boyer, *The history of the reign of Queen Anne digested into Annals, year the ninth* (1711), p. 165. For these addresses, see also J. Miller, *Cities Divided: Politics and Religion in English Provincial Towns, 1660–1722* (Oxford: Oxford University Press, 2007), pp. 269–74.
56 Boyer, *Annals*, p. 159.
57 Morphew, *Addresses*, pt 1 p. 6; *Post Boy*, 22–25 April 1710, no. 2332.
58 Morphew, *Addresses*, pt 2, p. 31; *Post Boy*, 17–19 August 1710, no. 2382.
59 Morphew, *Addresses* pt 1., p. 21.
60 J. Hoppit, *A Land of Liberty? England 1689–1727* (Oxford: Oxford University Press, 2000), pp. 302–3 also reflects on the importance of the language of passive obedience and hereditary right to successful Tory election propaganda.
61 Nicholas Rogers, *Whigs and Cities, Popular Politics in the Age of Walpole and Pitt* (Oxford: Oxford University Press, 1989), p. 365; H. Owen and J. B. Blakeway, *A History of Shrewsbury* (London: Harding, Lepard & Co., 1825) pp. 502–3 details the more enthusiastic reception he received elsewhere.
62 *The Post Man and Historical Account*, 8–11 April 1710, no. 1869; For Yewde see also P. Monod, *Jacobitism and the English People 1688–1788* (Cambridge: Cambridge University Press, 1993), pp. 171–2; Stuart Handley, 'Shropshire', in E. Cruickshanks, S. Handley, and D. Hayton (eds), *The House of Commons 1690–1715* (Cambridge: Cambridge University Press, 2002) www.historyofparliamentonline.org/volume/1690-1715/constituencies/shropshire, accessed 2 Aug 2017.
63 TNA SP 34/12/36 f. 62–3; A. A. Hanham, 'Lechmere, Nicholas, Baron Lechmere' *ODNB*; Lechmere was in Shrewsbury as part of his legal duties on the Oxford

circuit (he also met with hostility in Ludlow and Stafford), Cruickshanks, Handley and Hayton (eds), *House of Commons*, p. 603.
64 TNA SP 34/12/38 f. 65.
65 *Observator*, 10–13 May 1710, no. 34.
66 *A letter to the Right Honourable the Earl of Bradford, Lord Lieutenant of the county of Salop* (1710); *Post Man and the Historical Account*, 4–6 May 1710, no. 1880.
67 See [John Oldmixon], *History of Addresses* 2nd edn (1710), pp. 257–60; *Mercure historique et politique ... mois de Juin* (A la Haye, 1710), p. 641; *Europische Mercurius* (Amsterdam, 1710), p. 286.
68 Morphew, *Addresses*, pt 2, p. 5. BL 4705 g.16.
69 BL Add MS 70421 f. 170, John Dyer's newsletters, 20 July 1710. It is worth noting that most of the original addresses in BL Add MS Ch. 76109–23 either show evidence of having seals attached or, in the case of Appleby, still have them affixed.
70 Morphew, *Addresses*, pt 2.,p. 20; BL Lansdowne MS 849 f. 97 contains another address 'supposed from Salop', Whiggish in tone but with a different text from that printed in Morphew's collection. This attacked 'Modish Addressors' who only spoke of the Queen's 'Hereditary Title' while they, in contrast, were ready to state that the throne belonged to her as result of the 'joyful Revolution' and the Act of Settlement. The addressers also promised never to impose upon her majesty with 'any Clandestine & Surreptitious Addresses' but only to present those that had been, like this, signed in open session and to the sense of all subscribers.
71 TNA SP 34/12/37 f. 64; further evidence of this can be seen in Morphew's repeated request that readers of his serial collections of addresses send him texts as soon as they came to hand, and by the combination of periodical and book publication that he utilised.
72 Morphew, *Addresses*, pt 2, p. 34.
73 BL Add MS. 70421, f. 203v, John Dyer's newsletters, 31 August 1710; The county, which typically had split representation, chose two Tories in 1710, partly as a result of successful local propaganda campaign which saw circulars sent to motivate local clergy to vote for the Tory candidates, *VCH Shropshire*, iii, p. 258.
74 Morphew, *Addresses*, pt 2, p. 30 – presented on 21 August 1710.
75 BL. Add MS. 70421, f. 211–212, John Dyer's newsletters, 9 September 1710; Morphew, *Addresses*, pt 2, p. 34.
76 For the texts of Whig addresses see Morphew, *Addresses*, pt 1 p. 4 (City of London Lieutenancy and City of Gloucester); pt 1 p. 8 (Worcestershire address); pt 1, p. 12 (Hampshire address); pt 1, p. 16 (Westminster Justices); pt 1, p. 20 (Berkshire and Middlesex); pt 1, p. 24 (Northamptonshire address); pt 1, p. 32 (Wiltshire address); pt 1, p. 36 (Pembrokeshire address); pt 1, p. 47 (City of Norwich address); pt 2, p. 12 (Hertford and West-riding Yorks); p. 2, p. 15 (Hyth address); pt 2, p. 16 (Nottingham address); pt 2, p. 20 (Shropshire address); pt 2, p. 23 (Isle of Ely); pt 2, p. 24 (Kent address); pt 2, p. 28 (Cambridge address); pt 2, p. 36 (Chester address). For original texts see BL Add MS Ch. 76111 (Middlesex address); Add MS Ch. 76112 (Northamptonshire address); Add MS Ch. 76113 (Pembrokeshire address); Add MS Ch. 76114 (Wiltshire address); Add MS Ch. 76115 (Worcestershire address); Add MS Ch. 76118 (City of Gloucester); Add. MS. Ch. 76121 (Norwich); Add. MS. Ch. 76122 (Wallingford, Berks); Add MS Ch. 76123 (Westminster JPs). Dyer reproduced a Whig address from

Berwick-upon-Tweed, Add MS 70421 f. 185v, John Dyer's newsletters, 5 August 1710. See also NRO MC 42/136, 527 X4 for a draft Whig address to the Queen.

77 BL Add MS 70421, f. 78, John Dyer's newsletters, 10 April 1710. Dyer's comments were supported by Oldmixon who claimed that the Queen herself personally intervened to prevent the publication of the Gloucestershire address, Oldmixon, *History of Addresses pt 2.* (1711), p. 29.

78 *London Gazette*, 22–24 August 1710, no. 4734 (address from London clergy). *Post Boy* 19–22 August 1710, no. 2383 claimed that a number of the clergy refused to sign this address. Dyer gave the names of the refusers as 'Dr. Barton, & Mr. Baker, and those wch did not appear to ye Bishops Sumons were Dr. Kennet [Dr.] Bradford, Dr. Hancock, & Mr. Hoadly', Add MS 70421 f.198, John Dyer's newsletters, 24 August 1710.

79 *Review*, 18 May 1710, no. 23; Very similar accusations were made on the Tory side – see Dyer's comments on the counter-address from Worcester signed by 'Presbiterians, Anabaptists, Occasionall men, Porters, Scavingers, Journeymen, Weavers & all Riffe Raffe yt can be procured for love or money so yt it is Joakingly called ye begging Address', BL Add MS 70421 f. 208, John Dyer's newsletters, 5 September 1710.

80 *Flying Post*, 13 May 1710 referred to and refuted in *Post Boy*, 6–8 June 1710, no. 2351.

81 *Review*, 13 July 1710, no. 47.

82 *Observator*, 22–26 April 1710, no. 29.

83 Add MS 70421 f. 212, John Dyer's newsletters, 9 September 1710; *Post Boy* 2–4 May 1710, 2336.

84 *Observator*, 12–15 July 1710, no. 52. See also the earlier commentary on the University of Oxford's address *Observator*, 6–10 May 1710, no. 33 and *An Address to the Oxfordshire Addressors* (1710).

85 *Supplement*, 14–17 April 1710, no. 352; *Supplement*, 19–21 April 1710, no. 354.

86 For the former Morphew, *Addresses* pt 2, p. 12, for the latter see ibid,. pt 1, p. 37, Orford corporation and pt 2, p. 1, Coventry clergy.

87 Morphew, *Addresses*, pt 1, p. 2 (City of London); pt 1, p. 10 (City of Westminster); pt 1, p. 17 (Westbury, Wiltshire); pt 1, p. 21 (University of Oxford – here 'truly Tender'); pt 1, p. 22 (Clitheroe, Lancashire); pt 1, p. 29. (Wallingford); pt 1, p. 35 (Haverfordwest), pt 2, p. 3 (New Windsor); pt 2, p. 31 (County Durham); pt 2, p. 34 (Shropshire); pt 2, p. 35 (City of York).

88 Ibid., pt 1, p. 45 (City of Hereford); pt 2, p. 30 (Shropshire clergy).

89 Ibid., pt 2, p. 24 For disputes in Canterbury over loyal addresses see Knights, *Representation and Misrepresentation*, pp. 141–2.

90 For inversion in partisan discourse, see Ibid., p. 243.

91 Morphew, *Addresses*, pt 1., p. 11.

92 Ibid., pt 2., p. 17.

93 See *A second test offer'd to the electors ... impartially COLLECTED out of the ADDRESSES of both parties* (1710). This used a key to differentiate between the types of addresses: 'Addresses mark'd H are what's call'd High, and those L Low-Church' (p. 3).

94 Ibid., pt 1, p. 6 (Warwickshire); pt 1, p. 7 (Exeter); pt 1, p. 12 (Suffolk) for examples. Dyer referred to the Suffolk address as of 'soe Low a Straine yt [hole torn in page here] has[?] disapp[oin]ted everybodyes extacta-tion from yt Loyall County'. BL

Add MS 70421, f. 102, John Dyer's newsletters, 2 May 1710, though in his next newsletter (4 May) f. 103v., Dyer stated that 'upon 2d reading [it] appeares a very Loyall one'.

95   Morphew, *Addresses*, pt 1, p. 25. The St Albans address spoke of Anne's title as being derived from the 'King of Kings alone; and that therefore Your Majesty is accountable to no Power on Earth, except to Your own Conscience'. It was attacked by the *Observator*, 17–20 May 1710, no. 36. Anne reportedly asked for the wording of a similar address from the City of London to be changed when it was presented to her, see A. Somerset, *Queen Anne: The Politics of Passion* (Harper Press: London, 2012), p. 200.

96   B. Cowan, 'The spin doctor: Sacheverell's trial speech and political performance in the divided society', *Parliamentary History*, 31 (2012), 28–46 at 29–30.

97   Morphew, *Addresses*, pt 2, p. 24. And see also the Grand Jury of Cheshire address which condemned those who claimed that the 'Means of Revolution were unjust, or represent the Principles of it as Antimonarchical', ibid., pt 2, p. 36.

98   Ibid., pt 2, p. 31.

99   See, for example, the popularity of the former non-juror William Higden's *A View of the English Constitution* (1709) which deployed a plethora of legal precedents to demonstrate the legitimacy of giving allegiance to de facto rulers, Vallance 'William Higden', *ODNB*; and Vallance, 'The decline of conscience as a political guide: William Higden's view of the English constitution 1709', in H. E. Braun and E. Vallance (eds), *The Contexts of Conscience in the Early Modern World* (Palgrave: Basingstoke, 2004), ch. 6. The complexities of the debates around Anne's succession have recently been explored in greater detail by Joseph Hone, J. Hone, *Literature and Party Politics at the Accession of Queen Anne* (Oxford: Oxford University Press, 2017).

100 Morphew, *Addresses*, pt 1, p. 14.

101 BL Add MS Ch. 76109.

102 BL Add MS Ch. 76110 for the Devon address.

103 See for example the Coventry address Add MS Ch. 76118 or that from Ipswich Add MS. Ch. 76119. The Coventry address in MS form appears different from that reproduced in Morphew, *Addresses*, pt 1, p. 16 which referred to the actions of some 'unquiet spirits' prompting another address – presumably a reference to the address from Coventry featured on pt 1., p. 8 of Morphew with its references to 'levelling Republicans' 'Atheists' and 'Heretics'.

104 Morphew, *Addresses*, pt 1, p. 26. For a similarly vague address see that Monmouth in ibid., pt 1, p. 46.

105 Ibid, pt 2, p. 31.

106 See the attention paid in the *Post Boy* to correct an address published with no indication of the presenter: 27–29 June 1710, no. 2360 and see below Chapter six on connections between patronage, preferment and addressing.

107 See Chapter six.

108 [Simon Clement], *Faults on both sides* (1710), p. 47. On the authorship of this tract see Paul B. Patterson, 'Harley, Defoe, Trapp and the "Faults on both sides" controversy', *Albion*, 11 (1979), 128–42.

109 [Defoe], *A new test*, p. 16.

110 On the increasingly popular, if not populist, stance of the Tory party during this decade, see the comments in T. Harris, *Politics under the Later Stuarts: Party Conflict in a Divided Society, 1660–1715* (London: Longman, 1993), pp. 199–202.

111 See *Daily Courant*, 9 August 1715, no. 4303 (Exeter); *Flying Post or The Post Master*, 9–11 August 1715, no. 3682 (shire of Edinburgh); *Daily Courant*, 13 August 1715, no. 4307 (Aldborough, Yorkshire) for just three examples of many in 1715.

Chapter 5

Who were the 'public'? Identifying the addressers

The ubiquity of petitioning activity in early modern England and the wealth of surviving manuscript petitions is in stark contrast to the scarcity of manuscript loyal addresses. In many cases, those that do survive are drafts or fair copies without subscriptions. Extant manuscript addresses with subscriptions, such as the address from the 'well-affected' of Leicestershire to Richard Cromwell explored in detail below, demonstrate that though the language of status was critical to loyal addresses, such descriptions often disguised the more mixed background of the subscribers. The surviving manuscript evidence, however, tells us not only about who subscribed to these texts but also how these addresses were produced and their subscriptions obtained.

This chapter will begin by exploring the nature of surviving manuscript addresses and what these can tell us about addressing activity before moving on to a detailed examination of the 3,000 subscribers who added their names to the Leicestershire address to Richard Cromwell. By exploring this return, it is possible not only to map the geography of support for Richard Cromwell's Protectorate across the county, but also to explore at a micro level the political divisions revealed by his succession. Unusually, the Leicestershire address incorporated two variant texts, one of which offered a much more equivocal endorsement of the Protectoral regime. These variant texts may also have been the product of confessional divisions within the county. While the analysis of this address demonstrates the considerable social depth of some addressing activity, including those on the margins of society, the absence of women from this and other manuscript addresses highlights a key difference between addressing and mass petitioning.

The chapter will then move on to discuss how addressing activity shifted from such overt displays of 'popularity' during the interregnum to reasserting social hierarchy in congratulatory addresses to Charles II on his restoration to the throne in 1660. As will be shown, mass subscription nonetheless resurfaced as an addressing strategy from the 1680s onwards, as addressing once again came to be highly politicised. Subscriptional texts were a feature of post-revolutionary political culture as well, though, as we will see, mass subscription, especially to loyalty oaths and associations, was in tension with 'revolution principles'. While these changes in political culture were important, so too was a longer-standing consensus on the management of popular involvement in subscriptional activity, a consensus enshrined in law which predated the Restoration and survived intact well beyond the early modern period.

MANUSCRIPT ADDRESSES: THE SURVIVING EVIDENCE

The relatively limited numbers of surviving manuscript addresses are indicative of the different purposes of addresses in contrast to petitions. Thousands of loyal texts were reproduced in the pages of contemporary newsbooks and as separate broadsheets. The purpose of the address was primarily to display the loyalty of communities and the nation as a whole. Subscribing to an address, as we've already seen, was not without risk and it is also possible that deliberate destruction may explain the paucity of manuscript evidence: the Leicestershire address to Richard Cromwell, discussed in detail later, includes a number of folios where names have clearly been cut out, though whether by individuals wary of further recriminations or by later holograph signature collectors is not clear.[1] While the symbolic burning of the Northamptonshire address in 1661 may only have been of a facsimile (as with other emblems of the revolutionary period such as the Solemn League and Covenant), this occasion perhaps points to more extensive but secretive destruction of these records.[2]

Typically, what survives in local record offices are draft texts (usually without subscriptions) and fair copies (sometimes accompanied with the names of subscribers).[3] Subscriptions to surviving fair copies of addresses rarely exceed a few hundred names and sometimes feature a bare handful of signatories.[4] The positioning and number of names on these fair copies can give a deceptive picture of the subscription process: it is evident that in some cases names were added to fair copies though the individuals concerned signed at a later date.[5] The remaining drafts highlight the revising process before a final version of the text was agreed and made the public statement of that community. The drafting process could lead to the excision of potentially controversial statements or arguments.

As Derek Hirst has noted, the draft Gloucester address to Richard Cromwell featured claims that could be read to suggest that sovereignty resided with the people, an argument that was increasingly problematic in the late 1650s.[6] A later draft address from Gloucestershire Independents and Baptists, complete with the names of signatories, included a more pointed statement about the need for toleration to protect dissenters from legal prosecution by magistrates. This was dropped in the final draft and the support for greater toleration framed in the blander terms of liberty for tender consciences, perhaps as a way of avoiding antagonising local opinion.[7] The existence of variant drafts of an address could also point to political divisions within the community: the Guestling or Brotherhood of the Cinque Ports clearly produced two texts condemning the Rye House Plot in 1683, deciding by forty-three votes to twenty-six to have the first text engrossed on parchment.[8]

Draft addresses may also have been circulated both for their newsworthiness and to provide templates for other communities to adapt. The papers of the clerk and later mayor of Hastings, John Collier, contain a number of draft addresses in manuscript.[9] One address, from the justices, grand jury, clergy and freeholders of Kent to George I was sent to Collier by John Brewer, seemingly to offer an example for Hastings to follow.[10] These processes of circulation and imitation are further illustrated by an amended printed proclamation declaring George II king on the death of George I: Collier simply crossed out the words 'Lords Spiritual and Temporal' on the text, replacing them with the 'Mayor and Juratts of the Town & Port of Hastings'.[11] The preservation of fair copies with subscriptions in local archives may also have been a means of providing a resource that could be employed in any future instances where a public demonstration of loyalty was required. In the case of the fair copies of addresses from the borough of Lyme, produced in the 1680s, the desire to record subscriptions may have been borne out of civic pride: not only were fair copies of the texts of addresses and subscriptions kept but also manuscript transcriptions of press reports of the warm reception they received from Charles II and James II.[12]

As we have seen, from the very beginning, addresses were employed as propaganda for an international as well as national audience. In the early eighteenth century, addressing activity came to be closely connected to the dynastic struggles between the houses of Bourbon, Habsburg, Orange and Stuart. Addresses seemingly provided a European audience with a running commentary on public support for first the revolution settlement and then the Hanoverian succession. The texts of these addresses clearly circulated in manuscript as well as through European newsbooks. The Hanover papers which form part of the Stowe manuscripts in the British Library frequently include French translations of loyal addresses or English texts introduced in French.[13]

Where originals rather than drafts or copies of addresses exist (most frequently in State papers) we can gain an insight into subscription patterns and practices. Contemporaries were often sceptical about the means used to gather subscriptions and what this meant as a result about the quality of the addressers. As we have seen, alleging the use of bribery, subterfuge and intimidation in securing subscriptions to addresses was a common way of questioning their validity. As Roger North wrote of the petitions against the dissolution of the first Exclusion Parliament:

when this Hand-Tax was gathered, the Parchment Petition was sent up to a select Assembly or Club, who had the Administration in Charge. And there the Bead-Roll of Hands and Marks was cut off the several Petitions out of one County, except one, and to that all the rest were glued. So there appeared a fair Petition, entitled, *From all the Freeholders, &c.* And, the Roll being opened and extended, there appeared more Shapes than ever Dreams presented, looking as if they were alive, and like Insects, crawling about, or as the half formed equivocal vermin in the Mud of *Nile*; but looking closer, they all showed themselves no other than Hieroglyphics of Clowns.[14]

The presence of the signatures and marks of the unfranchised on addresses and petitions might though have been as much as a result of confusion as much as a desire to strengthen the impression of public support. As we will see, local officials sought guidance from government concerning from whom subscriptions should be sought.

Identifying who should subscribe was more difficult in the case of addresses where there was no established convention, in contrast to petitioning, that only those concerned in the matter of the address should add their names. One remedy was for addresses to come from bodies such as grand juries which had traditionally acted to represent the 'voice' of the county. This did not fully answer questions about the authenticity of such addresses as an expression of public opinion. Juries could be 'packed' by the sheriff, as occurred in Somerset in 1648 so that the body would support the policies of the radical John Pyne.[15] Borough corporations too could be heavily influenced by local magnates: in 1682 the Earl of Yarmouth ensured that the Norwich address to the Crown, surrendering the city's charter, would include a clause permitting the Crown to veto all civic elections (though Yarmouth notably did not 'thinke it prudent or Safe, to Insert the Names of the Corporation into ye body of this Instrument wch is a Record in ye Citty'). The revised address was approved by Yarmouth at a dinner also attended by the mayor, Bondish Freemen, the town clerk, Thomas Corie, two common council men and the Secretary of State Leoline Jenkins. Jenkins' presence again confirms the importance attached to government 'pre-approval' of the text of addresses.[16]

If this did not constitute direct central coordination, it certainly cast doubt on the claim of these addresses to offer unmediated expressions of public loyalty. Doubts about the legitimacy of these texts explain not only the preference for them to come from official bodies but also for addresses to be presented by individuals of requisite status and with the seal of the corporation or county affixed. These authenticating marks were especially important in the case of colonial addresses. For example, several addresses presented to Edward Hyde, Viscount Cornbury, in his role as governor of New York, were endorsed as 'billa vera' by his secretary Daniel Honan. These endorsements were particularly important at this moment in 1702 when Cornbury's government in New York and especially New Jersey was coming under severe public attack.[17]

Consequently, while far less abundant than printed addresses, manuscript texts can provide us with important evidence of the drafting process and occasionally give us an insight into how these texts were subscribed. We can also see how texts were circulated among local officers to aid the drafting and subscription process. This evidence suggests that the similarity of these texts was not necessarily a product of central manipulation and or coordination, but rather the result of communities adopting a successful template that had been employed elsewhere. Finally, manuscript evidence makes clear the importance of the original, handwritten and sealed texts in conveying the authoritative sense of a particular community. This was especially true in the case of communities far removed from the political centre, where direct, personal contact with the monarchy had to be substituted by clearly verified texts.

THE LEICESTERSHIRE ADDRESS

The majority of the surviving manuscript evidence, however, gives us little insight into processes of mass subscription. One surviving example of a mass address, though, containing roughly three thousand names, is the address of the 'well-affected inhabitants' of Leicestershire to Richard Cromwell. The manuscript survives as part of John Thurloe's papers within the Rawlinson MS held in the Bodleian Library. One possible reason for its preservation, as we will see, is that it provided a record of the names of potential political dissidents as well as loyalists.[18] The description of the addressers as 'well-affected' engaged with the common use of the term to describe those loyal to the Parliamentarian side. It was a description, as Rachel Weil has shown, which was often evidenced through material or physical aid, as much as internal, intellectual commitment to the cause. Allied with the relative lack of descriptions of rank and status in the text of the address (a notable contrast with post-Restoration addresses), it gave the impression of a community unified in thought and action to the Cromwellian regime.[19]

The names that immediately succeeded the text of the county's address added further to the sense of this as a sectional document. The subscriptions were led by the county's MPs, the regicide Francis Hacker and the Cromwellian baronet Thomas Beaumont, who was also selected to present the address to the Lord Protector.[20] Their names were followed by Thomas Pochin, named as one of the MPs for the county in 1654 and 1656.[21] Next were listed significant local committee-men, commissioners and militia officers such as John Goodman, William Hubbert, Clement Nedham (a former captain in Hacker's regiment), Thomas Cockram, Daniel Dale and William Hartropp.[22] The right hand column was filled with the names of godly ministers such as John Yaxley of Kibworth, accused after the Restoration of preaching and praying for the execution of Charles I.[23] Mapping the places where subscriptions were made reveals that coverage across the county was patchy to say the least. With the exception of the minister of Castle Donington, Thomas Smith, no

Who were the 'public'?

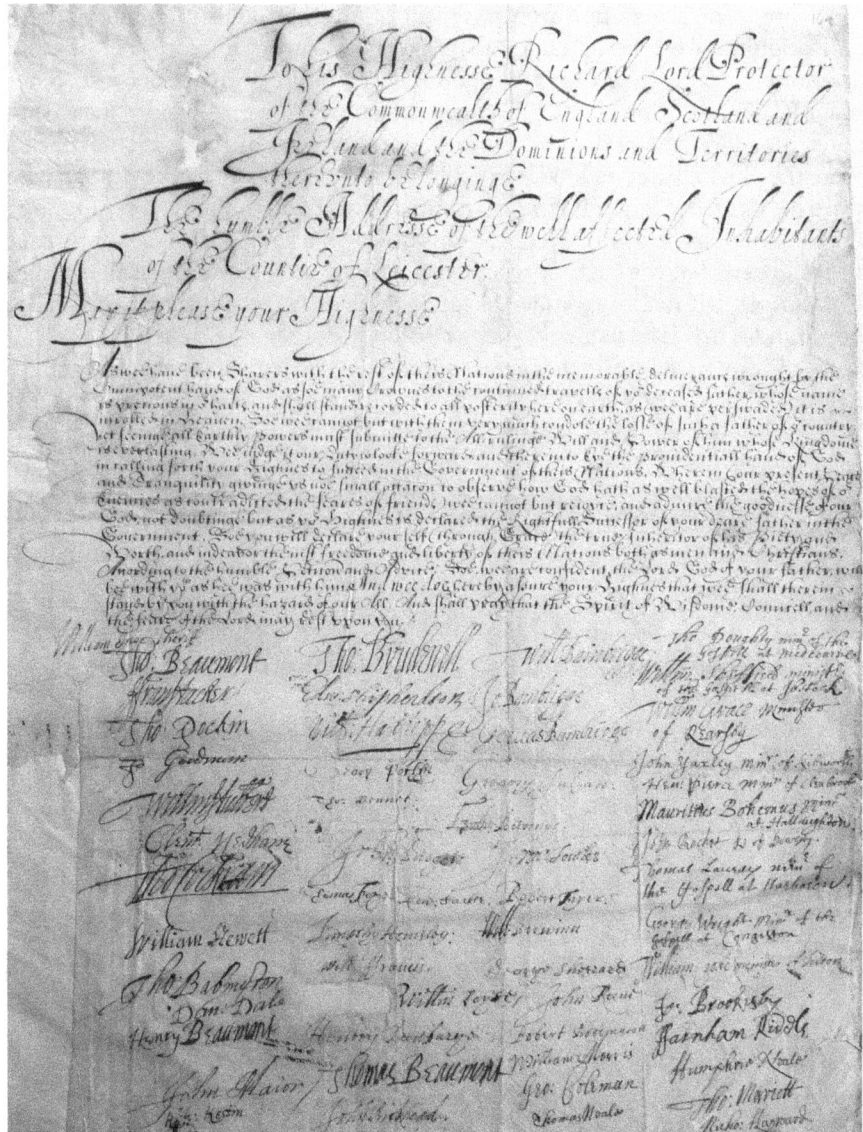

Figure 1. Loyal address of the 'well-affected' of Leicestershire to Richard Cromwell, Bodleian Library MS Rawl A61* f. 164–86

subscriptions appear to have been taken in the hundred of West Goscoate and in the adjoining hundred of East Goscoate, only a handful of places subscribed.[24] Major towns such as Ashby de la Zouch and Loughborough do not appear on the return, nor do they appear to have produced separate addresses.

Loyalty, memory and public opinion in England, 1658–1727

It should be stressed, however, that it is often difficult to identify where subscriptions were being taken: several folios feature no place names at all and other locations can only be identified through comparison with other records. For example, that the oath was subscribed in Twyford has been determined by the fact that the name of James Wright, minister for that parish after the Restoration, is surrounded by the names of other individuals who were local freeholders.[25] It is worth noting as well that though the first folio of the address claimed only to come from the 'well-affected' of the county, later pages stated that the text represented the town of Leicester as well, though comparison with other records has failed to identify any subscribers from the borough on this list.[26]

Significantly, though, the areas where no subscriptions were taken fit neatly with areas of known Royalist strength during the civil war.[27] The distribution of subscription across the county also fits reasonably well with the

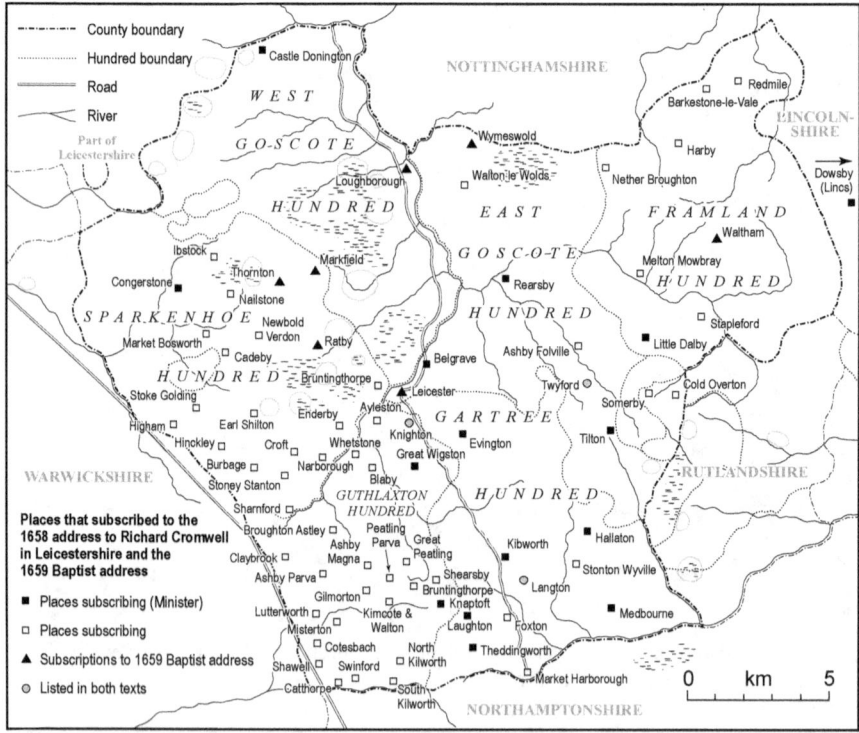

Figure 2. Distribution of subscription to 1658 address to Richard Cromwell in Leicestershire and 1659 Baptist address to the Rump (*A further testimony to truth ... by some baptized congregations, and other cordial lovers and assertors of the publick good old cause* (1659)).

geographical concentration of non-conformist conventicles recorded in a survey of 1669, which, according to R. H. Evans, predominately lay 'south of a line drawn roughly from Atherstone to Leicester and from Leicester to Market Harborough'.[28] Several subscribers to the address were identified as leading lay conventiclers in the same survey, including Elias Goadby, a mercer, and James Swinfield, a husbandman, both identified as frequenting a Presbyterian meeting at Ibstock.[29] Others, such as Humphrey Chapman and William Wykes or Wickes of Newbold Verdon were noted as having informed against 'delinquent' clergy.[30] This pattern and the leading signatories to the address might lead us to think that the text was the largely subscribed by Cromwellian loyalists. The absence of important local figures who were known critics of the Protectorate, such as the leading 'Commonwealthsman' Sir Arthur Hesilrige and the regicide Peter Temple, further strengthens this picture.[31] There was also a notable lack of subscriptions around Mountsorrel and Groby, the areas dominated respectively by the radical General Baptist Henry Danvers, and the aristocratic Grey family, both staunch critics of the Cromwellian regime.

Yet, closer examination of the returns qualifies the impression that the subscribers were clearly ideologically committed to the Protectorate. The first pages of the address appear to have been subscribed by those identified as figures of some status within the county. Yet, alongside Cromwellian MPs, office-holders and godly ministers, we can find the name of a family more commonly associated with the Royalist cause, the Brudenells.[32] The Thomas Brudenell who subscribed here was the cousin of Thomas, Lord Brudenell who had been committed to the Tower for levying war against Parliament in 1646 and whose estates had been sequestered for recusancy and delinquency.[33] Thomas Brudenell Esq. of Stonton Wyville's biography is harder to trace, but records suggest that he served as a JP during the interregnum and he was one of those appointed as a militia commissioner by the restored Rump in 1659.[34] Nonetheless, his son, also Thomas Brudenell, had served as a major in a Royalist regiment of horse at Ashby, and Brudenell senior's involvement with James Hay, Earl of Carlisle, in a composition case on behalf of the wife and children of his kinsman Robert Brudenell of Rutland, suggest that he also retained Royalist connections and perhaps sympathies.[35]

The initial impression that the address was the production of those 'well-affected' to the Protectorate is further complicated by exploring the backgrounds of the fifty-four ministers whose names feature within it. Some of the ministers had clear and strong ties to the Parliamentarian cause. Job Grey, rector of South Kilworth, was the brother of the Earl of Kent, who, along with Lord Grey of Groby, represented the major Parliamentarian aristocracy in the region.[36] John St Nicholas, rector of Lutterworth, had, like his brother, the lawyer and poet Thomas St Nicholas, been nominated to the Barebones Parliament of 1653.[37] Matthew Clarke, minister of Narborough, had served as a New Model Army chaplain and after the Restoration would be the most active dissenting preacher in the county.[38] It seems, however, that not all of the county's dissenting ministers could be brought to subscribe to this address. While we can identify fourteen subscribing clergymen who became non-conformists after the Restoration of monarchy, there were also some notable clerical absentees from the Leicestershire address. The Presbyterian minister Joseph Lee, rector of Cotesbach until his ejection in 1660, attracted considerable attention in the 1650s as John Moore, rector of Knaptoft's main disputant in a pamphlet battle over the benefits of enclosure. Lee did not subscribe to the Cromwellian address, although two men (Henry Wilde and Edward Smith), who he named as major enclosers in the area, did.[39]

Moreover, the number of dissenting ministers was exceeded by those clergymen, twenty-one in all, who retained their livings after 1660.[40] These included figures such as William Cotton, minister of Broughton Ashley. The son of Thomas Cotton Esq., Lord of Laughton manor, he inherited a twelve-room parsonage from his father and an annual income of £200. Thomas Cotton was identified as a supporter of Parliament and his son was a signatory to both the address of 1658 to Richard Cromwell and the 1659 address from Leicestershire ministers to the restored Commonwealth.[41] Yet, despite these previous public commitments to first the Protectorate and then the revived Rump, Cotton retained his living until his death in 1691 and has been identified by one historian as the epitome of the gentry clergyman in Restoration Leicestershire.[42]

Those clergy listed on the return even included several deemed 'scandalous' by the Parliamentarian authorities. Charges of drunkenness against ministers were commonplace and need to be viewed with some scepticism (Fiona McCall notes that 20 per cent of the charges against Leicestershire clergy related to drinking).[43] Some of these accusations, though, clearly had more substance to them. One subscriber to the Leicestershire address, Thomas Sturges, sometime vicar of Higham, was charged with drunkenness and causing scandal by the county committee in 1646. Sturges was accused of being too inebriated to officiate on repeated occasions, and of letting his family and others play games on a Sunday. While Sturges denied these charges, McCall has observed that this was qualified in his response by his 'prayer to God to bee of better Conversation'. It is notable too that Sturges did not regain his living post-Restoration, apparently for 'moral reasons', though he continued to reside in the area, dying in 1667.[44] Another subscriber to the Cromwellian address, Joseph Foster, curate under the sequestered minister of South Kibworth, William Hunt, was accused of being so 'much in drink', even at ten in the morning, that he was unable to read a warrant from the county committee.[45] We should note that these ministers were those deemed 'scandalous' rather than 'delinquent', so there is no clear evidence that active Royalist clergy subscribed the address.[46] Even so, though the Cromwellian return featured a smattering of the godly, it also included men such as

Edward Penton, minister of Bruntingthorpe, recorded by the Parliament's own surveyors as 'weak, negligent and worldly'.[47]

The varied character of the ministers subscribing to the address almost certainly reflects broader problems with religious provision within the county (and indeed nationally): as Bernard Capp has noted, by the early 1650s parishes in Leicester were dependent upon ministers from outside of the town for the provision of religious services.[48] Similarly, some parishes listed on the address, such Ayleston, appear to have had no incumbent at the time.[49] These considerations may also explain why four ministers who later conformed at the Restoration (Cotton, along with Thomas Jenkyns, John Pitts and Joseph Hulls or Hulse) were prepared to subscribe the 1659 address to the restored Rump.[50] The address was presented to the Commons as a sincere testimonial of the ministers' commitment to Parliament and a public denunciation of Sir George Booth's recent rising.[51] The text of the address itself, on the other hand, while bewailing the 'enraged malice of the old Common Enemy' was primarily concerned with the need for a 'Godly and Preaching Ministry', reflecting the inadequacies in religious provision in the county noted above.[52]

Looking beyond the clergy, the subscription returns suggest that the status of other subscribers was equally mixed. In some parishes, such as Gilmorton, there was a very close correlation between those who subscribed the 1658 address and the names that appeared on the Lady Day Hearth Tax return six years later, suggesting that those who took the address in these areas were the more significant householders.[53] Comparison with the Hearth Tax returns can also tell us something about the process of subscription. In the parish of Stoke Golding, even the order in which subscribers to the address were listed was almost identical to the ranking of those assessed for the Hearth Tax.[54] This suggests that, at least in this parish, subscriptions to the Cromwellian address were collected by going from door to door, perhaps also indicating a significant degree of official pressure to subscribe. Similar subscription patterns have been noted by John Walter and Alex Craven in the respective cases of the 1641 Protestation and the Engagement to the Commonwealth.[55] These similarities in administration are strengthened by the fact that both exercises appear to have been primarily the responsibility of constables: the John Cheney of Huncoat who subscribed the Cromwellian address also endorsed the parish's Hearth Tax return.[56] The targeting of householders may also explain the repetition of some names on returns. Gabriel Sleath appeared on the lists for both Gilmorton and Ashby Magna, perhaps because, as revealed by Hearth Tax records, he owned property in both parishes.[57]

In other towns and parishes that appear on the address, however, such as Melton Mowbray and Cadeby, the names appearing on the address were completely different from those on the 1664 Hearth Tax return.[58] In the case of a small parish such as Cadeby, listed as having fifty-three communicants

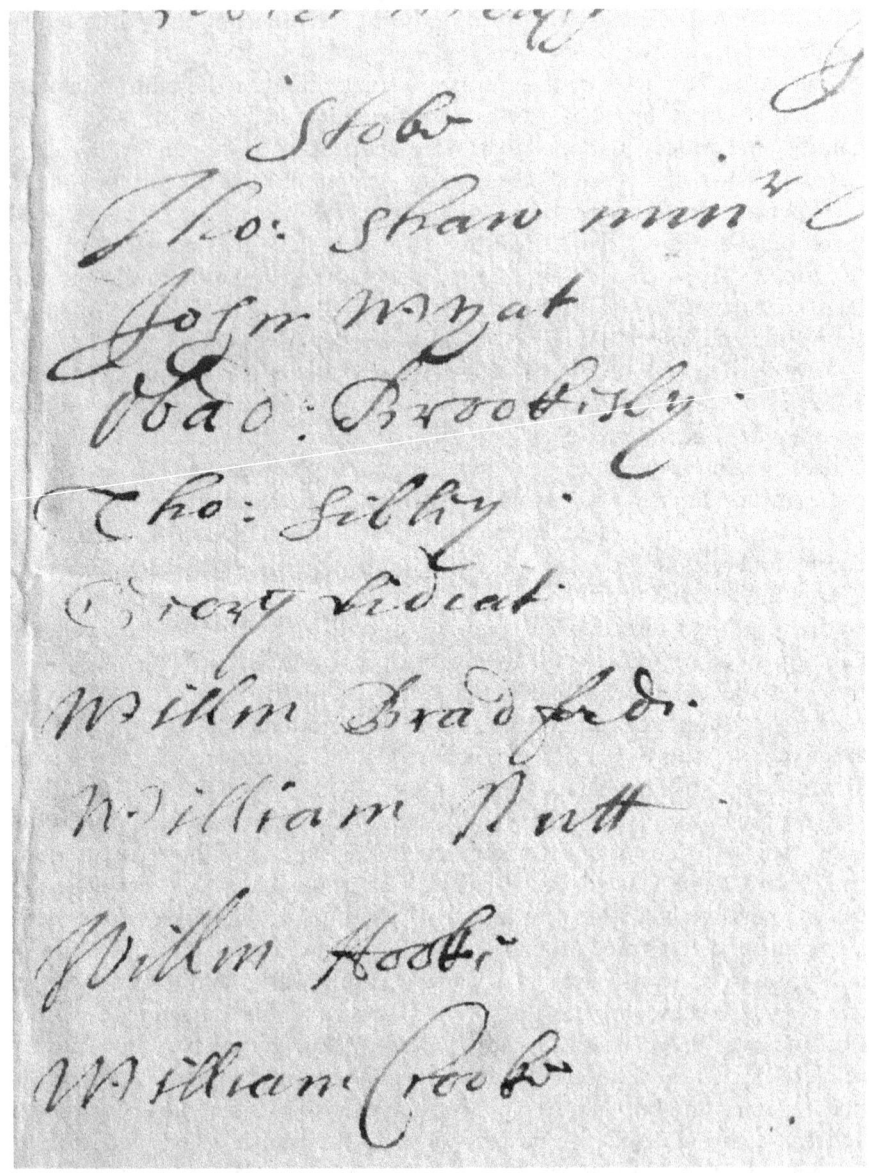

Figure 3a. Image of the Stoke Golding address, Bodleian Library MS Rawl A 61* f. 175

Who were the 'public'?

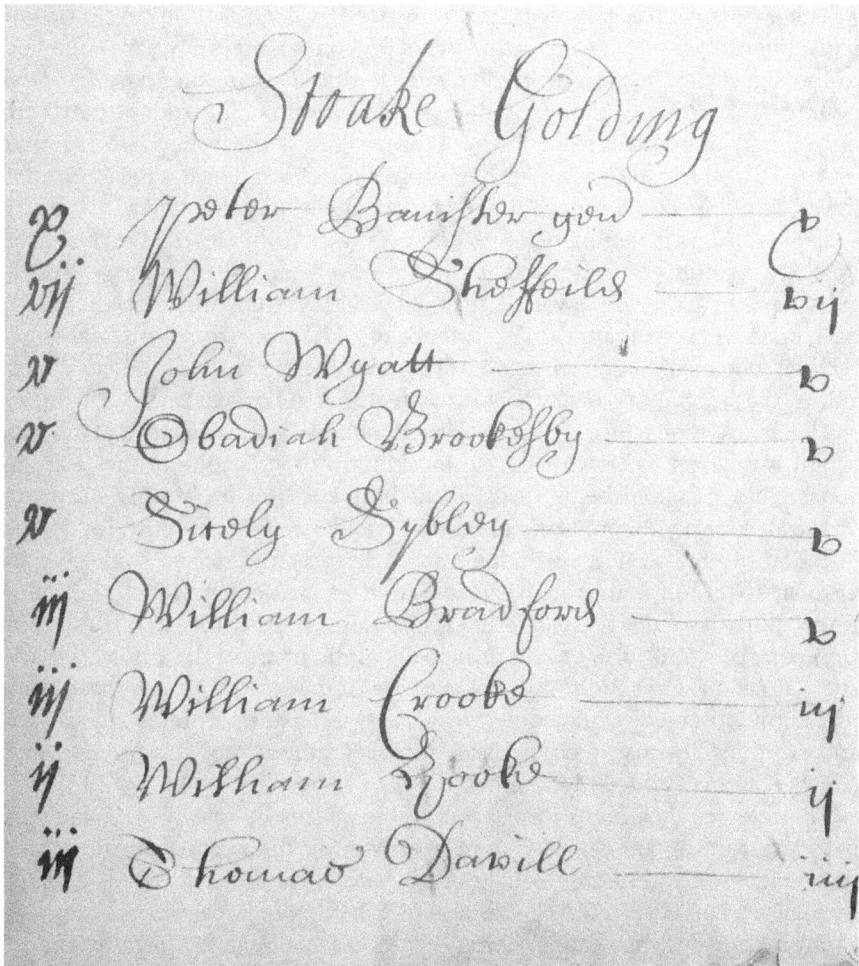

Figure 3b. Image of the Stoke Golding Hearth Tax return, The National Archives, Kew, E 179/251/4/8 f. 230

in the 1676 Compton Census, this is perhaps less surprising, but in the case of Melton Mowbray, listed as having some 1,078 communicants in the same census, it appears that significant sections of the population were either not approached to subscribe the Cromwellian address or could not be persuaded to do so.[59] If this was the case, however, it doesn't appear as if those tendering the address resorted to taking the subscriptions of the very poor (as we will see they were later accused of doing). The only individual on the Melton return appearing on surviving Hearth Tax exemption certificates was the church warden, William Reade, who helped compile the list.[60]

131

The evidence from Hearth Tax returns may suggest, however, that if subscribers were not usually recipients of poor relief, they may have belonged to the significant section of English society that lived on the margins – too poor to pay tax but not poor enough to be classed among the exempt.[61] In total, only ninety-one subscribers to the Cromwellian address have been found on the 1664 Hearth Tax return (with a further eleven listed as exempt), far fewer than one would expect on the basis of the multipliers typically used by social historians to generate population estimates from Hearth Tax returns.[62] Post-Restoration accusations that the Cromwellian addresses largely drew subscriptions from the lower reaches of social hierarchy may not, therefore, have been wide of the mark. The absence of addressers from parochial or tax records indicates that many may have come from the ranks of the 'just managing', that section of society that rarely features in the historical record.[63]

The instructions on the address itself nonetheless indicate that no direction was given as to who should or should not subscribe to the text; the constable of Higham being directed by the justices of the county simply to 'make all your neighbours aquainted with it and see who will subscribe'.[64] The question of who should subscribe nonetheless clearly excised some. On 16 October 1658, John Fitzjames begged Marchamont Nedham to let him know if the addresses submitted so far had been subscribed 'either by a numerous Company of hands, or by some Principalls in the name of the whole'.[65] If any such direction was sought in Leicestershire, it does not appear to have been uniformly observed: while some areas seem to have interpreted the call for subscriptions liberally, in other places such as Catthorpe only the minister and a few gentleman added their names.[66]

The role of magistrates in promoting the addresses may also explain the patchy nature of the Leicestershire return given the reports already noted that judges were refusing to take office before Richard had been formally recognised Lord Protector by Parliament.[67] In this regard, it may be significant that none of those subscribing the address in Melton Mowbray appear to have been office-holders.[68] These difficulties in securing the backing of local office-holders are also reflected in the problems encountered by James Winstanley with the Leicester address, noted by Derek Hirst. Unable to get any members of the borough to accompany the loyal address to Whitehall, Winstanley was forced to 'gather upp such as I could find fitt persons in habite and gravity' to present it.[69] The fact that relatively few press reports concerning the Cromwellian addresses name the individuals who presented the texts to the Protector suggests that the problems Winstanley encountered in Leicester were not unique.[70]

THE MICRO-POLITICS OF ADDRESSING

The unevenness of the Leicestershire address – geographically, socially, confessionally and politically – suggests that, in the case of many subscribers, the language of the 'well-affected' was here being adopted strategically by those who were not ideologically committed to the regime but who wished to avoid reprisals for failing to recognise it. As we have already seen, counties that had neglected to proclaim Richard as Protector, such as nearby Rutland and Northamptonshire, had certainly been very firmly reminded of their duty to do so by the Council of State.[71]

The presence of the term 'well-affected', however, was relatively unusual in the addresses to Richard Cromwell: only four other addresses (from Chard, Taunton, Tiverton and Pembrokeshire) made use of it.[72] The fact that three of these addresses came from Somerset may even indicate that the phrase had the whiff of disloyalty about it, suggesting support for 'Commonwealthsmen', given that the county was the stronghold of the anti-Cromwellian John Pyne.[73] It may, though, have simply been a means to overcome the kind of practical difficulties experienced by James Winstanley in producing and presenting the Leicester address. The majority of civilian addresses to Richard Cromwell preferred to present themselves as originating not from informal groups of the ideologically committed but either from civic corporations (such as 'The Mayor, Aldermen, Bayliffs, and Burgesses of the Town of Bedford') or from the county elite (for example 'The Knights, Justices, Gentlemen, Ministers and other Free-holders of the County of Cambridge').[74]

The use of the term 'well-affected' might then not only be an attempt to obscure the politically and religiously heterogeneous nature of the gathered subscriptions, but also to overcome the lack of support for the document among local office-holders. Similar strategies seem to have been adopted later in 1659 by supporters of the restored Rump. Humble petitions from groups of the 'well-affected' to the revived republic were more numerous than those from borough corporations or county benches.[75] Employing the language of horizontal, ideological affiliation, nonetheless, was problematic in that it cut against the fundamentally vertical ties of deference and loyalty which were implicit in both petitioning and addressing activity.[76] Of course, for some members of Richard's Parliament, simply acknowledging the rule of a single person, especially in the fulsome terms of some of these addresses, represented a 'blasphemous' act of sycophantic submission.[77] For some of Richard's supporters, however, the addresses clearly did not simply represent popular acclamation of the new Protector but instead the legitimation of his title by the people, the one truly authoritative body in the nation.[78]

The type of loyalty being proffered to Richard in the Leicestershire address was also contested, pointing to further political divisions at a local level. As has already been noted, while the opening folio claimed only to come from the county, from the second page of the address onwards the text was issued in the name of the 'County and Towne' of Leicester.[79] There were significant differences between the texts issued from the county and that presented by the borough of Leicester. The county text, given below, was essentially an echo of the official proclamation announcing the accession of Richard Cromwell as Lord Protector, recognising Richard as 'Rightfull Successor' according to the Humble Petition and Advice.

> To his Highnesse Richard Lord Protector of the Commonwealth of England Scotland and Irland and the Dominions and Territories thereunto belonginge
> The humble Addresse of the well affected Inhabitants of the Countie of Leicester
> May it please your Highnesse
> As wee have been Sharers with the rest of theis Nations in the memoriable deliverance wrought by the Omnipotent hand of God as soe many Crownes to the continued travells of yor deceased father, whose name is precious in or harts, and shall stand recorded to all posterity here on earth, as we are perswaded it is inrolled in heaven, Soe wee cannot but with them very much condole the losse of such a father of or country Yet seeinge all Earthly powers must submitte to the All-rulinge Will and Power of him whose Kingdome is everlasting. Wee judge it our duty to looke forward, and therein to Eye the providentiall hand of God in calling forth your Highnes to succeed in the Government of theis Nations. Wherein (our present Peace and Tranquility giving us noe small occacon to observe how God hath as well blasted the hope of or Enemies as contradicted the feares of friends) wee cannot but reioyce and admire the goodnesse of our God, not doubtinge but as yor Highnesse is declared the Rightfull Successor of your deare father in the Government, Soe you will declare yourself (through Grace) the true Inheritor of his Piety and Worth, and indeavor the iust freedome and liberty of theis Nations both as men and Christians, According to the humble Peticon and Advice: Soe wee are confident the Lord God of your father will bee with you as hee was with him, And wee doe hereby assure your Highness that wee shall therein stand by you with the hazard of our All. And shall pray that the Spirit of Wisdome Councell and the feare of the Lord may be rest upon you.[80]

While there was a muted reference to providence in the proclamation, the heaviest emphasis was laid on Richard's legal title as established by the second protectoral constitution. In contrast, the borough address, like many of the addresses that appeared in the pages of *Mercurius Politicus* and the *Public Intelligencer*, was suffused with providential language, and employed the common allusion to Richard as a new Joshua succeeding Oliver's Moses.[81] Both contemporary and subsequent observers read the use of providence in these texts as evidence that they offered no more than empty flattery. As the antiquary William Dugdale later dryly put it, the late Protector was compared to 'Moses, Zerubabel, Joshua, Gideon, Elijiah; to the Chariots and Horsemen of Israel; to David, Solomon, and Hezekiah. Likewise to Constantine the Great; and to whomsoever else that either Sacred Scripture, or any other History, had celebrated for their Piety, and Goodness.'[82] Although the use of providential language might have been sincere, as we have seen, it was frequently employed in addresses that did not explicitly acknowledge Richard's legal title. Furthermore, given some contemporary hostility to these Biblical comparisons as blasphemous, the use of the language of providence might also have been a marker (intentional or otherwise) of a particular religious outlook, less sensitive to the praise of mere human 'creatures'.

Moreover, the nature of Leicestershire's support for Richard was further complicated by the fact that there was also a variant of the county address. It is notable that not only did later folios of the county address claim to come from both the county and town of Leicester, but also that several returns were headed with a text quite different from that subscribed by the county's MPs, committee-men and godly ministers. This version of the address, given below, pointedly dropped both the reference to the late Protector being 'precious' in the subscribers' hearts and the description of Oliver as 'father of o[u]r country'.

> To his Highnesse Richard Lord Protector of ye Commonwealth of England Scotland and Ireland and the Dominions and Territories thereunto belonginge
>
> The humble Addresse of the well affected Inhabitants of the County and Towne of Leicester
>
> May it please your Highnesse
>
> As wee have beene Sharers with the rest of the Nation in the memorable deliverances wrought by the Omnipotent hand of God, as soe many Crownes to the endeavo^{rs} of you^r deceased father, whose name shall stand recorded to all posterity here on earth (as we are perswaded) it is inrolled in heaven; So wee cannot but wth them condole the losse of so faithfull and eminent an Instrument: Yet seeinge all earthly Powers must vaile to the all-ruling will and Power of him whose kingdome is everlasting, Wee iudge it our duty to looke forward, and therein to eye the providentiall hand of God in callinge forth your Highnes to succeed in the Government of these Nations,wherein (our p[re]sent peace and tranquility giving us noe small occasion to observe how God hath as well blasted thee hopes of our enemies, as contradicted the feares of friends) We cannot but reioyce and admire the goodnes of our God, not doubting but as yor Highnesse is declared the rightfull Successor of your father's goverm^t, So you will declare yo^{r}selfe (through Grace) the true Inherito^r of his piety and worth, and endeavo^r the iust freedome and liberty of these Nations both as men and Christians, according to the humble peticon and advice: And soe doe hereby assure yor Highness that wee shall therein hazard our all with you, and shall pray that the Spirit of wisdome Counsell and the Feare of the Lord may be rest upon you.[83]

It therefore provided a text which involved only minimal acknowledgement of the previous regime and avoided personal declarations of affection towards Richard's father, perhaps offering a form that could more easily be subscribed by those who were not wedded to the Cromwellian State. It may be significant that this variant text first appeared in the return including the parish of Knighton, an area dominated at the time by the Baptist Inge family.[84] The text of the address reverted back to the more pro-Cromwellian text as the subscriptions moved from the hundred of Gartree to that of Sparkenhoe, indicating the importance of constables not only in administering the address, but seemingly also in helping to determine the political stance of the locality.[85] The lack of a relatively uniform text of the county address also suggests that there was no commonly circulated pro-forma but that instead local communities were drawing up their own texts as they saw fit.[86] In the case of the Leicestershire address, we have what appears to be a unique example, not of cross- or counter-addressing, but of alternative texts included within notionally the same return.

As we have already seen, the different texts of the Leicestershire county and borough addresses reflected a wider debate about the legitimacy of Richard's title and the nature of the Protectoral regime. If some of the addresses were to be believed, this was a debate that also reached down the social scale. While these addresses generally sought to establish their credentials as authoritative texts, originating from local government and the politically enfranchised, several also asserted their popular appeal. In many texts, this was simply through the inclusion of the catch-all category of 'inhabitants', appended after the enumeration of knights, ministers, gentry, mayors, aldermen and burgesses etc. In the case of a few of the county addresses, however, sheer weight of numbers was referred to. The Leicestershire address itself was noted as being subscribed by 'some Thousands of hands', a claim also made of several other Cromwellian addresses.[87] As has already been noted, Fitzjames stated that the Dorset address had already secured 'allmost 2000 hands' by November 1658, though his letters urging subscription had targeted the clergy and gentry. (The address was finally presented in December of that year).[88] If the figures reported in the press are treated as reliable, the largest of these returns came from Lincolnshire and featured some 6,000 subscribers.[89]

As has already been demonstrated though, these claims to popular support were hotly contested by opponents of Richard's rule during the debate over the act recognising his title in February 1659 with MPs claiming that these numbers were fraudulent or that, if correct, simply indicative of the ease with which the people could be brought to subscribe to anything. Others, such as Richard Baxter and the Quaker William Caton, contended that the addresses were essentially generated by Baptist and Independent churches. The evidence of the Leicestershire address, and that of later manuscript addresses, suggests that the numbers reported in the press were reasonably accurate. The uneven pattern of subscription across the county and the mixed religious and social background of the subscribers, however, also indicates that the claims of the address to represent the whole county and to consist only of the 'well-affected' were more problematic.[90] Yet, despite the apparent readiness of local officials in the county to gather the subscriptions of the poor, the need to show popular support for Richard's regime was not so acute as to lead to the relaxation of contemporary gender norms: no women are present in the return.

LOYALTY AND SUBSCRIPTION PRACTICES FROM THE END OF THE PROTECTORATE TO THE RESTORATION

The reputed gulf between the public pronouncements of loyalty to Richard Cromwell and genuine popular support was at the heart of later critiques of mass addressing. Here the Cromwellian regime was doubly damned both for courting popularity and for failing to secure it. Certainly, the addressing campaigns that followed the downfall of Richard's protectorate appeared much more hostile to the idea of seeking mass subscriptions. As has already been noted, Richard's government was first directly challenged via a 'subscriptional text', Samuel Moyer's petition presented to Parliament in February 1659 and addressed only to the 'Commonwealth of England' with no mention of the Lord Protector or the Cromwellian Upper House.[91] After Richard's resignation in May 1659, the revived Commonwealth itself employed very similar strategies to attempt to legitimate its own authority. As has been shown, the humble petitions made to the restored Rump were fewer in number than the addresses made to Richard Cromwell, came from a narrower geographical range, were more commonly styled as coming from informal groups of the 'well-affected' or 'Assertors of the Good Old Cause', and were occasionally explicitly hostile to popular government.[92]

As the republic itself faltered, the language of addresses continued to be anti-populist but shifted from prizing intellectual consistency to reasserting social hierarchy. The addresses and declarations presented to General Monck urging him to support a free Parliament frequently described themselves as coming from the nobility and gentry of the area. The distinction between these declarations and those addresses and petitions which had preceded them was put bluntly by Thomas Fuller in an anthology of these texts published in 1660. 'Factious Petitions,' he said, 'gave the beginning, and *Loyal Declarations* must give the end to our Miseries. But here is the difference, the first were made by the *Scum*, these by the *Cream* of the Nation.'[93] (It is worth noting here not only Fuller's damning verdict on the quality of subscribers to Parliamentarian petitions but also the clear distinction being made here between petitioning and other, superior subscriptional forms.)[94]

Reassertions of the social hierarchy of this kind, however, continued to be disrupted by ideological divisions. Fuller's collection included an address to Monck ostensibly from the nobility and gentry of Leicestershire, promoted by the sheriff of the county, George Faunt.[95] Both contemporary press reports and the borough records indicate that the corporation and other Leicestershire gentry refused to join in this address. *Mercurius Politicus* alleged this was because the prime movers of it were known Royalists.[96] (It is also worth noting that no congratulatory address to Charles II appears to have been sent from the county or corporation.)

Even when the promotion of an address does not appear to have been contested, the tension between demonstrating public support and maintaining social distinctions resurfaced. The address to Monck from the gentry and nobility of Norfolk was printed in two variant broadsheet editions. One contained only the names of the presenters and a reference to the text as being subscribed by some three hundred of the gentry, while the other displayed the names of forty-five of the leading signatories adding that it had been signed by 'hundreds more' of the gentry, citizens and freeholders. The manuscript fair copy of the address in fact featured over eight hundred names.[97] The forty-five subscribers whose names were reproduced on the broadsheet were not displayed in the order that they appeared on the fair copy but were rearranged in order of social importance, with five individuals appearing only on the broadsheet.[98] As with the address to Richard Cromwell from Leicestershire, the subscribers were also from a more restricted geographical range than the title of the address suggested (primarily from Norwich and the surrounding area).[99] Again like the Leicestershire address, the subscribers included both former Royalists and Parliamentarians.[100]

This may reflect genuine attempts at coalition building: while contemporary newsletters alleged that addresses to Monck were the product of local Royalists, and some letter writers suggested that prominent local Royalists were deliberately left off these addresses to avert suspicion, the category of 'Royalist' by 1659 could certainly have included men such as Sir William Doyley, a former county committee man and MP for Norfolk under the Protectorate. Doyley had been excluded from Parliament by Cromwell in 1656 and by January 1660 was writing to the leading royalist in the area, Sir Horatio Townshend, promising that he was willing to do anything in his power 'for the country's peace, ease of grievances, and settlement of the nation'.[101] It may be that this desire for settlement and peace also explains the heterogeneous nature of the subscriptions to the address from Leicestershire to Richard Cromwell in 1658. On this basis, the fact that men such as John Cheney of Huncoate, who had subscribed to the 1658 address, were also leading contributors to the 'Free and Voluntary Present' to Charles II in 1661, is not necessarily evidence of their political hypocrisy.[102]

The addresses and declarations sent to Monck (followed by the congratulatory addresses sent to Charles II) signalled a shift in the printed format of these texts: from material predominately being reproduced in newsbooks to being issued as separate broadsheets. We might see this as signalling a shift of intent too, with these texts operating first and foremost as publicity for the addressers rather than propaganda for the State: in contrast to the texts reproduced in newsbooks, these broadsheet addresses usually included the names of subscribers as well as the words of the address itself. Indeed, Fuller claimed that one motivation for producing his anthology was to preserve such ephemeral texts given that '*Leaves* or *single Papers* ... are soon lost, not to say, The best of Papers so printed, are oft consigned to the worst of uses.'[103]

THE DECLARATION

Of the GENTRY, of the COUNTY of

NORFOLK,

And of the COUNTY and CITY of

NORVVICH.

WE the Gentry of the County of *Norfolk*, and County and City of *Norwich*, being deeply affected with the fence of our sad Distractions and Divisions, both in Church and State, and wearied with the miseries of an Unnatural Civil War, the too Frequent Interruptions of Government, the Imposition of several heavy Taxes, and the loud Out-cries of multitudes of undone, and almost Famished People, occasioned by the General decay of Trade, which hath spread it self throughout the whole Nation, and these Counties in particular; and having met together, and consulted what may best remedy, and remove our, and the Nations present Grievances and Distractions, Do humbly conceive, that the chief Expedient will be, the recalling of those Members that were secluded in 1648, and sat before the Force put upon the Parliament (We of the County of *Norfolk*) being by such Seclusion, deprived of any Person to represent us in Parliament,) and also by filling up the Vacant Places thereof; and all to be Admitted without any Oath, or Engagement, previous to their Entrance; which being done, We shall be ready to acquiesce, and submit in all things, to the Judgment and Authority of Parliament, without which Authority, the People of *England* cannot be obliged to pay any Taxes.

This Declaration, subscribed by three hundred Gentlemen, was delivered to the Honourable Will: Lenthall, *Speaker of the Parliament, on Saturday the Eight and Twentieth of January,* 1659. *By the Lord* Richardson, Sr John Hobart, *and* Sr Horatio Tounsend, *Baronets.*

Figure 4. Variant broadsheet declarations of the gentry of Norfolk to General Monck (1660): *The declaration of the gentry, of the county of Norfolk, and of the county and city of Norvvich* (BL, Thomason, 669 f. 23 [21]) and *A letter and declaration of the gentry of the county of Norfolk, and the county of the city of Norwich, to his excellency the Lord General Monck* (BL, 190 g. 13 [148])

A LETTER
AND
DECLARATION

Of the Gentry of the County of NORFOLK, and the County of the City of NORWICH, To his Excellency the Lord GENERALL MONK. √ Decr 18 1659

Right Honourable,

Ee the Gentry of the County of *Norfolk*, and of the County and City of *Norwich*, do cordially rejoyce, with many others of these Counties, and of the Nation, for your Excellencies return into your Native Countrey with honour and safety : And that the late Differences in the Armies are now so happily composed without blood-shed ; We are desirous to blesse our good God for these mercies, and to acquaint your Lordship, That we have signified the Resentment of our grievances to the Speaker of the Parliament ; A true Copie whereof we have here inclosed, sent to your Excellency, least any persons should in our absence mis-represent us or our intentions to your Lordship : We rest.

The Declaration.

WE the Gentry of the County of *Norfolk*, and County and City of *Norwich*, Being deeply affected with the sence of our sad Distractions and Divisions, both in Church and State ; And wearied with the Miseries of an unnaturall Civil War, The too frequent Interruptions of Government, the Impositions of severall heavy Taxes, And the loud out-cryes of multitudes of undone and almost famished people, occasioned by a generall decay of Trade, which hath spread it self throughout the whole Nation, and these Counties in particular : And having met together and consulted what may best remedy and remove Our and the Nations present greivances and Distractions ; Do humbly conceive, That the chief Expedient, will be, the Recalling of those Members that were secluded in 1648. and sate before the Force put upon the Parliament (We of this County of *Norfolk*, being by such Seclusion deprived of any person to represent us in Parliament) and also by filling up the vacant places thereof ; And all to be admitted without any Oath or Engagement, previous to their Entrance ; Which being done, We shall be ready to acquiesce and submit in all things to the Judgment and Authority of Parliament ; Without which Authority, the People of *England* cannot be obliged to pay any Taxes.

The Letter to Generall *MONK*, and this Declaration was signed by

Thomas Lord *Richardson*.	*Edmond Bacon*.	*Philip Woodhouse*.
John Hobart.	*N. Le Strange*.	*Ralph Heure*.
Horatio Townesend.	*Thomas Pettus*.	*John Tracy*.
John Asteley.	*Wil. Doyley*.	*Arthur Jenny*.
Wil. Hewitt.	*Thomas Guybon*.	*Augustin Sotherton*.
John Palgrave.	*John Windham*.	*John Buxton*.
Thomas Berney.	*James De Grey*.	*Francis Norris*.
Wil. Rant.	*Butts Bacon*.	*Thomas Johnson*.
Adrian Parmenter.	*Thomas Rant*.	*Thomas Le Gros*.
Edmund Burman.	*Chr. Jay*.	*John Hevile*.
John Rawley.	*Joseph Payne*.	*Richard Catelyne*.
Henry Watts.	*Rob. Bendish*.	*Suck. Jay*.
John Maum.	*Richard Wenman*.	*Rob. Suckling*.
John Andrewes.	*John Laurence*.	*Samuel Smith*.
John Salter.	*Thomas Wisse*.	*Rob. Holmes*.

With many hundreds more of the Knights, Gentry, Citizens, and Freee-holders.

LONDON,
Printed for *John Place*, at *Furnivals Inne* Gate in *Holborne*, 1660.

Figure 4. (Cont.)

Clearly, though, many of these broadsheets did not end up as 'bumfodder'. The publication of broadsheet addresses and petitions with the names of leading figures, though intended to gain credit for the subscribers and increase the credibility of the texts themselves, posed problems for a number of individuals. The pressure to subscribe to addresses to first the Protectorate, then the Rump, then for a free Parliament and finally to the King left individuals open to charges of hypocrisy and disloyalty. A prime example is the case of Thomas Beaumont, who had presented the Leicestershire address to Richard Cromwell. After the Restoration, Beaumont sought to have his Cromwellian baronetcy recognised by royal letters patent. This was eventually forthcoming but, as Beaumont complained in a petition to the King, the patent had been delayed by some twelve months, due to the 'untrue suggestions' of some concerning his loyalty.[104]

The exact nature of these suggestions was clarified in a petition of April 1661 supporting Beaumont's request signed by some sixty-six Leicestershire gentlemen. The gentlemen noted that it had been alleged that Beaumont had signed a petition from Leicestershire in 1648 calling for the King to be brought to justice.[105] The broadsheet copy of this petition bears no names, though it is entirely plausible that Beaumont did sign it: in his role as a justice of the peace in the late 1640s and early 1650s, Beaumont had informed on local Royalists and promoted the Commonwealth's orders to remove and deface the royal arms and/or pictures of the late King.[106] Perhaps more remarkable is the fact that many of the gentlemen who supported Beaumont, and asserted that he had been 'very Instrumentall' in the restoration of the King, such as Thomas Pochin, had earlier been prominent signatories of the address to Richard Cromwell.[107] The reputation of communities as well as individuals could potentially be damaged by past addressing activity. As we have seen, a number of the congratulatory addresses to Charles II issued in 1660 included apologies for past addresses to the Protectorate or Rump (usually qualified with claims that the earlier texts did not represent the true voice of area but were manufactured by small groups of activists). Others emphasised their pristine loyalty in that they had never been brought to address usurpers.

These texts glossed over the reality of rapidly shifting allegiances over the course of the 1640s and 1650s. The contemporary denigration of the Cromwellian addressers as mendacious, therefore, ignored the degree to which compromises and accommodations were inevitable in the turbulent last years of the interregnum. This was recognised even by some of the Stuart dynasty's staunchest supporters. Sir Geoffrey Palmer, appointed Attorney General 31 May 1660, would be actively involved in the trials of the regicides. Edmund Ludlow characterised Palmer's actions against the King's judges as those of 'one of the Tyrant's bloodhounds, at the bar'.[108] Yet, if Palmer was a royalist bloodhound, he seems not to have picked up much of a scent in the case of Thomas Beaumont. Instead, Palmer wrote to Secretary Nicholas on behalf of his 'neighbour' (as the letter described him), asking that Beaumont be given an explanation as to why the patent for his baronetcy had been stopped. It was, after all, Palmer argued, common knowledge that Beaumont had originally received the title from Cromwell and that he had 'acted with him'. More important than this outward conformity with the regime though, Palmer argued, was the fact that Beaumont had been 'helpful to manie against the opr[e]siones of those tymes'.[109] While Beaumont kept his title, his service to the Cromwellian regime was not without consequences: he appears to have been excluded from the county bench for most of the 1660s.[110]

Beaumont's case was not unique. Indeed it bore close comparison with that of another subscriber to the 1658 address, Thomas Pochin. Pochin, like Beaumont, had been identified in print early in the 1640s as one well-affected to the Parliament's cause and by 1647 he had been appointed sheriff of Leicestershire.[111] As has already been noted, Pochin also served as a magistrate and MP under the Cromwellian Protectorate. Pochin was a significant landowner and by 1660 the Barkby estate was valued at some £1,000. Despite his service to the regimes of the 1640s and 1650s, Pochin's wealth and status appears to have been little affected by the Restoration, no doubt helped by the fact that he had married the daughter of Sir Wolstan Dixie, one of the major Royalists in the county.[112] Pochin's father George was probably the Pochin named as a 'knight of the oak' (a mooted order of knighthood for those who had aided the exiled Stuart dynasty) for Leicestershire in 1660 and he and his father both made significant contributions to the Free and Voluntary Present of 1661.[113] Yet, like Beaumont, Pochin would also have to endure a period in the political wilderness, not returning to the county bench until 1670.[114]

SUBSCRIPTIONAL PRACTICES AFTER THE RESTORATION

The reassertion of social hierarchy evident in the addresses and declarations to Monck was emphasised even more vigorously in the congratulatory addresses sent to Charles II, the majority of which referred to themselves as the products of the nobility and gentry (for example, 'A Declaration of the Nobility, Knights and Gentry of the County of Oxon Who Have Adhered to the Late King').[115]

In many of the congratulatory addresses sent to Charles II social distinctions were made even clearer. The jumbled mess of subscriptions on the original Dorset address, for example, was carefully unpacked in the printed broadsheet copy, with subscribers ordered first by peers, then knights, then esquires and finally mere gentlemen.[116] Similar reordering and repackaging can be seen in the printed congratulatory addresses from Somerset, Gloucestershire and Rutland.[117] Further emphasising the role of the printed broadsides in advertising the loyal credentials of the subscribers, not only did these texts provide information on who had had the honour of presenting the address but in some cases, they also included names which had not featured on the original manuscript. The congratulatory address from Somerset in its original form only contained eighty names but the broadside featured a further fifteen, in a number of cases seemingly to give greater space to members of major county families like the Paulets, the Waldrons and the Horners.[118] Heightening their social exclusivity, these addresses also featured much smaller numbers of subscribers than the biggest Cromwellian addresses: the largest of the congratulatory addresses sent to Charles II was notably not one from the nobility and gentry but the loyal address of the 'Mayor, Recorder, Aldermen, Sheriff and the rest of the Commonalty of the Town and County of Newcastle upon Tyne'.[119]

This seeming retreat from popular petitioning was given statutory backing in 1661 with the passage of the Tumultuous Petitioning Act. As has already been noted, this was less of an unprecedented clampdown on popular political activity than first appears. The act, as with much post-Restoration legislation, was based on an interregnum precedent, the 1648 declaration against tumultuous assemblies. We should note too that addressing activity under the Cromwellian Protectorate largely avoided either direct invocations of popular support or emphasising horizontal, ideological ties in place of vertical social obligations. Most addresses were put forward as those coming from authoritative bodies rather than from the mass of the 'well-affected'. As has been emphasised, even those that did secure large numbers of subscribers, such as those from Leicestershire to Richard Cromwell or the Norfolk address to Monck, may represent attempts to build local coalitions to achieve political stability and security as much as a desire to show popular support.

As we have seen, the Exclusion Crisis revived political mass petitioning. Yet, though Roger North in his *Examen* presented addressing as providing the antidote to this practice, it was clear that Whig 'monster' petitions encouraged the loyalist press to emphasise that addresses also garnered popular support.[120] The most glaring example of this was the humble address of the loyal apprentices of the city of London, thanking the King for his declaration following the dissolution of the Oxford Parliament 'Signed by many thousands'.[121] Many other press reports concerning loyal addresses were keen to emphasis the numbers subscribing to these texts.[122] Some of these loyal addresses, such as that from the gentlemen, freeholders and inhabitants between the rivers of Dudden and Esk, which was reportedly 'Signed by 825 persons', must have amounted to a high proportion of the adult male population.[123]

The stress on popular subscription, however, remained in some tension with the language of status that also continued to be deployed in these texts. The address from the citizens of Worcester, presented at Windsor in August 1681 was reportedly,

> Subscribed by 610 Citizens, whereof there are three Lords and 43 of the Common Council. The Mayor and four Aldermen refused to subscribe the same: But it is informed that twenty of the Subscribing Citizens to this Address, are capable to Purchase the whole Number of the Non-subscribing Citizens within the City of Worcester.[124]

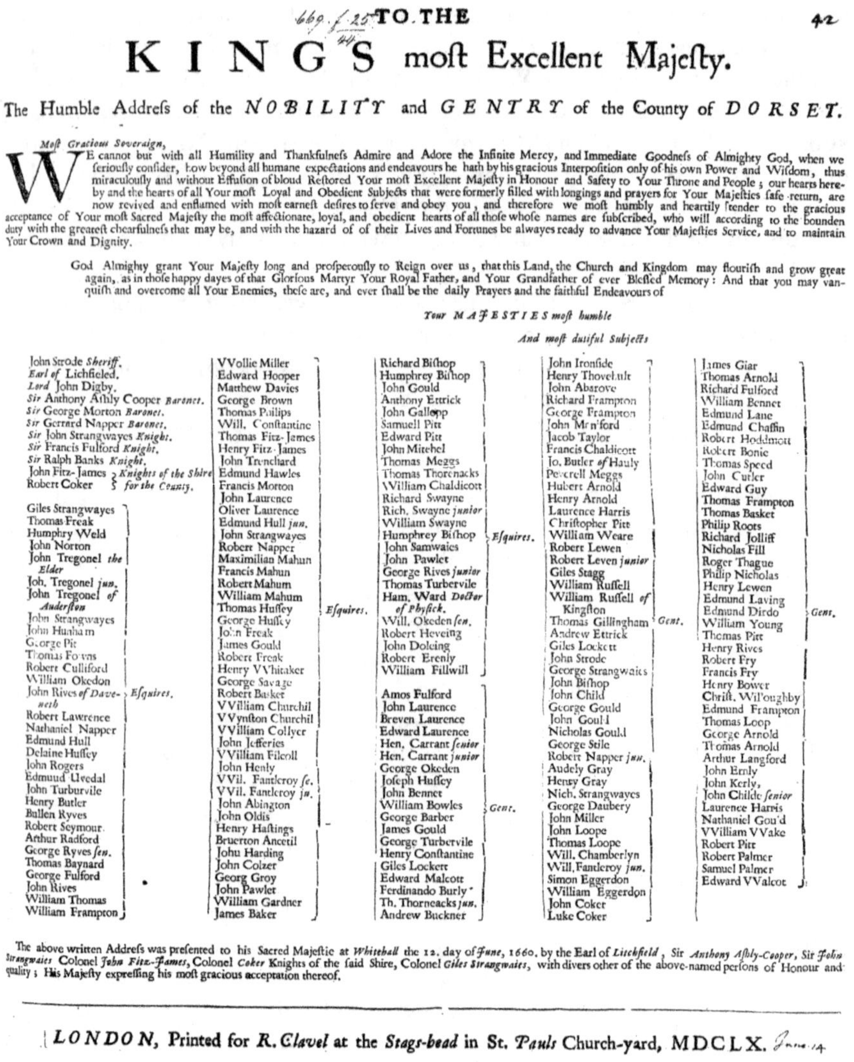

TO THE

KINGS moſt Excellent Majeſty.

The Humble Addreſs of the *NOBILITY* and *GENTRY* of the County of *DORSET.*

Moſt Gracious Soveraign,

WE cannot but with all Humility and Thankfulneſs Admire and Adore the Infinite Mercy, and Immediate Goodneſs of Almighty God, when we ſeriouſly conſider, how beyond all humane expectations and endeavours he hath by his gracious Interpoſition only of his own Power and Wiſdom, thus miraculouſly and without Effuſion of bloud Reſtored Your moſt Excellent Majeſty in Honour and Safety to Your Throne and People; our hearts hereby and the hearts of all Your moſt Loyal and Obedient Subjects that were formerly filled with longings and prayers for Your Majeſties ſafe return, are now revived and enflamed with moſt earneſt deſires to ſerve and obey you, and therefore we moſt humbly and heartily ſtender to the gracious acceptance of Your moſt Sacred Majeſty the moſt affectionate, loyal, and obedient hearts of all thoſe whoſe names are ſubſcribed, who will according to the bounden duty with the greateſt chearfulneſs that may be, and with the hazard of of their Lives and Fortunes be alwayes ready to advance Your Majeſties Service, and to maintain Your Crown and Dignity.

God Almighty grant Your Majeſty long and proſperouſly to Reign over us, that this Land, the Church and Kingdom may flouriſh and grow great again, as in thoſe happy dayes of that Glorious Martyr Your Royal Father, and Your Grandfather of ever Bleſſed Memory: And that you may vanquiſh and overcome all Your Enemies, theſe are, and ever ſhall be the daily Prayers and the faithful Endeavours of

Your MAJESTIES moſt humble

And moſt dutiful Subjects

John Strode *Sheriff.*
Earl of Lichfieled.
Lord John Digby.
Sir Anthony Aſhly Cooper *Baronet.*
Sir George Morton *Baronet.*
Sir Gerrard Napper *Baronet.*
Sir John Strangwayes *Knight.*
Sir Francis Fulford *Knight.*
Sir Ralph Banks *Knight.*
John Fitz-James, Robert Coker — *Knights of the Shire for the County.*

Giles Strangwayes
Thomas Freak
Humphry Weld
John Norton
John Tregonel *the Elder*
Joh. Tregonel *jun.*
John Tregonel *of Anderſton*
John Strangwayes
John Hunham
George Pit
Thomas Fowns
Robert Culliford
William Okedon
John Rives *of Daveneth*
Robert Lawrence
Nathaniel Napper
Edmund Hull
Delaine Huſſey
John Rogers
Edmuud Uvedal
John Turburvile
Henry Butler
Bullen Ryves
Robert Seymour
Arthur Radford
George Ryves *ſen.*
Thomas Baynard
George Fulford
John Rives
William Thomas
William Frampton — *Eſquires.*

VVollie Miller
Edward Hooper
Matthew Davies
George Brown
Thomas Philips
Will. Conſtantine
Thomas Fitz-James
Henry Fitz-James
John Trenchard
Edmund Hawles
Francis Morton
John Laurence
Oliver Laurence
Edmund Hull *jun.*
John Strangwayes
Robert Napper
Maximilian Mahun
Francis Mahun
Robert Mahum
William Mahum
Thomas Huſſey
George Huſſey
John Freak
James Gould
Robert Freak
Henry VVhitaker
George Savage
Robert Basket
VVilliam Churchil
VVynſton Churchil
VVilliam Collyer
John Jefferies
VVilliam Filcoll
John Henly
VVil. Fantleroy *ſe.*
VVil. Fantleroy *ju.*
John Abington
John Oldis
Henry Haſtings
Bruerton Ancetil
Johu Harding
John Colzer
Georg Groy
John Pawlet
William Gardner
James Baker — *Eſquires.*

Richard Biſhop
Humphrey Biſhop
John Gould
Anthony Ettrick
John Gallopp
Samuell Pitt
Edward Pitt
John Mitchel
Thomas Meggs
Thomas Thorenacks
William Chaldicott
Richard Swayne
Rich. Swayne *junior*
William Swayne
Humphrey Biſhop
John Samwaies
John Pawlet
George Rives *junior*
Thomas Turbervile
Ham. Ward *Doctor of Phyſick.*
Will. Okeden *ſen.*
Robert Heveing
John Dolcing
Robert Erenly
William Fillwill — *Eſquires.*

Amos Fulford
John Laurence
Breven Laurence
Edward Laurence
Hen. Carrant *ſenior*
Hen. Carrant *junior*
George Okeden
Joſeph Huſſey
John Bennet
William Bowles
George Barber
James Gould
George Turbervile
Henry Conſtantine
Giles Lockett
Edward Malcott
Ferdinando Burly
Th. Thorneacks *jun.*
Andrew Buckner — *Gent.*

John Ironſide
Henry Thovehult
John Abarove
Richard Frampton
George Frampton
John Mrn'ford
Jacob Taylor
Francis Chaldicott
Jo. Butler *of* Hauly
Peverell Meggs
Hubert Arnold
Henry Arnold
Laurence Harris
Chriſtopher Pitt
William Weare
Robert Lewen
Robert Leven *junior*
Giles Stagg
William Ruſſell
William Ruſſell *of* Kingſton
Thomas Gillingham
Andrew Ettrick
Giles Lockett
John Strode
George Strangwaies
John Biſhop
John Child
George Gould
John Gould
Nicholas Gould
George Stile
Robert Napper *jun.*
Audely Gray
Henry Gray
Nich. Strangwayes
George Daubery
John Miller
John Loope
Thomas Loope
Will. Chamberlyn
Will. Fantleroy *jun.*
Simon Eggerdon
William Eggerdon
John Coker
Luke Coker — *Gent.*

James Giar
Thomas Arnold
Richard Fulford
William Bennet
Edmund Lane
Edmund Chaffin
Robert Hoddmott
Robert Bonie
Thomas Speed
John Cutler
Edward Guy
Thomas Frampton
Thomas Basket
Philip Roots
Richard Jolliff
Nicholas Fill
Roger Thague
Philip Nicholas
Henry Lewen
Edmund Laving
Edmund Dirdo
William Young
Thomas Pitt
Henry Rives
Robert Fry
Francis Fry
Henry Bower
Chriſt. Wil'oughby
Edmund Frampton
Thomas Loop
George Arnold
Thomas Arnold
Arthur Langford
John Ernly
John Kerly,
John Childe *ſenior*
Laurence Harris
Nathaniel Gou'd
VVilliam VVake
Robert Pitt
Robert Palmer
Samuel Palmer
Edward VValcot — *Gent.*

The above written Addreſs was preſented to his Sacred Majeſtie at *Whitehall* the 12. day of *June*, 1660. by the Earl of *Litchfield*, Sir *Anthony Aſhly-Cooper*, Sir *John Strangwaies* Colonel *John Fitz-James*, Colonel *Coker* Knights of the ſaid Shire, Colonel *Giles Strangwaies*, with divers other of the above-named perſons of Honour and quality; His Majeſty expreſſing his moſt gracious acceptation thereof.

LONDON, Printed for *R. Clavel* at the *Stags-head* in St. *Pauls* Church-yard, MDCLX.

Figure 5a. Printed version of the address of the Dorset nobility and gentry to Charles II: *To the Kings most Excellent Majesty. The humble address of the nobility and gentry of the county of Dorset* (1660), BL Thomason 669 f. 25 [44]

Similarly, the *Loyal Protestant and True Domestick Intelligence* attacked the compendium *Vox Patriae* as containing but,

> Twelve (not allowable either) Addresses for Counties, whereas England, And Wales hath more than 52 counties in them. And but four Addresses from Cities, and 11 from Borough Towns (reckoning up the zeal of the young men of Taunton also) whereas there are near 250 Borough Towns in England and Wales.[125]

Who were the 'public'?

Figure 5b. Excerpt from the manuscript address of the Dorset nobility and gentry to Charles II in 1660, TNA SP 29/1 f. 55–6

In part, the effort made to stress the popularity of these texts was intended to counter allegations in the Whig press that these numbers had either been inflated in fraudulent ways or were less impressive than might be expected from supposedly 'loyal' counties and towns.[126] Yet these claims to mass support strained the credibility of some of these descriptions: one of the largest addresses issued in the wake of the dissolution of the Oxford Parliament, claimed to have been signed by 'above 16,000 of the principal Gentlemen, and Freeholders of Devonshire', though the text of the address itself employed the less precise and more plausible claim that it was from the King's 'Loyal Subjects.'[127] Likewise, the Tory press disputed Whig claims concerning the quality and number of the London apprentices who subscribed the loyal address, the *Loyal Protestant and True Domestick Intelligencer* asserting that it was subscribed by those of 'the most Eminent Rank (viz.), 4 Merchants, 2 Mercers, a Drapers [sic.], and a Goldsmith' but at the same time reported that Benskin's *Intelligencer* had wrongly claimed that only 2,000 apprentices had put their hands to it rather than the actual 20,000.[128] Nonetheless, what limited evidence we have to corroborate these press reports with original MS suggests that the numbers reported in the *London Gazette* were probably accurate.[129] Those addresses, however, issued in 'abhorrence' of Shaftesbury's 'Association' typically failed to declare the numbers of subscribers, partly because (as has already been shown) the general thrust of these addresses was overtly hostile to popular petitioning and partly too because many originated as addresses from grand juries.[130] References to the numbers of subscribers

145

appear to be almost completely absent from press reports of those addresses issued in the wake of the Rye House Plot, though there were a handful of exceptions such as the Derbyshire address presented 30 July 1683 which Morrice reported was 'signed by 9175'.[131]

As will be demonstrated in Chapter seven, Tory rhetoric, especially during the Exclusion Crisis, embraced populism, suggesting that loyalty to the monarchy was a more important qualification for participating in political life than social status or education. Yet, as we have seen, despite some vociferous Whig defences of the right to petition, statutory limitations on mass petitioning or addressing went unchallenged. Indeed, the language of Whig addresses tended to emphasise the quality of the subscribers as a means of countering accusations that they were reviving the strategies of the 1640s.[132] Overall, incidences of mass subscription in the post-Restoration period appear to have been driven by partisanship and political expediency. They did not represent or acknowledge the popular 'voice' as authoritative in the way that texts had occasionally done during the interregnum.

Popular petitioning and addressing were re-energised after the revolution of 1688 but the revolution posed new challenges in the employment of these devices. As has been shown earlier, while both Whigs and Tories used mass petitions and addresses during the 1680s, neither party strove to outlaw subscriptional activity altogether nor to repeal the post-Restoration restrictions on 'tumultuous' petitioning or addressing. This broad agreement about the desirability of some limitation on lawful petitioning was not fundamentally altered by the Revolution of 1688. Though the English Bill of Rights upheld the right of subjects to petition the Crown, the revolution settlement did not change the statutory restrictions on petitioning Parliament. Even during seemingly vociferous public controversies in which subscriptional texts were central, such as that over the 1701 Kentish petition, neither the Junto Whigs' supporters nor their opponents sought to challenge the guidelines established by the 1661 statute, a statute that continued to enjoy the full force of law until the 1980s.[133]

References to mass subscription to these addresses were rare (I have identified only two instances) and in the case of the largest of these (Northamptonshire) qualified by the claim that the subscribers were all freeholders.[134] This fits with the general downward trend in the number of subscribers to post-1688 addresses identified by Knights.[135] When mass subscriptional texts were employed, in 1696 and in 1723, it was in the form of sworn associations or oaths of loyalty. In the case of the 1696 Association in particular, contemporaries and later observers did confuse the texts with loyal addresses, in part because county and borough associations were often subscribed in conjunction with the drawing up of a loyal address. As Richard Edge wrote to Roger Kenyon on 29 February 1696 the 'address presented formerly by the Earle of Macclesfield, signed by 28,000 persons in Lancashire' was the same 'in effect' as the Williamite Association.[136] Similarly, John

Oldmixon was only able to claim that one post-revolutionary 'address' contained more names than all of the loyalist addresses of 1681 put together because he treated the Association and the loyal addresses that accompanied them as one and the same.[137] The confusion here between the addresses and the Association was also evident in some of the surviving returns for the oath. The surviving Association rolls for parts of Lancashire demonstrate that subscriptions were being taken under the text of the loyal address rather than the oath itself.[138]

The only women subscribers so far identified on a surviving manuscript loyal address were the five women whose names feature on this 1696 loyal address to William III.[139] The general absence of women from the list of subscribers to loyal addresses was connected to their primary aim of representing public loyalty, as well as their association with office-holding. So, whereas oaths and covenants bound subscribers to perform particular actions, rendering the securing of women's subscriptions occasionally politically expedient, addresses offered more generalised expressions of support.[140]

After 1688, however, oaths of allegiance were being used in distinctly different ways than they had been earlier in the century. While the many oaths and covenants imposed during the 1640s had been intended to mobilise partisan support and sort the 'disaffected' from the 'well-affected', post-revolutionary oaths and associations were used in similar fashion to loyal addresses, to project the image of public support for the revolution settlement.[141] The problem, however, was that the post-revolutionary ideal of political life was based around voluntary association, an ideal that it was hard to accommodate with penal 'state oaths', such as those tendered after the Atterbury Plot of 1722.[142] Addresses, on the other hand, presented at least the image of spontaneous public support even if, as earlier exercises showed, they were often prompted and carefully encouraged by authority. Consequently, whereas the 'state oath' was finished after 1723, addresses and voluntary associations flourished in the eighteenth century and continued to proliferate into the Victorian era.

CONCLUSION

It was often alleged that the thousands of names that featured upon mass petitions and addresses were the product of fraud or force. In the case of petitioning, 'monster' texts seemed to subvert some of the established conventions about legitimate petitioning, in that the petitioners could not be solely those directly concerned in the matter of the petition.

There was no such clear direction governing mass addressing, leaving it open as to whether the address should 'virtually' or directly represent the community it came from. Under both Oliver and Richard's protectorate, mass addresses occasionally seemed to involve a very broad understanding of political participation.[143] The Leicestershire address to Richard Cromwell certainly included gentlemen and esquires, MPs and ministers, but it also took in shearsmen, mercers, husbandmen and locksmiths. The very varied background of the subscribers, from regicides to 'scandalous' ministers, may raise questions about the description of the address as originating from the 'well-affected'. The evidence of subscription patterns in some areas suggests that a certain amount of coercion may have been involved. Yet, when viewed in conjunction with later addresses, especially those calling for a free parliament, the subscribers may appear less of a cobbled together hodgepodge and more of a political alliance seeking stability and security. As the Protectorate came under threat from a variety of radical groups both political and religious, such alliances must have seemed attractive to 'moderates' of a variety of ideological stripes. The case study of Leicestershire, however, also demonstrates the difficulty of forming these alliances, as variant texts were produced for subscription within the same county return.

With the Restoration, addressing and the subscriptional activity that accompanied it changed, reasserting social hierarchy and exclusivity and seemingly pre-empting the legislative ban on popular petitioning. Even so, this type of addressing activity and the statute that enforced it was less novel than it initially appeared. The majority of addresses produced during the Cromwellian period emphasised their legitimacy through status descriptors and claims to 'official' status – claims based on outright popularity were rare. Moreover, as with post-Restoration petitioning and addressing, these Cromwellian texts had also operated in an environment in which subscriptional culture was deemed legitimate, but only within certain proscribed limits. While the Leicestershire address may have contained the names of those eking out a living on the margins of society, the return was, nonetheless, ordered with the county's 'better sort' heading up the list. It also indicated an acceptance of established gender norms by entirely excluding women.

These restrictions appeared to come under considerable strain during the Exclusion Crisis, as both Tory and Whig supporters resorted to mass petitioning or addressing as means of both lobbying authority and demonstrating popular support. This breach was arguably deceptive: those texts that touted their popular appeal simultaneously attempted to claim that they were nonetheless only subscribed by the better sort. This period of popular subscription activity was also brief: by 1682 the addresses issued in 'abhorrence' of Shaftesbury's 'Association' were notable for their lack of reference to the numbers subscribing, with emphasis placed ever more heavily on the authority of those addressing (predominately grand juries). The shift from any sense of 'direct' representation to virtual representation via well-established avenues such as grand juries was made even clearer in those texts issued in defiance of the Rye House Plot which, with a few notable exceptions, did not advertise the number of individuals subscribing.

While subscriptional activity was carried on with renewed vigour after the revolution of 1688, it largely took the form of associations and oaths of loyalty, though these exercises in canvassing public loyalty were usually accompanied with addresses. Surveying the public in this way was problematic, however, in an era where government was both accepted to have been founded on public consent but also where avenues for popular political participation (elections, demonstrations) were increasingly closed off.

Addresses thrived in the post-revolutionary period because they were able to virtually represent communities while at the same time being far more exclusive subscriptional texts: one feature of addressing throughout the period explored in this chapter is that women, in contrast to the largely accepted customary practice of women's petitioning in early modern England, do not appear as subscribers of addresses. It could be argued that addressing in England finished the early modern period as it had begun in the 1650s: offering the perfect medium for a nation which acknowledged that some form of popular political participation was legitimate but which wished to keep that participation tightly bounded and subservient to notions of deference, hierarchy and patriarchy.

NOTES

1 See Bodl MS Rawl A61* f. 174–5. For evidence of the later use of these addresses to attack or discredit individuals see Richard Bower's employment of the Yarmouth address above and the case of Sir Thomas Beaumont described below.
2 And note too the orders to destroy the Yarmouth address discussed above in Chapter three.
3 For examples of drafts see HRO, 44 M69 G3/264 (Hampshire address to Queen Anne, 1702); HRO 44 M 69/G3/1127 (Hampshire Grand Jury address abhorring Shaftesbury's Association); HRO 18 M51/636/84 (Hampshire address to William III, 1701); HRO WF/F2/6 (Winchester City Ledger Book, vol. 6, 1691–1713), f. 73v. (loyal address of the Mayor, Bailiffs and Commonalty of Winchester to William III following the 1696 assassination plot); LRO, HMC 404 (address from Corporation of Wigan thanking Charles II for his declaration explaining the dissolution of the Oxford Parliament); LRO HMC 448 (draft address from Preston abhorring the Association, 1682); LRO HMC 591 (Lancashire grand jury address on accession of James II, 1685); LRO HMC 596 (Clitheroe address thanking James II for his declaration of indulgence); LRO HMC 1169 (Corporation of Wigan address to George I, 1715); LRO DDKE 2/20/1 (Grand Jury of Lancashire's address to Charles II for his declaration, 12 July 1681); LRO DDKE 2/20/2 (Grand Jury of Lancashire's address abhorring the Rye House Plot, 1683); LRO DDKE 2/20/6 (Address from Lancashire Lord Lieutenant, Deputy Lieutenants, Militia Officers, Justices of the Peace, Gentlemen and Freeholders to James II in the wake of the Monmouth Rebellion, 1685); LRO DDKE 2/20/7 (Address of the Nobility, Gentry, Militia and Commonalty of the County Palatine of Lancashire to Queen Mary II, c.1690s); Northumberland Archives,1 DE 12–17 (draft address to James II on his accession, 1685); WYAS, WYL 150/MX/R/30/4 (Address of Lords, Deputy Lieutenants, Justices of Peace and Gentlemen of Yorkshire to James II after the Monmouth Rebellion); WYAS,

WYL 156/MX/12/29/15 (Address of Mayor and Commonalty of York to James II on his accession).

4 See, for example, the run of loyal addresses in Kingston History Centre, KB 10/1–7.

5 LRO, HMC 447, 'Humble address of the Lord Lieutenant, High Sheriff, Deputy Lieutenants, Justices of the Peace and other officers of Lancashire at a general meeting at Preston the 21 April 1682'; LRO HMC 458, Thomas Hodgkinson to Roger Kenyon, 30 May 1682, 'When ye have received it [the address] bee pleas'd to send to Mr James Ashton & Cousan Winckley to signe it. All ye rest of ye Aldrmen & councell have already subscribed.' For similar evidence see WYAS, WYL 150/MX/R/30/3, Sir John Boynton to Sir John Reresby, 22 February 1684.

6 Hirst, 'Making Contact', 47 but see also J. Fitzgibbons, 'Rethinking the English Revolution of 1649', *Historical Journal*, 60 (2017), 889–914.

7 Gloucestershire Record Office, D747/2/A-B.

8 Kent Archives and Library Service, CP/Bp/289, Brotherhood papers. draft minutes and accounts, 1683. For a similar example see Centre for Buckinghamshire Studies, D193/5/2 which contains the texts of two addresses issued by the county's grand jury in 1701 with lists of the subscribers and non-subscribers.

9 ESRO, Say 1/1/1/1–6.

10 ESRO, Say 1/1/1/2.

11 ESRO, Say 1/1/1/5.

12 Dorset History Centre, DC/LR/A/3/1 f. 1–9.

13 BL Stowe MS 222 f. 78 (MS Copy of 'Kentish Petition'); BL Stowe MS 223, f. 307–307v. (Gloucestershire address in support of Sacheverell); BL Stowe MS 225 f. 395–6 (address from Gloucestershire, 1713); BL Stowe MS 228 f. 77–77v. (address from Lieutenancy of London (in French) denouncing the 1715 rebellion) and f. 86, copy of London Gazette including many loyal addresses abhorring the rebellion; BL Stowe MS 229, f. 22v.–23 (address, in English, from High Sheriff, Grand Jury, JPs, clergy and gentlemen of Cornwall, 1 July 1716). See also BL Stowe MS 219, f. 149 (Lord Chandos' Letterbook) includes address to James II on his accession to the throne from his factory at Constantinople.

14 North, *Examen*, p. 542.

15 J. S. Morrill, *The Cheshire Grand Jury 1625–1659: A Social and Administrative Study* (Leicester: Leicester University Press, 1976), pp. 37–9.

16 BL Add MS 27448 (Paston letters), f. 147–9.

17 Longleat House, Thynne MS LXVII, f. 188–212 (BL Microfilm 904/36).

18 Bodl MS Rawl A 61* f. 164–87; The same reasons may also explain why Thurloe kept a copy of the address from the officers of the army of England, Ireland and Scotland, Bodl MS Rawl A. 61/3 f. 187.

19 R. Weil 'Thinking about allegiance in the English Civil War', *History Workshop Journal*, 61 (2006), 183–91.

20 *A true catalogue*, p. 42. Beaumont, MP for Leicestershire, 1654, 1656, 1659; created a baronet by Oliver Cromwell in 1658 History of Parliament Trust, London, unpublished article on Thomas Beaumont/Leicestershire for 1640–1660 section by David Scott. Hacker, MP for Leicestershire, 1656, 1659, executed for his part in the regicide in 1660, see ODNB; History of Parliament Trust, London, unpublished article on Francis Hacker/Leicestershire for 1640–60

section by David Scott. I am grateful to the History of Parliament Trust for allowing me to see these articles and subsequent articles listed in draft.

21 MP for Leicestershire, 1654, 1656; History of Parliament Trust, London, unpublished article on Thomas Pochin/Leicestershire for 1640–60 section by David Scott.

22 For Goodman see Bodl MS J. Walker C. 5 f. 77; Hartrop see MS J. Walker C. 11 f. 145v. –146. Nedham was with Hacker when the latter interviewed George Fox, see G. Fox, *The Journal*, N. Smith (ed.) (London: Penguin, 1998), p. 148. Fox refers to Nedham as Hacker's 'son' but he is referred to as a captain in Hacker's regiment in R. H. Evans, 'Nonconformists in Leicestershire in 1669', *Transactions of the Leicestershire Archaeological and Historical Society*, 25 (1949), 98–143, 112. See also C. H. Firth with G. Davies, *The Regimental History of Cromwell's Army*, (2 vols, Oxford: Clarendon Press, 1940) i, pp. 236–7. Nedham, Cockram and Dale were named as commissioners for Leicestershire in a letter to Thurloe dated 26 November 1655, *Thurloe State Papers*, iv, pp. 235–50. Cockram, Hartropp and Nedham were listed as militia commissioners in 1659, *A & O.*, ed. Firth, pp. 1320–42.

23 On Yaxley, see J. Nichols, *The History and Antiquities of the County of Leicester* (4 vols, Wakefield: S. R. Publishers, 1971 facsimile of 1795–1815 edition), ii, pp. 650–2.

24 Bodl MS Rawl A61* f. 179. Smith is listed as minister of Castle Donington on a 1659 address to the restored Rump, reproduced in W. Dugdale, *A short view of the late troubles in England* (Oxford, 1681), p. 473.

25 Bodl. MS Rawl A 61* f. 182; Nichols., *Leicester*, iii, p. 493; J and J. A.Venn, *Alumni Cantabrigienses* (6 vols, Cambridge: Cambridge University Press, 1922–1954), iv, p. 473.

26 W. Hartropp (ed.), *Leicester and its Inhabitants in 1664, being a transcript of the original Hearth Tax returns* (Leicester: privately printed, 1900).

27 As identified in D. Fleming, 'Faction and Civil War in Leicestershire', *Transactions of the Leicestershire Archaeological and Historical Society*, 57 (1981–82), 26–36.

28 Evans, 'Nonconformists in Leicestershire', 110.

29 Ibid., 106. For other examples, see Bodl MS Rawl A 61* f. 176, John Lewis of Foxton, reportedly a former 'captaine in Cromwell's army' whose house was used for conventicles, Evans, 'Nonconformists in Leicestershire', 129 or Henry Hartshorne (Bodl MS Rawl A 61* f. 176), husbandman, identified as a teacher of 'Anabaptists' in Lubenham, Evans, 'Nonconformists in Leicestershire', 130.

30 Bodl. MS J. Walker C.5 f. 70–71v where both men are recorded as having accused the minister of Newbold Verdon, Mr Nicolls, of having gone to the Royalist garrison at Ashby de la Zouch and having preached in support of the king's cause there.

31 Hesilrige's sympathies in relation to Richard Cromwell's regime are indicated by the fact that he owned a copy of *A second narrative of the late parliament*, discussed above Chapter two p. 41 (Leics RO, DG 21/283). The pamphlet notably exempted Hesilrige from the near blanket condemnation of MPs and Cromwellian peers within the text, p. 33.

32 Fleming, 'Faction and civil war in Leicestershire', 32.

33   See J. Wake, *The Brudenells of Deene* (London: Cassell & Co, 2nd edn, 1954), pp. 101–174, 480; M.A.E. Green (ed.), *Calendar of the Proceedings of the Committee for Compounding,1643–1660* (5 vols, London: HMSO, 1889–93), ii, pp. 1078–9.
34   Nichols, *Leicester*, ii, pp. 803–4; Leics RO, BRII/18/29, f. 868 (Leicester Hall Books); *A & O*, ed. Firth, pp. 1320–42.
35   M. Bennett, 'Leicestershire's Royalist officers and the war effort in the county, 1642–1646', *Transactions of the Leicestershire Archaeological and Historical Society*, 59 (1984–5), 44–72, at 46; P. R. Newman, *Royalist Officers in England and Wales, 1642–1660: A Biographical Dictionary* (New York: Garland, 1981), p. 46; *Calendar of the Committee for Compounding*, v, p. 109; TNA SP 23/49 f. 273v; TNA SP 23/70, f. 345, 347, 348, 363, 398; *Calendar of the Committee for Compounding*, ii, p. 1079; Nichols, *Leicester*, ii, pp. 803–4. Note that a 'Major Brudenell' (presumably the younger Thomas) was named as a mooted 'Knight of the Royal Oak' in 1660 (see below), providing further evidence of Royalist commitment.
36   *VCH, Leicestershire*, i, pt 2, p. 382.
37   H. Neville Davis, 'St Nicholas, Thomas', ODNB.
38   D. L. Wykes, 'Clarke, Matthew (c.1630-c.1708)', ODNB; Evans, 'Nonconformists in Leicestershire', 111.
39   J. Lee, *Eutaxia tou agrou: or, a vindication of a regulated enclosure* (1656), p. 15; A. G. Matthews, *Calamy Revised: being a revision of Edmund Calamy's Account of the Ministers and Others Ejected and Silenced* (Oxford: Clarendon Press, 2nd edn, 1988), p. 320.
40   This number assumes that the Thomas Whatton listed on f. 181 of the address was the Leicestershire Whatton who became rector of Knaptoft 1662–70 (Venn, *Alumni Cantabrigienses*, iv, p. 379), not the Whatton accused of gross indecency, A. G. Matthews, *Walker Revised: Being a Revision of John Walker's Sufferings of the Clergy during the Grand Rebellion, 1642–1660* (Oxford: Clarendon Press, 1948), p. 87; F. McCall, *Baal's Priests: The Loyalist Clergy and the English Revolution* (Farnham: Ashgate, 2013), p. 75.
41   BL, Harley MS 911, f. 27–27v. offers a list of leading Leicestershire families, identified with a 'K' for supporters of the king and 'R' for rebels. Cotton is listed on f. 27 with an 'R' by his name.
42   J. H. Pruett, *The Parish Clergy Under the Later Stuarts: The Leicestershire Experience* (Urbana, IL: University of Illinois Press, 1978), p. 173.
43   McCall, *Baal's Priests*, p. 72.
44   Pruett, *Parish Clergy*, p. 17; Matthews, *Walker Revised*, p. 246; McCall, *Baal's Priests*, p. 79; Bodl. MS J. Walker C. 11 f. 28–28v.
45   Bodl. MS J. Walker C. 5 f. 73v.
46   Thomas Player, rector of Gilmorton, was supposedly ejected for refusing the Covenant but appears to have been reinstated later, see Matthews, *Walker Revised*, p. 242. However, M. Bloxsom, *A History of the Parish of Gilmorton in the County of Leicester* (Lincoln: Lincolnshire Chronicle, 1918), pp. 38–9 suggests that Player was only dispossessed in 1648 (by which point ejection for refusing the Covenant seems unlikely) and may have been readmitted as early as 1652. In any case, refusal to swear Parliamentary oaths and covenants was another 'stock' charge used against conformist clergy. Some clerical subscribers did have Royalist connections. The minister of Walton le Wolds, Samuel Blunt or Blount's

father Edward was a royalist frequently in trouble with the county committee, see Matthews, *Walker Revised*, p. 232.
47 Nichols, *Leicester*, iv, pp. 67n, 68.
48 B.S. Capp, *England's Culture Wars: Puritan Reformation and its Enemies in the Interregnum, 1649–1660* (Oxford: Oxford University Press, 2012), p. 111.
49 Bodl MS Rawl A 61* f. 167; Nichols, *Leicester*, iv, p. 30; *Leicestershire Parish Registers*, ed. W. P. W. Phillimore (12 vols, London: Phillimore & Co., 1908–1914) xii, p. 10.
50 Dugdale, *A short view*, p. 473.
51 *C. J.*, vii, p. 775, 9 September 1659, 'That the Petitioners, all Ministers of the Gospel in the County of Leicester, faithful Servants to the Parliament, and embarked in the same Bottom with yourselves; some of us marched along with your Forces, to suppress the late Rebellion of Sir George Booth, and others.'
52 Dugdale, *A short view*, pp. 471–2. Another one of the subscribers to the 1659 address, Immanuel Bourne, minister of Waltham, was the author the same year of a work justifying maintenance by tithes against Baptist objections, *A defence and justification of ministers maintenance by tythes* (1659). Bourne publicly maintained that he had remained neutral during the civil war and conformed after the Restoration, Rosemary O'Day, 'Bourne, Immanuel', ODNB but see also A. Henstock and S. Band, 'Immanuel Bourne's "Letter" describing the civil war at Ashover: eyewitness account or Victorian Hoax?', in P. Riden and D. G. Edwards (eds), *Essays in Derbyshire History Presented to Gladwyn Turbutt* (Chesterfield: Derbyshire Record Society, 2006), pp. 147–75, esp. pp. 154–5.
53 Bloxsom, *History of Gilmorton*, pp. 41–2.
54 TNA E 179/251/4/8 f. 230; Bodl. MS Rawl A 61* f. 175.
55 Walter, *Covenanting Citizens*, pp. 155–6; Alex Craven, '"For the better uniting of the nation": the 1649 Oath of Engagement and the people of Lancashire', *Historical Research*, 83 (2010), 83–101 at 92–3. I am grateful to Ed Legon for the point regarding compulsion.
56 TNA E 179/251/4/8 f. 219. This strongly suggests that Leicestershire was not one of those counties where responsibility for the collection of the Hearth Tax had already been conceded to the 'receivers' and their 'chimney-men' brought in to administer the Michaelmas collection. See Elizabeth Parkinson, 'Understanding the Hearth Tax returns: historical and interpretative problems', in P. S. Barnwell and M. Airs (eds), *Houses and the Hearth Tax: The Later Stuart House and Society* (York: Council for British Archaeology, 2006), ch. 2, pp. 10–11.
57 Bodl MS Rawl A 61* f. 181, TNA E179 251/4/7 fols. 205–6. According to Bloxsom, *History of Gilmorton*, pp. 41–2, Sleath was the largest landowner in the parish after the Restoration.
58 TNA E 179/251/4 /2 (Melton Mowbray); E 179/251/4/7 (Cadeby).
59 Figures on census taken from *VCH, Leicestershire*, iii, pp. 173–4.
60 TNA E 179/332 pt 1, printed pro-forma certificate for Melton Mowbray dated 13th March 1672. Admittedly, only certificates from 1670s survive.
61 Searching through contemporary parochial records for Melton enables us to identify only a couple of individuals on the address (Thomas Hackett, a locksmith, and Roger Wayle or Waile, parish constable and mercer), Leics RO DG 32/2, Melton Mowbray burials, marriages, baptisms, 1642–62. One subscriber to

the address in nearby Somerby, Henry Trigge, is also listed as 'gent' in the 1645 parish registers for Melton.

62 Tom Arkell suggests a multiplier of 4.3 outside of London. Even taking into account the fact that no women signed the address, the overall number of subscribers on the 1664 return is still well below what one would expect from a sample of 3,000: T. Arkell, 'Multiplying factors for estimating population totals from the hearth tax', *Local Population Studies*, 28 (1982), 51–7. Given that enforcement of the tax did improve in its later iterations, more subscribers might be identified in later Hearth Tax returns, but a preliminary examination of those that survive has not indicated substantial differences, see TNA E 179/251/5–6, Leicestershire Hearth Tax 'for ye 3 half yeares at Michmas 1665'; E 179/251/9, Leicestershire Hearth Tax return, Lady Day 1666; E 179/240/279, Leicestershire Hearth Tax return, 1670. I am grateful to Andrew Wareham for the point about enforcement.

63 I have been influenced in this assessment by C. Ferguson's 'The hearth tax and the poor in post-restoration Woking', in T. Dean, G. Parry and E. Vallance (eds), *Faith, Place and People: Essays in Early Modern English History in Honour of Margaret Spufford* (Woodbridge: Boydell and Brewer, 2018), ch. 5.

64 Bodl. MS Rawl A 61* f 171v.

65 Alnwick Castle, DNP: MS 552 f. 37v (BL Loan Microfilm 331).

66 Bodl. MS Rawl A 61* f. 180; *Leics Parish Reg*, v, pp, 132, 136 has Tho Calvercott and Edward Smith described as 'armiger'. Henry Wilde is the major encloser mentioned above in Joseph Lee's tract.

67 See above Chapter two, pp. 47.

68 See Leics RO DG 25/1/1, Melton Mowbray town warden's book, f. 78–84: a number of entries, mainly dealing with the nomination of the borough's school masters in 1659. Henry Trigge, however, listed under Somerby on the address, does appear in these pages.

69 *Records of the Borough of Leicester: Being a Series of Extracts from the Archives of the Corporation of Leicester, 1603–1688*, ed. H. Stocks (Cambridge: Cambridge University Press, 1923), p. 449 and Hirst, 'Making Contact', 48.

70 I have identified eight addresses to Richard Cromwell where presenters are noted: *Mercurius Politicus*, 30 September to 7 October 1658, no. 436 (Sussex, presented by 'Mr Vintner' a minister); *Mercurius Politicus*, 14–21 October 1658, no. 438 (Address from 100 congregational churches, presented by Thomas Goodwin and address from ministers of Southwark presented by revd William Cooper); *Mercurius Politicus*, 28 October to 4 November 1658, no. 440 (Chesterfield address presented by Gabriell Waine); *Nouvelles Ordinaires de Londres*, 14–21 October 1658, no. 439 (presentation of address from London ministers by Dr Spurstow, Dr Seaman, Mr Ash, Mr Calamy, Manton, Jenkins, Bates and Poole); *Nouvelles Ordinaires de Londres*, 4–11 November 1658, no. 442 (address of the inhabitants of Bucks, presented by Whitelock, address from JPs and Grand Jury of Worcester, presented by procurer general of Duchy of Lancaster); *Nouvelles Ordinaires de Londres*, 23–30 January 1658/9, no. 452 (address of Isle of Wight, presented by William Sydenham).

71 TNA PRO 31/17/33 Transcript of the Council of State Order Book 3 September 1658 to 18 January 1658/9, pp. 38–40.

72 *A true catalogue*, pp. 39–40; *Mercurius Politicus*, 21–28 October 1658, no. 439.
73 D. Underdown, 'Pyne, John', ODNB.
74 *A true catalogue*, pp. 30–31. (Borough addresses outweighed those from counties 46 to 30).
75 Vallance, 'Harrington, Petitioning and the Construction of Public Opinion'.
76 A point well made in Waddell, 'Was early modern England a petitioning society?', https://manyheadedmonster.wordpress.com/2016/11/07/was-early-modern-england-a-petitioning-society/, accessed 8 August 2017.
77 Packer commented that the blasphemies contained within them were worse than those for which James Nayler was punished in 1656, *Diary of Thomas Burton*, iii, pp. 152–194; BL Add MS 15862, 9 February 1659.
78 See Starkey's quote above in Chapter two, pp. 47.
79 Bodl MS Rawl A61* f. 165.
80 Bodl MS Rawl A61* f. 164; John Prestwich, *Prestwich's respublica*, pp. 204–6; TNA PRO 31/17/33, pp. 3–4.
81 *A true catalogue*, pp. 37–8. For examples see Devizes, *Mercurius Politicus*, 28 October to 4 November 1658, no. 440; Leicester, *Mercurius Politicus*, 4–11 November 1658, no. 441; Coventry, *Mercurius Politicus*, 11–18 November 1658, no. 442.
82 Dugdale, *A short view*, pp. 461–2.
83 Bodl. MS Rawl A 61* f. 166.
84 A. Betteridge, 'Early Baptists in Leicestershire and Rutland II & III', *Baptist Quarterly*, 25 (1974), 272–85; 354–78 at 278, 364.
85 Bodl. MS Rawl A* 81 f. 171.
86 See transcription of the Leicestershire return available at https://drive.google.com/file/d/1DJOj0vux2keDJ4RG9aUlKAXTVADvEiWA/view?usp=sharing for variation across the address.
87 *Mercurius Politicus*, 14–21 October 1658 no. 438. Similar reports of mass addresses from Sussex, *Mercurius Politicus*, 30 September to 7 October 1658, no. 436 and County and City of Hereford, *A true catalogue*, p. 41; *Mercurius Politicus*, 21–28 October 1658, no. 439.
88 Alnwick Castle, DNP: MS 552, f. 47 (BL Loan Microfilm 331). The address was reproduced in *Nouvelles Ordinaires de Londres*, 16–23 December 1658, no. 448.
89 *Mercurius Politicus*, 17–24 March 1659, no. 559
90 While it has been noted that leading 'conventiclers' can be identified on the address, both the preachers and laypersons identified ranged across Protestant denominations and included Presbyterians as well as Baptists and Congregationalists.
91 A. H. Woolrych, 'The good old cause and the fall of the Protectorate', *Cambridge Historical Journal*, 13 (1958), 133–61 at 138; *Diary of Thomas Burton*, iii, pp. 288–96; G. Davies, 'The army and the downfall of Richard Cromwell', *Huntington Library Bulletin*, 7 (1935), 131–67, at 146.
92 See above Chapter two.
93 T. Fuller, *A happy handful, or Green hopes in the blade* (1660), 'To His Highness the Lord General MONCK'.
94 I am grateful to Brodie Waddell for this point.
95 Fuller, *A happy handful*, pp. 24–5.

96 H. Stocks and W. H. Stevenson (eds), *Records of the Borough of Leicester: Being a Series of Extracts from the Archives of the Corporation of Leicester, 1603–1688* (Cambridge: Cambridge University Press, 1923), p. 459; *Mercurius Politicus*, 9–16 February 1660, no. 607; Knights, *Representation and Misrepresentation*, pp. 120–1; Worden, 'Campaign for a Free Parliament', 193–4.

97 *An Address from the Gentry of Norfolk and Norwich to General Monck in 1660: Facsimile of a Manuscript in the Norwich Public Library*, with an introduction by Hamon Le Strange and biographical notes by Walter Rye (Norwich: Jarrold and Sons, Ltd, 1913); Knights, *Representation and Misrepresentation*, p. 138; Worden 'Campaign for a Free Parliament', 191.

98 *Address from the Gentry of Norfolk*, p. 14.

99 Ibid.

100 Ibid., p. 12.

101 M. W. Helms/E. Cruickshanks, 'Doyley, Sir William c. 1614–1677', in *History of Parliament*, ed. Henning, www.historyofparliamentonline.org/volume/1660-1690/member/doyley-sir-william-1614-77, accessed 8 August 2017; *Address from the gentry of Norfolk*, p. 19.

102 TNA E 179/134/317; It is worth noting, however, that the 'Free and voluntary present' was criticised in Parliament as a means by which wealthy 'Presbyterians' could ingratiate themselves with the Restoration monarchy, S. K. Roberts, '"Ordering and methodizing" William Dugdale in Restoration England', in C. Dyer and C. Richardson (eds), *William Dugdale, Historian, 1605–1686. His Life, His Writings and His County* (Woodbridge: Boydell, 2009), pp. 66–88 at p. 74. I am grateful to my colleague Andrew Wareham for the suggestion to look at the Free and Voluntary Present.

103 Fuller, *A happy handfull*, 'To His Highness the Lord General Monck'. See Worden, 'Campaign for Free Parliament', p. 196 n.31 for comment on the unusual address given to Monck in this tract.

104 TNA SP 29/39 f. 247. The exact date that it was confirmed is, however, unclear. Nichols gives the patent as dated 21 February 1660 (Nichols, *Leicester*, ii, p. 860), probably taking the date from William Dugdale, *The antient usage* (1682), p. 127. The Crown docket book for 1660–75 lists the patent as granted on 21 February 1660/1 (TNA C231/7 p. 81) but the petitions relating to the case show that confirmation had been delayed until at the summer of 1661. At some stage the intercession of significant local Royalists, including the sheriff Richard Roberts (TNA SP 29/39 f. 253), and the attorney general Geoffrey Palmer (TNA SP 29/31 f. 60 and see above p. 142), who testified to Beaumont's work protecting the king's supporters during the 1650s, seem to have swung the case in Beaumont's favour.

105 TNA SP 29/39 f. 250. See petition of Dr Joseph Rhodes and Sir John Duncombe, 22 February 1661, TNA SP 29/39 f. 248. Beaumont made an attestion before Dr J. Bird, Master of Chancery, that he never signed or promoted the 1648 petition, 22 May 1661, TNA SP 29/39 f. 252.

106 *Records of the Borough of Leicester*, eds. Stocks and Stevenson, pp. 385, 394–5; *The humble petition of the committee, gentry, ministry, and other the inhabitants of the county of Leicester* (1648), Thomason E. 465 [36]; *C.J.*, vi, p. 41.

107 Besides Thomas Pochin, signatories included Beaumont's son (also Thomas), Robert Fryer, Farnham Riddle or Readell, Thomas Marriott, Randolph Boulter,

Clement Noone and James Winstanley, the recorder of Leicester who presented the borough address.
108 L. A. Knapfa, 'Palmer, Sir Geoffrey', ODNB.
109 TNA SP 29/30 f. 61. For a similar case see A. J. Hopper, 'The reluctant regicide? Thomas Wayte and the civil wars in Rutland,' *Midland History*, 39 (2014), 36–52.
110 Beaumont did not return to the bench til August 1667, TNA C231/7 p. 311; Scott, 'Beaumont', HoP.
111 J. Innes, *An examination of a printed pamphlet, entitled, a narration of the siege of the town of Leicester* (1645), p. 5 and see also A. P. Pochin, *The Pochins of Barkby* (privately printed, 1980), unpaginated.
112 H. E. Broughton, *Family and Estate Records in the Leicestershire Record Office* (Leicester: Leicestershire Museums, Arts and Records Service, 1991), p. 26; J. Burke, *A Genealogical and Heraldic History of the Commoners of Great Britain and Ireland* (4 vols, London,1835–38), i, p. 234.
113 Pochin, *Pochins of Barkby Hall*, has father as 'Matthew' but 'George Pochin Esq, Tho. Pochin gent' head up the return for Barkby Thorp, E 179/134/317. The description of the two Pochins makes it likely that it was George, not Thomas, who was named as a potential 'knight of the oak' – see Burke reference above.
114 TNA C 231/7 p. 387. He was appointed again in 1680, *A catalogue of all his majesties justices of the peace* (1680), p. 10. Pochin also appears as a sheriff of Leicestershire on Hearth Tax exemption certificates for Barkby, 9 December 1672, Walton le Wolds, 17 December 1672, Cossington, 12 December 1672 and Barsby, 24 December 1672, E 179/332 pt 1.
115 See the broadsides contained in BL Thomason 669 f. 25 for other examples.
116 TNA SP 29/1/f. 55–6 printed as *To the king's most excellent majesty ... the humble address of the nobility and gentry of Dorset* (1660), (Thomason 669.f 25[44]). Bowie observes similar practices in Scotland in anti-Union addresses, *Scottish Public Opinion*, p. 127.
117 Somerset (TNA SP 29/1 f. 85; Thomason 669 f. 25 [43]); Gloucestershire (TNA SP 29/1 f. 57; Thomason 669 f. 25 (48); Rutland (TNA SP 29/1 f. 83; Thomason 669 f. 25[55]).
118 Comparison of TNA SP 29/1 f. 85 and Thomason 669 f. 25 [43]. The Earl of Winchester, John Paulet, was the leading signatory to the address on both versions. For the Waldrons see Michael A. LaCombe, 'Waldron, Humfrey', ODNB. George Horner was MP for the county in the Convention Parliament (and one of the presenters of this address) and a Samuel Horner appears only on the printed broadside, M. W. Helms/I. Cassidy, 'Horner, George I (1605–77) of Cloford, Som.', in Henning ed., *History of Parliament*, www.historyofparliamentonline.org/volume/1660-1690/member/horner-george-i-1605-77, accessed 8 August 2017.
119 TNA SP 29/1 f. 75–77 (about 360 signatures).
120 North, *Examen*, p. 548.
121 *London Gazette*, 30 June to 4 July 1681, no. 1630.
122 In the same issue above, Town and Port of Deal (362), Inhabitants of Great Marlow (222); *London Gazette*, 4–7 July 1681, no. 1631, Officers of Militia, other gentlemen and loyal inhabitants of Canterbury (400); *London Gazette*, 7–11 July 1681, no. 1632, Inhabitants of Westminster and its liberty ('signed by some thousands'); *London Gazette* 11–14 July 1681, no. 1633, Brecon (2700); 'Loyal

Inhabitants' of Aylesbury (270); *London Gazette*, 15–18 July 1681, no. 1634, Nobility, gentry, clergy and other freeholders of N. Riding of Yorkshire (185).
123 *London Gazette*, 21–25 July 1681, no. 1636.
124 *London Gazette*, 11–15 August 1681, no. 1642.
125 *Loyal Protestant and True Domestick Intelligence*, 16 April 1681, no. 12.
126 *Impartial Protestant Mercury*, 28 June to 1 July 1681, no. 20 alleged that those signing the Hereford address included honorary freemen residing out of town. *Impartial Protestant Mercury*, 11–15 July 1681, no. 24 attacked the Herefordshire address as signed by only 59 individuals 'no great number for so Loyal a County as that is'.
127 *London Gazette*, 1–5 September 1681, no. 1648.
128 *Loyal Protestant and True Domestick Intelligencer*, 5 July 1681, no. 35. A report supported by the *Impartial Protestant Mercury*, 2–6 September 1681, no. 39, which stated that the addresses was presented with 20,000 names, none subscribing who 'is either Journeyman, Tapster, Hostler, Waterman or the like'.
129 See report of the Address of the Bailiffs and Freemen of Kingston upon Thames, *London Gazette*, 15–19 September 1681, no. 1652, reporting 139 subscribers; and Kingston Borough Archives, KB 10/1.
130 For some limited examples of popular subscription to these addresses *London Gazette*, 20–24 April 1682, no. 1714, Derbyshire grand jury address 'Signed by above 2000 Freeholders'; *London Gazette* 13–17 July 1682, no. 1738, address of the loyal young freemen and apprentices of the City of London 'Signed by about 12000 Hands'.
131 *The Entring Book of Roger Morrice*, ii. p. 430. Note too the comment from Charles Duncombe to Sir Thomas Thynne in January 1682 that the abhorrences would 'keepe the people warme some time', Longleat House, Thynne MS, 21 f. 350 (BL Loan Microfilm 904/11).
132 See below Chapter seven.
133 It was finally repealed in 1986 as part of schedule 3 of the public order act, www.legislation.gov.uk/ukpga/1986/64/schedule/3, accessed 8 August 2017.
134 See above Chapter four, p. 98.
135 Knights, *Representation and Misrepresentation*, p. 137.
136 HMC Kenyon MSS, p. 406.
137 [Oldmixon], *History of Addresses*, (1710), pp. 196–9, ibid., pt 2., pp. 6–7; Knights, *Representation and Misrepresentation*, p. 123.
138 See for example TNA C213/138/1 (West Derby and Lonsdale Hundreds).
139 W. Gandy (ed.), *Lancashire Association Oath Rolls 1696* (London: Society of Genealogists reprint, 1985), p. 4 (Rebecca Riselton of Halewood); p. 60 (Frances Edmondson – Borwich); p. 90 (Elizabeth Readhead of Blawith); p. 101(Aliz Nowell and Frances Turner – Clitheroe). Further Association rolls for Lancashire can be found in LRO QDV/10 but these exclusively feature the names of male office-holders.
140 See my 'On and off the page: women, citizenship and subscriptional culture in early modern England', in C. Cuttica and M. Peltonen (eds), *Democracy and Anti-Democracy in Early Modern Europe* (forthcoming, Brill, 2019). For political expediency as a motivation for encouraging women to subscribe, see Walter, *Covenanting citizens*, p. 204, inspired, Walter suggests, by the prominence of

Who were the 'public'?

women in the Scottish Covenanter movement on which see L. A. M. Stewart, *Rethinking the Scottish Revolution* (Oxford: Oxford University Press, 2016), pp. 97–114.

141 Though there is some evidence of the Association of 1696 being used to purge Tories from office, Vallance *Revolutionary England and the National Covenant*, pp. 201–2.

142 P. Langford, *Public Life and the Propertied Englishman, 1689–1798* (Oxford: Clarendon Press, 1991), pp. 98–114; E. Vallance, 'Women, politics and the 1723 Oaths of Allegiance to George I', *Historical Journal*, 59 (2016), 975–99 and note that some anti-Jacobite loyal addresses were clearly created in conjunction with the formation of volunteer armed associations: Dr Williams' Library, Baxter Treatise, V, fo. 320–1, item 186, 'The Humble Address & Association of us Ministers of ye Gospel in ye Counties of Nottingham, Derby, Leicester & places adjacent.' The ministers refer to 'our hearty subscribing ye Associaton, wth ye rest of our fellow-subjects.' On these loyalist associations, see F. O'Gorman, 'Origins and trajectories of loyalism in England, 1580–1840', in A. Blackstock and F. O'Gorman (eds), *Loyalism and the Formation of the British World, 1775–1914* (Woodbridge: Boydell and Brewer, 2014), pp. 19–42.

143 See the declaration from Coventry to Oliver Cromwell, signed by over 1,100 individuals (in a city of 1,400 households) in 1657 discussed in A. Hughes, 'Coventry and the English Revolution', in R. C. Richardson (ed.), *Town and Countryside in the English Revolution* (Manchester: Manchester University Press, 1992), ch. 4, p. 92; TNA SP 18/158 f. 170.

Chapter 6

The performance of loyalty: ritual in loyal addressing

Sir John Reresby's memoirs contain an account of a violent altercation between Reresby and a fellow Yorkshire magistrate, Mr 'Gysop' [or Jessop] at a meeting held on 18 July 1682. According to Reresby, Jessop was a lone voice of complaint against the harsh execution of laws against dissenters in the county. Reresby responded that Jessop was 'saucy' for describing the actions of his fellow justices in this way. Jessop in turn denounced Reresby's remarks as 'impudent'. Enraged by Jessop's comments, and finding himself sat too far away to administer admonition directly, Reresby threw a 'leaden standish' (a sort of inkstand) at his opponent which struck Jessop and cut his cheek 'quite thorow'. Both men then drew their swords but further bloodshed was avoided through the intercession of the other members at the meeting.[1]

Reresby was notoriously quick to anger and this altercation might be seen simply as further evidence of what one historian has described as his addiction to violence.[2] A letter from Reresby to the Earl of Halifax on 19 July to explain his actions reveals, however, that there were longer-standing tensions behind the clash. Reresby told Halifax that 'Mr Gysop hath ever had a resentment of my gaining an address from Sheffield and Hallamshire (that being his own nest), when he publiquely refused to sign it himselfe, saying he would not intermeddle in any disputes twixt his father and mother (meaning the King and Parliament), and endeavoured to prevent it in others.'[3]

The dispute between the two men stretched back to September the previous year. Invited along with other Yorkshire gentlemen to a feast at the Hallamshire Cutler's Hall on 1 September, Reresby had advised the Cutlers that they should present the King with an address from their corporation, thanking him for the declaration explaining his reasons for dissolving the Oxford Parliament. The Cutlers heeded Reresby's advice and a week later presented him with an address (he reported signed by 550), which they asked him to deliver to the Crown. Reresby accepted and on 19 September at Newmarket presented Charles II with the Hallamshire Cutlers' address. The text was well received, even though Reresby's *Memoirs* suggest that the

King was not terribly familiar with either Hallamshire or its cutlers. Reresby, however, did not miss the opportunity to use his audience with Charles to score political points, informing the King 'of a neighbouring justice of the peace (presumably Jessop), who refused to sign of the addresse, though he lived within the compas of Hallamshire, and to discourage others from doing it'. Charles promised Reresby that the offending magistrate would not be in post for long.[4] The Hallamshire Cutlers' decision to address the King was equally driven by self-interest. The Cutlers had a long-standing complaint that their forges were assessed for the Hearth Tax even though, as commercial 'hearths' like bakeries, they believed they should have been exempt.[5] By securing Reresby's services, the Cutlers hoped that they had acquired a powerful ally who would be able to intercede directly with the Crown on their behalf.[6]

The bloody encounter between Reresby and Jessop, and the rivalries and special interests that helped provoke it, demonstrate that, as well as the texts of the addresses themselves, the ritual and performative aspects of addressing were also highly significant. Producing, presenting or introducing an address could bring honour and royal preferment upon both individuals and groups but equally such activity could lead to disputes over precedence and seniority. Addressers who were deemed not to have delivered their texts correctly could find themselves the object of royal disfavour. Choices about who to get to present addresses and ask to introduce the addressers were also far from straightforward – not only could influential individuals be offended if they were not approached to present or introduce addresses, the choice of presenters and introducers sent out important signals about the political and religious affiliations of the addressers.

Critically, these choices and this performance had to be done correctly to secure access to the monarch. It was through this access, increasingly restricted at Court after the Restoration, that honour, preferment or concessions such as an exemption from the Hearth Tax could be secured. The performance itself was costly, not just in terms of the drafting, subscription and creation of a fair copy of the address, but also in paying for the travel, food and accommodation of presenters on their way to Court. The expense was not limited to the addressing itself, as many communities chose to offer cash gifts to the Crown along with their expressions of thankfulness and fidelity. Some historians have seen the readiness of even very small communities to meet this expense as evidence of their ideological commitment to the governing regime. This is debatable. As we will see, there were practical considerations which simply made addressing a much more expensive activity than other related means of approaching authority, namely the petition. Yet, the readiness of both communities and the Crown occasionally to spend large sums of money on addressing and 'treating' addressers does demonstrate that addressing mattered both to individuals (and the localities they were representing) and to the government.

The willingness to expend time and cash on addressing activity was often driven by pragmatic considerations, as in the case of the Cutlers. Addressing had the potential to provide communities and individuals with political access, influence and preferment. Yet, the motivations behind addressing activity were not purely instrumental. Addressing activity was engaged in for the honour it was seen to bring upon the addressers, and recalled as a way of connecting people and places to national history. As we will see, this is no better demonstrated than in the prominence that some figures, such as Reresby, gave to addressing activity in their autobiographical writing.

THE PERFORMANCE OF ADDRESSING

The creation of a loyal address can be described as a three stage process. First, typically with prompting from significant local powerbrokers and occasionally with central direction as well (Brian Weiser, for example, notes that Charles II urged the issuing of loyal addresses from dissenting churches in response to his second declaration of indulgence), an address would be drafted.[7] Though these drafts were the initial products of grand juries, common councils and county benches, they too were often vetted by major figures with connections to the political centre. The Earl of Yarmouth, for example, made sure his instructions concerning the framing of the Norwich address abhorring the Association had been followed by reviewing a draft at a dinner with the mayor of the city.[8] Second, the address was subscribed, again with local office-holders and important community figures usually heavily involved in the distribution of the text and the gathering of names. Finally, the text was delivered at Court by presenters nominated by the community and the presenters themselves were introduced to the Crown by a leading courtier previously approached by the addressers. As we will see, the choice of this 'introducer' was not straightforward and a number of approaches occasionally had to be made.[9]

The denouement of this addressing activity also followed a gestural script, with the addressers kneeling or prostrating themselves before the monarch when delivering the address. Once this action was completed, the monarch (or occasionally their representative) would respond to the address and allow them to come forward to have the honour of kissing their hand. (The significance of the Crown instructing a surrogate to respond will be discussed below.)

The ritual aspects of addressing were also mirrored in addresses presented to MPs during the 1680s. Sir John Knight, MP for Bristol, was accompanied on his journey back from London by 196,

> of the most Eminent and Loyal Protestants in this City, all on Horse-back; who came to wait upon him home, and to testifie their Respects to him for his Faithful Service in the last Parliament [in the city's address]: And had not his Letters been

kept at the Post-Office longer then ordinary, whereby his coming down was hardly known, he would have been attended by a much greater number.[10]

Mark Knights has argued that one of the reasons for the popularity of the addressing form in the post-Restoration period was because it offered a relatively cheap way of delivering a 'gift' to the Crown.[11] Certainly, it involved less expense than the hospitality and gift-giving that typically accompanied a royal visit. Charles II, for example, was given four golden herrings worth £200 to £250 when he came to Great Yarmouth in September 1671.[12] Nonetheless, producing and presenting a loyal address could still be costly: the Guestling or Brotherhood of the Cinque Ports spent £20 in 1683 in drawing up an address and covering transport, food and accommodation for the appointed presenters.[13]

In contrast to petitioning, costs could not be reduced by employing the distribution of printed petitions as a cheaper alternative because it was the delivery of the manuscript address which provided the opportunity to lobby government.[14] Yet, the perceived value of addressing was such that many corporations and counties appeared ready to meet these costs – so many that Sir John Reresby reported that beds could barely be had at Newmarket in 1683, such was the throng of people waiting on the King to deliver their addresses.[15] In contrast to the argument of Scott Sowerby, however, this readiness to commit significant resources was not solely a consequence of ideological commitment to the Crown's policies, but recognition of the esteem and advantage that individual addressers and those they represented could gather from participating in this public ritual.[16]

ADDRESSING AND THE INDIVIDUAL

The importance of addressing as a marker of status both for individuals and groups/communities can be seen in the prominence given to addressing activity in some examples of early modern life-writing. Lengthy reports of addressing activity are a feature not only of Reresby's memoirs, but also Edmund Calamy's 'Accounts', Benjamin Stinton's 'journal' and Bulstrode Whitelocke's 'Diary'.[17] Mark Knights has also noted the way in which William Holgate of Saffron Walden, Essex, filled his commonplace book with the texts of addresses sent from his borough and the county during Queen Anne's reign.[18]

Reresby, Calamy, Stinton and Whitelocke were all directly involved in presenting addresses and the encounters that their actions afforded with the monarch (or in Whitelocke's case chief magistrate) were clearly important in terms of these individuals' estimation of their self-worth. Reresby reported that, having delivered the Middlesex Justices' address abhorring Shaftesbury's Association to Charles II that,

> His Majesty amongst several other expressions to me at the same said thes words, that he thanked me for my endeavours in this and other perticulars of his service,

> that whenever I had a mind that I should freely have accesse to him, for he had a kindenesse for me and a good opinion of my judgement.[19]

Calamy's audience with George I in 1717 was recalled in particularly vivid detail, though more it seems out of shock than awe:

> His Majesty Used to Receive us upon such Occasions Standing on his Feet, But was now Sitting on a Chair of State, under a Canopy, and I was Led up to him under my Arm by Mr Secretary Stanhope (who Introduced us) thro' a Lane of Noblemen, and Attendants at Court. When I Came near him, I Observed his Lips Quiver'd and his Hands Shook, and Saw Several Signs of a great Langour and Faintness which Sensibly Struck me. Telling the Secretary afterwards what I Observed with Concern, he Signified to me, that his Majesty had an Indisposition that Morning upon him, which was pretty Usual with him, But that there was not the Least Hazard in it, and it would soon be over, which made me Easy.[20]

As David Wykes has observed, the opportunity to present loyal addresses was particularly important for the London 'Committee of the Three Denominations (of Presbyterians Congregationalists and Baptists)', because it made them one of the few private bodies granted the privilege of addressing the Crown.[21] This privilege, granted to the committee in the reign of Queen Anne, conferred official legitimacy upon both these churches and their ministers.[22] The honour afforded the dissenting ministers, however, was clearly not felt appropriate by some. The Tory paper, the *Weekly Journal with Fresh Advices Foreign and Domestick*, reported that an address had been made to the King 'by the whole Body of Dissenting Ministers viz., Presbyterians, Independents, and Anabaptists'. The presenters, it alleged,

> though they were all formerly of very mean Occupations have since their Call been look'd upon as the most eminent Preachers among that Dipping Set of People. A Man of Parts that hath raised himself from a low Degree by his Talents, is so far from deserving our Censure, that he deserves our Applause.[23]

The Weekly Journal then employed the not entirely flattering example of Cardinal Wolsey to illustrate the point. Calamy noted the slight in his 'Account', stating that the paper had represented the Baptist ministers presenting the address as 'Illiterate Tradesmen', but concluded that the slur was 'not Thought worth while to take any Publick Notice of'.[24] The attack, however, clearly stung Benjamin Stinton, one of the five presenters of the address. Stinton devoted some six pages of his journal to rebutting the charge, rehearsing the biography of the lead presenter, Nathaniel Hodges, to show that he had never been in trade but had gone from grammar school to the dissenting academy at Taunton, and was then called to the ministry. Even if some Baptist preachers had been working men, Stinton said, this had been the practice of churches through the ages, citing the example of the Jews who had called for their 'greatest Rabbies & Doctrs to be Trained up in some Mechanic Act'. Stinton closed by admitting that

The performance of loyalty

> It was not worth while I Confess to have said so much in Answer to such a Scandalous and Lying paper as the Journal; but I find that most Authors who have Writ against the Baptists, have gone upon this as the Common Topick to render them Odious & Contemptible to ye People.[25]

The presence of discussions of addressing in life-writing produced by those involved in presenting addresses is unsurprising given the importance attached to the activity in conferring honour on an individual. We can also find discussions of addressing, however, in autobiographical works by those typically excluded from political activity of this kind. In her 'Remembrances', the gentlewoman Elizabeth Freke included a transcript of the address of the clergy of London and Westminster to Queen Anne, presented by the bishop of London. The text could have been taken from either the *London* or *Norwich Gazettes*, though Freke appears to have added some details of her own (the number of clergy accompanying the address).[26] Freke's 'Remembrances' included comment on high politics in the late seventeenth and early eighteenth century.[27] The incorporation of this address into her autobiographical collections, however, may have been prompted by personal experience. Freke was the holder of the advowson for the parish of West Bilney, even referring to herself as 'parson' when asserting her right to appoint the curate.[28] Freke's 'Remembrances' also include her lengthy correspondence with the bishop and diocese of Norwich, centring on her rights of appointment and the costs of supporting the minister and church at Bilney.[29] These disputes became heated: Freke was summoned to the consistory court to answer for her appropriation of the tithes and profits belonging to the living but did not attend on the grounds of illness. The chancellor of Norwich's response to Freke's letter excusing her absence, in which she maintained that she had shown great 'charrity to this church and the sopportt of itt ... that were nott obliged to itt', was blunt:

> I crave leave to differ from you in my sentyments aboutt the allowance of twenty pound per annum by your self and father and predycessours to the curratt of Billney which you say has been pure charrity. I think you are of rightt obliged to itt by the laws of God and man.[30]

Freke would ultimately be excommunicated by the court for her failure to appear.[31] Perhaps in reproducing the address of the London clergy, an incident which she gave more space than any other national event, Freke was reasserting her authority over the church at Bilney: if the bishop of London and 150 male clergymen could come to make public homage to Queen Anne, should not the bishop and chancellor of Norwich bend the knee to the 'parson' of Bilney?

Yet, aside from their personal importance to individuals, it was surely again the mnemonic quality of loyal addressing that gave it such prominence in some life-writing. Certainly, the regular appearance of addresses in contemporary newsbooks may explain their presence in contemporary 'Diurnals', such as that compiled by Thomas Rugg.[32] The ubiquity of loyal addresses in newsprint may also account for their prominence in chronicles and histories, such as those produced by White Kennett, bishop of Peterborough, which relied heavily on printed sources.[33] As has already been noted, however, loyal addressing also quickly generated its own compendia and histories, establishing it as a particularly reflective genre.

Here, in terms of its presence in examples of autobiographical works, there may be a comparison to be drawn between addressing and another inherently ephemeral genre, the almanac, which has recently been identified by Adam Smyth as a vehicle for life-writing.[34] Addresses, as with almanacs, were also a form ready-made for adaptation, as the circulation of drafts and amendment of printed copies in John Collier of Hastings' papers demonstrate.[35] Moreover, just as addresses and printed commentaries on addressing showed an awareness of the history of past addressing activity, so these texts also came to be incorporated in personal and corporate histories. It is worth noting that while some of the works discussed above appear in diary form, they were all later productions, created with the intent of forming a coherent narrative of that individual or community's life. For example, Reresby's 'Memoirs' were part of a broader biographical project which included the writing of the Reresby family's history.[36] Bulstrode Whitelocke's pride in being approached to present the Buckinghamshire address to Richard Cromwell might be viewed as simply another example of his egotism. The differences between the fuller discussion of his role in addressing activity in his 'Diary', however, and the briefer notices in his published *Memorials* are arguably significant.[37] As Blair Worden noted in his review of Ruth Spalding's edition of the 'Diary', Whitelocke actually referred to the text as his 'history' or 'private history'.[38]

Broadly speaking, the distinction between the texts that formed the basis of his *Memorials* and those that formed the 'Diary' was that the former was intended as a 'public' record of events, while the latter was a more personal narrative of the period that Whitelocke had lived through.[39] By the time that Whitelocke came to write his account of the later 1650s, Worden argues that this distinction had effectively broken down and the source material for the 'Diary' and the published *Memorials* were one and the same.[40] Even so, given the prominence of accounts of addressing activity in other autobiographies, Whitelocke's touting of his role in the framing of addresses in 1658–9 speaks less of his 'incurable self-importance' and more of the significance of recording an activity that was publicly acknowledged to confer honour and status.[41] Stinton's 'Journal' might be read in a similar way: while this was certainly a personal account (Stinton's bruised ego was patently on display in his discussion of the 1715 address) it was also meant as a denominational history (the full title of the work was 'A Journall of the Affairs of the Antipaedobaptists').[42]

Addresses featured in life-writing because they represented an important means (as we will see in more detail) for individuals of gaining credit both within their communities and at the centre of power. It was also through addressing activity that direct access could be gained to the monarch or chief magistrate. They were also incorporated into these biographical texts, however, because of the way in which they connected the individual or the group or the community to a wider historical narrative. This also made addresses an important reference point for later local histories, which attempted to place the history of their community within a larger national story.[43] In turn, this was connected to the public nature of addressing, not only in terms of the publication of these addresses in the contemporary press (again providing source material for autobiographers, chroniclers and historians) but also the very public ceremonial that accompanied them. The readiness of individuals and communities to participate in this ritual was a consequence of the significant rewards that could come from successful addressing activity, and there were similar benefits for the Crown in permitting these approaches. Yet, there were also significant risks involved for both sides in the exchange.

Some of the benefits for individuals in participating in addressing activity have already been touched upon. The importance of acting as a presenter of an address is evidenced by the regularity with which the press reported both presenters and those introducing the addressers. John Morphew's compendia of addresses prompted by the trial of Henry Sacheverell included an index covering presenters and introducers of texts as well as place names.[44] When this was omitted or given incorrectly, corrections were swiftly issued as was the case with the Exeter address condemning the 1715 rebellion: 'N.B. The Address from the City of Exeter was not presented by Dr. Lynford, as was said by Mistake in the Gazette of the 9th Instant'.[45] Failure to accurately record who had presented an address could generate local disputes. In the case of a loyal address to George II sent from Middlesex's JPs, it was alleged that one of the justices, John Gonson, had influenced the press to ensure that only his role in delivering the text was acknowledged.[46] The effort to capture the names of those presenting addresses was not only made in print: Gregory Alford's role as a presenter, and the praise he received at Court as reported in the *London Gazette* for these displays of loyalty was also reproduced along with the manuscript draft addresses in Dorset archives.[47] As has been noted, the choice of certain presenters was loaded with political significance: Lord Kilmorey who introduced the Shropshire address in 1710 was a former nonjuror and his readiness now to take the oaths to Queen Anne was used as evidence of the loyalty the pro-Sacheverell addresses were inspiring.[48]

Presenting an address was also a route to preferment. Reresby used his addressing activities as part of his strategy to secure the governorship of York – a route that his rival, Sir Thomas Slingsby, also sought to employ, 'he haveing just at that time brought up an address to his Majesty from grand jurys and the gentry at the assizes at Yorke'.[49] Besides the traditional courtesy of permitting the addressers to kiss the monarch's hand, some presenters, such as Thomas Walker who presented the Exeter address in 1681, were knighted for their services.[50] It was also common for addressers to be entertained at Court or by leading courtiers. The lawyers of Middle Temple were 'very splendidly' hosted by Sir Leoline Jenkins at a dinner in their honour following the presentation of their address abhorring the Association.[51] Edmund Calamy reported that when the London dissenting ministers presented their address to Queen Anne in 1706, they were not only permitted to kiss the Queen's hand but were 'Nobly Entertain'd at Dinner at the Board of Greencloth, which was a Favour we never had had before'.[52] The most extravagant example of hospitality of this kind was the feast laid on for the loyal London apprentices who addressed Charles II in 1681: according to contemporary letters, the entire cost of the dinner at Mercers' Hall was a staggering £750 (nearly £86,000 in present day terms).[53]

The favour shown to addressers did bring accusations that the loyalty of the addressers had simply been bought: in reference to the loyal London apprentices, that hopes of royal venison had inspired their 'Cackling Loyalty'.[54] Accusations of this kind made it necessary for the loyalist press to dispute that communities had only been brought to address through the promise of gifts and honours:

> And whereas in some Pamphlets it is said, That the motive which induced Gentlemen to promote Addresses, was to get Honour; those worthy Persons Col. Windham and Aldermen James Bennet, who presented our Address, modestly declined the Honour of Knighthood, though His Majest my graciously proffered to confirm it upon them, begging His Majesty to excuse them, lest the Enemies of King and Church should object it as their prospect.[55]

ADDRESSES, COMMUNITIES AND POLITICAL ACCESS

Tim Harris has argued convincingly that we should not view such 'treating' of addressers as outright bribery, seeing it instead as part of 'a dialectical process, with the activities of the propagandists helping to prompt an initiative from below, which in turn is encouraged by elite rewards'.[56] James Daybell has also noted that petitions, specifically petitionary letters, had a gift-like aspect to them.[57] A correctly framed petition, couched in respectful, humble and supplicatory language was itself a part of this gift exchange. The emotional content of addresses and petitions, with promises of fidelity and service returned with thankfulness and gratitude, also spoke of the transactional nature of these texts.

In the case of addressing, this gift-giving was certainly not just one way: the Crown was a recipient as well as distributor of loyal bounty. Many of the addresses sent to Charles II congratulating him on his restoration to the throne were also accompanied with the surrender of fee-farm income, acquired during the interregnum, to the Crown.[58] A number of boroughs also presented cash gifts as well as transferring ownership of fee-farms. The recorder and principle burgesses of St Albans gave Charles II £100 in gold, as well as the fee-farm.[59] Thomas Clifford and Thomas Chaff, MPs for Totnes in Devon, presented the King with 'an hundred pieces of Gold in a Gold-wrought Purse' along with the address from the town.[60]

As with the statements already noted in these addresses concerning past petitioning and addressing activity, this gift-giving might have been partly intended to make amends for past disloyalty. The surrender of fee-farms was accompanied in some cases with exculpatory speeches in which towns excused their purchase as not an attempt to materially benefit from the circumstances of the interregnum but an act of necessity undertaken to preserve their community.[61] The giving of cash gifts was not solely an attempt to smooth over previous accommodations with the interregnum regime, it was also another potential way of securing preferment. The Earl of Yarmouth's unsuccessful drive for a gift of a thousand guineas to accompany the Norwich address abhorring the Association was alleged to have been an attempt to secure a knighthood for one of the presenters.[62]

One other critical 'gift' that corporations could offer the Crown, besides cash, was their charters. The use of quo warranto writs during the 1680s to remodel English boroughs into a more politically pliant mould has been much discussed.[63] Addresses encouraging the creation of new charters played a key role in this process but, again, this was not simply a top-down operation but one in which the Court's supporters could employ addressing as a strategy to exclude political rivals. As Yarmouth reported to Leoline Jenkins on 27 October 1682,

> The Loyall party of my friends in ye Towne of Yarmouth have made an Address to His Maty wch they will soon present: they also have given mee in and assigned several breaches in their Charter for wch they will pray a Quo Warranto for there is a most notorious opposite faction of men of Comonwealth principles, yet must be purged as you will see ye necessity when I present their Actions.[64]

Above all, for communities the value of addressing was the political access that it bought: as a draft address from the Lancashire grand jury put it, it was the 'gracious accesses to papers of this nature' that the Crown gave that made loyal addressing valuable.[65]

This access became an even more valuable commodity after the Restoration as regulations over access to the Court were tightened, the architecture of the Whitehall palace altered to reduce the number of 'public' spaces and, in the 1680s, the Court itself removed to less central locations, whether at Windsor or Newmarket.[66] As we have seen, securing an audience with the King allowed Reresby to not only press his own case but also to represent the interests of his clients, the Cutlers of Hallamshire. In turn, by securing Reresby's services, the Cutlers hoped that they had acquired a powerful ally who, as a justice, would be able to offer legal protection and, as a well-connected courtier, would be able to intercede on their behalf directly with the Crown.⁶⁷ Prior to encouraging the Cutlers to address the King, Reresby's interventions with the then Lord Treasurer, Thomas Osborne, Earl of Danby, appear to have been critical to the Hallamshire Cutlers receiving a unique temporary exemption from paying the tax on their forges.⁶⁸ Reresby's offer of services was itself not completely selfless: as he said in his memoirs, 'I did not please at Court by this proceeding, but whatever I lost ther I gained in my country.'⁶⁹ Reresby expected that in return for his intervention on behalf of the Cutlers that he would have their support for Court candidates in parliamentary elections. Yet, Reresby was to be disappointed: the Cutlers preferred to back the Whig candidates in the election of 1679. Reresby, nonetheless, was convinced to continue to work with the Cutlers through the presentation to him of some fine silver-capped razors (offering a reminder that gift-giving was integral to the preparation of addresses as well as their presentation).⁷⁰

The Cutlers, however, continued to pursue alternative strategies to secure a permanent exemption for their forges. It is worth noting here that, while Reresby's intervention was undoubtedly important, Danby had initially been persuaded to halt collection of the Hearth Tax from the Cutlers because an Act of Parliament, sponsored by the company, clarifying grounds for exemption, was already before the Commons.⁷¹ The former Master Cutler, John Pearson, and the clerk of the corporation, John Stirynge, were particularly active in this regard, with the Master Cutler's accounts indicating regular payments to both men for trips to London to lobby Parliament.⁷² The Cutlers were also spending a considerable amount on legal fees to contest the imposition of the tax on their forges (Reresby estimated £200), had previously petitioned the Privy Council about their case and had even produced a pamphlet highlighting their plight.⁷³ In comparison to the amounts disbursed on legal fees and lobbying Parliament, the single shilling recorded in the Cutlers' accounts as being spent on copying the address represented only a very small part of the significant financial expenditure aimed at securing a permanent exemption. In fact, the Cutlers would later spend much more money in producing a loyal address to William III.⁷⁴ In addition, though Reresby was lauded for the 'miracle' of persuading a company associated with Whiggery and dissent to make a public declaration of support for Charles II's decision to dissolve the Oxford Parliament, the actual text of the Cutlers' address was much more reserved than some in its expression of loyalty. While it thanked Charles for his words of respect for Parliament, his readiness to prosecute 'Popery' and his determination to rule within the law, it made no mention of using penal laws to prosecute Protestant dissenters, nor did it acknowledge the King's prerogative power to dissolve Parliament.⁷⁵ Most importantly, though, the Cutlers were not content to limit their patronage of local justices to Reresby but were also providing hospitality to Sir John's bitter rival, Jessop, as well.⁷⁶

The performance of loyalty

The Cutlers' case demonstrates that gaining political access was not straightforward and the role of those introducing the addressers was very important. The Cutlers were prepared to secure a patron such as Reresby, whose political outlook was different from their own, because of the connections and influence he possessed. Later instances also highlight the importance of the choice of presenter and introducer. For example, John Greensfield informed Dr Charlett, Master of University College Oxford that the address from the 'Northern Clergy' to George I in 1714 'wd not have been presented yt day if I had not got Mr Cook Vicechamberlain to gett notice to the Duke of Montrose who was with ye King, & who was to Introduce us'.[77] Securing access enabled the addressers, ostensibly present only to declare their loyalty to the Crown, to seek concessions from authority. Calamy used his audience with the King, but more importantly Secretary Stanhope, to press for the payment of promised royal compensation to the dissenters for the damage suffered to their meeting houses in anti-Hanoverian rioting in 1715.[78]

Occasionally, however, too much appears to have been invested in the (often formulaic) responses of authority to loyal addresses. James Winstanley, the recorder of Leicester who presented the borough's address to Richard Cromwell, read a great deal into the new Protector's use of the word 'Citty' to describe the place. The prolix new Protector spoke for half an hour in response to the address referring to Leicester as the 'Citty of Leicester ... as if his desire had been to have a Citty'.[79] It is worth noting too that the London dissenters had to make repeated approaches to George I before the Crown could be brought to make good on its original promise to offer compensation for the damages suffered in the recent rioting.[80]

For communities as well as individuals, addressing also provided an opportunity to establish superiority over rivals. For the 'Committee of the three denominations' the question of precedence was resolved by establishing a rota in which Presbyterians, Independents and Baptists would all take turns to present the committee's address.[81] In other federal structures, however, disputes broke out, as in the Guestling or Brotherhood of the Cinque Ports over producing a congratulatory address to Charles II in 1660. New Romney and Hastings were at odds as to which held the speakership for this year, which would in turn determine where the 'Guestling' would be held to draft the loyal address.[82]

The phrasing of addresses could also provoke conflict. The *Impartial Protestant Mercury* reported in July 1681 that the loyal address from the North Riding had been delayed as it was 'mentioned, *We the Nobility, Gentry and Clergy*, in the Head of the said Address; and not *We the Nobility, Clergy and Gentry*. Whereupon, the *Clergy* not gaining the Point, many of them withdrew, and refused to subscribe therein.'[83] Morrice claimed that a similar dispute was provoked by the 1683 address from the Dublin Grand Jury titled

'The humble Addresse of the Grand Jury, Deputy Lieutennants, Justices of Peace, Clergy and Gentlemen &c':

> Justice Keating desired them very calmely to alter the title, because it was indecorous to put the Court upon the Bench after the Grand Jury, after much discourse the foreman of the Jury Sworre God Damne him so it was and so it should goe, ... he was a better man than that Judge was, and if he had him off the Bench he would slapp his sides.[84]

Whether or not these reports were accurate, as we have already seen, social hierarchy was fundamentally ingrained into addressing activity. Questions of status were not trivial, as demonstrated in James Winstanley's efforts to secure individuals of sufficient wherewithal to present Leicester's address to Richard Cromwell discussed above.[85]

The necessity of securing persons of quality to present an address became more important after the Restoration, especially as new regulations at Court in the 1670s severely restricted access to those other than the gentry.[86] By the 1680s, a clear preference was being noted for addresses to be presented by gentlemen only. As the Earl of Yarmouth wrote to Roger L'Estrange in July 1681, 'Itt is now ye fashion that all addresses com well attended by gentlemen.'[87] When it proved impossible to secure an entourage of this kind to accompany an address, explanations needed to be made. Leoline Jenkins reported to Lord Weymouth in 1683 that he had presented the Wiltshire address 'in the best manner I could', which the King had received graciously, and 'was pleased fully to approve of the reasons that His Lo[rdshi]p gives why it was not attended wth some of the Gentlemen of that County in the Presenting of it'.[88]

Failure to present an address or petition properly could lead to its legitimacy being questioned, as when the Common Hall of London presented their petition to the King in July 1681, claiming that it was unanimously agreed to. The Crown's response was terse: 'The King sees no Aldermen come with You to own this Sense; And the King knows the City much better, than to believe This to be their Sense.'[89]

Disputes over precedence and status were not restricted to those drafting or presenting addresses. While introducers were often critical to addressers gaining an audience at court, identifying a suitable introducer was a complex task. The addressers had to consider the signals that approaching a particular individual would send and also weigh up the risks of alienating other powerful patrons by failing to approach them. These complicated calculations could lead to addressers being used as pawns in the power games of the political elite. The politics of securing an introducer were described in detail in Calamy's account of the London dissenting ministers 1706 address to Queen Anne. Calamy reported that,

> there was a Pretty Warm Debate whether Lord Sunderland, or Mr Secretary Harley should be desir'd to do us the honour to Introduce us to his Majesty, and a Majority being for the Former, it was by Common Consent put upon me, to wait upon his

Lordship with the Request of the Whole Body, and to give Notice to those deputed of the Time and place that should be fix'd on, for their Waiting on the Queen.

Sunderland, however, appeared to have other designs, asking Calamy when he called upon him,

> why we did not make that Motion to our friend Mr Harley, who he was satisfied would be very Ready to bring us in to the Queen's Presence upon such an Occasion. I thereupon took the Freedom to Ask him on the other Hand, whether it was kind and generous in his Lordship to slight the Sincere Respect of those who had with some Warmth given his Lordship the Preference in that Application. He told me he had heard of our Debate, and knew what had pass'd ... But he said if we would Listen to him, it should not be either Mr Harley or himself, but my Lord Treasurer that should Introduce us. I frankly told his Lordship, it was more than I knew that any of our Body, had that Freedom with any Lord Treasurer, as to Ask his Lordship to do us that Honour. And added that I had nothing of that Nature in any Commission: and that in such as Case as this, I was as much oblig'd to keep to the Instructions of those that deputed me, as his Lordship when he was one of the Lords Committees in Parliament, was to the Instructions given him by the House of Peers.

Sunderland acknowledged the obligations that were placed upon Calamy by his fellow ministers and therefore promised that he would personally request the Lord Treasurer introduce the dissenters' address, sending a letter to this effect by one of his servants. Calamy,

> submitted to his Lordship's Judgement and told my Brethren of it, who were well Satisfied. I had his Lordship's Letter by his Servant on the Saturday Morning, which Signified the Lord Treasurer's Readiness, and fix'd Monday Morning for us to be at Windsor with our Address: and I had Work eno' to give Notice to the Several Persons Deputed who Liv'd in several Parts of the Town, and to Fix them with Coaches, so as that we might get to Windsor in Time on the Monday.

The plan, as outlined to Calamy by Sunderland, however, appeared not to have been put into execution:

> When we came there, I sent my Servant to Lord Sunderland's, to let his Lordship know, we were Come and Ready to Receive his Directions: and Word was brought that his Lordship went out of town that Morning; at which my Companions (and Particularly Mr Spademan) were not a Little disturb'd. To make them Easy, I went myself, and Enquir'd of Lord Sunderland's Gentleman, whether his Lordship had left no Directions for me and my Company. Upon which he told me, he had left Orders, that if we Call'd, we should Wait on the Lord Treasurer in his Name. Without going back, I went up to the Castle, and found the Lord Treasurer's Lodgings, and told the Centinel that stood at the Entrance, that if he would help me to the Speech of any Lord Treasurer's Gentleman, I would give him something in order to his drinking her Majesty's Health. He Rang a Bell and a Footman Presently Came up, of whom he enquir'd for Lord Treasurer's Gentleman, who soon Appearing, I Told him my Business, and he went in and told my Lord, who sent for me

in: And I Acquainting his Lordship that I waited on him by the Direction of Lord Sunderland, who had Encourag'd us to hope his Lordship would do us the Honour to Introduce us with our Address to the Queen; he told me that If I would bring my Brethren up thither, he would readily go with us to her Majesty.

Calamy's audience with the Lord Treasurer, despite this positive response, was clearly an unexpectedly awkward encounter:

> I Observed Mr Harley was there with his Lordship: And he gave me a Look upon the Occasion, the Language of which was very Intelligible to me, considering what had Pass'd. We soon came up thither together, and were Standing in my Lord's Antichamber when Mr Harley came out from him, and he Pass'd thro' the Midst of us: But none that were Present, could help Observing, what a Look he gave us.[90]

While it is possible that Sunderland had simply been busy and forgotten the arrangements made with Calamy, it is tempting to see him as having passed the job of introducing the dissenters' address on to Lord Treasurer Godolphin as a means of offering a conscious snub to Harley. (Harley had advised Queen Anne against appointing Sunderland as Secretary of State, arguing that he would be difficult to work with and that it would signal too clearly that she was favouring the Whig party.)[91]

There were clearly political hazards for introducers to negotiate as well. Aligning themselves with an addressing campaign could be politically injudicious, especially given the prominence with which the names of presenters and introducers were advertised in the press. In July 1683, Reresby was approached by Richard Boyle, Earl of Burlington, about drawing up an address to Charles II, condemning the Rye House Plot. Reresby suspected that the purpose of the approach was to cast off political suspicion from the earl who 'was looked upon above as a cautious man, that had noe mind to venture too far for fear of his great estate'.[92] (It is notable that Burlington appears to have played a much more active role in promoting addresses under James II than during Charles' reign.)[93] Burlington reportedly consented to sign whatever address the gentlemen of Yorkshire should agree to but ultimately never subscribed as a result of decisions taken at a dinner on 25 July attended by the high sheriff of the county, Reresby and a number of the Marquis of Halifax's friends (whom Reresby had gathered there):

> as soon as dinner was done I moved for a ressolution which way, and to whom to be presented to the King, this addresse ought to be convayed (haveeing found the sheriff inclining the day before that all that matter should be left to the Earl of Burlinton, and then I knew that my Lord Rochester, his son-in-law, would be the person appointed to present it to the King).

As in the case of Calamy, Sunderland and Harley, political rivalries seem to have been at play: Halifax was one of Rochester's opponents and would later play a significant role in his fall from grace in 1684 (accusing him of peculation).⁹⁴ Reresby developed a strategy to support his aristocratic patron Halifax without offending another locally influential figure in Burlington:

> I would not appear very pressing in it myselfe that it should be sent up to my Lord Halifax, haveing a mind to keep fair with my Lord Burlinton, but had soe laid the things that it being after a long debate putt to the question, it was carried that it ought to be sent up to my Lord Halifax. This being agreed, I sent away my servant that night to my Lord Burlinton to acquaint him how the gentlemen had resolved, and that in case he thought not fitt to joine with them under Thos circumstances I would prevent the sending of the address to him at all, and take it upon myself that soe it might not be ill taken that he did not signe it as he had promossed. This he well approved of, and thanked me for it, by this means he avoiding this or any construction for his refusing to sign.⁹⁵

Similar concerns seem to have excised the Duke of Montrose when approached by Greenhill to introduce the address from the northern clergy in 1715: while Montrose was prepared to undertake this, he

> wd not so far Disoblige the Kirk as to inform them in any publick print yt He introduced me with Mr Gray to present yt foresaid Address, thus were so much countanencing me, so yt by my appearing agt ye Kirk has lost me all my Scots interest with the Nobility there, so yt I have been confused on all hands.⁹⁶

ROYAL RITUAL AND LOYALTY

The performance of addressing, as much as the content of addresses, therefore provided a medium for furthering factional and ideological struggles. This was as true for the Crown as for the addressers. The benefits to the monarchy of addressing could be assessed in practical terms – the transfer of valuable fee-farms, cash gifts and, most of all, the surrendering of corporation charters, enabling the Crown to fashion a more pliant civic political culture and pack Parliament.

The ritual of addressing, however, was also a political tool. Both Anna Keay and Brian Weiser have noted Charles II's sophisticated use of Court ceremonial to project power and to manage political relationships. The King's approach to addressing and petitioning was a key part of this strategy.⁹⁷ (The use of ritual under the Protectorate is less clearly documented, though what brief mentions we can find suggest that it did not directly ape royal ceremonial, with kneeling and kissing of hands absent from reports.)⁹⁸ As Narcissus Luttrell noted, if petitioning was not legally proscribed, a clear difference emerged during the Exclusion Crisis in the Crown's reception of loyal addresses in comparison to mass petitions: 'those meet with a kind reception at any time, these are alwaies distastfull; these petition him in times of danger to call the representative body of the nation, and those give him thanks for dissolving them.'⁹⁹

The different responses were sometimes thrown into sharp relief when multiple addresses and petitions were presented at the same time. Morrice reported that on 21 May 1681, the Lord Mayor of London and Sir Robert Clayton had gone to Windsor to present the city's petition but 'At the same time The Leiutenancy went to present another of a different aspect. The Lord Chancellor by appointment told them how well his Majestie tooke the latter. But for the first they medled with matters that concerned them not &c.'[100] Anna Keay has noted that the delivering of a response by the Lord Chancellor, rather than the King himself, was also a clear indication that an address had not found favour. In the case of the petition from Common Hall, the verbal rebuke was also accompanied with a gestural snub as the King turned his back on the petitioners rather than offer them his hand.[101] Just as presenting an acceptable loyal address could be a path to preferment, so sponsoring an unwelcome petition could potentially stymie a political career. Baron Chandos' appointment as ambassador to Constantinople was almost blocked because of his involvement in petitioning activity. Chandos assured Charles that in this, 'he was drawn in and misled, but that now he abhorred all such practices' and the King's objections were waived.[102]

As has already been noted, loyal addressing was also employed by James II to legitimate his religious policies. An incident recorded by Morrice, however, suggests a shift in the employment of ritual under his reign. On 10 July 1686, a number of Baptist ministers addressed the Crown to give thanks for the King's pardon (issued in the wake of the Monmouth Rebellion). Morrice's longhand account is rather bland, noting that they received a response that if they 'carryed themselves Loyallty [sic], they should find protection'. Much more detail was offered in his shorthand notes. The Baptists were, Morrice said,

> kept long upon their knees ¼ of an hora almost/while his Majesty showed the petition to several about him at which they were very merry/The Quakers had petitioned very freely and very full for liberty &c. and have got nothing of those but a verbal order for impunity from his Majesty notwithstanding which they are disturbed and punished/They that came after with a shallower address can not expect it[.][103]

In spite of this surely humiliating audience with the King, Morrice stated that it was 'credibly said' a week later that the Baptists had received assurances not only of pardons for past actions but also of freedom to hold meetings in the future.[104]

Of course, as has already been noted, Charles II also employed gesture to punish those who presented unwelcome petitions and occasionally delivered spoken admonishments as well.[105] Yet this incident is suggestive of a blunter and less considered approach to the politics of gesture and ritual. The fact that a month later, James was offering a much warmer welcome to similar addresses from Baptist ministers suggests that he had miscalculated both the extent of his own authority and the strength of support for his tolerationist policies.[106] These policies may have been endorsed by numerous loyal addresses but, as we've noted, they appear to have been drawn from a narrower constituency than those which were sent to Charles II. Moreover, in accepting addresses presented by groups such as the Baptists, James was relaxing a now well-established protocol that only the gentry and aristocracy should deliver and introduce these texts. Morrice's remark, noted above, that these addresses were 'no way considerable' can be read as a verdict on the social status of the subscribers as well as their number.[107] Certainly, in Reresby's eyes, the issuing of such addresses, whether encouraged by promises of religious toleration or manufactured by freshly purged corporations, 'much deceaved' the King 'as to the opinion of his subjects concerning the indulgence, three or four men in divers places pretending to represent the thoughts of a whole corporation or county'.[108]

CONCLUSION

The signs of public favour given through the ritual of addressing remained important after the revolution of 1688, especially for non-conformist churches for whom the activity represented an important avenue not only through which to influence the government but also to gain legitimacy as religious institutions. While at moments of crisis, such as after the 1715 rebellion, their support might be openly welcomed, the Crown also had to consider the risk of alienating Anglican opinion, a fact which frustrated nonconformists' hopes for greater public recognition.[109] In the later eighteenth century, the presenting of petitions to the Crown involved fewer personal audiences with the monarch, as the Home Secretary came to be the main point of contact for petitioners. Steven Poole has argued, nonetheless, that the idea that petitioning brought individuals into virtual, if not physical, contact with the monarch remained important.[110] The reciprocity embodied in the exchange of both compliments and gifts in addressing remained a feature of the activity into the Victorian period: the hundreds of addresses that the Queen received on the occasion of her Diamond Jubilee were frequently gifts in themselves, lavishly bound in Morocco leather or beautifully mounted and illuminated.[111]

Overall, the patterns we can discern in the ritual performance of addressing over the course of the later seventeenth and early eighteenth century parallel those noted in relation to subscription: barring exceptional moments of crisis, there was a desire to limit participation in this ceremonial to the social elite. The exclusivity of the drafting and presenting of addresses helps explain the importance attached to the activity in some early modern life-writing. In providing a tangible link between the periphery and the centre, addresses also helped communities assert their importance and connect their history with that of the nation. As Mark Knights has suggested, this may in turn have helped foster a stronger sense of British identity, especially as addresses came to be focused upon the imperial struggle with France.[112] As with the material text of the address, authorised by signatures and official seals, ritual itself could be used to evaluate the authenticity of the text. Those communities that could not find appropriate representatives to present their loyal texts need to provide a clear explanation for their failure to do so or risk a rebuff.

Communities, such as the corporation of Cutlers, sometimes displayed a sophisticated awareness of both the national political context and the specific requirements for successfully gaining access at Court. We have seen that the Cutlers' addressing activity was motivated by material concerns rather than loyalty. Even texts produced for reasons of expediency, however, could be valuable to the Crown. In the case of the Cutlers', it provided Charles II with a declaration of (albeit equivocal) loyalty from a community normally associated with Whiggery and dissent. The Cutlers' address also demonstrated the importance of local powerbrokers both to securing addresses from communities and to ensuring that those communities' texts were well received at the political centre.

While Charles' successful use of court ritual as tool of political management has been noted by historians including Brian Weiser and Anna Keay, these strategies were being deployed to support policies that were already targeted at securing the support of the most influential group in the country at large, the Anglican-Tory gentry. James' relative failings consequently were not simply a result of a less nuanced approach to court etiquette but also a product of pursuing policies that were anathema to the political hierarchy in many English counties. The post-revolutionary political and religious context, especially the advent of limited religious toleration, changed conditions to a certain extent but, as the Tory press's mocking of the Baptist addressers suggested, the social status of addressers and the connections of those they approached to introduce their texts remained critical.

NOTES

1 J. Reresby, *Memoirs of Sir John Reresby: The Complete Text and a Selection from his Letters*, A. Browning (ed.) revised by M. K. Geiter and W. A. Speck (London: Royal Historical Society, 1991), pp. 271–2.
2 J. Sharpe, *A Fiery and Furious People: A History of Violence in England* (London: Random House, 2016), p. 256 and ibid., pp. 255–60 for Reresby's violent behaviour more generally. I discuss this case in more detail in Vallance, 'Une démonstration stratégique de loyauté dans l'Angleterre de la fin des Stuart: le cas des couteliers du Hallamshire', *Revue Histoire, Économie et Sociétié*, 38, no. 1 (2019), 67–84.
3 Reresby, *Memoirs*, p. 272n.
4 Ibid., pp. 230–1, quote at p. 231. The text of the Cutlers' address reproduced in *Vox Angliae*, pt 2, pp. 5–6, however, recorded that only 510 people subscribed to it.
5 For this dispute see R. E. Leader, *History of the Company of Cutlers in Hallamshire in the County of York* (2 vols, Sheffield: Company of Cutlers, 1905), i, p. 146. See

also David Hey, *The Fiery Blades of Hallamshire: Sheffield and its Neighbourhood, 1660–1740* (Leicester: Leicester University Press, 1991), pp. 136–9; J. D. Purdy, *Yorkshire Hearth Tax Returns* (Hull: University of Hull Centre for Regional and Local History, 1991) pp. 25–9. For the Hearth Tax and the Cutlers more generally in the seventeenth century, see M. J. Unwin, 'The Hallamshire cutlery trades in the late seventeenth century: a study of the Hearth Tax returns and the records of the Cutlers' Company' (PhD dissertation, University of Sheffield, 2002). I am grateful to Dr Unwin for discussing the Cutlers' dispute with me.

6   Reresby, *Memoirs*, p. 270 and for earlier complaints by the Cutlers, ibid, pp. 104–5, 119, 125.
7   B. Weiser, *Charles II and the Politics of Access* (Woodbridge: Boydell and Brewer, 2003), p. 72.
8   BL Add MS 36988, f. 147–9, Paston letters. See also Kenyon MSS, p. 127. The address from 'Mayor, Aldermen, Bayliffs, and Burgesses of the Borough and Corporation of Wigan' was the product of the Mayor, the 'two Sir Rogers' and the recorder.
9   Kenyon MSS, p. 142, Thomas Hodgkinson to Roger Kenyon, 30 May 1682, asked Kenyon to pass on the address from Preston which was to have been presented by Lord Derby to Lord Arlington instead.
10 *Protestant (Domestick) Intelligence*, 15 February 1681, no. 97.
11 Knights, 'The Loyal Address', p. 319.
12 NRO, Y/C 19/8, f. 160, Yarmouth Corporation Assembly Book, 1662–80, 18 September 1671.
13 Kent Archives and Library Services, CP/Bp/288, Draft minutes of the Guestling, 24 July 1683.
14 Peacey, *Print and Public Politics*, pp. 275–80.
15 Reresby, *Memoirs*, p. 259.
16 Sowerby, *Making Toleration*, pp. 35–6.
17 BL Add MS 50958–9, Edmund Calamy's Accounts; DWL MS 38.17, Stinton's Journal; *The Diary of Bulstrode Whitelocke 1605–1675*, R. Spalding (ed.) (Oxford: Oxford University Press, 1990).
18 Knights, 'The Loyal Address', p. 326.
19 Reresby, *Memoirs*, p. 246.
20 BL Add MS 50959 f. 164, Edmund Calamy's Accounts.
21 David Wykes, 'George I, the Hanoverian succession, and religious dissent', in A. Gestrich and M. Schaich (eds), *The Hanoverian Succession: Dynastic Politics and Monarchical Culture* (Farnham: Ashgate, 2015), pp. 73–88, pp. 82–5.
22 DWL MS, 38.17, f. 16, Stinton's Journal.
23 *Weekly Journal with Fresh Advices Foreign and Domestick*, 20 August 1715. The address was also reported in *London Gazette*, 16–20 August 1715, no. 5356 which also reported the King's dismay at the 'unchristian and barbarous' treatment that dissenters had met with as a result of their defence of the Hanoverian succession, perhaps explaining the particular hostility of the Tory press to this address.
24 BL Add MS 50959, f. 140, Calamy's Accounts.
25 DWL MS 38.17 f. 38–41, Stinton's Journal.
26 *The Remembrances of Elizabeth Freke, 1671–1714*, R. A. Anselment (ed.) (Camden Soc., 5th series, 18, London, 2001), pp. 154–5.
27 Ibid., pp. 142–52.

28 B. J. Todd, 'Freke, Elizabeth', ODNB.
29 *Remembrances*, ed. Anselment, pp. 112–13; 115–16; 117–27.
30 Ibid, pp. 120–1.
31 Ibid., p. 17.
32 *Diurnal of Thomas Rugg, 1659–1661*, pp. 40–1, 50, 69, 82, 99, 102, 104–5.
33 W. Kennett, *A Register and Chronicle Ecclesiastical and Civil* (1728), pp. 35, 43, 132, 163,180–1, 206, 209–10, 222, 226, 239, 361, 376, 405, 457; Kennett, *A Complete History of England* (3 vols, 1706), iii, pp. 191, 212, 224, 378, 382, 419, 465, 469, 501, 504–5, 522, 824–5. For Kennett's reliance on printed sources, especially in *A Register*, see Bennett, *White Kennett*, pp. 168, 176–7. Similarly, see the regular commentary upon petitioning and addressing in Luttrell's *Relation* and Abel Boyer's *Annals*.
34 A. Smyth, *Autobiography in Early Modern England* (Cambridge: Cambridge University Press, 2010), ch. 1.
35 See Chapter five.
36 Reresby, *Memoirs*, pp. xvii-xviii; BL Add MS 29442–3 Reresby's 'Family History', the last folios of the second volume provide the beginnings of his autobiography (f.11–17).
37 Compare, for example, Whitelocke, *Memorials*, pp. 675–77 to *Whitelocke's Diary*, ed. Spalding, p. 500.
38 *Whitelocke's Diary*, ed. Spalding, p. 544 'This private history'; B. Worden, 'The "Diary" of Bulstrode Whitelocke', *English Historical Review*, 108 (1993), 122–34 at 123.
39 Ibid., 126.
40 Ibid., 127.
41 Ibid., 134.
42 DWL MS 38.17 f. 14, Stinton's Journal.
43 See below conclusion.
44 [J. Morphew], *A Collection of Addresses*, pt 2 p. 42.
45 *London Gazette*, 13–16 August 1715, no. 5355,
46 Tim Hitchcock, 'The body in the workhouse: death, burial, and belonging in early eighteenth-century St Giles in the Fields', in M. J. Braddick and J. Innes (eds), *Suffering and Happiness in England, 1550–1850: Narratives and Representations. A collection in honour of Paul Slack* (Oxford: Oxford University Press, 2017), ch. 7, p. 160.
47 Dorset History Centre, DC/LR/A/3/1 f. 1–9. For a further instance of the preservation of material from newsbooks, see Bedfordshire Archive Services, Bor BA3/6, Bedfordshire address abhorring the Rye House Plot, 1683, taken from *London Gazette*, 5–8 November 1683, no. 1875, originally framed but frame removed in 1980s/90s. My thanks to Kirsty McGill, digitisation technician at Bedfordshire Archives for this information.
48 See above Chapter four.
49 Reresby, *Memoirs*, p. 259.
50 *London Gazette*, 30 May to 2 June 1681, no. 1621.
51 *Loyal Protestant and True Domestick Intelligence*, 21 February 1682, no. 119.
52 BL Add MS 50958, f. 194, Calamy's Accounts. The Board of Green Cloth was the body which audited the accounts of the royal household.

53 Kent Archives and Library Services, U269 C356/5, William Eldred to Thomas Whitfield, 9 August 1682. Folger, L.c. 1257, Newdigate newsletters, 8 August 1682 reported that provision had been made for 1000 guests with tickets distributed for free. For more on this feast, see T. Harris, *London Crowds* in the reign of Charles II: Popular Politics from the Restoration until the *Exclusion Crisis* (Cambridge: Cambridge University Press, 1987), pp. 177–8.
54 *Impartial Protestant Mercury*, 26–30 May 1682' no. 115.
55 *Loyal Protestant and True Domestick Intelligence*, 5 July 1681, no. 35. The same edition mistakenly reported that the borough of New Sarum had been presented with two new gilt maces, worth £300 and such 'as no corporation in England can boast of' by the king for their loyalty. A subsequent edition (no. 37) was forced to enter the correction that the maces had in fact been bought by the recorder of the borough.
56 Harris, *London Crowds*, p. 177.
57 J. Daybell, 'Scripting a female voice: women's epistolatory rhetoric in sixteenth-century letters of petition', *Women's Writing*, 13 (2006), 3–22.
58 TNA SP 29/1 f. 52 (Mayor, Bailiffs and Commonalty of Coventry); TNA SP 29/3 f. 17 (Mayor, Bailiffs and Commonalty of Oxford); *Mercurius Publicus*, 2–9 August 1660, no. 32 (Mayor, Bailiffs and Burgesses of Preston). See also Stocks, *Leicester Borough Records*, p. 466.
59 *Parliamentary Intelligencer*, 2–9 July 1660, no. 28.
60 *Mercurius Publicus*, 26 July – 2 August 1660, no. 31.
61 See the Oxford address TNA SP 29/3 f. 17.
62 *Impartial Protestant Mercury*, 14–17 February 1682, no. 86; BL Add MS 27448, f. 34, Paston letters, Edward L'Estrange to Yarmouth, 15 July 1681.
63 J. Miller, 'The Crown and the borough charters in the reign of Charles II', *English Historical Review*, 100 (1985), 53–84; Miller, *Cities Divided*, ch. 8; P. D. Halliday, *Dismembering the Body Politic: Partisan Politics in England's Towns, 1650–1730* (Cambridge: Cambridge University Press, 1998); Sowerby, *Making Toleration*, ch. 5.
64 BL Add MS 27448, f. 187, Paston letters.
65 HMC Kenyon MSS, p. 68.
66 On these shifts see Weiser, *Politics of Access*, ch. 2; A. Keay, 'The Ceremonies of Charles II's Court' (PhD dissertation, University of London, 2004), esp. pp. 84–90; see also Anna Keay *The Magnificent Monarch: Charles II and the Ceremonies of Power* (London: Continuum, 2008).
67 Reresby, *Memoirs*, p. 270 and for earlier complaints by the Cutlers, ibid, pp. 104–5, 119, 125.
68 Reresby, *Memoirs*, p. 150, and see *Calendar of Treasury Books*, ed. W. A. Shaw (31 vols, London, 1904–62), vi, p. 785 where the Hearth Tax 'farmers' reported that over £516 had been lost to the Treasury through this concession.
69 Reresby, *Memoirs*, p. 105.
70 Leader, *History of the Cutlers*, i, p. 146.
71 Reresby, *Memoirs*, p. 119.
72 Cutlers' Company Archives, Sheffield, D1/1, 'Accounts of the Masters Cutler, 1625–1790', unpaginated, entries for 1677–1680. For Pearson and Stirynge see D. Hey and J. Unwin, 'The company, its freemen, and its apprentices,

73 Reresby, *Memoirs*, p. 104; TNA PC 2/64, f. 225, 347–8, 463, Privy Council Registers 1673–75; Purdy, *Yorkshire Hearth Tax*, p. 26; *The case of the company of Cutlers in Hallamshire* ([London?, 1680]). It is worth noting that the Cutlers' petition was made on behalf of other smiths in Yorkshire, Warwickshire and Derbyshire as well.
74 Cutlers Company Archives, Sheffield, D1/1, 'Accounts of the Masters Cutler, 1625–1790', 1682, records payment of one shilling for drawing up three copies of the address; ibid., 1698, charges recorded about 'Addressing his Maiesty', £1 1s 8d.
75 Reresby, *Memoirs*, p. 230n.; *Vox Angliae*, pp. 5–6.
76 Leader, *History of the Cutlers*, i, p. 147; Cutlers Company Archives, Sheffield, D1/1, 'Accounts of the Masters Cutler, 1625–1790', 1683, records the cost of six bottles of white wine and two of sack to Mr Jessop when 'divers of ye Companie went to drink with him' and from 1684 onwards the Company was renting land from the Jessop family.
77 Bodl., MS Ballard 36 f. 162.
78 BL Add MS 50959 f. 165, Calamy's Accounts; DWL MS 38.17 f. 71v.–73v., Stinton's Journal.
79 *Leicester Borough Records*, ed. Stocks, p. 450.
80 BL Add MS 50959 f. 155–6, May 1716, Calamy's Accounts. Calamy notes that the dissenters had 'waited long and found nothing done towards their Relief.'
81 DWL MS 38.17 f. 36v, Stinton's Journal.
82 Kent Archives and Library Services, NR/CPc/170, Circular letter, with answers, from Hastings, 2 June 1660.
83 *Impartial Protestant Mercury*, 26–29 July 1681, no. 28
84 *The Entring Book of Roger Morrice*, ii, pp. 392–3.
85 See Chapter two.
86 Weiser, *Politics of Access*, pp. 38, 42.
87 BL Add MS 27448, f. 36, Paston letters.
88 Longleat House, Thynne MS 22 f. 39, Newsletters, (BL Loan Microfilm 904/11), Jenkins to Weymouth 17 July 1683.
89 *Impartial Protestant Mercury*, 9 July 1681, no. 36.
90 BL Add MS 50958, f. 192–4.
91 Hoppit, *Land of Liberty*, p. 294.
92 Reresby, *Memoirs*, ed. Browning p. 307.
93 See WYAS, WYL 150/MX/12/31/20, 22, 24v., Mexborough MSS, Letters from Burlington, February 1684/5.
94 W. A. Speck, 'Hyde, Lawrence', ODNB.
95 Reresby, *Memoirs*, ed. Browning. p. 312.
96 Bodl. MS Ballard 36 f. 162.
97 See also B. Weiser, 'Access and petitioning during the reign of Charles II', in E. Cruickshanks (ed.), *The Stuart Courts* (Stroud: Sutton, 2000), pp. 203–13.
98 See J. Walter, 'Body politics in the English Revolution', in Taylor and Tapsell, *English Revolution Revisited*, ch. 4.

99 Luttrell, i, p. 108. For similar comments from a Court perspective see J. Wright, *A compendious view of the late tumults and troubles* (1685), pp. 115–16.
100 *The Entring Book of Roger Morrice*, ii p. 278.
101 Keay, 'Ceremonies', p. 89.
102 Luttrell, *Relation*, i. 43. Chandos' notebook shows that he had learned his lesson, including as it does both the text of an address to James II on his accession to the throne from the factory at Constantinople and orders from Chandos for other factories at Aleppo and Syrmna to follow suit, BL Stowe MS 219 f. 149, 160.
103 *The Entring Book of Roger Morrice*, iii, pp. 164–5.
104 Ibid., iii, p. 174.
105 See Chapter three.
106 *The Entring Book of Roger Morrice*, iii, p. 238.
107 See Chapter three, p. 83.
108 Reresby, *Memoirs*, p. 494. Reresby was specifically referring to the attempt of Sir John Bointon '(who aspired, I presume, to be made a judge)' to secure an address from the Yorkshire grand juries. None would agree but the Catholics, Bointon and a 'Mr Bull' who presented it 'as the act of the whole sessions'.
109 BL Add MS 50959, f. 155–6, Calamy's Accounts.
110 S. Poole, *The Politics of Regicide in England 1760–1850: Troublesome Subjects* (Manchester: Manchester University Press, 2000), ch. 2.
111 The addresses can be found in TNA, PP 1/1–666. For an example of a lavishly illustrated address, see that from Port Elizabeth, Cape Colony TNA PP 1/647/14. For the Diamond Jubilee see J. Morris, *Pax Britannica: The Climax of an Empire* (London: Faber and Faber edn, 2010), ch. 1.
112 Knights, *Representation and Misrepresentation*, pp. 150–1.

Chapter 7

From subjects to objects: the language of loyalty

> There is one essential point wherein a political liar differs from others of the faculty, that he ought to have but a short memory, which is necessary, according to the various occasions he meets with every hour, of differing from himself, and swearing to both sides of a contradiction.
>
> Jonathan Swift, *The Examiner*, 9 November 1710, issue 14

Swift's essay on political lying was only one of many works in the later years of Queen Anne's reign which claimed that the credibility of political discourse had been fundamentally undermined. As we will see, the rapid succession of addressing campaigns to different monarchs was produced as evidence of just the kind of convenient public 'forgetting' identified by Swift. This Augustan crisis of credibility resonates with present day anxieties concerning the distorting effect of partisan loyalties on the public's critical reasoning. Academic studies have highlighted how party loyalty creates a ' "perceptual screen" filtering information and exaggerating what is favourable to one's own party'.[1] Supporters' sense of identification with their party may even lead them to endorse policies in conflict with their own intellectual beliefs: Democrat voters in the USA given a choice between a stringent welfare policy and a more generous one were found to back the less liberal policy package if told it was supported by the party. When given a free choice, they supported the alternative proposal.[2]

The emotional aspects of loyalty, it will be argued here, are crucial for understanding the changing nature of the value and also its shifting objects. The threat to rational debate, political credibility and decision-making that was sometimes seen in emotive party polemic needs to be qualified. Loyalty, it will be argued, was fundamentally expressed in affective terms and it remained so across the period under consideration. The emotional aspects of loyalty were also critical to the development of a public memory of past political activity, which in turn helped foster a critical political public.

Beginning with an exploration of recent philosophical and historical readings of loyalty, the chapter moves on to explore how the language of loyalty changed within collections of addresses produced from 1659 to 1756. Using Optical Character Recognition (OCR) software, it maps the shifting vocabulary of political fidelity across these works, demonstrating the persistence of emotional language post-1688. It then explores contemporary critiques of addressing discourse as not simply emotive but also meaningless, showing that these works nonetheless provided enduring testimony to the affective quality of loyalty in their stress upon sincerity. Indeed, it will be argued that it was precisely the emotional quality of addressing which ensured its continued vitality while other forms of expressing public loyalty were abandoned.

LOYALTY: PHILOSOPHICAL AND HISTORICAL READINGS

Modern philosophical discussions of loyalty have stressed its emotional, partial nature. For Judith Shklar, what distinguished loyalty was that it was 'deeply affective and not primarily rational'. Moreover, many loyalties may not even be a matter of choice: we may feel a sense of loyalty to our ethnic group, our nationality or to our family, though we have not been able to meaningfully choose any of these things.

For Shklar, this emotional character and its powerful connection with both group and individual identity distinguished loyalties from other forms of association, such as obligation. Shklar defined obligation as essentially 'rule governed conduct', defined by duties that had been consented to either tacitly or explicitly and which were legitimated on the grounds of fairness or security.[3] Under the umbrella of loyalty itself, Shklar distinguished between loyalty to groups or communities, and fidelity, given to individuals. For Shklar, this was the most personal form of loyalty and 'the most expressive of our personality and emotional life'. Though fidelity might be used to describe the bonds of friendship or love, it could also be used to describe the relationship between political leaders and their followers.[4] Even political loyalty, then, is typically personified rather than being affixed to ideals.[5]

Indeed, some formulations of loyalty have presented the concept as requiring a competing 'other': for George Fletcher, loyalty 'by definition, generates interest, partiality, an identification with the object of one's loyalty rather than with its competitors'. For Fletcher, loyalty operates in a triad: A is loyal to B because C is a competitor with B.[6] John Kleinig questions whether this formulation is always true of loyalties: we can be loyal to our family without necessarily having to see it as being in competition with or better than other families.[7] Fletcher's view nonetheless touches upon an aspect of loyalty identified in most recent discussions: individuals hold multiple loyalties which will often come into conflict with each other (and our obligations), in turn generating 'non-chosen duties'.[8] As Shklar put it: 'One thing ties all these notions [of loyalty] together: They all invite conflict; trouble is their middle name.'⁹

The partial, emotional and, at times, irrational nature of loyalty identified by these scholars has also been connected to a grand narrative of political development. Much of the discussion of loyalty has been prompted by the perceived failure of liberalism and its universalised morality to co-exist with the particularised ethics generated by loyalty. Indeed, Kenneth Minogue has argued that liberalism's defining characteristic is its aversion to 'excessive loyalty' – meaning any commitments that jeopardise individual autonomy: 'The history of the modern state, from its beginnings in the sixteenth century,' Minogue argues, 'may be viewed as a centuries-long experiment in loosening the bonds of loyalty demanded from the subjects.'¹⁰

A similar view has been articulated by a number of historians and literary scholars mapping the changing 'politics of affectivity' (as Steven Zwicker has described it) in early modern England.¹¹ For Zwicker, Locke's critique of Filmer's patriarchalism was part of a broader attempt to contain,

> a mode of thought whose implications had become all too clear in the 1640s and, which once again, though for different reasons, had made the costs of a passionate state in which sovereign and subject are variously figured in paternal, patriarchal, conjugal, domestic, and filial embrace too burdensome to endure.¹²

Matthew McCormack has noted the very different objects of Whig and Tory loyalty: for Whigs, the prime object of loyalty, English law, was depersonalised; for Tories it resided in the person of the prince and any attempts to separate the office of king from the body of the monarch were, in the words of one clergyman, 'pernicious'.¹³

After the revolution of 1688, emotionally laden understandings of loyalty came to be closely associated with Jacobitism and the idea of personalised, affective political bonds did not return to broader understandings of the 'loyal' until the emergence of the culture of sensibility in the later eighteenth century.¹⁴ McCormack and Zwicker's readings of loyalty as becoming at least temporarily disassociated from feeling are shared by Ute Frevert. Frevert argues that 'under conditions of parliamentary democracy trust supersedes fidelity'.¹⁵ Whereas loyalty was irreversible ('fidelity could not be broken'), 'trust' was fiduciary: 'Those who offered trust made demands, they stated conditions under which trust was granted and threatened to withdraw it in case those conditions were not met.'¹⁶ The replacement of the emotional ties of loyalty with the contractual bonds of trust can be placed within Norbert Elias' thesis of a European 'civilising process' in which control over the passions was increasingly privileged by eighteenth-century society.¹⁷ Taking the discussion forward in time to the modern liberal democratic state, Minogue characterises loyalty under these forms of government as sustained not by 'remote and awesome majesty, but by delivering the goods. In other words, the loyalty of subjects has become conditional'.¹⁸

From subjects to objects

There are elements of this broad narrative that can be traced in the shifting language of loyalty found in addresses across the late seventeenth to early eighteenth century. Through an analysis of word frequency within compendia of loyal addresses, it will be shown that there were clear, partisan distinctions in the use of loyalty, broadly corroborating the findings of McCormack. As we will see, the partisan use of loyalty meant that at times it conformed to Fletcher's definition, in being delineated primarily in relation to the 'disloyal' other. Equally, the use of addresses as party propaganda in the reign of Queen Anne especially generated claims from both Tory and Whig writers that the credibility of political discourse was being fundamentally undermined. These arguments, however, notably stopped short of calling for an end to all addressing activity. In contrast with other 'loyal' literary forms such as panegyric, once viewed as having fallen into disuse by the early eighteenth century, addresses continued to be issued with great regularity and frequency.

The persistence of the address as a vehicle for representing public loyalty, it will be suggested, may also be related to Russell Muirhead's arguments in support of party loyalty. Effective political action, Muirhead argues, requires both 'memory and patience' – that is, an awareness of past achievements (and, therefore, what it is that needs to be secured), and a commitment to action that may only generate benefits at some later date.[19] We have already seen that the memory of past addressing activity was deployed both to defend and attack individual and group loyalties. As much as successive addressing campaigns could be invoked to demonstrate the inconstancy of public affections they also offered reminders of past commitments and guided future political action. Equally, though we can identify a shifting language of loyalty which, post-1688, included loyalty to sets of principles (the constitution) and institutions (the state), this did not mean that loyalty was entirely divested of its emotional content. Arguably, the continued viability of addressing activity rested on its affective aspects, the notion that it was a spontaneous and sincere expression of public fidelity to the monarch.

THE LEXICON OF LOYALTY

The first lexicographical references to loyalty associated the term with personal values: Robert Cawdry's *A table alphabetical* (1604), defined 'loyal' as 'obedient, trustie, constant'. The word did not appear in any editions of Thomas Blount's influential *Glossographia* (first published in 1656), however, and it was not until the 1696 edition of Edward Phillips', *The New World of Words* (first published in 1658 and highly derivative of Blount's work) that loyalty was listed. Here the term was described as 'Fidelity and Truth in Observance of the Oaths of Submission and Obedience to Authority'. The 1706 edition of the same text included entries for both 'Loyal', meaning 'observant of the Law: faithful, trusty, honest' and also for 'Loyalty', representing 'Fidelity or Faithfulness, especially to a Sovereign Prince or State'.[20] These early eighteenth-century definitions combined Whiggish readings of loyalty as synonymous with being law-abiding and obedient to the State, with potentially apolitical associations with moral qualities (honesty, trustworthiness, fidelity).

Tools such as the Early English Books Online (EEBO) N-gram browser, developed by Anupam Basu and Stephen Pentecost, indicate that the use of 'loyal' in early modern print peaked in the 1680s. In 1639, for example, there was only one occurrence of 'loyal' in the EEBO Text Creation Partnership (TCP) corpus. In comparison, in 1682, the peak of the word's frequency over the period 1473–1700, 'loyal' occurred 1,165 times. A similar pattern can be observed for 'loyalty' with eighty-seven occurrences in 1639 compared with 976 in 1682 (again the peak year).[21] Similar patterns can be observed through exploring word use within compendia of loyal addresses. A corpus of compendia of addresses from 1659–1756 have been converted into Microsoft Word documents using the OCR software ABBY Finereader.[22] Given the length of these works (close to 100,000 words in the case of the 1727 compendium of addresses to George II), no attempt has been made to manually correct the transcriptions produced by the software. As a result of the difficulty of current OCR software in recognising early modern typeface, this means that the transcriptions are of limited accuracy and offer only a rough sketch of word use within the text. These transcriptions were then uploaded to the corpus analysis software, Voyant Tools, developed by Stefan Sinclair and Geoffrey Rockwell.[23]

The Cromwellian addresses gathered in the two 1659 collections, as has already been noted, were heavy with providential language. In *A true catalogue*, 'God' is the second most frequently used term (fo/so is listed as first), followed by government, lord and people. The sixth most commonly used word, 'father' reflects the consist references to Oliver in the addresses to Richard Cromwell. Notably, 'commonwealth' is fairly low in the ranking of terms (thirty-eight) and the majority of these references when viewed in context are relatively apolitical (commonwealth as synonym for nation/state rather than a particular form of government without a single person). The language of godly magistracy is here much more prominent than that of loyalty: 'loyal' is only ranked as 293 in the most commonly used terms in the compendium, while loyalty barely scraps into the ranking of 500 most frequently used words at 479.

Other linguistic tools, such as EEBO-TCP Key Words in Context, developed by Anupam Basu and Stephen Pentecost, support the impression that, at this point, 'loyal' and 'loyalty', if employed in a political context, were predominately used in Royalist works such as Sir William Sanderson's *A compleat history of the life and raigne of King Charles* (1658).[24] This is confirmed by an analysis of Fuller's *A happy handfull*. Unsurprisingly, as this was a collection of texts calling for a free Parliament, 'Parliament' is the second most commonly found term, 'free' the third. Fuller's emphasis on the social status of the addressers, noted above, is also confirmed through the frequency of status terms such as 'sir' (eleventh), 'lord' (nineteenth), 'esq.' (thirty-first), 'gentlemen' (forty-third), and 'gentry' (sixty-fifth). In contrast, there is only one use of the word 'loyal' and no mention at all of 'loyalty'. Given what has already been said about the association of loyalty with fidelity to the monarch, the use of this term would have both been inappropriate in texts directed at an army officer and also have threatened to reveal the Royalist intent of many of these works.

The infrequency with which the terms 'loyal' and 'loyalty' were used in the addresses of 1658–60 may also provide further support for the argument of modern commentators that loyalty's primary objects are persons or groups of people. While the Protectorate restored a single head of State, the language of Cromwellian addresses continued to cast the Protector as a public servant or, more commonly, a divine instrument, diminishing their individual agency. See for example the address to Oliver Cromwell from Colonel Read's regiment which depicted the Protector as the pilot of the ship of the commonwealth leading it to 'so safe an Harbour'. Those addresses, such as that from the Lord Mayor, Aldermen and Commons of the City of London to Oliver in March 1658, which acknowledged the legitimacy of the Humble Petition and Advice, were expressing their support for a form of government ('a happy, lasting and well-grounded form of Government' according to the address) rather than pledging fidelity first and foremost to the individual at the head of that government.[25] Very few of the addresses dedicated to Richard Cromwell had much to say about the personal qualities of the new Protector, preferring instead to depict this new 'Joshua' as a vessel for God's will – in the words of the Cheshire address as the one 'the Almighty hath designed' to see 'the advancement of his Glory, the propagation of his Gospel, the vindication of his precious Truth against all Heresies, Errors and Schisms'.[26] The complaints already noted that the addresses to Richard Cromwell were 'blasphemous' were indicative of the sensitivities around acclaiming an individual at this point in time. This depersonalised understanding of political obligation became even more pronounced, of course, in the humble petitions to the restored Rump, where commitment was being expressed to that ever-changing entity 'the Good Old Cause' rather than to any individual or set of individuals.[27]

The association of 'loyal' and 'loyalty' with the monarchy's supporters persisted into the 1680s. Though this was the decade across the whole seventeenth century in which the terms appear most frequently, they were remarkably scarce in the collection of Whig addresses, *Vox Patriae* (1681). 'Humbly' was the seventieth most commonly used term in this collection, 'loyal' was only ranked as 162nd, and there were only five uses of 'loyalty' in the whole volume, placing the word outside the top five hundred terms found in the collection. Status terms, however, feature much more frequently with 'esq.' the number one term, 'sir' second, earl at eight and baronet at ten. Partly we can explain the prominence of these terms by the fact that these were addresses primarily directed at Members of Parliament but it is also, arguably, indicative of a broader attempt to deflect accusations that the Whig party were reviving the strategies of the civil wars by emphasising instead the social status of their addressers. This was in contrast to the Tory collection *Vox Angliae* (1682). Here 'loyal' was the fourth most commonly used word in the collection, while other similar terms featured within the top fifty: dutiful (twenty-fifth), humbly (twenty-eighth), obedient (thirty-fourth), loyalty (forty-fifth).

The different patterns identified within these rival collections support McCormack's view that there were distinct Whig and Tory understandings of loyalty, one privileging obeying the law, the other fidelity to the prince. This argument is also supported by White Kennett's later comment that, during the Exclusion Crisis, the Tory Party carried 'Principles of Loyalty' 'Higher than Law or Reason' and that 'Loyalty' was at this time, viewed as equivalent to 'Adherence to the Interest of the Court'.[28] The differences also reflect different responses to popular politics in the 1680s. The poem, *True Loyalty in its Collours* (1681), a verse in praise of the loyal apprentices of London, was a pugnacious paean to plebeian loyalty: 'No Name, because you can't Write well? A *Fist* Is a *Good Hand*, that can Writ **Loyalist**.'[29] This defence of the illiterate or semi-literate loyalist connected with stories in Tory newsletters of loyal apprentices whose masters attempted to bully them into subscribing to Whig petitions or counter-addresses.[30] The Tory endorsement of populism was also indicated in the regular recording in *Vox Angliae* of the numbers of subscribers to these addresses. It was, in contrast, the Whig press which disparaged the London apprentices as 'Ruffians and Beggerly Vermine, drawn in by Pots of Ale' and which, as we have seen, preferred to emphasise the social status of subscribers.[31] Later collections of addresses to James II, published in 1710 and 1722 respectively, sustain this identification between loyalty and the Stuart Court.[32]

The connection between loyalty and the Stuart dynasty may also be a product of the relationship between addresses and other literary forms. Addressing, as Mark Knights has noted, shared a number of obvious features with panegyric.[33] Unlike encomia, panegyric was typically occasioned by some special event and or subject, including moments that were also a frequent trigger for addressing activity (the succession of a new monarch).[34] As with loyal addresses, panegyric could be used to deliver advice or criticism as well as praise: both Thomas Eliot and James VI and I included panegyric within the broader genre of 'advice to princes' in providing an image of virtue for the monarch to follow. This advice was also directed at the monarch's subjects, to remind them of the debt of loyalty to the Crown.[35] As White Kennett stated in his translation of Pliny's panegyric to Trajan (a translation dedicated to James II that, as we have seen, came back to haunt Kennett): 'We have a Monarch so indulging, that our onely yoke is a pressure of inability to raise him a deserved commendation.'[36]

Literary scholars such as James Garrison have argued, however, that this form was exhausted by the early eighteenth century, with writers of the calibre of Dryden, Pope and Swift either indulging in heavy criticism of the genre, exploiting it for satirical purposes, or declaring its death.[37] Other laudatory poetic types, such as the Pindaric ode, have also been declared 'moribund' by the turn of eighteenth century.[38] Changing political circumstances must have played a part as well: the direct connection of this poetry to individual Stuart monarchs (as an English genre it emerged during the reign of James VI and I) caused problems for individual authors such as Kennett and Aphra Behn as it did for the genre as a whole.[39] Though Behn continued to write congratulatory poetry (to Mary II) after the revolution, it was notable that her praise of the Queen, in whom she traced the 'Lines of your great Father's face' seemed largely a proxy for praising James, the 'Great Lord, of all my Vows'.[40] Equally, the genre was threatened by the decline of the Court as a cultural as well as political centre under the last two Stuarts, with Robert Bucholz noting the minimal attempts made during the reign of Anne 'to produce art for the purpose of glorifying the monarch'.[41]

The adversarial addressing that followed the trial of Henry Sacheverell to some extent reflects the weakened connection between loyalty and the monarchy. In John Morphew's two part collection of addresses, some of the language relates directly to the specifics of the Sacheverell case and its aftermath – 'Church' was ranked as the second most common word, followed by 'tour'. 'Loyal' ranked highly in both the 1710 and 1711 editions (at eleven and fourteen respectively). Yet, it also indicated that, post-revolution, new objects of loyalty had been created. A rival compendium published in 1710 which exclusively featured the more 'Whiggish' addresses, while retaining some similarities with Morphew's texts (the prominence of 'church' (fourth)), also added some terms to the loyal lexicon: 'glorious' was the twelfth ranked term, 'Protestant' the fourteenth and 'revolution' the thirtieth. In addressing produced during the 1690s and 1700s, we can also see a growing emphasis on the role of Parliament and parliamentary elections in delivering the 'sense of the people'.[42] As many of these addressing campaigns were connected with the war with France, the more reserved praise of royal authority in English addresses came to be seen as a way of distinguishing the limited monarchy of England from French absolutism. If the English addresses were less effusive, one address commented, this was because 'We stand upon another bottom than France.'[43]

As the work of Arthur Williams and Abigail Williams has demonstrated, congratulatory verse under William and Anne similarly adapted its tone to the new international political context. Poets such as Matthew Prior carefully distinguished between the qualified praise offered in their verse and the flattery lavished upon Louis XIV by his Court poets such as Nicolas Boileau-Despréaux.[44] We have already noted that addresses sent to William III occasionally adopted a similar line, explaining that their more measured praise was more fitting to English constitutional arrangements than the sycophantic texts sent to the French King.⁴⁵ Yet, in endorsing England's constitution, Whiggish addresses continued to eschew populism, arguing instead (in reference to the pro-Sacheverell texts) that men of estate and substance would be found in the lists of non-subscribers.⁴⁶ (And it is worth noting that in the 1710 compendium of Whig addresses, 'gentlemen' came higher in the ranking of commonly used terms, at eleven, than 'people', at thirteen.)

The less effusive nature of post-1688 addresses, however, should not be over-exaggerated. If William and Anne were honoured less for their personal qualities than as figureheads protecting the virtue of liberty and the constitution that enshrined it, there were heroic surrogates to whom individual praise could be directed instead. Two collections published in 1710 and 1712 respectively employed the addresses of both Parliament to the Crown and the public to Parliament to demonstrate popular support for the Queen's leading general, the Duke of Marlborough.⁴⁷ In early 1710 Marlborough had been pressing for Parliament to appoint him captain-general for life.⁴⁸ The first collection, *The Sense of the Nation* detailed the many addresses of thanks sent by Parliament to John Churchill for his services and the honours and gifts of land and money that were conferred upon him. By 1711, however, with the strength of the Tory party growing and with Anne's relationship with Sarah Churchill having irreparably broken down, Marlborough was under serious attack, accused of having profiteered from the award of supply contracts. The Duke was dismissed from his office by the Queen on 30 December 1711.⁴⁹ The second collection, *The Sense of the Nine in Ten*, indirectly presented Marlborough's loss of office as an affront to national feeling, cataloguing the many addresses of congratulation that had been made to the general on the occasion of his military victories. Indeed, these addresses were so numerous, the editor noted, that many had not been published: 'The Addresses on the Victory at Ramellies were not printed; but mention is made in the Gazettes of about 250 presented on that Occasion, from several Parts of England and Wales.'⁵⁰

While Marlborough might have provided an alternative object for public affection, there remained significant emotional content in the addresses sent to William and Anne. As has been noted, those occasioned by Louis XIV's recognition of the 'Old Pretender' were dominated by expressions of indignation at the French King's actions. The address from Winchester conveyed the city's 'detestation' and 'resentment' at the 'late affront' offered to William by Louis. In the same issue of the *Gazette*, the University of Cambridge and the borough of New Woodstock spoke of their dismay at the 'indignity' suffered by William through the acknowledgement of James Francis Edward Stuart.⁵¹ Addresses not only offered a public declaration of the locality's love for the King but also, in some cases, assured William that they would select 'well-affected' MPs. The address from the Grand Jury of Cumberland assured the King that their 'hearts' were 'full of affection' towards him, and promised to elect only representatives who shared their ardour. The borough of Ludgershall in Wiltshire assured William that they would only choose members of parliament who were 'entirely affected' to the King.[52] Similar expression can be found in some of the addresses sent to Queen Anne in 1710.[53]

The depersonalisation of loyalty did become more apparent, however, with the succession of the Hanoverian dynasty. The compendium of addresses to George II on his accession, published in 1727 by John Cluer, maintained loyalty's affective character – 'happy' was the sixth most commonly occurring term, loyal the nineteenth, dutiful ranked twentieth, joy at twenty-seven, happiness at fifty-one and love at sixty-one. This outpouring of the public's hearts (the twenty-eighth most commonly used term in the compendium) overshadowed references to 'rights' (sixty-second), the state (at eighty-six) and the constitution (104). The public's love for George II, however, was not unconditional: the address from Great Yarmouth made clear that their fidelity was merited by the King's delivering to them 'those valuable Blessings they enjoy as a free People'.[54] Equally, the source of public happiness might be identified in the revolution settlement, rather than in the King.[55] By the end of George II's reign, public loyalty appeared to be almost entirely disconnected from the monarch's person. A later, more critical compendium of addresses, issued in 1756 in the wake of the loss of Minorca to the French (a failure which precipitated the outbreak of the Seven Years' War), associated loyalty primarily with institutions and other corporate entities (the 'people' at five, 'parliament' at six, 'nation' at seven, 'public' at nine, 'country' at ten).[56]

Reviewing the language of addresses from the mid-seventeenth century to the middle of the eighteenth century reveals that while the words 'loyal' and 'loyalty' retained their association with fidelity to the monarchy, loyalty as a concept had shifted in its associations, by the Hanoverian age becoming associated with institutions (Parliament) and concepts (the state, the nation). Even so, loyalty continued to be invested with emotional meaning, supporting the arguments of scholars such as Michael Walzer that affective loyal bonds can be forged with ideals as well as with persons.[57]

It was the objects of loyalty, then, rather than the emotional register of addresses, which most clearly changed after 1688. While there is much to McCormack's assessment that Tories and Whigs developed different understandings of loyalty, it remained consistently a value expressed in affective language. The constitution which Whigs identified as the primary object of their loyalty was, after all, frequently described as 'happy'.[58] As McCormack has convincingly shown, the emotional quality of loyalty strengthened in the later eighteenth century as a result of a combination of developing ideas of sensibility with the broadening imperial crisis facing the British monarchy, necessitating a more active form of public fidelity.[59] The affective content of addresses remained to the fore even as these texts once again became vehicles for public criticism of authority. While the collection of addresses occasioned by the loss of Minorca began with a rebuttal of public attacks upon them as unconstitutional, it also asserted their legitimacy on the grounds of feeling as well as law:

The people have indeed authored their representatives in parliament to make laws, grant money, and support their rights. But they have not transferred their rights themselves, nor alienated the sense of feeling; nor given up the important right of expressing what they feel.[60]

HISTORIES OF LOYAL ADDRESSING

Contemporaries also observed the shifting objects of public loyalty across the seventeenth century. The minister of Richmond, Abiel Borfet's 'reasons' for refusing the Association to William III in 1696 included the poor precedent of all the 'Voluntary addressers' to first the Cromwells, then Charles II and finally James II.[61]

These successive waves of addressing activity raised questions about the emotional as well as political content of these texts. If loyalty was synonymous with love then there was considerable evidence of the infidelity of the English public. We have already seen that past addressing activity was recalled and redeployed to political effect throughout the period under consideration. Reprinted collections of addresses had the potential to embarrass specific individuals or groups and to deliver implicit criticism of their current political stance. Without more extensive editing and comment, however, they were relatively limited weapons for tackling popular mass addressing campaigns. The mnemonic quality of addressing, though, provided the opportunity for a far more thoroughgoing critique of the address, delivered through histories of the genre. These demonstrated the apparently fickle nature of political loyalty in late Stuart England, at the same time undermining the credibility of addresses as reliable indicators of public opinion.

Yet, some histories went further to suggest that the language of loyalty in these addresses was fundamentally too unstable to convey any fixed political meaning. Ultimately, these authors stepped back from discrediting addressing altogether and instead sought to distinguish between inappropriate 'modern addresses' and legitimate forms of 'opinion politics'. In so doing, these writers, by adopting the more detached persona of the historian rather than the party polemicist, attempted to cast themselves as moderate figures striving to restore the integrity of political discourse. Their critiques of addressing, however, continued to be framed in emotional terms, defining the legitimate loyal address in terms of the sincerity of its affective content as well as the appropriateness of its objects.

The historicising of addressing activity may point to further similarities with the older tradition of verse panegyric. As Mark Knights has noted, panegyric included an element of historical comparison, demonstrating how the rule of the ideal prince had established order out of disorder (in much the same way as the ante-masque provided a contrast with the harmony of good government in the Court masque).[62] During the reign of Queen

Anne, however, a historical perspective was deployed primarily to evaluate addressing activity itself rather than its objects. Daniel Defoe's intervention in the controversy over the pro-Sacheverell addresses, *A New Test of the Sence of the Nation* (1710), written at time when he had moved back into the employ of Robert Harley, represents the most far-reaching critique of this kind. Defoe did not simply point towards the dramatic shifts in loyalties evident in addresses to successive regimes and dynasties as proof of the political hypocrisy of many addressers, he argued instead that they demonstrated that these texts were no more than vacuous formalities. Of the addresses offering the lives and fortunes of English subjects to James II, Defoe said they were 'a customary Piece of Extravagance' which the King foolishly took 'to be in Earnest'. As with polite forms of greeting, those addressed should not expect their addressers to fulfil these promises in reality: 'Sir, Your most Obedient Servant, says a Man to me in the Street; if I shou'd bid him to go of an Errand for me, he wou'd answer, What, Sir, do you take me for a Porter!'[63] Defoe's long view of loyal addressing in England delivered an image of these texts as fundamentally meaningless:

> Thus King *James* was serv'd with His Addressors, I cou'd have brought a List of the Universal Addressings of the Nation just in this Manner, and ev'ry Way as extravagant, to *Richard Cromwell* of Old, not Two Months before they depos'd him: Ditto to King Charles the second, when they abhorr'd Petitioning; when they gave up their *Charters, Laws* and *National Priviledges* to Him: *Ditto* to King WILLIAM upon Occasions quite Differing, and Contradicting to them all.

These examples proved that 'for many Years past, [addressing has] been reckoned to stand for nothing; and is therefore, by Custom determin'd to be no Manner of Signification'.[64] This historical line of attack mirrored Whig arguments in the contemporary press, *The Observator* claiming that the pro-Sacheverell addresses were the same in substance as those to Charles II and James II which had attacked Parliament.[65] To drive home this point, Defoe's pamphlet juxtaposed pro-Sacheverell addresses attacking dissenters and religious toleration with earlier addresses from the same places thanking James II for the liberty of conscience granted by his two Declarations of Indulgence.[66] Unlike Whig periodicals such as the *Observator*, however, Defoe was also ready to criticise Whig counter-addressing activity. Instead of correcting the mistaken notions expressed in High Church addresses, all these alternative texts did, Defoe said, was to 'let the Queen know, the People of the Place are most horribly divided and no Body knows which Side was the strongest; for Hands to an Address seldom, if ever, are any Trial of the Strength of the other Parties.'[67]

The difficulty for Defoe, as his critics both south and north of the Tweed were keen to point out, was that he had earlier in his political career been a staunch advocate of Parliament listening to the demands of the people as communicated through addresses and petitions. In 1701 Defoe had written in support of the imprisoned Kentish gentlemen. These gentlemen had petitioned Parliament to vote the King the necessary money for his war with France, but it was deemed an insult to the honour of the two Houses. As we have seen, that in turn had prompted a major Whig addressing campaign. Six years later, however, Defoe, now operating as a pro-Union writer and spy for Harley, specifically used the case of the Kentish petitioners as an example of addressing or petitioning that had overstepped its legitimate bounds:

> In all Nations such Addressings have been esteemed contrary to the Duty of Subjects, contrary to the Nature of Addressing, and contrary to the Dignity of Authority; and therefore the Parliament of *England*, in the Case of the Famous *Kentish Petition* show'd their Resentment, not at Petitioning in General, for that every Body allowed, was the Privilege of the Subject, but at the manner or Expression, the Words of which were, *That they would turn their Humble Addresses into Bills of Supply*. Now, tho' it was no Breach of Duty to Petition the Parliament to supply the King's wants for the Publick Good; yet in this particular turn, the Parliament thought the Petitioners took upon them to Reproach the House, with trifling their time away in Complements and Addresses when the necessity of the Nation called for supplying the Publick for Action.[68]

Defoe's 1707 essay was prompted by vigorous anti-Union addressing campaign in Scotland which has been well-documented in the work of Karin Bowie.[69] The seemingly dramatic volte-face in Defoe's attitude to addresses and petitions was noted by his Scottish opponents who took the opportunity to reprint sections of his work in defence of the Kentish petitioners, thereby using Defoe's own words against him.[70] The same tactic was adopted by Defoe's English critics in 1710, as they employed sections of *The Original Right of the People of England* (1701) to demonstrate that Defoe had once vigorously defended the freedom of petitioners to criticise Parliament or reflect on its conduct, indeed had argued that to view such criticism as illegal was 'a Doctrine wholly New, and seems to be a Badge of more slavery to our own Representatives, then ever the People owed them, or then every they themselves expected'.[71]

It was not only Sacheverell's supporters who attacked Defoe. John Oldmixon, the Whig propagandist whose *History of Addresses* was once attributed to Defoe, was one of Defoe's fiercest critics. Oldmixon's *History of Addresses* was first published in 1709 in reaction to the addresses against war with France. A second edition was printed in 1710 with some seemingly hastily inserted sections directly dealing with pro-Sacheverell texts.[72] The second part of this edition was published later the same year and now concentrated wholly on tackling the High Church addresses. The first part of Oldmixon's history offered a chronological survey of loyal addressing from the 1650s to its year of publication. The similarities of argument between Oldmixon's text and Defoe's were clear. Like Defoe, Oldmixon argued that language in the addresses had been cast adrift from its usually accepted meanings. Speaking of the addresses produced during the 'Tory Reaction' under Charles II, Oldmixon said,

> Loose Principles, in the Phrase of that Time, were Principles of Liberty; and disaffected, is the being uneasy under Apprehension of Popery and Slavery. For, as has been hinted, if we do not translate that Court-Dictionary, 'twill be impossible to understand the History.[73]

And as with Defoe, Oldmixon also appeared keen to cast at least the first part of his *History* as moderate and unpartisan. For example, he dwelt on dissenting churches' addresses of thanks to James II when such examples might seem to have been prejudicial to the Whig cause.[74] The conclusion to be drawn, according to Oldmixon, was that the history of addresses was not one of party politicking but the pursuit of self-interest:

> he that hopes to win, or fears to lose either Pension or Place, is neither Tory nor Whig, he's of no Side but his own; he'll address or not address, swear or not swear, vote or not vote, as he thinks 'twill conduce most to his gaining or keeping what tempted him to do so ...[75]

There were also significant differences, however, in approach between Oldmixon and Defoe. Oldmixon, for all his play at political impartiality, was much clearer than Defoe that there had been periods of 'good' loyal addressing, namely under William III, addresses which though they were 'few indeed in Number' in quality far exceeded 'all that had gone before, as coming from the Hearts of the People of England by the Mouths of their Representatives'.[76] For Oldmixon, 'good' addresses were not only communicated through the people's legitimate representatives in Parliament, but also were sincere expressions of public affection. Oldmixon saw sincerity and popularity as compatible. Unlike Defoe, Oldmixon laid more emphasis on the weight of numbers being on the Whigs' side, at least in terms of those subscribing to addresses, a claim encapsulated in his comment that the number of all those signing up to the addresses supporting the dissolution of the Oxford Parliament could be exceeded by the numbers subscribing just one of the addresses to William III in 1696. (A claim which, as has already been noted, rested on blurring the distinction between the loyal addresses which sometimes accompanied the rolls of the 1696 Association to William III and the oath rolls themselves which were indeed voluminous.)[77]

Despite the accusations of plagiarism made against Defoe within it, organisationally, Oldmixon's later second volume was actually closer in style to Defoe's *A New Test*, rejecting the straightforward chronological structure of the earlier work to instead tackle individual boroughs and counties in turn, examining their addresses to Queen Anne in comparison with their earlier protestations of loyalty to the Stuart monarchy. The result was a far lengthier and, it must be said, more repetitive work. What the second part of Oldmixon's work lacked in literary élan, however, it made up for in forensic attention to the detail of the 1710 addresses and their predecessors. The work focused upon aspects of the High Church addresses, which suggested that their claims to speak for whole communities were of dubious credibility, noting, for example, that the Haverfordwest and Pembrokeshire addresses were made at the same assizes and on the same day.[78] Essentially offering an extensive address-by-address critique of Morphew's collection, Oldmixon demonstrated that 'there is no more Dependence to be made on them, than on a Mountebank's Words who promises Wonders from his Drug'.[79]

The similarity of Oldmixon's approach to that adopted by Defoe in *A New Test* did not, though, lead to a similar argument. Oldmixon instead asserted that, despite the unreliability of many of them, it was 'every whit as Whimsical as the Addresses themselves' to believe, as Defoe ostensibly claimed in *A New Test*, that they 'meant nothing'. Their intent, he said, was in fact plain, to 'affront the Revolution, attack the Toleration, excuse the Criminal, insult the Parliament, to change the M____ry, and oblige the clergy.'[80]

Defoe's and Oldmixon's positions on these addresses, however, were perhaps not as far apart as these comments suggested. As we have seen, Defoe was not alone in suggesting that these 'modern addresses' undermined the stability of political language by inverting the meaning of commonly understood political terms. Benjamin Hoadly in his *True Genuine Tory Address* (quoted at length in part two of *The History of Addresses*) provided a glossary of words repeatedly found in High Church addresses.[81] Elsewhere Hoadly stated that the addresses had created a 'New Dialect' by which well-understood words such as 'toleration' had been cunningly re-branded as 'Legal Indulgence', despite the fact that the former term was the one used by both the Crown and Parliament.[82]

Moreover, although Defoe had gone further than other authors in his comments regarding the unreliability of addresses, he stepped back from totally condemning them. Stating that the remarks concerning addresses in the foregoing part of *A New Test* had been 'ironical', Defoe clarified that he was not suggesting that the public should never address either the Crown or Parliament again but that the practice should return to its 'proper terms' and addresses be made with 'due solemnity'.[83] Earlier in the same tract Defoe had given some indication of what the 'proper' moments for addressing were – 'it would be agreeable enough to any Prince, to receive the Congratulations, hearty Expressions of their Subjects Joy upon Occasions of Success, the Protestations of their Fidelity, and Zeal in National Exigencies, and the like'.[84]

Properly framed and issued at the appropriate moment, emotional public expressions of loyalty were for Defoe perfectly legitimate. His pamphlet finished with a call for addressers to 'mend their stile' rather than cease their activities altogether.[85] Arguably, in both *A New Test* and his response to the anti-union addresses, Defoe was attempting to distinguish between legitimate and illegitimate addressing rather than to reject it wholesale. We can even see here some element of consistency between this position and that adopted in his earlier pamphlets of 1700–1. As Katherine Penovich has noted, Defoe had argued that while Parliament was required to receive petitions and addresses, it did not need to consider or debate them unless they involved an infringement of the rights of freeholders. In the case of union, Defoe's argument was that the treaty did not extinguish the freeholders' right to representation but only altered the context in which that representation was delivered (Westminster instead of Edinburgh).[86] It is also worth noting that in his defence of the Kentish petitioners, Defoe had supported the substance of their complaint but not the language in which it was delivered, nor the addressing campaign which followed it.[87] This line of argument was also followed by Defoe in his correspondence. In a letter to Harley sent in 1704, Defoe explained that while the people, through petitioning, had recovered their 'Just Rights', they had in the process 'Usurpt Some, That are Not Their Due, Vizt Censuring Their Superiors, But the Govornmt is bound to Submit to the Grievance because tis Incurable.'[88] By the people, Defoe was also clear that he specifically meant freeholders, not the mass of the population.[89] It was essential in a country like England where the people had such a share in the government that they were permitted to petition and address but this did bring with it the negative consequence of them over-stepping their bounds and criticising those in authority.

Defoe, Oldmixon, Hoadly and others were not arguing that addressing should be prohibited but insisting that it should be kept within appropriate limits. The use of the phrase 'modern addresses' by the critics of the High Church texts suggested that addressing itself was not bad, only the contemporary corruption of it. As Oldmixon said in the dedication to the first edition of *The History of Addresses*:

> You and I who have sign'd so many Loyal Addresses, to his late *Majesty* and our present Gracious Sovereign, cannot be against *Addressing*. But we shall ever be against the inconsiderate Manner of managing of 'em, the *Levity* and *Inconstancy* of People in changing their *Stile* and *Sentiments* which is all that is Expos'd, or meant to be Expos'd in these *Sheets*. For as to *Addressing* Queen *Anne* with sincere and hearty Tenders of our *Lives* and *Fortunes*, in Vindicating her Rightful and Lawful Title to this Empire, the Protestant Succession, and the Constitution Ecclesiastical and Civil against all Opposers, there's no true English Man who will not be always ready, and none are more so than our selves....[90]

This line of argument fitted in with earlier Whig criticisms of addressing in the 1680s which had stressed the importance of directing these texts at MPs as the true representatives, through Parliament, of the voice of the kingdom. Again, though, it also asserted that determining between legitimate and illegitimate addresses involved an evaluation of the emotional quality of the address. Sincere affections were here being prized at least as highly as the principles to which they were attached: empire, the Protestant succession and the constitution.

Rather than suggesting that addresses were meaningless, Defoe, Oldmixon and Hoadly's response to the language of these texts resonates with Olivia Smith's observation that claiming that popular petitions were incorrectly presented or expressed was a valuable way of delegitimising them.[91] Indeed, arguments about the threat posed to the credibility of political language by 'subscriptional texts' were not exclusive to Whig authors. In critiquing White Kennett's account of popular petitioning in his *Complete History*, Roger North warned readers of his *Examen* that they were entering 'a Wilderness of odd and disorderly Passages, about which the Court, City Country and almost all Estates and Degrees of People were huddled together in a Confusion of Language like *Babel*'.[92] Broader arguments about the unreliability of Whig writers were made by John Arbuthnot in his *Art of Political Lying*.[93] For Arbuthnot, this 'art' could be expressed through gestures and spoken words as much as texts: 'The Promissory Lyes of Great Men are known by Shouldering, Hugging, Squeezing, Smiling, Bowing; and Lyes in Matter of Fact, by immoderate Swearing.'[94] The use of these sorts of arguments also allowed Whig authors to sidestep to a certain degree accusations that they were betraying 'revolution principles' by ignoring the voice of the people as communicated through these addresses. That approach was also consistent with the emphasis on the quality of the subscribers, noted above, to be found in Whig compendia of addresses.

J. A. Downie suggested that the Whig response to the Tory challenge over the trial of Henry Sacheverell had failed to build on the literary success of Defoe's *Review* and was consequently ineffective.[95] Defoe and Oldmixon's responses to the High Church addresses, however, arguably represent an innovative and sophisticated development of printed collections to undermine claims that these texts were representative of national political opinion.

The production of histories of addressing went some way to remedy the obvious disparity in numbers between Whig and Tory addresses in 1710. At the same time, by adopting a historical standpoint, Defoe and Oldmixon were able to create the impression of keeping an objective distance from contemporary controversies. The very nature of loyal addresses as a running commentary on major national events (wars, peace, the birth and death of princes) made them well-suited to such an approach. At the same time, in stepping outside of immediate party political struggles, histories and compilations of addresses encouraged a greater awareness of the role of public opinion in contemporary debate. In suggesting that *some* addresses or addressing campaigns were poor indicators of public opinion, these writers were conceding (implicitly or explicitly) that the 'sense of the nation' was something worth determining. As the use of the word 'sense' implied, the legitimate expression of public feeling continued to be supported in these historical accounts of addressing. Targeting the inappropriate tone and language of these addresses also allowed these authors to avoid questions of popularity and square dismissing these texts with a continuing attachment to the principle that the English government was fundamentally a 'popular' government. Furthermore, by targeting only 'inappropriate' addressing, these authors left the door open for the continued exploitation of mass addressing by the Whig party in the 1720s.

Critical histories and compendia did not, therefore, fundamentally alter the nature of loyal addresses or the practices used to promote them. There was, after all, no long-standing political impetus to suppress loyal addressing: both Whigs and Tories had successfully exploited the medium in the past. What compendia and histories of addressing did do was to reveal in great detail a number of significant facets of loyal addresses. Reading Morphew's collection or Oldmixon's history, it was impossible to come away without seeing them as adversarial, combative texts.

In the case of both Whig and Tory compendia of the 1710 addresses, their partisan nature was made visually apparent through the shared tactic of displaying addresses and counter-addresses side by side, or with different fonts or keys attached to them. As Muirhead has suggested, however, with reference to partisan loyalty in a modern political context, the 'perceptual screen' it fashioned (or 'the Curtain' as it was earlier described by Oldmixon) was not impenetrable.[96] Indeed, for Oldmixon, the lesson of the history of addressing was not that the practice should be abandoned, but that its emotional content should be reaffirmed:

> let it be a Lesson to us who have the Happiness to live under the Government of so Good and so Great a Princess as our present Soveraign, never to Address her with our Pens only, but with our Hearts, and to look upon all the Addresses we have made to her, as so many Sacred Engagements of our Loyalty and Zeal for her Service.[97]

Memory, in the case of addressing activity, not only served to recall past political commitments but also to direct and shape future action. Kept within appropriate bounds and sincere of affect, addressing could continue to be a legitimate means of conveying and representing public loyalty.

CONCLUSION

Kenneth Minogue has described loyalty as a 'mere, brute sentiment'.[98] While his treatment of loyalty associates it very closely with power, his recognition of its sentimental aspects complicates his analysis. As Minogue notes, Jacobites continued to be loyal to the exiled James II and his descendants though he exercised little 'power'.[99] Equally, the picture of bonds of loyalty being replaced with a contractual, transactional relationship between subject and ruler depicted by Minogue and Frevert also requires modification. As Angela McShane has noted, following the work of Victoria Kahn, loving relationships, notably marriage, were also contractual and, in turn, love was necessary to generate consent to such a contract.[100] Like interpersonal relations, it was possible for nations to fall out of love with their sovereigns and McShane notes the lack of a significant material culture of loyalty surrounding James II as perhaps indicative of the lack of public affection for him.[101] As the survey of terms used in addresses above indicates, the lexicon of loyalty may have changed after 1688, but its objects continued to be invested with emotional value. The 'affective economy' of loyalty, as McShane has termed it, remained in place.[102] Indeed, it arguably became more important in a post-revolutionary political and cultural landscape which valued voluntary association above 'rule-based' understandings of political obligation. It was these conditions that permitted the prose panegyric of the loyal address to continue to thrive as its poetic equivalent went into artistic decline. It was vital that it did so, as the same conditions ensured that other means of securing and displaying public loyalty, such as the oath of allegiance, were falling into disuse.

NOTES

1. Russell Muirhead, 'The case for party loyalty', in S. Levinson, J. Parker and P. Woodruff (eds), *Loyalty* (London: New York University Press, 2013), pp. 229–56, at p. 244.
2. Ibid., p. 245.
3. J. N. Shklar, 'Obligation, loyalty and exile', in S. Hoffman (ed.), *Political Thought and Political Thinkers* (London: University of Chicago Press, 1998), pp. 38–55 at p. 41.
4. Ibid., p. 42.
5. J. Kleinig, *On Loyalty and Loyalties: The Contours of a Problematic Virtue* (Oxford: Oxford University Press, 2014), p. 27.
6. G. P. Fletcher, *Loyalty: An Essay on the Morality of Relationships* (Oxford: Oxford University Press, 1993), p. 8; Kleinig, *On Loyalty and Loyalties*, p. 22. See also J. Connor, *The Sociology of Loyalty* (New York: Springer, 1997), p. 48.
7. Kleinig, *On Loyalty and Loyalties*, p. 22
8. The phrase is John Perry's *The Pretenses of Loyalty: Locke, Liberal Theory and American Political Theology* (Oxford: Oxford University Press, 2011), p. 42.
9. Shklar, 'Obligation, loyalty and exile', p. 43.
10. K. Minogue, 'Loyalty, liberalism and the state', in G. Feaver and F. Rosen (eds), *Lives, Liberties and the Public Good* (New York: St Martin's Press, 1987), pp. 203–28, at p. 203, discussed in Kleinig, *On Loyalty and Loyalties*, p. 4.
11. S. N. Zwicker, 'The politics of affectivity in early modern England', in R. H. Wells, G. Burgess and R. Wymer (eds), *Neo-Historicism: Studies in Renaissance Literature, History and Politics* (Studies in renaissance literature, 5, 2000), ch. 9.
12. Zwicker, 'Politics of affectivity', p. 212.
13. Matthew McCormack, 'Rethinking "loyalty" in eighteenth-century Britain', *Journal for Eighteenth-Century Studies*, 35 (2012), 409–11. See also F. O'Gorman and A. Bradstock, 'Loyalism and the British world: overviews, themes and linkages', in Bradstock and O'Gorman (eds), *Loyalism and the Formation of the British World 1775–1914*, pp. 1–18 at p. 5. It is notable too that in eighteenth-century historiography loyalty, as distinct from 'loyalism', tends to be used most frequently in

association with Jacobitism, for example P. Monod, M. Pittock and D. Szechi (eds), *Loyalty and Identity: Jacobites at Home and Abroad* (Basingstoke: Palgrave Macmillan, 2010).

14   McCormack, 'Rethinking "loyalty"', pp. 411–18.
15   U. Frevert, 'Does trust have a history?', Max Weber lecture 2009/10, Central European University, p. 10, available at http://cadmus.eui.eu/handle/1814/11258, accessed 18 April 2017.
16   Frevert, 'Does trust have a history?', p. 7.
17   U. Frevert, *Emotions in History – Lost and Found* (Budapest: CEU Press, 2011), pp. 27–8.
18   Minogue, 'Loyalty, liberalism and the state', p. 218.
19   Muirhead, 'Party loyalty', p. 230.
20   This wording was copied in B. N. Defoe's *A compleat English dictionary* (1735) but omitting the words 'or State' and, under 'loyal' leaving out the observance of the law.
21   https://earlyprint.wustl.edu/, accessed 18 April 2017.
22   Texts analysed in this way include, [V. Powell], *A true catalogue* (1659); W. Caton, *Truths caracter* (1660); T. Fuller, *A happy handfull* (1660) [EEBO-TCP full text used]; *Vox patriae* (1681); *Vox Angliae* (1682); *A collection of the several addresses in the late King James's time* (1710); *A collection of addresses presented by the English and Scottish Presbyterians to King James VII* (1722); *A collection of the addresses which have been presented to the Queen since the impeachment of the reverend Dr. Henry Sacheverell* (Pts 1 & 2, 1710–11); *A collection of addresses &c.* (1710); *The addresses to King George II on his accession to the throne* (1727); *The voice of the people* (1756).
23   https://voyant-tools.org, accessed 18 April 2017.
24   https://earlyprint.wustl.edu/toolwebgrok.html, accessed 18 April 2017. Searching for 'loyal', 'loyalty' across date range 1656–60.
25   Both in *Mercurius Politicus*, 11–18 March 1658, no. 407.
26   *Mercurius Politicus*, 17–24 February 1659, no. 555.
27   See, for example, the Herefordshire petition in *Mercurius Politicus*, 12–19 May 1659, issue 567.
28   Kennett, *Complete History*, iii, p. 419.
29   *True loyalty in its collours: or, a survey of the laudable address of the young men and apprentices of the city of London* (1681).
30   See *Loyal Protestant and True Domestick Intelligence*, 16 August 1681, no. 47, and 27 August 1681, no. 50.
31   See *Impartial Protestant Mercury*, 17–21 June 1681; *Impartial Protestant Mercury*, 1–5 July 1681, no. 21.
32   *Addresses to James II on birth of prince of Wales* (humble ranked 8, loyal at 9); *Presbyterians addresses to James II* (loyalty at 8, humble at 15).
33   Knights, 'Loyal address'.
34   J. D. Garrison, *Dryden and the Tradition of Panegyric* (London: University of California Press, 1975), pp. 4–5. For an alternative view, emphasising the persistence of the panegyric form see J. Hone, 'Politicising praise: panegyric and the accession of Queen Anne', *Journal for Eighteenth-Century Studies*, 37 (2014), 147–57.
35   Garrison, *Dryden and the Tradition of Panegyric*, pp. 20–4.
36   Ibid., p. 25. And for this tract see also Knights, 'Loyal Address', pp. 327–8.

37 Garrison, *Dryden and the Tradition of Panegyric*, pp. 32–4. D. N. Deluna, '"Modern Panegyrick" and Defoe's "Dunciad"', *Studies in English Literature, 1500–1900*, 35 (1995), 419–35.
38 E. Rothstein, *Restoration and Eighteenth-Century Poetry* (London: Routledge, 1981, 2014 reprint), p. 8.
39 A. S. Williams, 'Panegyric decorum in the reigns of William III and Anne', *Journal of British Studies*, 21 (1981), 56–67 at 56.
40 Quoted in Janet Todd, 'Behn, Aphra', ODNB.
41 R. Bucholz, *The Augustan Court: Queen Anne and the Decline of Court Culture* (Stanford: Stanford University Press, 1993), p. 229. See also P. Rogers, *Pope and the destiny of the Stuarts: History Politics and Mythology in the Age of Queen Anne* (Oxford: Oxford University Press, 2005), ch. 4.
42 See *London Gazette*, 23–27 November 1701, no. 3761, address from Warwick.
43 *Post Man and Historical Account* 24–26 November 1696, no. 242.
44 Williams, 'Panegyric decorum', 57–62; A. Williams, *Poetry and the Creation of a Whig Literary Culture 1681–1714* (Oxford: Oxford University Press, 2005), esp. ch. 3.
45 *Post Man and the Historical Account*, 22–24 October 1696, no. 228.
46 *Review of the State of the British Nation*, 18 May 1710, no. 23.
47 *The Sense of the Nation, Concerning the Duke of Marlborough* (1702 [actually later, 1710?]); *The Sense of the Nine in Ten* (1712). For the importance of print to Marlborough's public persona see T. Claydon, 'A European general in the English press: the print image of Marlborough in the Stuart realms', in J. B. Hattendorf, A.J. Veenendaal Jnr and R. Van Hövell tot Westerflier (eds), *Marlborough: Soldier and Diplomat* (Rotterdam: Zutphen, 2012), ch. 6. See also Williams, *Whig Literary Culture*, pp. 139–40 for Marlborough as a surrogate for Anne and ibid., Chapter four in general.
48 J. B. Hattendorf, 'Churchill, John', ODNB.
49 Hattendorf, 'Churchill', ODNB.
50 *Sense of the Nine in Ten*, p. 24.
51 *London Gazette*, 6–10 November 1701, no. 3756.
52 *London Gazette*, 6–10 November 1701, no. 3756 (Cumberland); *London Gazette*, 13–17 November 1701, issue 3758 (Ludgershall).
53 Morphew, *Addresses*, pt 1, p. 9 (Radnor).
54 *The addresses to King George II*, p. 32. For a similarly conditional expression of loyalty see the address of the University of Cambridge to George I, *London Gazette*, 16–20 August 1715, no. 5356, which stated that as the King had promised to defend the constitution, so the people should 'make the same Constitution the Rule of their Obedience'.
55 *The addresses to King George II*, p. 99.
56 *The voice of the people* (1756).
57 M. Walzer, *Obligations: Essays on Disobedience, War and Citizenship* (Cambridge, Mass.: Harvard University Press, 1970), p. 5 (although for Walzer 'commitments to principles are usually also commitments to other men'). See also Kleinig, *On Loyalty and Loyalties*, p. 27; R. Devetak, 'Loyalty and plurality: images of the nation in Australia', in Michael Waller and Andrew Linklater (eds), *Political Loyalty and the Nation-State* (London: Routledge, 2003), pp. 27–43, at pp. 37–8.

58 Morphew, *Addresses*, pp. 24 (Kent), 27 (Cambridge).
59 McCormack, 'Rethinking "loyalty"', 415–17.
60 *Voice of the People,* A2 and see the address from Boston, Lincolnshire, ibid., pp. 40–1 and for this tract, McCormack, 'Rethinking "loyalty"', 421.
61 *Postman and the Historical Account,* 5–7 May 1696, no. 155. Also produced as a separate pamphlet, Abiel Borfet, *The minister of Richmond's reasons for refusing to subscribe the association* (1696).
62 Knights, 'Loyal address', p. 328.
63 [Defoe], *A new test,* p. 15; The pamphlet is attributed to Defoe in P. N. Furbank and W.R. Owens (eds), *A Critical Bibliography of Daniel Defoe* (London: Pickering and Chatto, 1998), p. 102.
64 [Defoe], *A new test,* p. 16.
65 *Observator,* 8–12 April 1710, no. 25; see also *Review of the State of the British Nation,* 13 July 1710, no. 47.
66 [Defoe], *A new test,* pp. 22–3.
67 Ibid., pp. 82–3.
68 [D. Defoe] *Two great questions considered* (1707), p. 8.
69 Bowie, *Scottish Public Opinion,* esp. ch. 6.
70 Ibid., pp. 101, 108.
71 Anon. *The modern addresses vindicated, and the rights of the addressers asserted, by D. De Foe extracted out of his book, intitled, The original right of the people of England examined and asserted* (n.pl., n.d.), p. 2.
72 [John Oldmixon], *History of Addresses* (1710), for evidence of the haste with which this was put together see p. 244 where the original index break remains, even though the work then continues for another fifteen pages with the index actually starting at p. 261. It is also noticeable that the new content on the Sacheverell addresses contained markedly less editorial comment than that given in the earlier pages.
73 [Oldmixon], *History of Addresses* (1710), p. 21.
74 Ibid., pp. 105–16. This may also have represented another opportunity for the conformist Oldmixon to needle his dissenting rival, Defoe.
75 [Oldmixon], *History of Addresses* (1709), p. 216.
76 Ibid., p. 186.
77 Ibid., pp. 196–9. For the addresses and associations of 1696 see above Chapter four. As already noted there, some areas of Lancashire did substitute subscription to a loyal address for subscription to the Association.
78 [Oldmixon], *History of Addresses,* (1711), p. 307–8.
79 Ibid., p. 183.
80 Ibid., p. 329.
81 Ibid., pp. 269–71. B. Hoadly, *True genuine Tory address* (1710) in *A fourth collection of scarce and valuable tracts,* vol. iii (1751), pp. 264–8 at pp. 267–8. Counter glossaries were produced in *The true genuine Tory-address and the true genuine Whig-address set one against another* (1710), pp. 11–12 and *The true genuine modern Whig-address* in *A fourth collection,* pp. 271–3.
82 [Benjamin Hoadly], *The voice of the addressers, or a short comment on the chief things contain'd, or condemn'd in our late modest addresses* (1710), pp. 26–7. On broader fears in this period about private political languages see Knights, *Representation and Misrepresentation,* pp. 295–8.

83 [Defoe], *A new test*, p. 88.
84 Ibid., p. 80.
85 Ibid., p. 91.
86 K. R. Penovich, 'From "revolution principles" to union: Daniel Defoe's intervention in the Scottish debate', in J. Robertson (ed.), *A Union for Empire: Political Thought and the British Union of 1707* (Cambridge: Cambridge University Press, 1995), pp. 228–43 at p. 238.
87 See Defoe, *Original Right*, p. 4, 'the Representative Body of the People ought not to be Banter'd or Affronted neither, at the Will and Pleasure of any private Person without Doors' and p. 23.
88 *Letters of Defoe*, ed. Healey, p. 33.
89 Defoe, *Original right*, pp. 18–19, noted in Gunn, *Beyond Liberty and Property*, p. 75.
90 [Oldmixon], *History of Addresses* (1709), [unpaginated p. 14]
91 O. Smith, *The Politics of Language, 1791–1819* (Oxford: Clarendon Press, 1984) at p. 34 and see pp. 30–4.
92 North, *Examen*, p. 540.
93 J. Arbuthnot, *Proposals for printing a very curious discourse...A treatise of the art of political lying* (1712), p. 16.
94 Ibid., p. 21.
95 J. A. Downie, *Robert Harley and the Press: Propaganda and Public Opinion in the Age of Swift and Defoe* (Cambridge: Cambridge University Press, 1979), pp. 98–9.
96 [Oldmixon], *History of Addresses*, (1711), p. 2.
97 [Oldmixon], *History of Addresses*, (1710), p. 12.
98 Minogue, 'Loyalty, liberalism and the state', p. 221.
99 Ibid., p. 221.
100 A. McShane, 'Subjects and Objects: Material Expressions of Loyalty in Seventeenth-Century England', *Journal of British Studies*, 48 (2009), 871–886. V.A. Kahn, *Wayward Contracts: the Crisis of Political Obligation in England, 1640–1674* (Princeton: Princeton University Press, 2004).
101 McShane, 'Subjects and objects', 877.
102 Ibid., 873.

Conclusion

The loyal address was a product of the broader growth in subscriptional activity during the civil wars. Employed as a means of legitimating the Cromwellian Protectorate, the address offered a form similar to the petition. Like the petition, it was notionally the spontaneous product of that group or community, but more open to central coordination and control. In this way, the emergence of the address as a political genre can be seen as part of wider attempts by the interregnum regime to manage the press (for example, through semi-official newsbooks) and popular politics (through measures against mass petitioning).

From their inception, however, these texts were employed in ways which subverted their supposedly acclamatory role. The Corporation of Great Yarmouth, for example, used its address of congratulation to Oliver Cromwell on assuming the Protectoral title to remind their new head of State of the town's financial burden in maintaining the haven and the pier.[1] As we have seen, texts that were intended to lend authority to the Cromwellian regime, during the short protectorate of Richard Cromwell, were regularly employed instead to question the legitimacy of his rule, as well as being used as vehicles for religious controversy. If these addresses failed to successfully shore up Richard Cromwell's authority, they nonetheless demonstrated the value of these texts as a means to apply political pressure and challenge government while maintaining the outward appearance of loyalty to the regime. They also demonstrated the capacity of these texts to provoke the discussion of national issues, such as the eligibility of a new ruler, at a local level. The value of these devices was recognised by the restored Stuart monarchy which, like its Cromwellian predecessor, chose to regulate petitioning and addressing activity rather than attempt to suppress it entirely. This response was not simply recognition of the Crown's limited power to contain popular political activity but also an acknowledgement of the political value of addresses as demonstrated first in campaigns for a free Parliament, and then, in lending public approval to the restoration of Charles II.

The 1680s saw the revival of strategies of mass petitioning and addressing which the Restoration monarchy's supporters (and the Crown itself at points) connected back to the civil wars. This reflected the mnemonic aspects of these subscriptional texts and their capacity to act as vehicles for the historical, as well as the social or political imaginary. Past subscriptional activity was used to attack the reputations of individuals ranging from the Tory party's chief propagandist, Sir Roger L'Estrange, to the relatively lowly members of the Yarmouth corporation.

For the Court's opponents, however, history could also provide a resource for questioning the legitimacy of subscriptional practices, specifically loyal addressing campaigns in support of the Crown. Equally, loyalist 'abhorrances' issued repudiating Shaftesbury's 'Association' and then the Rye House Plot, appeared to suggest that all subscriptional activity conducted without royal approval might be illicit and smack of conspiracy. Yet, neither the Court nor its opponents during the Exclusion Crisis were committed either to removing a right to petition or address, or to repealing the post-Restoration limitations on mass petitioning. This, and the emphasis especially in Whig discourse on male freeholders as constituting the political nation, suggests that mass petitioning and addressing represented an expedient rather than a principled admission of the formally excluded into the public sphere. Of course, whether explicitly authorised or not, the involvement of the lower orders in debates on matters such as the royal succession represented a dramatic transgression of established social and political norms. Moreover, the political deployment of popular memory and the mobilisation of popular support had important ramifications for the Stuart monarchy during the reign of James II. The consistent connections made between post-Restoration non-conformity, civil war Puritanism and political radicalism made the pursuit of a policy of toleration (and the alliances with dissenting churches that it necessitated) deeply problematic.

These same alliances also challenged the prior emphasis in addressing activity upon the importance of social hierarchy and the production of addresses from official bodies (such as corporations or grand juries). Similarly, the exploitation of popular hostility against both Catholics and non-conformists encouraged a public mood that was profoundly unsympathetic to the king's religious objectives. As in the 1650s, the failure of James' addressing campaigns to achieve their goals also reveals that such subscriptional activity did not simply fabricate 'public opinion' but was directly connected to actual levels of public support. As during the brief protectorate of Richard Cromwell, campaigns alone could not transform public opinion and could instead often provide opportunities to mount political opposition.

The potential of these campaigns for challenging rather than legitimising authority was realised after the revolution of 1688. In 1701 and 1710, addressing campaigns significantly influenced electoral outcomes and led to changes in government. These campaigns not only affected national politics but also represented interventions in European affairs as the addresses commented on both foreign policy (war or peace with France) and dynastic claims (the Spanish succession). This influence was in part derived from the revival of popular petitioning and addressing strategies.

As in the 1680s, however, even the seemingly most strident assertions of the popular voice, such as Defoe's *Legion's Memorial*, tended to limit legitimate political petitioning and addressing to freeholders. Equally, though the Bill of Rights had affirmed the liberty of subjects to petition the Crown, it did not relax the post-Restoration restrictions on subscriptional activity and there was no indication even in the most heated petitioning and addressing controversies during the reigns of William and Anne of a willingness to open up this arena of popular politics in the way in which restrictions on the press had been relaxed by the lapsing of the Licensing Act.[2]

Nonetheless, the success of addressing campaigns initiated by the government's critics (in the case of the supporters of Henry Sacheverell) and the increasingly sophisticated use of print in these controversies (the growing number of compendia and histories of addressing produced in the 1700s), saw addressing activity display some of the 'dialogic' characteristics identified by David Zaret in petitioning during the civil wars. The presentation of text and counter-text within some compendia implicitly invited the volume's readership to adjudicate between these texts. The use of addresses in such obviously partisan ways, however, provoked anxiety about the ability of the public to evaluate these different political claims. Yet these collections and histories of addresses themselves exaggerated the degree of political division and overlooked the many texts which attempted to occupy a less controversial middle ground. Moreover, despite the vehemence of their attacks on some addressing activity, neither Daniel Defoe, nor John Oldmixon nor Benjamin Hoadly advocated the suppression of this subscriptional form: once again the remedy was regulation.

This is not to deny the considerable social reach of addressing activity. As demonstrated by an analysis of the Leicestershire address to Richard Cromwell, those subscribing to these texts could include many on the margins of society as well as representatives of the county elite and local office-holders. Mass subscriptional activity of this kind has been seen as evidence of the broadening of the English political nation: for Steven Pincus, 'the number of subscriptions in 1696' to the Association in defence of William III 'suggests that most English men and some women assigned themselves a political role'.[3]

The evidence provided by subscription returns, especially those for loyal addresses, is arguably more ambiguous than this. In the case of the Leicestershire address, subscription patterns which are suggestive of coercion raise doubts on whether we can view subscriptions as expressions of autonomous political agency. Addresses, as statements of corporate or community loyalty, in any case placed less emphasis upon individual consent and action than other subscriptional forms such as oaths. The involvement of the poor (if not the very poor) in this subscriptional activity did undoubtedly challenge established norms concerning political participation but their involvement in this activity was not consistent nor was it regularly given express official approval. Post-Restoration there was a marked retreat from securing mass subscriptions to these texts, with the display of subscriptions instead designed as a reassertion of political and social hierarchy, as well as being a demonstration of the individual subscriber's loyalty to the monarchy.

The Exclusion Crisis made mass mobilisation of public opinion again expedient but, as has already been noted, did not prompt any significant revaluation of the legislative restrictions on popular petitioning and addressing. The social and political breadth of subscriptions to addresses tendered between 1658 and 1660, however, does indicate the value of these devices for bringing together political coalitions, an important facet of addressing activity already highlighted by Scott Sowerby in his work on addresses in support of James II's policy of toleration.

Again, though, what groups of subscribers were associating for was not always transparent. The process of addressing could be costly because of the need to pay the costs of presenters travelling to Court, as well as the expense of 'treating' presenters and introducers to encourage them to take on these roles. This expense was justified because it was the ceremonial aspects of addressing that provided the greatest opportunity for reward both for the community and individual presenters. A properly presented, and well-expressed, address was that which was most likely to secure vital political access to central authority.

The willingness of communities to expend considerable sums of money on this activity consequently did not mean that this financial outlay was an expression of their ideological commitment either to the current government or its policies. As the case of the Hallamshire Cutlers indicates, communities could invest in addressing activity as one of a number of strategies designed to secure material concessions (in this case tax relief) largely detached from the matter of the address. The Cutlers' actions nonetheless demonstrate that local communities could have a fairly sophisticated understanding of which individuals and what sorts of expressions of loyalty were needed in order for their material concerns to be dealt with.

This instrumental approach to addressing was not without value for the Crown either, because it could bring typically dissident groups to make public declarations of (albeit strategic) loyalty. The value of these displays was also in the opportunities they provided the Court for managing opposition. Under Charles II, access to Court became more tightly regulated and socially exclusive. Gestural and sometimes verbal rebuke was used to indicate when petitions or addresses were deemed inappropriate or potentially seditious. Charles' effective use of ceremony contrasted with his brother's less sophisticated approach to these encounters. The comparative ineffectiveness of James' addressing campaigns, however, was not simply a result of personality differences between the two monarchs. Charles' policies from 1681–5 were geared towards appealing to the Tory-Anglican gentry who represented the majority of the political and social elite. These policies also chimed with a significant section of popular opinion. James' tolerationist policies, on the other hand, seemingly threatened the social and political hierarchy in ways in which no amount of deft manipulation of Court access and ceremony arguably could have overcome.

The importance of the ritual connected to addressing activity, however, did not seriously diminish with the changing nature of the English Court after 1688. Formerly proscribed groups such as England's dissenting churches saw the opportunity to present addresses to the Crown as an important way of legitimising their denominations as well as winning important dispensations from the Hanoverian monarchy.

The consistency in the performance of addressing activity was matched by a relative consistency in the language of loyalty used in these texts. Addresses were dependent less on 'rule-based' notions of political obligation but more upon an emotionally defined idea of loyalty. Loyalty in this way retained potentially subversive aspects: if loyalty was commonly understood as love and faithfulness towards a ruler, this assumed that that prince was in some way 'loveable' – criteria against which, again, James II might be found wanting. While the language of loyalty did shift post-revolution, to incorporate ideals (liberty) and institutions (the constitution) as well as the person of the monarch, the emotional register remained in place but was directed at new objects. The passionate language in which loyalty was often expressed, however, was occasionally seen as being problematic: either becoming dangerously over-heated or, conversely, being reduced to empty sycophancy. The argument that addressing had spawned a new and bewildering political vocabulary, however, was itself a particular rhetorical strategy. By adopting a historical perspective, critics of post-revolutionary addressing such as Defoe, Oldmixon and Hoadly were able to undercut the credibility of this political medium. Defoe, however, was exceptional in maintaining that some post-revolutionary addressing had rendered political language meaningless. Instead, the intent of analysing the lexicon of these texts was again to discriminate between legitimate and illegitimate forms of subscriptional activity. This process of regulating addressing was in turn managed through precisely the action of remembering or historicising subscriptional activity which, it has been suggested, encouraged a developing awareness of 'public opinion'.

Addressing campaigns were typically initiated at the political centre. The argument of this book concerning their role in fostering a sense of a political public therefore complements other accounts of the emergence the early modern 'public sphere' (notably that provided by Peter Lake and Steve Pincus), which have argued for the importance of the State in facilitating this development. As has been shown, however, this large-scale subscriptional activity was not simply an example of the successful projection of State propaganda. Equally, the scope of these exercises on its own does not indicate the growing capacity of the State: the failure of addressing campaigns in 1658 and 1687–8 to achieve their core goals indicates the degree to which subscriptional activity continued to be reliant on negotiation with and support from local elites and the population at large. Even the related example of the Association of 1696 is arguably less indicative of the transformation of the post-revolutionary State than is sometimes claimed: the Association returns vary markedly in their content and form, perhaps indicating less the increasingly long reach of the fiscal-military State and more the successful co-option of local government into administering these exercises.[4] This dependence on local power networks also meant that even campaigns initiated at the centre could stimulate public criticism and debate (again as clearly evidenced during the rule of Richard Cromwell and James II).

The discursive and critical aspects of addressing activity bear comparison with the 'democratic' features of mass petitions during the 1640s identified by David Zaret. The partisan perspectives delivered within these texts have led other historians, notably Mark Knights, to follow some contemporary observers in questioning whether readers could exercise rational judgement in evaluating such subjective claims. Here, however, it has been argued that the partisan nature of much addressing activity in fact promoted the kind of self-awareness that scholars such as Zaret have seen as important for the development of a critical public.[5]

Addressing, even more than petitioning, generated an enduring public record of political activity through its close connection to national political events. Its commemorative capacity was heightened by its intrinsic publicness: in contrast to petitioning, the only point of printing addresses was to publicise public support and/or the loyalty of the community and individual addressers. Addressing, even more than petitioning, therefore lent itself to being employed as a resource in both individual, local and national historical narratives. A case in point is the Yarmouth address to Richard Cromwell sent by Richard Bower to Secretary Williamson. The very fact that Bower acquired a text which the corporation had ordered obliterated indicates the importance that Bower attached to it as a record of political activity. By the late eighteenth century, the Yarmouth address had been integrated into printed histories of the town and, by the Victorian age, addressing activity had taken centre stage in Charles Palmer's narrative of the borough's political life from the Stuart to Georgian era.[6] In contrast to more quotidian petitioning, it was the extraordinary nature of addressing – its ability to connect the locality with national events – which made it memorable.

Bower's original intent in copying the address, of course, had not been to provide a resource for future historians. Partisanship, a desire to mark out political opponents through evidence of their past collusion with the Cromwellian regime, had driven him to contact Williamson. Bower's discriminatory intent sits uneasily with accounts of subscriptional activity, most notably Zaret's, which connect it with emergent democracy and broadening notions of citizenship.[7] While it has been argued that partisanship was integral to the developing awareness of public opinion communicated through these texts, the language of addresses and their ostensibly 'acclamatory' purpose makes them a seemingly poor fit with a narrative of democratic development. In other respects, however, addresses were better accommodated with eighteenth-century political landscape than other subscriptional forms such as oaths of loyalty. They placed less emphasis upon individual agency, making the act of subscription less overtly transgressive.

Equally, as texts predominantly representing communities or corporate bodies, they could work with an idea of political representation as directed at reflecting different interests, economic, social, religious and political, within the nation. As notionally spontaneous expressions of loyalty, they were also easier to accommodate with the principle of voluntary association which was critical to public life in the post-revolutionary period. Vestiges of this outlook can still be seen in the addresses sent to Queen Victoria on the occasion of her Diamond Jubilee, attempting to represent the incredibly varied communities of the late nineteenth-century British empire, from the 'Society of Ancient Britons' to the Malay Royal Family.[8]

Within Britain at least, discordant voices in 1897 were rare: England and Scotland appeared unified in their declaration of loyalty to Queen Victoria. In contrast, during the political turbulence of the seventeenth century the 'sense of the people', as Defoe would later put it, was much harder to discern. This offers a reminder that these subscriptional texts, as Zaret has suggested, occupied a space somewhere between 'real' and 'normative' opinion. Communities were coerced, their opinions manipulated or spun, but the content of these texts could not be totally divorced from the opinions of the groups which produced them. If the anecdotes about them carried an element of truth, Richard Cromwell was as aware as his critics that many of the addresses contained in his trunks had offered highly equivocal pledges of loyalty. Yet, though Richard's rule would be short-lived, the form of the address survived both the Restoration and the revolution of 1688 to replace other subscriptional forms as the main means of representing loyalty.

The precise form that loyalty took would remain contested and addresses, especially in the later eighteenth century as Britain's imperial crisis developed, could still be vehicles for political controversy.[9] They endured, nonetheless, as a critical means of representing public opinion that implicitly acknowledged a broad political public. Yet, while addresses provided opportunities for wider political participation, they did so in a way that fundamentally conceded the legitimacy of social and political hierarchy.

Making loyalty the primary qualification for political participation did have potentially subversive implications, as underscored during the Exclusion Crisis in particular. Yet, qualifying political participation in this way also avoided conferring any permanent political agency or autonomy upon the addressers. The address was consequently perfectly suited to a fundamentally unequal society in which political life continued to be centred around the monarchy, even as mass democracy became a reality.

NOTES

1. NRO Y/C 19/7 f. 245, Yarmouth corporation assembly book, 1642–1662, 1 June 1654.
2. Although here it should be noted that the lapse of the Licensing Act only ended one form of censorship and did not signal the end either of press regulation or of the idea that some type of censorship was necessary. See A. W. Barber, '"Why don't those lazy priests answer the book?" Matthew Tindal, censorship, freedom of the press and religious debate in early eighteenth-century England', *History*, 98 (2013), 680–707; Ross Carroll, 'Ridicule, censorship, and the regulation of public speech: the case of Shaftesbury', *Modern Intellectual History*, 13 (2016), 1–28.
3. Pincus, *1688*, p. 468; A more cautious assessment is offered in Knights, *Representation and Misrepresentation*, p. 160.
4. See for example Jeremy Gibson's comments on the haphazard nature of the Oxfordshire Association rolls: J. Gibson (ed.), *Politics and Loyalty in Post-Revolution Oxfordshire: The 1690 County Parliamentary Poll; The Association Oath Rolls, 1695–96* (Bury: Oxfordshire Family History Society, in association with The Family History Partnership, 2011), p. 63. For a different assessment see M. J. Braddick, *State Formation in Early Modern England* (Cambridge: Cambridge University Press, 2000), pp. 327–30.
5. Zaret, *Origins of Democratic Culture*, p. 252.
6. H. Swinden, *The History and Antiquities of the Ancient Burgh of Great Yarmouth* (Norwich, 1772), pp. 578–9; 'C. Parkin', *The History of Great Yarmouth, Collected from Antient Records and other Authentic Materials* (Lynn, 1776), p. 317. David Stoker has demonstrated that this work was essentially a pirated version of Swinden's history, produced by the bookseller William Whittingham, see D. Stoker, 'Parkin, Charles', ODNB and Stoker, 'Mr Parkin's Magpie, the Other Mr Whittingham and the Fate of Great Yarmouth', *The Library*, series 6, 12 (1990), 121–31; Palmer, *History of Great Yarmouth*, pp. 247–70.
7. For the modern period in relation to women's subscriptions see Zaeske, *Signatures of citizenship*, pp. 109–11; P. A. Pickering, 'And your petitioners &c.': chartist petitioning in popular politics 1838–48', *English Historical Review* (2001), 368–88 at 378–80.
8. TNA PP 1/484 (Ancient Britons); TNA PP 1/647/1 (Loyal address of Tunku All bin Tunku Allum, the Surviving Representative of the Malay Royal Family in Singapore).
9. K. Wilson, *The Sense of the People: Politics, Culture and Imperialism in England, 1715–1785* (Cambridge: Cambridge University Press, 1998 edn), pp. 267–8, 357–8; M. Knights, 'The 1780 Protestant petitions and the culture of petitioning', in I. Haywood and J. Seed (eds), *The Gordon Riots: Politics, Culture and Insurrection in Late Eighteenth-Century Britain* (Cambridge: Cambridge University Press, 2012), pp. 46–68; J. E. Bradley, *Religion, Revolution and English Radicalism: Non-conformity in Eighteenth-Century Politics and Society* (Cambridge: Cambridge University Press, 1990), ch. 9 & 10.

Bibliography of archival and manuscript material consulted

ARCHIVE SERVICES, WEST YORKSHIRE JOINT SERVICES, MORLEY, YORKSHIRE
WYL 150/MX/12/31/20, 22, 24v., Letters from Lord Burlington, February 1684/5
WYL 150/MX/R/30/3, Sir John Boynton to Sir John Reresby, 22 February 1684
WYL 150/MX/R/30/4, Address of Lords, Deputy Lieutenants, Justices of Peace and Gentlemen of Yorkshire to James II after the Monmouth Rebellion
WYL 156/MX/12/29/15, Address of Mayor and Commonalty of York to James II on his accession

BEDFORDSHIRE ARCHIVES AND RECORDS SERVICE, BEDFORD
Bor BA3/6, Bedfordshire address abhorring the Rye House Plot, excerpted from *London Gazette*, originally framed

BODLEIAN LIBRARY, UNIVERSITY OF OXFORD
MS Ballard 36
MS J. Walker C. 5, Working papers for Sufferings of the Clergy
MS J. Walker C. 11, Leicestershire militia commissioners' proceedings
MS Rawl A. 61* f. 164–87, Address of the well-affected inhabitants of Leicestershire to Richard Cromwell
MS Rawl A. 61/1–3, State Papers of John Thurloe

BRITISH LIBRARY, ST PANCRAS, LONDON
Add MS 5138, Guybon Goddard's diary
Add MS 15862, Parliamentary Diary of Thomas Burton 1656–59
Add MS 27448, Paston letters
Add MS 29442–3 Reresby's 'Family History'
Add MS 50958–9, Edmund Calamy's Accounts
Add MS 70421, John Dyer's newsletters sent to Edward Harley and Dr Stratford at Christ Church, 1709–10

Bibliography

Add MS 75359, Althorp papers vol. I
Add MS 78195, Evelyn Papers vol. XXVIII
Add MS Ch. 76109–23, Addresses to Queen Anne on the occasion of the trial of Henry Sacheverell
Egerton MS 1048, A collection of Parliamentary documents, mostly originals relating to events in the years 1624–59
Harley MS 911, Richard Symonds' civil war diaries
Lansdowne MS 823, Letters to Henry Cromwell III, 1657–59
Lansdowne MS 849 'A volume containing a great number of articles, chiefly State papers'
Northumberland MS 552, Fitzjames letter books (BL Loan Microfilm 331)
Stowe MS 219 (Lord Chandos' Letterbook)
Stowe MS 222, Hanover papers, vol. I
Stowe MS 223, Hanover papers, vol. II
Stowe MS 225, Hanover papers, vol. IV
Stowe MS 228, Hanover papers, vol. VII
Stowe MS 229, Hanover papers, vol. VIII
Stowe MS 354, Speeches and other collections relating to Parliament
Stowe MS 746, vol. V, 1691–1702
Thynne MS, Longleat House, 67 (BL Loan Microfilm 904/36)
Thynne MS, Longleat House, 21–2, Newsletters (BL Loan Microfilm 904/11)

CENTRE FOR BUCKINGHAMSHIRE STUDIES

D193/5/2, '1701 Copyes of ye Addresses of the Grand Juryes etc.'

COMPANY OF CUTLERS IN HALLAMSHIRE, ARCHIVES

D1/1, 'Accounts of the Masters Cutler, 1625–1790'

DORSET HISTORY CENTRE, DORCHESTER

DC/LR/A/3/1, 'Misdemeanour Book, Counsels' Opinions, Loyal Addresses etc.'

DR WILLIAMS' LIBRARY, LONDON

Baxter Treatise, V, fo. 320–1, item 186, 'The Humble Address & Association of us Ministers of ye Gospel in ye Counties of Nottingham, Derby, Leicester & places adjacent'
Baxter Treatise, V, fo. 322–23, item 187, 'The Humble Address of ye Protestant Dissenting Minister of ye several Denominations in & about ye Cities of London and Westminster'
MS 38.17, Benjamin Stinton's Journal

EAST SUSSEX RECORD OFFICE (COLLECTION NOW HELD AT THE KEEP, BRIGHTON, SUSSEX)

SAY 1/1/1/1, 'Draft address (in John Collier's hand) of the Mayor, Jurats and inhabitants of Hastings to Queen Anne, in thanksgiving for peace terminating the war with France'

SAY 1/1/1/2, Letter from John Brewer at West Farleigh near Maidstone, Kent to John Collier, attorney-at-law at Hastings
SAY1/1/1/3, Fair copy of the address of the Mayor and Corporation of Hastings to George I, upon his accession
SAY1/1/1/4, Draft address of the Mayor, Jurats and Inhabitants of Hasting to George I, 23 February 1726
SAY1/1/1/5, Printed proclamation of the lords of the realm proclaiming George II king upon the death of George I
SAY1/1/1/6, Address of the Mayor, Jurats and Freemen of the Corporation of Hastings to George II

FOLGER SHAKESPEARE LIBRARY, WASHINGTON DC
L. c. 1–39500, Newdigate family collection of newsletters

GLOUCESTERSHIRE ARCHIVES, GLOUCESTER
D747/2, Draft and copy of loyal addresses from Independents and Baptists of the County of Glos, 1687 or 1688
GBR/H/2/3, 'A Booke for entering of letters sent from the Lords of the Councell & Lord Lieutenant beginning Anno Dm 1639'

HAMPSHIRE ARCHIVES AND LOCAL STUDIES, HAMPSHIRE RECORD OFFICE, WINCHESTER, HAMPSHIRE
44 M69 G3/264, Hampshire address to Queen Anne, 1702
44 M69/G3/1127, Hampshire Grand Jury address abhorring Shaftesbury's Association
18 M51/636/84, Hampshire address to William III, 1701
WF/F2/6, Winchester City Ledger Book, vol. 6, 1691–1713

KENT ARCHIVES AND LIBRARY SERVICES, MAIDSTONE, KENT
CP/Bp 286, 'Circular letter, with answers, from Rye arearing a Guestling'
CP/Bp 288, Draft minutes of the Guestling, 24 July 1683
CP/Bp 289, Brotherhood papers, draft minutes and accounts, 1683
CP/Bp 290, Draft loyal address, July 1683
NR/CPc/170, Circular letter, with answers, from Hastings, 2 June 1660
U269 C356/5, William Eldred to Thomas Whitfield, 9 August 1682

KINGSTON HISTORY CENTRE
KB 10, Draft loyal addresses

LANCASHIRE ARCHIVES, LANCASHIRE RECORD OFFICE PRESTON, LANCASHIRE
DDKE 2/20/1, Grand Jury of Lancashire's address to Charles II for his declaration, 12 July 1681

Bibliography

DDKE 2/20/2, Grand Jury of Lancashire's address abhorring the Rye House Plot, 1683
DDKE 2/20/6, Address from Lancashire Lord Lieutenant, Deputy Lieutenants, Militia Officers, Justices of the Peace, Gentlemen and Freeholders to James II in the wake of the Monmouth Rebellion, 1685
DDKE 2/20/7, Address of the Nobility, Gentry, Militia and Commonalty of the County Palatine of Lancashire to Queen Mary II, c.1690s
HMC 404, address from Corporation of Wigan thanking Charles II for his declaration explaining the dissolution of the Oxford Parliament
HMC 448, draft address from Preston abhorring the Association, 1682
HMC 447, 'Humble address of the Lord Lieutenant, High Sheriff, Deputy Lieutenants, Justices of the Peace and other officers of Lancashire at a general meeting at Preston the 21 April 1682'
HMC 458, Thomas Hodgkinson to Roger Kenyon, 30 May 1682
HMC 591, Lancashire grand jury address on accession of James II, 1685
HMC 596, Clitheroe address thanking James II for his declaration of indulgence;
HMC 1169, Corporation of Wigan address to George I, 1715
QDV/10, Association in support of William III

THE NATIONAL ARCHIVES, KEW

C 213/138/1, Association Oath Rolls. Lancashire. West Derby and Lonsdale Hundreds
C 231/7, Crown Office Docket Book, 1660–78
E 179/134/317, Leicestershire Free and Voluntary Present, July 1661
E 179/240/279, Leicestershire Hearth Tax Return, 1670
E 179/251/4/1–8, Leicestershire Hearth Tax Return, Lady Day 1664
E 179/251/5–6, Leicestershire Hearth Tax 'for ye 3 half yeares at Michmas 1665'
E 179/251/9, Leicestershire Hearth Tax, Lady Day 1666
E 179/251/10, Four additional membranes of Leicestershire Hearth Tax returns
E 179/332 pt 1, Leicestershire Hearth Tax exemption certificates, 1670
E 179/353 pt 2, Leicestershire and Rutland Hearth Tax exemption certificates, 1674
PC 2/64, Privy Council Registers 1673–75
PP 1, Jubilee addresses to Queen Victoria
PRO 31/17/33, Transcript of the Council of State Order Book 3 September 1658 to 18 January 1658/9
SP 18/158, Letters and papers, Council of State, December 1657
SP 18/181, Letters and papers, Council of State, May–June 1658
SP 18/184, Letters and papers, Council of State, December 1658
SP 23/49, Returns of sequestrated recusants, Committee for Compounding with Delinquents
SP 23/70, Committee for Compounding with Delinquents, Books and Papers, 1st series, no. 10
SP 28/148, Bedfordshire–Buckinghamshire, Commonwealth Exchequer Papers
SP 29/1, State Papers Domestic, May 1660
SP 29/3, State Papers Domestic, June 1660
SP 29/9, State Papers Domestic, Petitions July 1660
SP 29/12, State Papers Domestic, Petitions August 1660
SP 29/30–31, State Papers Domestic, Feb 1661
SP 29/39, State Papers Domestic, July 1661

Bibliography

SP 29/383, State Papers Domestic, July 1676
SP 29/408, State Papers Domestic, November–December 1678
SP 34/12/36, Copy of the affidavit of John Stainer of Aston, Salop on the insulting behaviour of Thomas Yewde
SP 34/12/37, 'Copy of letter dated 5 April 1710 from John Lawne to [?Earl of Sunderland], from Salop. Relative to an address which is about to be given by the High Sheriff'
SP 34/12/38, Certificate that Thomas Yewde refused to take the oath of abjuration
SP 44/6, Secretaries of State, State Papers, Entry Books, Sir Edward Nicholas, Ecclesiastical

NORFOLK RECORD OFFICE

MC 42/136, 527 X4, draft Whig address to Queen Anne
Y/C 19/7, Yarmouth corporation assembly book, 1642–62
Y/C 19/8, Yarmouth corporation assembly book, 1662–80
Y/C 36/19/20, letter from John Ramey, attorney for the prosecution in Rex vs Cotman, 10 March 1760

NORTHUMBERLAND ARCHIVES, WOODHORN, ASHINGTON, NORTHUMBERLAND

1 DE 12–17, draft address to James II on his accession, 1685

RECORD OFFICE OF LEICESTERSHIRE, LEICESTER AND RUTLAND, WIGSTON, LEICESTERSHIRE

BRII/18/29 (Leicester Hall Books)
DE 1241/1, Kimcote and Walton parish registers
DE 3575/1, Cadeby baptisms, marriages, deaths
DG 21/283, The Hazlerigg Collection, copy of *A Second Narrative of the Late Parliament*
DG 25/1/1, Melton Mowbray town warden's book
DG 32/2, Melton Mowbray burials, marriages, baptisms, 1642–62
DG 36/2, Melton Mowbray parish registers

ROYAL INSTITUTION OF CORNWALL

MEN/146, Loyal address to William of Orange from a general meeting held at Bodmin

YALE UNIVERSITY LIBRARY MANUSCRIPTS AND ARCHIVES, STERLING MEMORIAL LIBRARY, NEW HAVEN CONNECTICUT

MS 753, Box 2, English Miscellaneous Manuscripts Collection, 1362–1945

Index

abhorrences 69, 71–2, 75–7, 82, 107, 145, 148, 162–3, 168–9
abhorrers 70, 75–6, 176, 195, 208
Act against Tumults and Disorders (1661) 5, 25, 52–3, 84, 97
Act of Recognition (1659) 47–8
addresses
    compared to oaths 13–15, 31–2, 147, 210, 213
    compared to petitions 3–5, 10, 13–15, 21–3, 31–3, 44, 56, 74, 84, 94, 99, 120–3, 161, 163, 175, 207, 212
    as legitimating devices 2, 10, 13, 26, 28, 33, 40–1, 47–50, 56, 83, 133, 136–7, 176–7, 207–8, 211
    as performance 16, 161–3, 167, 175, 211
addressing, loyal
    characteristics of 2–4, 9–10, 13, 22, 24–5, 27–8, 31–2, 41, 51, 56, 71, 84, 94, 99–100, 110–11, 167–8, 192, 200–1, 209, 212
    discussion in life-writing 12, 163–8, 177
    expense of 15, 161–3, 210
    gendering of 9, 13, 15, 32, 120, 136, 147, 149
    origins of 3, 13, 16, 31, 40–1, 54–6, 67, 74, 207
    post-Restoration 15, 33, 51, 124, 147–9, 163, 177–8, 191–2, 202, 210
    process of 2, 12, 30–2, 44, 56, 82, 121–2, 124, 129, 162–3, 210
    risks involved in 71, 76, 121, 167, 174
    social breadth of 9, 13, 15, 52, 81, 120, 129–33, 136–8, 142–3, 147–8, 172, 177–8, 208–10
    value of 15, 41, 95, 163, 167, 208–10
affiliation
    political 11, 15, 30, 54, 82, 112, 141
    religious 11, 15, 161
agency
    individual 22, 28, 30, 32, 189, 213–14
    political 13, 21–2, 28, 209, 213
allegiance
    oaths of 14, 106, 147, 202
    shifting 16, 137, 141, 184, 194–5
alliances 14, 32, 49, 56, 58, 85, 148, 208
almanacs 166
Anglican clergy 51–2, 82, 105–6, 122, 127–9, 136, 165, 171–2, 175
Anne, addresses to 95, 101, 108, 110, 163, 165, 168, 172–4, 187, 191–3, 197
anti-petitions 68, 70
    see also counter-texts
anti-petitioners 70–1
    see also abhorrers
army, addresses from 40, 42–4, 51
authenticity, of addresses 11, 41, 104, 123, 178

authority
   challenges to 30, 78, 95–6, 193, 199, 208–9
   deference to 25, 28, 32
   demands on 10, 25, 31, 33, 56, 78, 171
   legitimating 16, 23, 25–6, 28, 33, 40, 46, 49, 68, 137, 207

Beaumont, Thomas 124, 141–2
Bower, Richard 66–7, 212
Bowie, Karin 2, 3, 5, 196
Boyle, Richard (Earl of Burlington) 174–5
broadsheets 11–12, 26, 32–3, 40, 69, 121, 138, 141–2
   see also newsbooks; newsletters; pamphlets

Calamy, Edmund 163–4, 168, 171–4
Catholics 14, 68, 75, 208
Caton, William 45, 53–4, 56, 136
Charles II
   addresses to 51–2, 57, 67–8, 73, 120, 142–3, 168, 174, 197
   use of ritual 175–6, 178, 210
Churchill, John, Duke of Marlborough 192
citizenship 23–4, 28–30, 33, 213
compendia of subscription texts 11, 16, 22, 28, 32, 53–7, 67, 80–1, 94, 103, 109, 144, 166–7, 187–8, 191–3, 200–1, 209
congratulatory addresses 1–4, 13, 31, 41, 50–2, 57, 69, 76, 99, 120, 137–8, 141–3, 168, 171, 192, 198, 207
counter-texts 11, 15, 22, 25–6, 29, 70, 94, 101, 103–4, 107, 109–10, 136, 190, 195, 201, 209
credibility
   of addresses 8, 16, 27, 48, 107, 141, 194, 198, 211
   political 95, 184, 187, 200
Cromwell, Henry 42–3
Cromwell, Oliver
   addresses to 31, 40, 72–4, 147, 189, 207
   death of 41–2, 50

Cromwell, Richard
   addresses to 3, 13, 15, 31, 40–51, 53–6, 66–7, 73–4, 76–7, 81, 98, 107, 120–1, 124–38, 141, 143, 147–8, 166, 171–2, 188–9, 207–9, 212
   Protectorate of 13, 41–50, 54–8, 136–7, 207–8, 212–13
   trunks of 13, 16, 55–6, 213
Cutlers, Hallamshire 15, 160–2, 169–71, 178, 210

Defoe, Daniel 9–10, 16, 94–9, 106–8, 111–12, 195–200, 209, 211, 213
democracy 6, 16, 21, 23, 30, 94, 186, 212–14
dialogic order 5, 26, 94, 209
disaffection 32, 106, 147
discourse, political 33, 56–7, 67, 94, 184, 187, 194, 208

Elizabeth II, addresses to 1–2, 4
emotions 3, 8, 10, 16, 22, 29, 34, 99, 168, 184–7, 193–4, 198–9, 201–2, 211
English Bill of Rights 68, 83–4, 146, 209
Exclusion Crisis 4, 25, 28, 66, 68, 71–2, 80, 143–4, 146, 148, 175, 190, 208, 210, 213

failure of addressing campaigns 26, 207–8, 212
fidelity 112, 187, 193, 198, 211
Fitzjames, Sir John 42, 48, 50, 132, 136
Fleetwood, Charles 42–4
Fletcher, George 185, 187
Freke, Elizabeth 34, 165

George I, addresses to 112, 122, 171
George II, addresses to 167, 188, 193
gift-giving 15, 161, 163, 168–70, 175, 177, 192

Habermas, Jürgen 6–9, 11, 33, 58
Harris, Tim 71, 82–3, 168
Hauser, Gerard 33–4, 56
Hearth Tax 15, 129, 131–2, 161, 170
High Church 5, 11, 95, 102–3, 105, 107–8, 195–6, 198–200

Index

Hirst, Derek 4, 45, 56, 121, 132
histories of addressing 9, 12, 22, 27, 58, 94, 107, 166, 194–201, 209
Hoadly, Benjamin 16, 107, 198–200, 209, 211
Humble Petition and Advice 43–4, 46, 134, 189

Indulgence, Declarations of 4, 69, 75, 82–4, 162, 195
inversion, tactics of 108, 111

James II
  addresses to 67, 69, 76, 82–3, 98, 107, 190, 195, 197, 208
  use of addresses 14, 49, 68, 76, 176
  use of ritual 176–7, 178, 210

Kennett, White 76–7, 79, 166, 190–1, 200
Kentish petitioners 94–101, 146, 196, 199
Knights, Mark 3, 5–6, 8, 12, 13, 33, 40, 56, 67, 72, 81, 82, 94–5, 97–8, 101, 146, 163, 177–8, 190, 194, 212

Lake, Peter 3, 6–7, 9–11, 67, 84, 211
language
  of addresses 16, 44, 171–2, 188–90
  emotional 3, 8, 10, 16, 22, 29, 34, 99, 168, 184–7, 193–4, 198–9, 201–2, 211
legitimacy
  addresses as devices of 2, 10, 13, 26, 28, 33, 40–1, 47–50, 56, 83, 133, 136–7, 176–7, 207–8, 211
  of addressing activity 14, 57, 67–8, 74, 77–8, 81, 84, 97, 101, 107, 112, 147–8, 172, 193–4, 196–201, 208–9
Leicestershire address 14–15, 48–9, 120–1, 124–26, 135–6, 147–8, 209
L'Estrange, Sir Roger 7–8, 14, 78–9, 84, 96, 172, 208
life-writing
  discussion of addressing 12, 163–8, 177
Locke, John 95, 97, 99, 186
London Gazette 2, 12, 67, 69, 75, 106, 145, 167

loyalty 22, 28–34, 103, 133, 137, 146, 184, 187, 192–4, 202
  addresses as record of 10, 67, 71, 74–6, 78, 84, 100, 110, 137, 207, 209–11, 213
  affectivity of 10, 16, 22, 34, 184–7, 193–4, 202
  formulations of 185–6, 187–8, 213
  language of 16, 56, 185, 187–94, 202, 211
  performance of 162–3
  public 22, 29, 33, 50, 58, 122, 193–4

mass subscriptional activity 2, 5, 13, 15, 21, 25–6, 28–30, 32–3, 42, 49, 52, 55–6, 68–71, 74, 79, 84, 94, 97–8, 100, 111–12, 120–1, 124, 137, 143, 146–8, 175, 194, 201, 207–10, 212
McCormack, Matthew 186–7, 190, 193
memory
  importance of 34, 187, 201
  politics of 14, 208
  public, of addressing activity 3, 13–14, 22, 28, 30, 38, 50, 53, 56, 66–7, 71–2, 76–7, 84–5, 107, 184, 187
Mercurius Politicus 12, 40, 43–4, 46–7, 49–50, 52, 56, 134, 137
mnemonic texts 13–14, 22, 32–4, 50–1, 57, 66–7, 72, 77, 84–5, 107, 165, 167, 177–8, 201, 184, 187, 200, 208, 211, 212
Monck, General George, addresses to 137–9, 142–3
Morphew, John 103–4, 106–9, 167, 191, 198, 201
motivations for addressing 12, 16, 121, 162, 168, 178

Nedham, Marchamont 41–2, 45, 47, 53, 132
newsbooks 11–12, 26, 32–3, 41, 44, 46–7, 56–7, 67, 94, 121, 138
  see also pamphlets; broadsheets
newsletters 27, 32, 69, 94, 106, 138, 190
non-conformists 14, 45, 53, 66, 69, 71, 73, 75, 79, 82–3, 85, 98, 100,

102, 108, 121, 127–8, 136, 160, 162, 164, 168, 170–4, 177, 195, 197, 208, 211
Nouvelles Ordinaires de Londres 40, 42, 46–7, 49, 51

oaths 21–2, 26, 28–30, 32
   of allegiance 14, 106, 147, 202
   compared to addresses 13–15, 31–2, 147, 210, 213
   parliamentary 29–30
   post-Restoration 147–9, 202, 213
Oldmixon, John 3, 5, 9, 16, 55, 107, 146–7, 196–201, 209, 211
opinion politics 2–3, 58, 194
Oxford Parliament 4, 69–71, 73, 78, 81–2, 97, 143, 145, 160, 170, 197

pamphlets 7, 26, 40, 69, 73, 81, 94–7, 105
panegyric 187, 190–1, 194, 202
parrot petitions 5, 23
partisanship 6, 9, 11, 14, 30, 32–4, 94, 97, 103, 146–7, 184, 187, 201, 209, 212–13
Paston, Robert, 1st Earl of Yarmouth 123, 162, 169, 172
petition, right to 67–8, 70, 77–81, 83–4, 95, 97
petitioning 5, 14, 21–30, 33, 42, 49–50, 52, 71, 77–9, 94–5, 99, 120, 146, 207–10
   tumultuous 14, 25, 70, 79, 84, 97, 143, 146
petitions, compared to addresses 3–5, 10, 13–15, 21–3, 31–3, 44, 56, 74, 84, 94, 99, 120–3, 161, 163, 175, 207, 212
Pincus, Steven 6–7, 9–11, 67, 84, 209, 211
political access 16, 31, 161–2, 164, 167–72, 178, 210–11
political affiliation 11, 15, 30, 54, 82, 112, 141
political culture 6, 21, 30, 94, 121, 175
political debate 5–6, 9, 66, 93–5
political participation 3, 5–6, 8, 10, 22–3, 30, 99, 147, 149, 210, 213–14

popular politics 3, 7, 9–10, 13–14, 22, 29, 71–2, 112, 143, 149, 190, 207, 209
popular support 13, 32, 49, 56–7, 100, 136–7, 143, 148, 192, 208
popular voice 8, 95, 146, 209
populism 52, 98, 146, 190, 192
Powell, Vavasor 40, 45
propaganda 12, 40–1, 73, 122, 187, 212
providential language 44, 46, 56, 134, 188
public opinion 2–3, 5–7, 9–12, 14, 16, 21–3, 33, 47–8, 56, 58, 82–3, 107, 123, 200, 208, 211, 213
public sphere 3, 5–9, 11, 27, 33, 57, 67, 94, 208, 211
Publick Intelligencer 40, 44, 50, 52, 56, 134

Quakers 1–2, 76

reflectiveness, of addressing 56–7, 84, 166
religious affiliation 11, 15, 161
religious differences 41, 45, 75–6, 108–9
religious toleration 3, 14, 44–5, 75–6, 82–4, 101–2, 108, 121–2, 176–8, 195, 198, 208, 210–11
Reresby, Sir John 160–1, 163–4, 166, 167, 169–71, 174–5, 177
revolution principles 102, 111, 121, 200
ritual 2–3, 167, 175, 177, 211
Rump Parliament
   addresses to 49, 52, 129, 133, 137, 141, 189
   use of addresses 41, 49, 58, 68, 85
Rye House Plot 4, 69, 72, 75, 77–8, 82, 122, 146, 148, 174, 208

Sacheverell, Henry 5, 94–5, 101–10, 167, 191–2, 200, 209
Savile, George, Marquis of Halifax 160, 174–5
Shibboleths 29, 43
sincerity 16, 185, 194, 197
Sowerby, Scott 3, 32, 84, 210
Spencer, Charles, 3rd Earl of Sunderland 104–5, 172–4

Index

status
  addressing as marker of 163, 165, 166–7, 172
  language of 120, 143, 148
  social 8, 11, 15, 21, 41, 123, 129, 146, 172, 178, 188, 190
Stinton, Benjamin 163–4, 166
subscribers, number of 9, 11–12, 21, 25, 48, 52, 79, 81, 98, 121, 123, 136, 138, 143, 145–8, 177, 190, 197
subscription process 14–15, 21, 48, 122–4, 129, 162
subversive potential 30, 33–4, 211, 213
Swift, Jonathan 98, 184, 191
sycophancy 1–2, 55, 133, 191, 211

Thurloe, John 15, 45, 47–8
Tories 11, 55, 67, 78, 81–2, 94–7, 101–8, 110–11, 146, 148, 186–7, 190, 192–3, 200, 211
Tory press 107, 145, 164, 178
True catalogue, A 40, 44, 45–7, 49, 50, 53–4, 188

Vox Angliae 80–1, 190
Vox Patriae 80–1, 144, 189

well-affected 15, 23, 29, 32, 45, 48–9, 52, 120, 124, 126–7, 133, 136–7, 143, 147–8, 192
Whig press 104, 106–7, 145, 190, 195
Whigs 11, 14, 55, 67, 69–72, 76–7, 80–5, 94–6, 98–112, 143, 146, 148, 170, 186–7, 189–93, 196–7, 199–201, 208
Whitelocke, Bulstrode 40, 42, 163, 166
William III, addresses to 83, 99–100, 191–2, 197
women's involvement in subscriptional activity 13, 15, 23–8, 30, 32, 120, 136, 147–9

Yarmouth corporation address 31, 46, 66–7, 193, 207–8, 212

Zaret, David 3, 5, 23–4, 26–7, 30, 33, 80, 94, 209, 212–13

EU authorised representative for GPSR:
Easy Access System Europe, Mustamäe tee 50,
10621 Tallinn, Estonia
gpsr.requests@easproject.com

www.ingramcontent.com/pod-product-compliance
Lightning Source LLC
Chambersburg PA
CBHW070237240426
43673CB00044B/1830